Chicago For Dummies
3rd Edition

D0684260

Chicago Transit

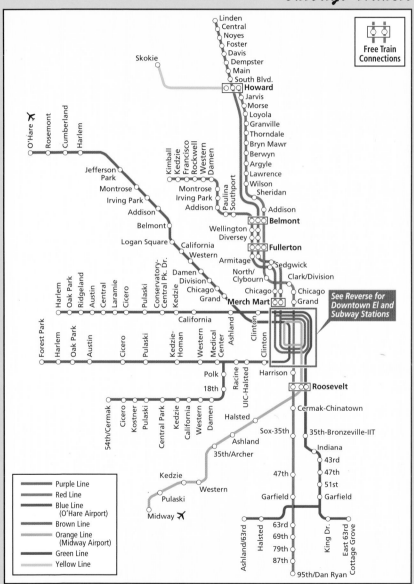

Free Train Connections

Linden
Central
Noyes
Foster
Davis
Dempster
Main
South Blvd.
Skokie
Howard
Jarvis
Morse
Loyola
Granville
Thorndale
Bryn Mawr
Berwyn
Argyle
Lawrence
Wilson
Sheridan

O'Hare
Rosemont
Cumberland
Harlem
Jefferson Park
Montrose
Irving Park
Addison
Belmont
Logan Square

Kimball
Kedzie
Francisco
Rockwell
Western
Damen
Montrose
Irving Park
Addison
Paulina
Southport
Addison
Belmont
Wellington
Diversey
Fullerton
California
Western
Armitage
Damen
Division
Chicago
Grand
Sedgwick
North/Clybourn
Chicago
Clark/Division
Chicago
Merch Mart
Grand

See Reverse for Downtown El and Subway Stations

Harlem
Oak Park
Ridgeland
Austin
Central
Laramie
Cicero
Pulaski
Conservatory-Central Pk. Dr.
Kedzie
Forest Park
Harlem
Oak Park
Austin
Cicero
Pulaski
Kedzie-Homan
Western
Medical Center
Ashland
Clinton
Clinton
California

Polk
18th
Racine
UIC-Halsted
Harrison
Roosevelt
Cermak-Chinatown

54th/Cermak
Cicero
Kostner
Pulaski
Central Park
Kedzie
California
Western
Damen
Halsted
Ashland
35th/Archer
Sox-35th
35th-Bronzeville-IIT
Indiana
43rd
47th
51st

Kedzie
Western
Pulaski
Midway

47th
Garfield
Garfield

Ashland/63rd
Halsted
63rd
69th
79th
87th
King Dr.
East 63rd
Cottage Grove
95th/Dan Ryan

Purple Line
Red Line
Blue Line (O'Hare Airport)
Brown Line
Orange Line (Midway Airport)
Green Line
Yellow Line

Downtown El and Subway Stations

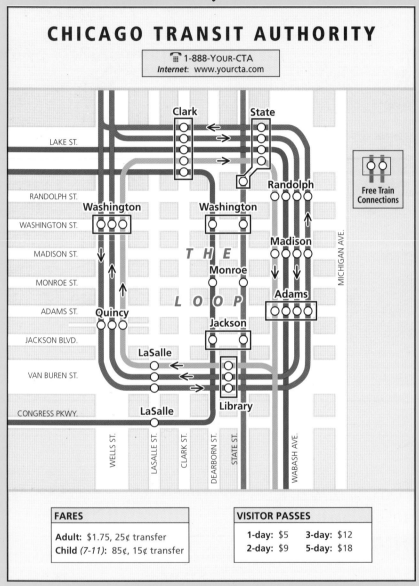

CHICAGO TRANSIT AUTHORITY

☎ 1-888-YOUR-CTA
Internet: www.yourcta.com

Free Train Connections

LAKE ST.

Clark

State

RANDOLPH ST.

Randolph

Washington

Washington

WASHINGTON ST.

MADISON ST.

Madison

MONROE ST.

Monroe

THE

ADAMS ST.

Adams

Quincy

LOOP

JACKSON BLVD.

Jackson

LaSalle

VAN BUREN ST.

CONGRESS PKWY.

LaSalle

Library

MICHIGAN AVE.

WELLS ST.

LASALLE ST.

CLARK ST.

DEARBORN ST.

STATE ST.

WABASH AVE.

FARES		VISITOR PASSES	
Adult: $1.75, 25¢ transfer		**1-day**: $5	**3-day**: $12
Child *(7-11)*: 85¢, 15¢ transfer		**2-day**: $9	**5-day**: $18

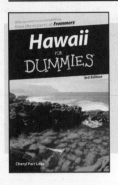
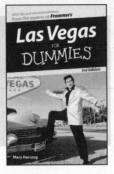

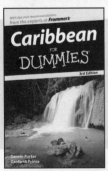
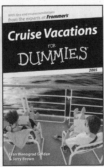

Chicago
FOR
DUMMIES®
3RD EDITION

by Laura Tiebert

Wiley Publishing, Inc.

Chicago For Dummies, 3rd Edition

Published by
Wiley Publishing, Inc.
111 River St.
Hoboken, NJ 07030-5774
www.wiley.com

Copyright © 2005 by Wiley Publishing, Inc., Indianapolis, Indiana

Published simultaneously in Canada

No part of this publication may be reproduced, stored in a retrieval system, or transmitted in any form or by any means, electronic, mechanical, photocopying, recording, scanning, or otherwise, except as permitted under Sections 107 or 108 of the 1976 United States Copyright Act, without either the prior written permission of the Publisher, or authorization through payment of the appropriate per-copy fee to the Copyright Clearance Center, 222 Rosewood Drive, Danvers, MA 01923, 978-750-8400, fax 978-646-8600. Requests to the Publisher for permission should be addressed to the Legal Department, Wiley Publishing, Inc., 10475 Crosspoint Blvd., Indianapolis, IN 46256, 317-572-3447, fax 317-572-4355, or online at http://www.wiley.com/go/permissions.

Trademarks: Wiley, the Wiley Publishing logo, For Dummies, the Dummies Man logo, A Reference for the Rest of Us!, The Dummies Way, Dummies Daily, The Fun and Easy Way, Dummies.com and related trade dress are trademarks or registered trademarks of John Wiley & Sons, Inc., and/or its affiliates in the United States and other countries, and may not be used without written permission. Frommer's is a trademark or registered trademark of Arthur Frommer. Used under license. All other trademarks are the property of their respective owners. Wiley Publishing, Inc., is not associated with any product or vendor mentioned in this book.

For general information on our other products and services, please contact our Customer Care Department within the U.S. at 800-762-2974, outside the U.S. at 317-572-3993, or fax 317-572-4002.

For technical support, please visit www.wiley.com/techsupport.

Wiley also publishes its books in a variety of electronic formats. Some content that appears in print may not be available in electronic books.

Library of Congress Control Number: 2005924067

ISBN-13: 978-0-7645-7748-2

ISBN-10: 0-7645-7748-4

Manufactured in the United States of America

10 9 8 7 6 5 4 3 2 1

3B/QW/QX/QV/IN

WILEY

About the Author

Laura Tiebert is a freelance writer whose travels have taken her from the frozen tundra of Dawson City in Yukon Territory to the wide beaches of Muscat, Oman. A native Midwesterner, she lived in New York City for years before returning to Chicago. Today, she stays a bit closer to home in Evanston, Illinois, where she lives with her husband, Andrew, and son, Joel.

Author's Acknowledgments

I would like to acknowledge the inspiration for this book. My grandparents, Ray and Monie Johnston, met in the late 1920s on the Burlington Northern commuter train between Chicago and the western suburbs and spent 60 years together. The colorful stories they told, about John Dillinger, the stockyards, the Loop, and nights out at the Palmer House Hilton, make me feel connected to the city today.

This book is better because of the insightful editing of Jennifer Reilly. Thank you!

Publisher's Acknowledgments

We're proud of this book; please send us your comments through our
Dummies online registration form located at www.dummies.com/register/.

Some of the people who helped bring this book to market include the
following:

Editorial

Editors: Elizabeth Kuball,
  Jennifer Reilly

Cartographer: Liz Puhl

Editorial Manager: Michelle Hacker

Editorial Assistant: Melissa Bennett

Senior Photo Editor: Richard Fox

Cover Photos: Front: Brett
  Patterson/Corbis; Back: AGE
  Fotostock/Superstock, Inc.

Cartoons: Rich Tennant
  (www.the5thwave.com)

Composition Services

Project Coordinator: Ryan Steffen

Layout and Graphics:
  Lauren Goddard, Joyce Haughey,
  Heather Ryan, Julie Trippetti

Proofreaders: Leeann Harney,
  Jessica Kramer, Joe Niesen,
  TECHBOOKS Production
  Services

Indexer: TECHBOOKS Production
  Services

Publishing and Editorial for Consumer Dummies

   Diane Graves Steele, Vice President and Publisher, Consumer Dummies

   Joyce Pepple, Acquisitions Director, Consumer Dummies

   Kristin A. Cocks, Product Development Director, Consumer Dummies

   Michael Spring, Vice President and Publisher, Travel

   Kelly Regan, Editorial Director, Travel

Publishing for Technology Dummies

   Andy Cummings, Vice President and Publisher, Dummies
     Technology/General User

Composition Services

   Gerry Fahey, Vice President of Production Services

   Debbie Stailey, Director of Composition Services

Contents at a Glance

Maps at a Glance

Table of Contents

Introduction

*L*et's get one thing straight right up front: Chicago is the best-kept big-city secret in the United States. A bold statement, you say? Bold it may be, but it's fitting for this straight-shooting metropolis on the prairie.

Chicago is loud and smart, crude and glamorous, brash and refined. In some ways it's casually elegant, and in others, unabashedly goofy. You see the contrasts in the glamour of Michigan Avenue's elegant hotels and the boisterousness of the fans screaming for "Da Bears" at Soldier Field. Flashy sports cars idle curbside at Rush Street's hot spots, while farther west, art-school hipsters look for the offbeat in Wicker Park. Then again, you can find Midwesterners in their conservative pullovers and khakis just trying to make sense of it all.

America's third-largest city, Chicago constantly reinvents itself and has pulled itself up by its bootstraps in the last two decades to become a vibrant, cosmopolitan place. It has been said that Chicago is the most livable city in the United States. It's also one of the most visitable. Firmly rooted on Midwestern soil, Chicago is very much its own kind of town. I think it'll be your kind of town, too. In this book, I give you the resources to make your Chicago experience a singular one.

About This Book

My favorite way to travel is with a person who has lived in that place. That's my intention for you with this book. Sure, I hit the must-see tourist destinations, and I highlight the sights that actually merit their popularity. But I also point you to off-the-beaten-path places that Chicagoans frequent. The beauty of this approach is that in Chicago, unlike in New York and Los Angeles, you can actually gain admission to these places. Chicago is much less elitist, much less concerned with the ultimate in trendy, than those cities. The City of Big Shoulders also has open arms.

This is a guidebook and also a reference book. You can read it cover to cover, or you can jump in anywhere to find the information you want about a specific task, such as finding a hotel, or an aspect of your trip, such as dining. Whether you're sitting in your living room trying to make a reservation or standing on the corner of State and Madison wondering where to eat, *Chicago For Dummies,* 3rd Edition, is set up so you can get the facts, descriptions, and recommendations you want, quickly. The book is written so that you can open it to any chapter and dig in to get the information you need without any hassles.

Dummies Post-it® Flags

As you're reading this book, you'll find information that you'll want to reference as you plan or enjoy your trip — whether it be a new hotel, a must-see attraction, or a must-try walking tour. Mark these pages with the handy Post-it® Flags included in this book to help make your trip planning easier!

For those hotels, restaurants, and attractions that are plotted on a map, I provide a page reference in the listing information. If a hotel, restaurant, or attraction is outside the city limits or in an out-of-the-way area, it may not be mapped.

Please be advised that travel information is subject to change at any time — and this is especially true of prices. I, therefore, suggest that you write or call ahead for confirmation when making your travel plans. The authors, editors, and publisher cannot be held responsible for the experiences of readers while traveling. Your safety is important to us, however, so we encourage you to stay alert and be aware of your surroundings. Keep a close eye on cameras, purses, and wallets — all favorite targets of thieves and pickpockets.

Conventions Used in This Book

In this book, I include lists of hotels, restaurants, and attractions. As I describe each, I often use abbreviations for commonly accepted credit cards. Take a look at the following list for an explanation of each:

AE: American Express

DC: Diners Club

DISC: Discover

MC: MasterCard

V: Visa

I divide the hotels into two categories — my personal favorites and those that don't quite make my preferred list but still get my hearty seal of approval. Don't be shy about considering the runner-up hotels if you can't get a room at one of my favorites or if your preferences differ from mine. The amenities that the runners-up offer and the services that each provides make all these accommodations good choices to consider as you determine where to rest your head at night.

I also include some general pricing information to help you decide where to unpack your bags or dine on the local cuisine. I use a system of dollar signs to show a range of costs for one night in a hotel (in a double room) or a meal at a restaurant (included in the cost of each meal is an appetizer, entrée, and nonalcoholic beverage). Check out the following table to decipher the dollar signs:

Cost	Hotel	Restaurant
$	$75–$125	$20 and under
$$	$126–$200	$21–35
$$$	$201–$300	$36–$45
$$$$	$301 and up	$46–$60
$$$$$		$61 and over

Foolish Assumptions

As I wrote this book, I made some assumptions about you and what your needs may be as a traveler. Here's what I assumed about you:

- You may be an inexperienced traveler looking for guidance when determining whether to take a trip to Chicago and how to plan for it.

- You may be an experienced traveler who hasn't had much time to explore Chicago and wants expert advice when you finally do get a chance to enjoy that particular locale.

- You're not looking for a book that provides all the information available about Chicago or that lists every hotel, restaurant, or attraction available to you. Instead, you're looking for a book that focuses on the places that give you the best or most unique experience in Chicago.

If you fit any of these criteria, *Chicago For Dummies,* 3rd Edition, gives you the information you're looking for!

How This Book Is Organized

This book is divided into six parts covering the major aspects of your trip. Each part is further broken down into specific components so you can go right to the subtopic you want (you don't have to read all about nightlife if you're just looking for a jazz club, for example). Following are brief summaries of the parts.

Part 1: Introducing Chicago

Get a panoramic view of Chicago as I scan the city's highlights, the not-to-be-missed attractions and activities. It's an exciting era in the city's history, and I help you decide when to go, based on weather considerations and event schedules.

Part II: Planning Your Trip to Chicago

By nature, I'm a planner. In fact, for me, planning the trip is half the fun. Ah, the possibilities! If you're a planner too, you'll love this part of the book. I debate the pros and cons of your travel options and even review airports. You'll be able to plan your budget; contemplate using trains, planes, or automobiles; join in a tour; and find particular advice for those with special travel needs and interests.

Part III: Settling Into Chicago

Being in a new city can be a bit like groping around in the dark. Reading through this part will have you navigating the city like a native. Maybe you'll even find yourself giving directions to hapless tourists on the street! Then, you'll get the lowdown on Chicago's hotels and restaurants — what's the latest and greatest, what's getting shabby around the edges, what offers the ultimate in luxury or the biggest bargain.

Part IV: Exploring Chicago

In this part, I guide you through Chicago's attractions. I point out the major sights and show you additional attractions, should you have the time, energy, and inclination. If you want to take a piece of Chicago home with you, turn to the chapter on shopping. And if this jumble of things to do and see is just too much for you, I provide a variety of ready-made itineraries.

Part V: Living It Up after Dark: Chicago Nightlife

Chicago offers culture hounds options that stack up favorably against anything you'll find anywhere else in the world. In this part, I cover the best of the sights and sounds of nighttime Chicago. I run the gamut of information on Chicago's live theater and performing arts scene (including symphony, opera, and dance), as well as Chicago's best bars and clubs.

Part VI: The Part of Tens

In this part, I provide lists of information to make your vacation perfect — from the top ten Chicago experiences to ten creative ideas for days when the weather isn't cooperating. Most importantly, you'll discover indispensable tips for experiencing Chicago as the locals do.

In the back of this book I've included an *appendix* — your Quick Concierge — containing lots of handy information you may need when traveling in Chicago, like phone numbers and addresses for emergency personnel or area hospitals and pharmacies, lists of local newspapers and magazines, protocol for sending mail or finding taxis, and more. Check out this appendix when searching for answers to lots of little questions that may come up as you travel. You can find the Quick Concierge easily, because it's printed on yellow paper.

Icons Used in This Book

These icons appear in the margins throughout this book:

Keep an eye out for the Bargain Alert icon as you seek money-saving tips and/or great deals.

The Best of the Best icon highlights the best Chicago has to offer in all categories — hotels, restaurants, attractions, activities, shopping, and nightlife.

This icon points out insider information on where locals eat, shop, and spend time in Chicago.

Watch for the Heads Up icon to identify annoying or potentially danger-ous situations, such as tourist traps, unsafe neighborhoods, budgetary rip-offs, and other circumstances to beware of.

Look to the Kid Friendly icon for attractions, hotels, restaurants, and activities that are particularly hospitable to children or people traveling with kids.

The Tip icon highlights useful advice on things to do and ways to sched-ule your time.

Where to Go from Here

Your next stop is Chicago, a living, vibrant, wonderfully diverse city that offers something for every taste, inclination, or budget. This book helps you make decisions about how you can tailor Chicago to be your kind of town.

Part I
Introducing Chicago

The 5th Wave
By Rich Tennant

"The closest hotel room I could get you to the Magnificent Mile for that amount of money is in Cleveland."

In this part . . .

When should you go to Chicago? What annual events hold the most interest for you? Which attractions are absolute must-sees, and which activities should be on the list of anyone visiting the city? Come with me as we survey Chicago from a bird's-eye view, taking in the big picture of all the attractions and activities that await you.

Chapter 1

Discovering the Best of Chicago

In This Chapter

▶ Kicking back: Baseball and the blues

▶ Getting highbrow: Performing arts, museums, and architecture

▶ Eating your way around town

> *Hog Butcher for the World,*
> *Tool Maker, Stacker of Wheat,*
> *Player with Railroads and the Nation's Freight Handler;*
> *Stormy, husky, brawling,*
> *City of the Big Shoulders*
>
> —Carl Sandburg, *Chicago*

*I*n this chapter, you get a sampling of the qualities that make Chicago the most American of American cities. Today, you'd hardly recognize Chicago by Sandburg's description. No longer home to stockyards, the city is a cosmopolitan, vibrant place. But Chicago still retains its unique identity: big and brawling, inventive, and wonderfully diverse. Chicago is the least pretentious and most livable metropolis in the United States — and maybe the most visitable, too.

Some activities just say "Chicago." They're the quintessential Chicago experiences, and no visit is complete without them. Read on for some of the activities that make Chicago a special place to visit. Throughout the book, the Best of the Best icon is attached to those places/activities mentioned in this chapter.

The Best Hotels

Most Family Friendly: With cribs, laundry service, free hot breakfast, and every room a suite, the **Embassy Suites Hotel Chicago–Downtown/Lakefront** is ideal for families looking for a little more space than the typical hotel room provides. The in-room Nintendo, indoor pool, and location near Navy Pier — plus hamburger joint P.J. Clarke's located in the same building complex — should keep Junior happy, too.

Best Room with a View: This isn't an easy call. Peering over the elevated tracks, **The Crowne Plaza Chicago/Silversmith** in the Loop, offers a distinctly urban vista. But consider several other hotels for their mix of lake and city views: the **Four Seasons Hotel Chicago, The Drake, The Ritz-Carlton Chicago,** and **Park Hyatt Chicago.**

Best Bet for Romance: A hip hotel that's known for its sense of romance and whimsy is **Hotel Burnham.** During the holidays, you're right across the street from the world-famous windows at Marshall Field's and within viewing distance of the massive Christmas tree at Daley Plaza. Inside, you'll get a feel for the handcrafted beauty of the former Reliance Insurance building, one of the city's first skyscrapers. Windows are huge — you won't feel left in the dark or cramped here. Rooms are clubby but glamorous, with plush beds, mahogany writing desks, and chaise lounges.

Best Place to Splurge: You want luxury? You've got luxury at three of Chicago's hotels, which rank among the best in the world. The attention to detail, regal pampering, and well-connected concierges you'll find at both the ultra-luxe **Ritz-Carlton Chicago** and **Four Seasons Hotel Chicago** make them the hotels of choice for travelers who want to feel like royalty while in town. The **Peninsula Hotel** has also ascended into the ranks of the Ritz and Four Seasons, when it won *Travel + Leisure* magazine's 2004 award for top service in North America (and ranked in the top ten in the world).

Best Place to Save a Buck: Red Roof Inn Chicago Downtown offers a fabulous location for a bargain price. But the **Hampton Inn & Suites Chicago–Downtown** gets bonus points for being a bargain stay, and for having a pool.

Best Swimming Pool: With its dazzling, all-tile, junior Olympic-size pool constructed in 1929, the **Hotel InterContinental Chicago** takes this award easily.

For more information on the hotels listed in this section, see Chapter 9.

The Best Restaurants

Best New Restaurant: A hot new spot featuring small plates is **Avec,** which is garnering kudos from foodies nationwide. It's small, it's crowded (you share a table with other diners), but it's a truly unique experience.

Best View: A location right on the Magnificent Mile means the **Hancock Observatory** (Chapter 11) offers an up-close-and-personal view of the city from its observation deck. For lunch, visit the **Signature Room at the 95th,** a sleek restaurant that offers a special lunch buffet. On a clear day, you can see 50 miles and part of three surrounding states — Michigan, Indiana, and Wisconsin. (Ladies, make sure to visit the restroom — it's got the best views in the restaurant!)

Best Ice Cream: Since the 1920s, **Margie's Candies** has been serving up mammoth sundaes in conch-shell-shaped dishes. Margie is gone now, but her husband Peter still mans the cash register. Don't miss the home-made hot fudge, real butterscotch, and caramel. The place is frozen in time — about 1940, to be exact — and is stuffed with kitschy dolls, boxes of homemade candy, stuffed animals, and news clippings through the years.

Best Outdoor Dining: Long tables and family-style dining reign in **Greektown,** making it a comfortable and fun destination for families and large groups. At **Pegasus,** a rooftop garden allows diners a panoramic view of the Chicago skyline. The restaurant is so family- and large-group-oriented, in fact, that when I called to make a reservation for a group of ten, the host replied, "Ten is not a big group!" So there you have it.

Best Burger: The hamburger at **Mike Ditka's Restaurant** tastes more like chopped steak and can easily feed two. Sports fans will be entertained by football memorabilia, and Bears fans can relive the glory days of former coach Mike Ditka, who owns the place. Take your kids to the main dining room, though, because the bar vicinity tends to get a little foggy with cigar smoke.

Best Barbecue: At longtime city favorite **Carson's,** $19.95 gets you a full slab (nearly 2 pounds' worth) of incredible baby-back ribs, accompanied by a bowl of Carson's almost-as-famous coleslaw and a choice of potatoes.

Best Vegetarian: Vegetarians and veggie lovers alike will delight in the twist on fine dining served up at **Green Zebra.** The restaurant features "small plates" of veggie specialties, such as fennel risotto cake with a syrah reduction, and Hawaiian heart of palm with kaffir lime and Thai basil chili.

Best Traditional Restaurant: Good German fellowship (known as *gemut-lichkeit*) flows — along with mounds of plump sausages — at several German restaurants. One of the most centrally located is the Loop's **The Berghoff,** with its own brews on tap (and its own root beer, for those not imbibing).

Best Family-Style Dining: Maggiano's is a mecca for Italian family-style dining. Heaping plates of pasta meant to be shared make Maggiano's a good choice for a budget-conscious family. In fact, everything on the menu is super-sized. Most steaks are more than a pound, and the full pasta dishes weigh in at over 25 ounces. (You can also get half-portions: You'd be amazed at how large even a 14-ounce portion of pasta can be!) You're expected to share dishes, pass things around, and try a little bit of everything.

Best Hot Dog: Gold Coast Dogs, a River North fast-food stand, serves up the authentic item, meaning a Vienna All-Beef Frank slathered with mustard, green relish, chopped onion, sliced tomato, hot peppers, and celery salt. Your kids may be brave enough to ask for and receive ketchup, but as an adult, I wouldn't risk the disapproving, raised-eyebrow look you'll get from the counter staff. You can round out the meal with cheese fries, made from Idaho potatoes and topped with a generous glob of Wisconsin cheddar.

Best Pizza: In the town where deep-dish pies were born, Chicagoans take their out-of-town relatives to either **Gino's East** or **Lou Malnati's** to taste the real thing: mouthwatering slabs of pizza loaded with fresh ingredients atop delectably sweet crusts. Lou's fan base is so enamored that the restaurant has even instituted a popular overnight mail-order business to get expatriate Chicagoans with a deep-dish jones over the hump.

Best Fast Food: Even though you're in the hometown of McDonald's, my vote goes to **foodlife** in Water Tower Place, a food court exemplar with everything from Asian noodles to pizza to smoothies.

Best Brunch: Cajun and southern cooking is in store for you at **Wishbone.** Primitive art, bright colors, and a bustling crowd make this a great place for kids. A diverse crowd, from Harpo Studios employees (Oprah is headquartered right around the corner) to businesspeople in suits and ad-agency types, frequent the place. For brunch, be sure to try the salmon cakes.

Best Neighborhood Hang-Out: Stanley's is a classic Lincoln Park restaurant with a family-friendly bent. When you walk in, there's a bar, but the adjacent dining room feels as though you've entered someone's family room, decorated with photos, quilts, bowling trophies, and children's drawings. On Saturday and Sunday from 11 a.m. to 4 p.m., there's an all-you-can-eat brunch buffet, featuring make-your-own omelets, build-your-own-Belgian waffles, home-fried potatoes, fried chicken, and mashed potatoes. Daily specials are posted on the chalkboard out front.

For more information on the restaurants listed in this section, see Chapter 10.

The Best Museums

Best Museum for Older Children: Yes, the biggest *T. rex* fossil ever unearthed resides at Chicago's **Field Museum of Natural History.** As long as you're going to see "Sue" (if you're on a first-name basis with the famous *T. rex*), you should know that an entire "campus" of museums is nearby, including **Adler Planetarium & Astronomy Museum** and the

John G. Shedd Aquarium. Farther south in Hyde Park, the incomparable **Museum of Science and Industry** wows kids and adults with a real-life U-boat submarine that's been completely refurbished and placed in a new indoor exhibit, airplane, ant colony, and more.

Best Museum for Younger Children: The **Shedd,** the nation's largest (and oldest) indoor aquarium, is housed in a spectacular 1929 Beaux Arts structure. The aquarium revamped and improved facilities to celebrate its 75th anniversary in 2005.

Best Art Museum: Downtown, the **Art Institute of Chicago** is a great starting point for seeing masterpieces.

Best Museum for Exploring the Outdoors Indoors: Located in Lincoln Park, the **Peggy Notebaert Nature Museum** is an environmental museum for the 21st century and boasts kid-friendly hands-on exhibits.

For more information on the museums in this section, see Chapter 11.

The Best Nature

Best Park: The city's newest park welcomed flocks of visitors in its first month alone, and for good reason. The 25-acre **Millennium Park** sets a new standard for what an urban park can be. With sculptures you can touch and feel (and in one case, splash around in), the park sets a nationwide example for what a modern city park can be. It's also home to a spectacular Frank Gehry–designed band shell and pedestrian bridge. And of course, the sentimental favorite is **Lincoln Park,** worth at least a few hours' stroll.

Best Golf Course: Within Grant Park, you may want to putt around at **The Green at Grant Park,** an 18-hole putting course (and with its beautifully landscaped greens, you'll recognize immediately that this is not your usual miniature golf course).

Second City, Third Coast

Although it may surprise residents of the first two coasts (East and West, that is), Chicagoans consider themselves residents of the *Third Coast* — Lake Michigan's shore. Thanks to the foresight of city founders who, in 1836, wrote that the lakefront was a public ground "to remain forever open, clear, and free" from construction, the shore has no warehouses or shipping docks. More than half of Chicago's 2,800 acres of lakefront were created by filling in the lake and building a string of splendid lakeshore parks. The result? 30 miles of sand beaches, green lawns, beds of flowers, and bicycle paths.

Best Beach: While in Lincoln Park, stroll the lakefront path, and whether you're coming from the north or south, eventually, you'll see the North Avenue pedestrian bridge that crosses Lake Shore Drive. Walk over the lanes of traffic, and you'll find yourself at Chicago's number-one summer fun destination: **North Avenue Beach.** While you're here, join Chicagoans at the lake in a game of beach volleyball, or simply walk, run, or relax.

Best View: Lively, renovated **Navy Pier** has become the city's number-one tourist destination since it reopened in 1995. The view of the city, as you walk out on Navy Pier, then turn and watch the city glimmer in the twilight, is among the best city views in the world.

For more information on the listings in this section, see Chapters 11 and 14.

The Best Culture

Best Opera: A perennial favorite is the **Lyric Opera,** one of the nation's best opera companies, which continually amazes with top-notch productions at the Civic Opera House on the banks of the Chicago River in the Loop. The opera continually sells out 100 percent of the time, but don't fear. Subscription holders routinely hand in unused tickets before the performance, so you can still get some great seats.

Best Symphony: Directed by well-known conductor Daniel Barenboim (his term will end in 2006, and we're waiting to see who will attempt to fill his shoes), the **Chicago Symphony Orchestra** is world-class.

Best Ballet: Chicago has adopted the **Joffrey Ballet,** which does a sumptuous production of *The Nutcracker* each holiday season in the spectacular setting of the Auditorium Theatre, one of Chicago's architectural gems (now newly renovated).

Best Theater: Excellent theater companies include the **Goodman, Steppenwolf,** and **Victory Gardens theaters.** Steppenwolf, located in Lincoln Park, focuses on original, edgy drama. The Goodman has a less cutting-edge repertoire and includes some musicals each season. Victory Gardens stages world-premier plays, some of which are making quite a splash, even on a national scale. Other theater highlights include the refurbished **Oriental** and **Palace theaters** and two top-notch facilities in their respective genres, the **Chicago Shakespeare Theater** on Navy Pier and the **Old Town School of Folk Music theater and education center,** which presents traditional and contemporary folk music from around the world.

If you skip Chicago's theater scene, you just may miss out on the next Broadway smash hit. Two of the most widely applauded Broadway productions of the past few years started at the Goodman Theater: Arthur Miller's *Death of a Salesman,* starring Brian Dennehy, and Eugene O'Neill's

Moon for the Misbegotten, with Cherry Jones and Gabriel Byrne. Plus, *The Producers,* starring Matthew Broderick and Nathan Lane, debuted in Chicago before taking New York by storm.

Best Comedy: Nobody does comedy better than **The Second City,** a training ground for comedians, such as John Belushi, Dan Aykroyd, Bill Murray, and Chris Farley.

For more information on the performing arts events listed in this section, refer to Chapter 15.

The Best Live Music

Best Blues: Chicago is the blues capital of the world. And if you get to know this style of music, you may gain a greater appreciation for other popular forms, such as jazz and rock 'n' roll. Nothing is quite as sweet as hanging out at **Buddy Guy's Legends** on a Thursday night and discovering that the man seated next to you is B.B. King's drummer, visiting Chicago on a rare night off. Even if you don't love the blues, do yourself a favor and check it out when you're here.

Best Rock: You can't do better than **Metro,** which is housed on North Clark Street in an old theater (they simply removed all the seats). It's one of Chicago's best live-music venues, intimate but not too small, and the launching pad for great local-bands-gone-international, like the Smashing Pumpkins and Ministry.

Best Small Venues: One of the city's most intimate rooms for live music is found at **Schubas Tavern and the Harmony Grill** on North Southport Avenue. The music styles here are eclectic, ranging from rock to funk to the occasional mariachi band. You'll find everything from local bands on their way up to national acts that are still loyal to Schubas. It's standing general admission, and has the added bonus of having the Harmony Grill connected to it — this atmospheric former Schlitz Brewery tap house built around 1900 still offers Schlitz Beer in bottles.

Best Eclectic Music: Elbo Room is one of the top five venues for music in the city, located on North Lincoln Avenue. Upstairs, there's a cocktail lounge with a full bar. Downstairs, you'll find the stage, with seating along the walls. It's sweaty, crowded, and filled with lovers of live music from ska to hip-hop.

For more information on music venues, head to Chapter 16.

Chapter 2

Digging Deeper into Chicago

. . . .

In This Chapter

▶ Immersing yourself in Chicago history
▶ Scoping out the skyline: our famous architectural heritage
▶ Familiarizing yourself through books and movies

. . . .

A little background can make it easier for you to hit the ground running, so you can better enjoy Chicago. In this chapter, you get easy-
to-digest cultural information, with a historical timeline, architectural
highlights, culinary tidbits, local lingo, and recommended reading and
films so that you can discover Chicago's uniqueness.

History 101: The Main Events

Chicago has a long and illustrious history that began in the late 1600s,
when two French explorers discovered a portage that linked the Great
Lakes with the Mississippi River valley. From then on, there was no looking back!

Chicago timeline: 1673–2004

1673   French explorers Marquette and Joliet discover portage at Chicago link-
ing the Great Lakes region with the Mississippi River valley.

1779   Afro-French-Canadian trapper Jean Baptiste Point du Sable establishes
a trading post on the north bank of the Chicago River. A settlement follows two years later.

1794   General "Mad" Anthony Wayne defeats the British in the Battle of Fallen
Timbers; the disputed Illinois Territory is finally ceded to the young
American Republic by treaty a year later.

1803	Garrison of Fort Dearborn is established in Chicago, commanded by the grandfather of artist James McNeill Whistler.
1812	Incited by the British in the War of 1812, Potawatomi Indians destroy Fort Dearborn and slay its residents.
1816	Fort Dearborn is rebuilt.
1818	Illinois is admitted to the Union as the 21st state.
1837	Chicago is incorporated as a city, with about 4,000 residents.
1847	The *Chicago Tribune* begins publishing.
1856	Chicago is chief railroad center in the United States.
1865	Chicago stockyards are founded.
1870	The city's population numbers almost 300,000, making it perhaps the fastest-growing metropolis in history.
1871	The Great Chicago Fire burns large sections of the city; rebuilding begins while the ashes are still warm.
1882	The ten-story Montauk Building, the world's first skyscraper, is erected.
1892	The city's first elevated train goes into operation.
1893	Completely recovered from the Great Fire, Chicago hosts its first World's Fair, the World's Columbian Exposition. The world's first Ferris wheel is a big draw.
1908	The Chicago Cubs win their second World Series. They haven't won one since!
1917	The Chicago White Sox win the World Series. They haven't won one since!
1919	"Black Sox" bribery scandal perpetrated by eight Chicago White Sox players stuns baseball.
1920–1933	During Prohibition, Chicago becomes a "wide-open town"; rival mobs battle violently throughout the city for control of distribution and sale of illegal alcohol.
1929	On St. Valentine's Day, Al Capone's gang murders seven members of rival George "Bugs" Moran's crew in a Clark Street garage.
1931	Al Capone finally goes to jail, not for bootlegging or murder, but for tax evasion.
1934	Bank robber and "Public Enemy Number One" John Dillinger is gunned down by police outside the Biograph Theater.

(continued)

(continued)

1942	Scientists, led by Enrico Fermi, create the world's first nuclear chain reaction under Stagg Field at the University of Chicago.
1953	Chicago native Hugh Hefner starts publishing *Playboy* (the original Playboy Mansion was located in Chicago's Gold Coast neighborhood).
1955	Richard J. Daley begins his first term as mayor; he is widely regarded as the "last of the big-city bosses."
1960	John F. Kennedy and Richard Nixon hold the first televised presidential debate in WBBM-TV's studios.
1966	Civil rights leader Martin Luther King, Jr., moves to Chicago to lead a fair housing campaign.
1968	After King's assassination, much of the West Side burns during heavy rioting. Anti–Vietnam War protests in conjunction with the Democratic National Convention end in a police riot and a "shoot to kill" order by Mayor Richard J. Daley.
1974	The 1,454-foot Sears Tower is completed, becoming the tallest building in the world.
1979	Jane Byrne becomes the first woman elected mayor of Chicago.
1983	Harold Washington becomes the first African-American mayor of Chicago.
1986	The Chicago Bears win their only Super Bowl to date.
1989	Richard M. Daley, the son of the long-serving mayor, is elected mayor.
1999	Michael Jordan, arguably the best basketball player ever, retires (for the second time) after leading the Chicago Bulls to six NBA Championships in the previous eight years.
2000	The Goodman Theatre opens its new $46 million theater complex in the Loop, completing the revitalization of the downtown theater district.
2001	Chicago's second airport, Midway, opens a new $800 million terminal, giving travelers more options for Chicago flights.
2004	Millennium Park, Chicago's largest public works project in decades, opens at the north end of Grant Park. The centerpiece is a modern, steel-sheathed band shell designed by famed architect Frank Gehry.

Building Blocks: Local Architecture

One advantage to having your city burn to the ground: You can rebuild it with style. Thanks to the Great Fire of 1871, Chicago's architects were able to start over and "make no small plans," as city planner and visionary Daniel Burnham said. Chicago is the birthplace of modern architecture and the skyscraper. Chicago is home to 45 Mies van der Rohe buildings and 75 Frank Lloyd Wright buildings, plus dozens by the first Chicago school and the second Chicago school. Enough said? The **Chicago Architecture Foundation** helps visitors discover the city's architectural gems (see Chapter 11).

Taste of Chicago: Local Cuisine

If you have to eat while you're here, you're in luck. Food doesn't get much better than the Mexican cuisine at **Frontera Grill,** the ribs at **Twin Anchors,** the burgers at **Mike Ditka's Restaurant,** the sushi at **Kamehachi,** or the Italian at **Tuscany on Taylor** in Little Italy. And if that's not enough, how about steak and mammoth baked potatoes slathered in butter at **Gibson's** or deep-dish pizza at **Gino's East?** Oh, I can't neglect to mention Italian beef sandwiches and garlicky Chicago hot dogs. (See Chapter 10 for restaurants and light bites.) And don't forget to finish off your meal with a Frango chocolate mint from **Marshall Field's** department store. (See Chapter 12 for more on shopping.) Feeling hungry yet?

Word to the Wise: The Local Lingo

National news anchors aspire to the flat vowels and plain language of the Midwest. You should have no problem understanding the inhabitants of this, the most Midwestern of cities. With the exception of "da Bears" and a few other local phrases, Chicago-ese is easy on the ears.

Background Check: Recommended Books and Movies

So many great American writers have come from Chicago, lived here during their productive years, or set their work within the city's confines that it's impossible to recommend a single book that says everything about Chicago. However, here are a few suggestions to get you started.

Master builders: Sullivan, Wright, and Mies

Visitors from around the world flock to Chicago to see the groundbreaking work of three major architects: Sullivan, Wright, and Mies. They all lived and worked in the Windy City, leaving behind a legacy of innovative structures that still inspire architects today. Here's the rundown on each of them:

Louis Sullivan (1865–1924)

Quote: "Form ever follows function."

Chicago buildings: Auditorium Building, 430 S. Michigan Ave. (Adler & Sullivan, 1887–1889); James Charnley House, 1365 Astor St. (Adler & Sullivan, with Frank Lloyd Wright, 1892); and Carson Pirie Scott & Co., 1 S. State St. (1899, 1903, with later additions).

Innovations: Father of the Chicago school, Sullivan was perhaps at his most original in the creation of his intricate, nature-inspired ornamentation, examples of which cover the entrance to Carson Pirie Scott & Co.

Frank Lloyd Wright (1867–1959)

Quote: "Nature is my manifestation of God."

Chicago buildings: Frank Lloyd Wright Home & Studio, 951 Chicago Ave., Oak Park (1889–1911); Unity Temple, 875 Lake St., Oak Park (1905–1908); The Rookery, 209 S. LaSalle St. (interior renovation, 1907); and Frederick C. Robie House, 5757 S. Woodlawn Ave., Hyde Park (1909).

Innovations: While in Chicago, Wright developed the architecture of the Prairie School, a largely residential style combining natural materials, an intercommunication between interior and exterior spaces, and the sweeping horizontals of the Midwestern landscape. (For tours of Wright's home and studio, see Chapter 11.)

Ludwig Mies van der Rohe (1886–1969)

Quote: "Less is more."

Chicago buildings: 860–880 N. Lake Shore Dr. (1949–1951); S. R. Crown Hall, 3360 S. State St. (1956); and Chicago Federal Center, Dearborn Street between Adams Street and Jackson Boulevard (1959–1974).

Innovations: Mies van der Rohe brought the office tower of steel and glass to the United States. His stark facades don't immediately reveal his careful attention to details and materials.

Upton Sinclair's *The Jungle* tells the tale of a young immigrant encountering the filthy, brutal city. Its 1906 publication caused an uproar that led to the passage of the Pure Food and Drug Act. James T. Farrell's trilogy *Studs Lonigan,* published in the 1930s, explores the power of ethnic and neighborhood identity in Chicago. Other novels set in Chicago include Saul Bellow's *The Adventures of Augie March* and *Humboldt's Gift,* Theodore Dreiser's *Sister Carrie*, and Richard Wright's *Native Son.*

For an engrossing overview of the city's history, read *City of the Century* by Donald Miller; an excellent PBS special based on the book is also available on video and DVD. For a contemporary look at life in Chicago, take a look at two books that give a human face to the city's shameful public-housing history: Daniel Coyle's *Hardball: A Season in the Projects,* the true story of youngsters on a Little League baseball team from Cabrini Green; and Alex Kotlowitz's *There Are No Children Here,* a portrait of children growing up in the Robert Taylor homes.

And, of course, no one has given a voice to the people of Chicago as have the estimable Studs Terkel, whose books *Division Street: America, Working,* and *Chicago* are based on interviews with Chicagoans from every neighborhood and income level; and the late newspaper columnist Mike Royko, author of perhaps the definitive account of Chicago machine politics, *Boss.* His columns have been collected in *One More Time: The Best of Mike Royko* and *For The Love of Mike: More of the Best of Mike Royko.*

Chicago became a popular setting for feature films in the 1980s and 1990s, and the trend continues today. For a look at Chicago on the silver screen, check out *Ferris Bueller's Day Off* (1985), the ultimate teenage wish-fulfillment fantasy; *The Fugitive* (1993), which used the city's El trains as an effective backdrop; and *My Best Friend's Wedding* (1996).

For many Chicagoans, though, the quintessential hometown movie scene is the finale to *The Blues Brothers* (1979), which features a multicar pileup in the center of downtown Daley Plaza. Of course, others would argue that the Oscar-winning musical *Chicago* (2002) sings the praises of Chicago — 1920s Chicago, that is — like no other. And don't forget *Barbershop* (2002) and its sequel, *Barbershop 2: Back in Business* (2004), both offering a view of contemporary South Side Chicago from a seat in a neighborhood barbershop.

Chapter 3

Deciding When to Go

In This Chapter
▶ Weighing the pros and cons of winter, spring, summer, and fall
▶ Spelling out the facts and fallacies about Chicago weather
▶ Checking out a month-by-month listing of events

*W*hen should you go to Chicago? That depends. What kind of weather do you like? Chicago has it all — sometimes within a day! No doubt you've heard the wisecracks about Chicago's weather (that is, the city has only two seasons — winter and August) and that tongue-firmly-in-cheek piece of advice: "If you don't like the weather, stick around for five minutes."

As with many sayings, both have an element of truth. Chicago weather does hit the extremes. And it's oh-so-changeable. I've left my apartment on a sunny, summer day in jeans and a T-shirt only to witness the temperature drop 15°F in 15 minutes. In this chapter, I tell you what you need to know about the city's ever-changing seasons, as well as its many festivals, so you can determine your ideal time to go.

Revealing the Secrets of the Seasons

Most Chicago visitors find that the ideal times to visit are late spring and early fall. In the **spring,** you soak up blossoms, blooms, and equable temperatures. Spring in Chicago may be short, but it's invigorating and widely welcomed. Some Chicagoans, eager for warm weather, lie out on roof-deck lounge chairs in 55°F April weather. **Fall,** with its golds, reds, and browns, provides crisp, clear days with idyllic balmy interludes. Pleasant weather sometimes lingers into late November.

Chicago has a reputation for being extremely cold in the **winter.** In truth, it's not much colder than any other northern city. Daunting days of sub-zero temperatures and –40°F wind chills do occur. Salt trucks rumble incessantly over Chicago's frozen streets, and potholes almost large enough to swallow cars bring rush-hour traffic to a halt. **Summer** isn't exactly a piece of cake, either: During the dog days, you may have whole strings of days when temperatures stay in the 90s and high humidity drains your energy.

But those are the extremes. Lake Michigan has a moderating effect on Chicago weather, air-conditioning the city in summer and warming the cold in the winter. (Of course, in the Windy City, the lake also has a negative effect — the same breeze that cuts the humidity in the summer can bite straight through the thickest down jacket in the winter.)

Table 3-1 gives you the lowdown on the average temperatures in Chicago. Remember, though, that these are only averages. You may want to pack an outfit or two for cooler or warmer weather, depending on when you plan to travel. For all of my tips on packing, see Chapter 7.

Table 3-1 Chicago's Average Temperatures and Precipitation

	Jan	Feb	Mar	Apr	May	June	July	Aug	Sept	Oct	Nov	Dec
High (°F/°C)	29/ −1.5	34/ 1	46/ 7.5	59/ 15	70/ 21	80/ 26	84/ 29	82/ 28	75/ 24	63/ 17	48/ 9	34/ 1
Low (°F/°C)	13/ −10.5	17/ −8	28/ −2	39/ 4	48/ 9	58/ 14.5	63/ 17	62/ 16.5	54/ 12	42/ 5.5	32/ 0	19/ −7
Rainfall (in./cm.)	1.6/ 4.1	1.4/ 3.6	2.7/ 6.9	3.6/ 9.1	3.3/ 8.4	3.7/ 9.4	4.2/ 10.7	3.8/ 9.7	2.4/ 6.1	2.9/ 7.4	2.8/ 7.1	2.5/ 6.4

What follows is a rundown of the pros and cons of each season.

Springtime in Chicago

Many of Chicago's 30-million-plus annual visitors choose spring for their travels. What follows are the best reasons to go to Chicago in the springtime:

- ✔ It's warming up! Days stay light longer. The city begins to wake up after a long winter's nap.

- ✔ Chicago plants thousands of tulips and daffodils, which pop up optimistically during the season and brighten the streetscape.

But keep in mind the following springtime pitfalls:

- ✔ Just because the days are warming up doesn't mean that the weather is necessarily nice. Strong winds can blow, and buckets of rain can fall during long strings of gray days.

- ✔ Spring is the time of year (along with winter) when theater shows may close for a week. *Remember:* Performers need vacations, too.

- ✔ You're a bit in limbo as far as events go. Festivals don't start until June, and you're too late for the holiday season and the decorations.

Summer in the city

Ahhh, summer. Lazy days and quiet nights. . . . Well, not in Chicago! Summer is festival time. Knowing what lies on the other side of the calendar, Chicagoans jam-pack summers full of outdoor activities — so much so that the choice of activities on weekends can be overwhelming. Consider these points:

- ✔ The air may be hot and humid, but you can usually count on a cool lake breeze. If you're venturing to the suburbs, however, the temperatures there can be 10°F higher.

- ✔ Everyone is outside, soaking up the good weather. People stay out late, eating and drinking at sidewalk cafes.

- ✔ The weather is often perfect for taking boat cruises, strolling along Navy Pier, and enjoying other activities on the lakefront.

But, again, keep in mind the following:

- ✔ Festivals can be hot and cramped. (Then again, that's the point, right?)

- ✔ Because of the heat, everyone is at the lake, making the area a congested free-for-all: inline skaters skating into bikers biking into runners running into Fido, who just broke off his leash!

- ✔ School is out, and the kid-oriented attractions are swarming. Be prepared to leave extra time for parking and standing in line at attractions such as the John G. Shedd Aquarium, Sears Tower Skydeck, and Museum of Science and Industry.

A fall to remember

In my opinion, fall is a beautiful time of year — no matter where you are. Here are some autumn bonuses for the Chicago scene:

- ✔ You get the best weather in the fall — still warm enough, but not so hot and humid that you're going to have a meltdown. You have the best shot at an uninterrupted string of beautiful days.

- ✔ The cultural scene is back in swing, with openings for the opera and symphony seasons.

You should look out for some things, however:

- ✔ Convention season is in full swing. Getting a hotel room or restaurant table can be a challenge. And if you do, you may find yourself surrounded by dozens of computer geeks . . . or dentists . . . or restaurant owners. Then again, you may enjoy that!

- ✔ Beware of unpredictable September or October Indian summer heat waves. (Don't forget the shorts and sunscreen — just in case.)

Winter in the Midwest

Winter brings visions of softly falling snowflakes, but the reality is that those lovely snowflakes result in slick roads and salt trucks. Consider the following when planning a winter vacation in Chicago:

✔ During the holidays, the city looks beautiful. All of Michigan Avenue is lit up. Chicago goes all-out with Christmas decorations.

✔ Hotel prices sink during the slowest weeks of the winter, making the search for that good room at a great rate much easier.

✔ After Christmas, a peaceful hush settles over the city. You can have Michigan Avenue to yourself on the weekdays. After-holiday sales keep the stores busy on the weekends, but otherwise, you can pretend that the city is all yours.

✔ Mayor Daley has made an effort to make Chicago attractive to tourists in the winter with events such as WinterBreak Chicago, which fills the month of February with a series of blues concerts and more.

Winter does have its downsides, however. Consider the following:

✔ December is a bad month for crowds. Michigan Avenue is packed, literally — so much so that making your way down the street can be a challenge.

✔ Between conventions, family vacations, and savvy travelers, winter is rapidly becoming a more popular time to visit. Tourists are discovering that winter is Chicago's bargain season, but (so far) the cold months are still the least crowded.

✔ Did I mention winter's chilly temperatures?

✔ Because business is slow, hotels, restaurants, and stores take the opportunity to renovate, meaning that various areas that serve the public may be closed for maintenance purposes.

✔ Winter is the other time of year (along with springtime) when shows may close for a week.

Perusing a Calendar of Events

Chicago abounds with ethnic parades and other lively events — most of them free and packed with residents. You can choose from among a wide array of events, no matter what the month. The food, music, art, and flower fairs have established niches in the city's yearly schedule, along with the national parades and street celebrations staged by many of Chicago's numerous ethnic groups. Pick your time, choose your interest, and enjoy.

The best way to stay on top of the city's current crop of events is to ask the **Chicago Office of Tourism** (☎ 312-744-2400) or the **Illinois Bureau of Tourism** (☎ 800-2CONNECT) to mail you a copy of *Chicago Calendar of Events,* an excellent quarterly publication that surveys special events, including museum exhibitions, concert and theatrical performances, parades, and street festivals. Also ask to be sent the latest material produced by the **Mayor's Office of Special Events** (☎ 312-744-3315) or the **Special Events Hot Line** (☎ 312-744-3370), which keeps current with citywide and neighborhood festivals. The Chicago and Illinois offices of tourism also jointly operate a useful Web site at www.877chicago.com.

Remember that new events may be added every year and that some events may be discontinued or rescheduled. Call ahead to the sponsoring organization, the Chicago Office of Tourism, or the Mayor's Office of Special Events to verify dates, times, and locations.

January

Opening Day seems far away, but those "wait-until-next-year" Cubbie fans never stop dreaming. The **Chicago Cubs Convention,** held at the Chicago Hilton and Towers, hosts players signing autographs and collectors buying, selling, and swapping memorabilia. Call ☎ 773-404-2827 for more information. Mid-January.

The **Chicago Boat, Sports, and RV Show** (☎ 312-946-6262), held at McCormick Place, is for those who dream of spring. A tradition for over 70 years, you'll find boats, recreational vehicles, a climbing wall, and seminars on boating and fishing. Last week in January.

Again, spring fever comes early at a time of year when a little color and fragrance are more than welcome. Go to the Lincoln Park Conservatory (☎ 312-742-7737) and Garfield Park Conservatory (☎ 312-746-5100) for the **Azalea and Camellia flower shows** featuring spring-blooming plants, such as azaleas, tulips, and hyacinths. End of January through February.

February

A twisting dragon joins a fierce-looking lion dancer in the **Chinese New Year Parade** that winds its colorful way from Wentworth Avenue at 24th Place to Princeton Avenue and Cermak Road in Chinatown. Call ☎ 312-326-5320 for more information on this parade. Sunday following the Chinese New Year (between Jan 21 and Feb 19, depending on the lunar calendar).

In the dead of winter, come fantasize about convertibles and get your hands on the shiniest, newest automobiles for the coming year at the **Chicago Auto Show.** Presented since 1901, this show at McCormick Place attracts close to a million car owners and wannabe owners. Call ☎ 630-495-2282 for more information. Mid-February.

Watch more than 10,000 American Kennel Club dogs strut their stuff at the **International Cluster of Dog Shows** held at McCormick Place South. Call ☎ 773-237-5100 for more information. Third week in February.

March

A Chicago tradition since the 1840s, the annual **St. Patrick's Day Parade** along Dearborn Street from Wacker Drive to Van Buren Street brings out a celebrity grand marshal, local pols, and union bosses. The Chicago River is dyed green for the big day. Saturday closest to March 17.

The **Spring Flower Shows,** held at Lincoln Park Conservatory (☎ 312-742-7737) and Garfield Park Conservatory (☎ 312-746-5100), feature lilies, daffodils, tulips, pansies, and other flowering perennials. Usually begins the week before Easter.

April

Neither rain nor sleet nor snow nor hail (all very real possibilities in early spring) keeps eternally hopeful Cubs fans away from Wrigley Field or Sox fans away from U.S. Cellular Field (formerly Comiskey Park) on **Opening Day.** Call ☎ 773-404-2827 for the Cubs, or ☎ 312-674-1000 for the White Sox. Generally during the first week of April.

May

Wright Plus Tour, at the Frank Lloyd Wright Home & Studio in Oak Park is an annual tour that allows for a glimpse inside the brilliant mind of the architect. The tour includes ten buildings, including Frank Lloyd Wright's home and studio, Unity Temple, and several other notable Oak Park buildings, in both Prairie and Victorian styles. Tickets go on sale March 1 and sell out quickly. Call ☎ 708-848-1976 for information.

What has historically been one of the country's largest contemporary art fairs, **Art Chicago,** held at Navy Pier Festival Hall, hosts more than 200 art galleries and 2,000 artists. With the show's fall from favor in art circles, Art Chicago is changing up its offerings, so we'll see what the future brings. Call ☎ 312-587-3300 for information. Mother's Day weekend.

"Sweet Home Chicago" is "sweet home" to the **Chicago Blues Festival,** a huge blues event in Grant Park. At festival time, a bus shuttles aficionados between the city's numerous blues clubs. Call ☎ 312-744-3315 for information. End of May or early June.

The Ferris Wheel and Carousel begin spinning again at Navy Pier. The rides operate through October. Call ☎ 312-595-7437 for information.

June

A week or so after the blues musicians leave Grant Park, music fans head to the same venue to listen to top gospel performers at the **Chicago**

Gospel Festival. Over 40 performances unfold on three stages. Call ☎ 312-744-3315. Early June.

Entertainment, readings, food, and books galore abound at **Printers Row Book Fair,** one of the nation's largest free outdoor book fairs, which is located on Dearborn Street between Polk and Congress. Call ☎ 312-222-3986. The first weekend in June.

Ravinia Festival in Highland Park is the open-air summer home of the Chicago Symphony Orchestra and many visiting performers from Tony Bennett to Lyle Lovett. Call ☎ 847-266-5100 to make ticket reservations. Mid-June through September.

Fine art from more than 200 painters, sculptors, and jewelry designers, plus an art auction, garden walk, food and drink, and children's art activities can all be found at the **Old Town Art Fair,** located in the Old Town neighborhood at Lincoln Park West and Wisconsin Street (☎ 312-337-1938; www.oldtowntriangle.com). Second full weekend in June.

The **Grant Park Music Festival** hosts free outdoor musical concerts. Bring your blanket, picnic basket, and maybe even a Frisbee. Call ☎ 312-742-4763 to obtain a schedule. Last week in June through August.

Park yourself on Broadway to see the creative floats and colorful marching units in the **Gay and Lesbian Pride Parade.** The route is Halsted Street from Belmont Avenue to Broadway, south to Diversey Parkway, and east to Lincoln Park. Call ☎ 773-744-3315 for more information. Last Sunday in June at noon.

Sample Carson's ribs, Eli's cheesecake, and Pizzeria Uno's pizza at **Taste of Chicago.** This huge festival at Grant Park has close to 100 food booths to feed 3 million hungry visitors. The busiest day is July 3, because Chicago launches its Independence Day fireworks that evening over the lake. Call ☎ 312-744-3315 for information. Late June to early July.

The **Chicago Country Music Festival**, held in Grant Park (☎ 312-744-3315), is less claustrophobic than the Taste of Chicago, and it's held at the same time — best of all, it's free. You'll see big-name entertainers of the country-music genre. Late June (during the first weekend of Taste of Chicago).

July

Fireworks (launched from barges in Monroe Harbor), concerts, and spirited marches mark the **Independence Day Celebration** in Grant Park. Concurrent with Taste of Chicago, the crowds are enormous: Take public transportation. Call ☎ 312-744-3315 for more information. July 3.

The 33-year-old **Sheffield Garden Walk** allows you to snoop around the private gardens of Lincoln Park homeowners at Sheffield and Webster avenues. Food and drink vendors, live bands, and more make this a hopping event for Lincoln Park singles. Call ☎ 773-929-9255 for information. Mid-July.

You won't believe the crowds — or the big-name bands — that the city's oldest church (700 West Adams at Des Plaines Avenue) turns out for the annual **Old St. Patrick's World's Largest Block Party** blowout. Okay, the admission price is steep — around $35 — but we're talking six bands over two nights on two stages, plus all the beer you can drink (and people do drink all they possibly can). Call ☎ 312-648-1021. Mid-July.

The **Venetian Night Boat Parade** of beautifully decorated and illuminated boats takes place to elaborate fireworks and music by the Grant Park Symphony Orchestra, performing works by Italian composers. Events take place along the water at Monroe Harbor. Call ☎ 312-744-3315 for information on the parade. End of July.

August

The **Chicago Air & Water Show** showcases action on, in, and over Lake Michigan, with stunt pilots and skydivers, wing walkers and precision flyers, plus water-skiing, windsurfing, and air-sea rescue. You'll have a hard time ignoring the show (unless you're oblivious to sonic booms, C-130 cargo planes, stealth bombers, and F-16 fighters roaring over your head). Hugely popular are the U.S. Air Force Thunderbirds, who usually make an appearance. If you bring a portable radio, you can tune into WBBM (780 AM) to hear the show. Then, you can plant yourself on any beach up and down the lakefront and avoid the crowds at North Avenue Beach. Call ☎ 312-744-3315 for information. Mid-August.

The **Chicago Jazz Festival** always attracts national names, and jam sessions at local jazz clubs stretch into the wee hours. Call ☎ 312-744-3315 for information on this event in Grant Park. Labor Day weekend.

September

Around the Coyote hosts one of the nation's largest concentrations of artists. Tour hundreds of artists' studios and see music performances and fashion shows in the Wicker Park and Bucktown neighborhoods. Call ☎ 773-342-6777 for details. Second weekend in September.

A relative newcomer to the Chicago music festival scene, **World Music Festival Chicago** — the City's Department of Cultural Affairs' major undertaking — brings in top performers from Zimbabwe to Sri Lanka and Hungary and points in between. It's been hugely popular, so call early for schedules and tickets (☎ 312-744-6630); many performances sell out. Shows are a mix of free and ticketed performances (most are $10 or less). The Museum of Contemporary Art, the Chicago Cultural Center, the Old Town School of Folk Music, and the Hot House host many of the performances. Throughout September.

October

One of Chicago's largest parades — the **Columbus Day Parade** — lasts two hours, includes more than 200 bands and floats, and features a celebrity grand marshal. (President George H. W. Bush and Barbara Bush have served, as did the late Joe DiMaggio.) The route is Columbus Drive from Balbo to Monroe streets. Call ☎ 312-828-0010. Closest Monday to October 12, at around noon.

The world-class **Chicago Marathon** begins and ends in Grant Park and usually attracts many elite runners who hope to attempt world-record times because the course is flat and, therefore, fast. Call ☎ 312-904-9800 or go to www.chicagomarathon.com for information. Mid-October.

The **Chicago International Film Festival,** the oldest competitive film festival in the country, has screenings for more than two weeks at theaters across the city. Call ☎ 312-332-3456 for a schedule. Mid- to late October.

November

State Street Thanksgiving Parade (☎ 312-751-5681) is an annual event that takes place on Thanksgiving morning beginning at 8:30 a.m. The parade marches up State Street, from Congress to Randolph.

Disney sponsors the **Magnificent Mile Lights Festival,** a colorful parade of characters that makes its way south on Michigan Avenue from Oak Street to the Chicago River. As the parade passes, lights are illuminated block by block. Carolers, elves, and minstrels appear with Santa along the avenue all day and into the evening. Call ☎ 312-642-3570. Saturday before Thanksgiving.

Chicago Humanities Festival takes over locations throughout downtown, from libraries to concert halls. Over a period of 11 days, the festival presents cultural performances, readings, and symposiums tied to an annual theme (recent themes included "Brains & Beauty" and "Crime & Punishment"). Expect appearances by major authors, scholars, and policymakers, all at a very reasonable price ($5 per event). Call ☎ 312-661-1028 or visit www.chfestival.org for information. Early November.

December

Performances of *A Christmas Carol,* an annual favorite for more than two decades, take place in the Goodman Theatre in the North Loop theater district. Call ☎ 312-443-3800 early for tickets because the show sells out. Thanksgiving to the end of December.

The colorful illuminated displays of the **Zoo Lights Festival** enliven the Lincoln Park Zoo, 2200 N. Cannon Dr. (☎ 312-742-2000; www.lpzoo.com). On a Saturday in early December, you can participate in Caroling to the Animals, a daylong tradition. Around Thanksgiving to New Year's Day.

The free tickets to Chicago's annual interactive choral event, the **Do-It-Yourself Messiah,** sponsored by LaSalle Bank, are much in demand. The choral director of the Chicago Symphony Orchestra conducts this event, held at Orchestra Hall. Visit www.lasallebank.com/messiah for more information. Mid-December.

On **New Year's Eve,** Chicago stages a massive midnight fireworks display at Navy Pier, where you also find a big party with dancing into the wee hours. Call ☎ **312-595-7437** for information. December 31.

Part II
Planning Your Trip to Chicago

The 5th Wave   By Rich Tennant

"Welcome to our nonstop flight to Chicago. Will you be sitting in first class or a bit nearer the stockyards?"

In this part . . .

Anticipation — it's one of the most enjoyable aspects of traveling. In this part, I help you plan your trip, starting with a review of the pros and cons of Chicago's two airports, and moving on to budgeting and transportation. Should you rent a car or take the El? Should you join a tour or create your own itinerary? What assistance is available for those with special travel needs and interests? You find all the information you need right here.

Chapter 4

Managing Your Money

. . . .

In This Chapter

▶ Figuring out how much money is enough
▶ Budgeting like a pro: where to splurge, where to save
▶ Locating ATMs
▶ Being streetwise with your wallet or handbag
▶ Coping with a lost or stolen wallet

. . . .

C hicago has a way of eating up your money: dinner at **Harry Caray's** (see Chapter 10), cabs, admission fees, tips for the bellhop and maid, the bottle of water bought at **Navy Pier** (see Chapter 11), coffee at **Corner Bakery** (see Chapter 13) — and all that wonderful shopping. Making matters worse, ATMs are on practically every corner. With cash and credit so accessible, spending can get out of hand fast.

Before you go, come up with a realistic idea of how much you can spend. You don't want to worry constantly about spending money, but you don't want to faint when you get your credit card bills, either. The idea is to have fun and enjoy yourself without agonizing over every dollar you spend. For peace of mind and for the sake of your bank account, know when you can afford to splurge and when to economize.

This chapter gives you some ideas of how to allocate your funds. After all, you don't want to find yourself still paying for this trip when you set off on your next adventure!

Planning Your Budget

Budgeting a trip to Chicago — or to anywhere else for that matter — is a matter of give and take. Unless your bank account is bottomless, you'll need to make some trade-offs. Are you prepared to sacrifice some hotel comforts to pay for tickets to a hit musical? Can you eat hot dogs for lunch in exchange for splurging on a couple of dinners at restaurants owned by superstar chefs? Are you just as happy taking home photos as expensive souvenirs? Then maybe you can have cocktails downtown on North Michigan Avenue in the **Signature Room on the 95th** at the top of the **John Hancock Center Observatory** (see Chapter 11). It's all a matter of your priorities.

Taxes and fees

These expenses aren't usually paid in cash, so they're easy to overlook. When you arrange any commercial transaction — booking a hotel room or renting a car, for example — be sure to ask for the total cost, which will inevitably be more than the great-sounding price the business initially quotes you. Read on to see how taxes and fees can expand the price.

- ✔ Chicago sales tax is 8.75 percent. Restaurants in the central part of the city add another 1 percent tax to your bill.

- ✔ Hotel room tax totals 14.9 percent.

- ✔ Many restaurants add a 15 to 18 percent gratuity to the bill if your party is larger than five people.

Gratuities

The average tip for most service providers, such as waiters and cab drivers, is 15 percent, rising to 20 percent for particularly good service. If you're looking for an easy way to calculate the tip in a Chicago restaurant, keep in mind that doubling the tax equates to 17.5 percent of the bill. A 10 to 15 percent tip is sufficient if you just have a drink at a bar. Bellhops get $1 or $2 a bag, hotel housekeepers should receive at least $1 per person per day, and valet parking and coat-check attendants expect $1 to $2 for their services.

Hotel phones

Your hotel may charge you $1 or more per call from your room — even if you're just calling a toll-free number or contacting a long-distance operator to use your telephone credit card. If you have a wireless phone with unlimited (or a large amount of included) minutes, you may want to use it rather than the hotel phone. But make sure to check with your wireless phone company to find out if you have to pay roaming charges outside your home calling zone.

Incidentals

You may not notice the little costs each time they occur, but if you're stopping for coffee twice a day, buying bottled water, or purchasing a second map because you left the first one in your hotel room, you could easily be spending $20 to $30 more per day than you need to. Buy water at a drugstore or supermarket, stash it in your hotel room, and take a bottle with you each time you head out. Have your morning cup of coffee from the coffeemaker in your hotel room and stop once at a coffee shop as a treat during the day (it's also a good opportunity to use the restroom, which can be hard to find in downtown Chicago). Make some trail mix from nuts and raisins and put it in individual baggies. Try to not waste too much on incidentals, and you'll have more to spend on entertainment and the like.

For tips on budgeting, see "Cutting Costs" at the end of this chapter. For information on Chicago's taxes, some of which are quite significant (like our 8.75 percent sales tax), see the appendix.

Table 4-1 offers some average costs for you to get started.

Table 4-1	What Things Cost in Chicago
Cab from O'Hare to downtown hotel	$32
Cab from Midway to downtown hotel	$27
Shuttle from O'Hare to downtown hotel	$19
Shuttle from Midway to downtown hotel	$14
Subway or bus ride	$1.75
Transfer (good for two additional rides)	25¢
Ticket to John Hancock Center Observatory	$9
Ticket to Sears Tower Skydeck	$9.50
Sightseeing boat tour (two hours)	$18
Hot dog at Gold Coast Dogs	$2.30
Dinner for one at Boston Blackie's	$14
Dinner for one at Café Luciano	$23
Steak dinner at Saloon Steakhouse	$37
Weekday *Chicago Tribune*	50¢
Movie ticket	$9–$10

Transportation

You don't need a car in Chicago. Hey, when I lived in the heart of the city, I didn't own a car. With the high costs of owning an automobile — insurance, registration, gas, parking, and wear and tear (on vehicle and nerves) — why would I own a car? You can get around easily, and usually safely, on Chicago's relatively efficient public transportation system and on foot. A bus or subway ride costs only $1.75, and a transfer that provides two additional rides (if taken within a two-hour window) is only an additional 25¢. Cabs are plentiful and relatively inexpensive. The average cab ride in the downtown area costs $5 to $7. All of which means that you won't need a rental car, even if you're not staying downtown. So, assuming you spend $20 a day on cabs and public transportation, you save a sizable chunk of the $40 to $50 that you may otherwise spend on a car rental, plus valet parking at your hotel, which runs as high as $36 a day. That could amount to more than $60 a day to apply to other expenses. (For more information about getting around the city, see Chapter 8.)

Watch the meter. Taxis cost $1.90 as soon as the driver starts the meter, and then $1.60 for each mile. The driver also adds 50¢ for each additional passenger aged 12 to 65. At press time, there was talk of raising the fare, so don't be surprised if you jump into a cab and it costs you even a bit more.

Lodging

Lodging is pretty easy to figure out. The cost is set after you book your accommodations and is less flexible than other areas of your budget, such as attractions. You have to have a place to stay. So, as in other real-estate matters, location, location, and location determine the cost of your lodgings. The more central you are to Chicago's **Magnificent Mile,** the more expensive the hotel. If you're prepared to stay a little bit away from downtown, you can save on lodging. But if being in the middle of the action is valuable to you, you can find other areas of your budget for economizing. For me, location is most important. I will take a smaller room in a hotel that's centrally located over a larger room in a hotel that's far from the main attractions. I like to walk everywhere and would rather spend a bit more on the room and less on cab fare. But that's just me. You need to decide if the time spent traveling on public transportation or the expense of taking cabs is worth the money you save by staying in a hotel that's located away from the center of the city.

According to the Hotel/Motel Association of Illinois, the average hotel room rate is about $155 for downtown Chicago and $110 for the metropolitan area, with Chicago's finest hotels averaging $370 per night, second only to New York City. When you figure in room tax, you're going to be spending at the very least $100 for a room — although you can shave off a few dollars by staying at the downtown Red Roof Inn or on the Near North side, for example. If you're able to spend $150, you can figure in a few extra comforts and conveniences. Push this up to $200 a night and you can get a comfortable and well-located hotel room. (See Chapter 9 for the lowdown on the Chicago hotel scene.)

Dining

Because Chicago has so many restaurants, inexpensive and moderately priced eateries are easy to find. Many have the equivalent of blue-plate specials. When you splurge at a top-tier restaurant, consider a multi-course tasting menu to keep costs down. In most cases, these fixed-price menus, which often showcase the chef's best efforts, are a much better deal than ordering à la carte.

You can save on breakfast if you choose a hotel whose room rates include continental breakfast or, in some cases, a full buffet. Otherwise, look for a coffee shop where you can get a roll or bagel, plus juice or other beverage, for about $5. With careful choices (especially if you opt for soup and salad), you can eat lunch for $7 to $10. You can have a decent dinner in a nonfranchise restaurant for $20 or less.

 Hit **Lou Mitchell's** in the Loop for breakfast (see Chapter 10), and you won't need lunch. The hearty portions and low prices make this spot a favorite with locals. You get free doughnut holes while you wait in line, and for about $9 you can get a gigantic omelet that will keep you — and maybe a travel companion, too — going 'til dinner. (P.S. Ladies also get a bonus box of Milk Duds when they finish!)

Sightseeing

Admission fees for museums, observation decks, and other attractions can add up quickly. To figure out how much to budget, refer to the chapters on sightseeing (Chapters 11 and 13), compile a list of must-see attractions, and total the price of admissions. For ways to trim your budget, see "Cutting Costs" at the end of this chapter.

Shopping

This category is, of course, highly flexible. Budgeting often involves at least one four-letter word: *sale.* Check the daily newspapers, such as the *Chicago Tribune* and *Chicago Sun-Times* (especially the Sunday editions), for announcements. To be sure of hitting the city's most spectacular sales, plan to visit in January. And when it comes to Chicago souvenirs, why not be creative? Instead of bringing home overpriced Chicago Cubs jerseys from the souvenir store, you can buy something unique, such as a package of money from your free tour of the **Federal Reserve Bank of Chicago.** The bills are shredded, of course, but it makes a fun gift.

Nightlife

Entertainment can be a tough category in which to economize. If you enjoy a cocktail or a glass of wine, figure on spending about $10 a pop at a downtown bar. If you're headed for a jazz or blues club, allow for a cover charge plus drinks (perhaps with a minimum drink requirement). However, some lively neighborhood bars serve reasonably priced drinks (see Chapter 16). And some entertainment won't cost you a dime, such as noontime **"Under the Picasso" concerts** at Daley Plaza, and free movies at the **Chicago Cultural Center** (located on South Michigan Avenue just north of the Art Institute of Chicago) and **Oriental Institute Museum** in suburban Hyde Park. In the summer, most music festivals in Grant Park are free, and the people-watching alone can keep you entertained all night long. (See Chapter 11 for information on these activities.)

Generally, you can see a show in Chicago for much less than you'd pay on Broadway, and tickets are cheaper still if you take advantage of discounts that are up to 50 percent the day of the show at **Hot Tix** booths. Locations include: 163 E. Pearson St. (the Chicago Waterworks Visitor Center), just off Michigan Avenue, and 78 W. Randolph St., in the Loop.

Check out www.hottix.org for current information. (See Chapter 15 for details on plays and the performing arts).

Cutting Costs — But Not the Fun

Let's say you tallied up your expected expenses and tried to make some trade-offs, but the grand total still seems too high. Now is the time to think about some serious ways to economize.

Planning tips

When you pull your trip together, consider

- ✔ **Asking for discount rates:** Membership in AAA, frequent-flier plans, trade unions, AARP, or other groups may qualify you for discounted rates on car rentals, plane tickets, hotel rooms, even meals. Ask about everything; you may be pleasantly surprised.

- ✔ **Going in the off season:** If you can travel during nonpeak months, airline tickets are much cheaper. And during the low season (the depth of winter) you can find hotel prices that are as much as half of what they are during peak months.

- ✔ **Traveling on off days of the week:** If you can travel on a Tuesday, Wednesday, or Thursday, you may find cheaper airfares. When you inquire about airfares, ask if you can obtain a lower rate by flying on a different day. Also remember that, for some airlines, staying over a Saturday night can cut your airfare by more than half.

- ✔ **Reserving your flight well in advance:** Fares that require a 21- or 14-day advance purchase can be a great deal.

- ✔ **Trying a package tour:** For many destinations, one call to a travel agent can net you airfare, hotel, ground transportation, and even some sightseeing, all for much less than if you tried to put the trip together yourself. See the section on package tours in Chapter 5 for specific suggestions.

Lodging tips

To trim your hotel bill, think about

- ✔ **Reserving a hotel room with a kitchen:** Doing your own cooking and dishes may not feel like a vacation, but you save a lot of money by not eating in restaurants three times a day. Even if you only make breakfast and an occasional bag lunch in the kitchen, you still save in the long run. And you won't be shocked by a hefty room-service bill.

- ✔ **Checking into a hotel that includes meals or drinks in its room rate.** Embassy Suites, for example, includes a hot breakfast buffet and an evening cocktail gathering. Two Kimpton hotels, Hotel

Monaco and Hotel Allegro, offer guests wine and cheese each evening. Three Near North hotels (City Suites, Majestic, and Willows) serve breakfast featuring legendary Ann Sather cinnamon rolls. (See Chapter 9 for hotel listings.)

✔ **Asking if your kids can stay in your room for no charge:** A room with two double beds usually doesn't cost more than a room with one queen-size bed. And many hotels won't charge you the additional person rate if the additional person is pint-size and related to you. Even if you have to pay $15 or $20 for a rollaway bed, you save hundreds by not taking two rooms.

✔ **Avoiding the hotel minibar:** If you have midnight cravings, stock up on beverages and snacks at a supermarket. Even premium prices at a grocery store are cheaper than the minibar.

✔ **Not paying for amenities you won't use:** If you don't expect to have time for a swim in the pool or a workout in the health club, choose a hotel that doesn't have (and charge for) those facilities.

Transportation tips

When planning your trips around town, I suggest:

✔ **Not renting a car:** Unless you do much traveling to the suburbs and beyond, a car can be a liability in Chicago and an unnecessary cost, especially when you add the high cost of parking — over $30 a day at most major hotels. Buses, trains, and cabs can save you big bucks.

✔ **Studying the public transit system and street pattern:** You can find plenty of advice in this book about riding the Chicago Transit Authority (CTA). Know in advance where taking a bus or train is advisable, and remember that the 25¢ transfer is a great deal. Chicago is a good walking city, and many of the attractions that you want to see can be explored on foot. Be sure to pick up a free public transit map at any CTA station, download maps from the CTA Web site at www.transitchicago.com, or call ☎ **888-968-7282.** For the lowdown on public transportation, see Chapter 8.

✔ **Taking advantage of the CTA Visitor Pass:** Passes are a good investment for visitors who plan to spend much time sightseeing around the city. For details, see Chapter 8.

Dining tips

Before you dive into your next Chicago meal, consider

✔ **Trying expensive restaurants at lunch instead of dinner:** Lunch tabs are usually a fraction of what dinner would cost at most top restaurants, and the menu often boasts many of the same specialties.

✔ **Keeping an eye on the time:** Breakfast specials may end at 10 a.m. or the early-bird dinner menu may run only until 6:30 p.m. — just when you realize that you're hungry.

✔ **Not drinking in hotel bars:** The only exceptions are bars such as the Palm Court at the **Drake** hotel and the Salon in the **Hotel Inter-Continental,** where the price of a drink includes excellent jazz.

Sightseeing tips

When penny-pinching matters, try

✔ **Buying a Chicago CityPass:** The CityPass includes admission to Adler Planetarium & Astronomy Museum, the Art Institute of Chicago, the Field Museum of Natural History, the Museum of Science and Industry, the John G. Shedd Aquarium, and the John Hancock Center Observatory (see Chapter 11). The adult rate is $49, and the youth rate (3 to 11 years) is $39. The value of an adult pass is $95, so you're saving loads if you plan to hit most of Chicago's attractions. After you present your CityPass at the first attraction, booklets are valid for nine days. You can purchase a CityPass at any of the six locations or online at www.citypass.com.

✔ **Taking advantage of freebies:** On certain days, some major museums, such at the **Art Institute of Chicago,** waive admission. Chicago also has many fine free museums, such as the **Museum of Broadcast Communications** (it's closed temporarily, but will reopen in a new home in 2006) and the **Oriental Institute Museum** (see Chapter 11).

Handling Money

With the proliferation of ATMs, getting cash away from home — even from your credit card — is rarely a problem. But if you're visiting the ATM every day, you may start racking up significant fees. In that case, consider traveler's checks. Here's the lowdown on the pros and cons of using various forms of payment.

Choosing traveler's checks or the green stuff

Traveler's checks are something of an anachronism from the days before the ATM made cash accessible at any time. The only sound alternative to traveling with dangerously large amounts of cash, traveler's checks were as reliable as currency. Unlike personal checks or cash, traveler's checks could be replaced if lost or stolen.

These days, traveler's checks seem less necessary because all American cities (including Chicago) have 24-hour ATMs that allow travelers to withdraw small amounts of cash as needed and avoid the risk of carrying a fortune around in an unfamiliar environment. Generally, carrying the smallest amount of cash possible — enough to pay for cabs, tips, and other incidentals — is wise.

Two major ATM networks are **Cirrus** (☎ **800-424-7787**; www.mastercard.com) and **Plus** (☎ **800-843-7587**; www.visa.com). Check the back of your card for the name of your bank's network. You may be linked to two or three networks.

Of course, as with anything else, you pay for the convenience of instant cash. Many banks impose a fee ($1, $1.50, or even $2) every time a card is used at an ATM owned by another bank. If you're withdrawing money every day, you may be better off with traveler's checks — provided that you don't mind showing identification every time you want to cash a check.

You can get traveler's checks at almost any bank. **American Express** offers denominations of $10, $20, $50, $100, $500, and $1,000. You pay a service charge of 1 to 4 percent. You can also get American Express traveler's checks over the phone by calling ☎ **800-221-7282**; by using this number, Amex gold and platinum cardholders are exempt from the 1 percent fee. AAA members can obtain checks without a fee at most AAA offices.

Visa offers traveler's checks at Citibank locations nationwide, as well as several other banks. The service charge is 1.5 to 2 percent; checks come in denominations of $20, $50, $100, $500, and $1,000. Call ☎ **800-732-1322** for information. **MasterCard** also offers traveler's checks; call ☎ **800-223-9920** for a list of vendors near you.

 Be vigilant when using ATMs. Whenever possible, choose machines in well-lighted locations where plenty of people are about. And stay alert while processing your request for cash. Robberies (and worse) can and do occur around ATMs.

Doting on debit cards

Another way of working with money you have — as opposed to the theoretical money of credit cards — is by using a debit card (an ATM card with a credit card logo). In many cases, your debit and ATM card are the same piece of plastic. Instead of getting cash, however, the debit card pays for purchases anywhere a credit card is accepted. The advantage? The money comes out of your checking account instead of pushing up against your credit card limit. Plus, you never pay an additional fee to use it, and you have less cash to carry around.

Using plastic

Invaluable when traveling, credit cards are a safe way to carry money and provide a convenient record of all your expenses. You can also withdraw cash advances from your credit cards at any bank (although you start paying hefty interest on the advance the moment you receive the cash, and you won't receive frequent-flier miles on an airline credit card). At most banks, you don't even need to go to a teller; you can get a cash advance at the ATM if you know your personal identification number (PIN). If you forget your PIN or didn't even know you had one, call the phone number on the back of your credit card and ask the bank to send it to you. It usually takes five to seven business days, though some banks provide the number over the phone if you tell them your mother's maiden name or pass some other security clearance.

Finding Chicago's ATMs

The two major ATM networks are MasterCard's **Cirrus** (☎ 800-424-7787) and Visa's **Plus** (☎ 800-843-7587). Most banks use one of these networks. Look for the logo on the back of your ATM card to see which network accepts your card.

In Chicago, **Bank One** (with its blue and white logo) has a large network of ATMs. On Michigan Avenue, you'll find Bank One ATMs in the John Hancock Center Observatory building and in the Bank One building at Ontario Street (near the northwest corner of the intersection with Michigan Avenue). If you aren't a Bank One customer, the charge to use the ATM is $1.50. If you are a Bank One customer, you won't get charged. Bank One is a member of the MAC, Cash Station, and Cirrus networks.

When using an ATM, exercise the same caution that you would at home (for example, protect your password). Don't be complacent just because you're in a busy foot-traffic area — that makes running off with your money easier, not harder.

Dealing with a Lost or Stolen Wallet

Most credit card companies operate toll-free numbers to call if your wallet or purse is stolen. Your card issuer may be able to wire you a cash advance and provide an emergency replacement card in a day or two.

Check the back of your card for the issuing bank's number before you leave home. Keep the number separate from your wallet. You also can call **toll-free directory assistance** (☎ 800-555-1212) to find your bank's number.

Visa and MasterCard have global service numbers: for **Visa,** ☎ 800-847-2911; for **MasterCard,** ☎ 800-307-7309. (Both suggest you contact your card issuer directly.) **American Express** cardholders and traveler's check holders should call ☎ 800-221-7282.

If you carry traveler's checks, keep a record of the serial numbers so you can handle an emergency. Keeping a record of your credit card numbers and the companies' emergency numbers also is a good idea. Be sure to keep a copy of all your travel papers separate from your wallet or purse, and leave a copy with someone at home in case you need it faxed in an emergency.

Always notify the police if your wallet is stolen. You probably won't get the wallet back, but you may need a copy of the police report for your insurance or credit card company. In Chicago, ☎ 311 is the **non-emergency police number.**

Chapter 5

Getting to Chicago

● ●

In This Chapter

▶ Debating the merits of a package tour
▶ Getting a great deal on a flight
▶ Flying in comfort and safety
▶ Discovering other ways to get here from there

● ●

*A*ll roads lead to Chicago: The city is a major hub in the interstate highway system and remains connected to the rest of North America with passenger rail service. In the center of the country, Chicago is an easy destination to access by train, plane, or automobile.

In this chapter, I show you how to go about making your travel arrangements, no matter what mode of transportation you choose.

Flying to Chicago

Most people get here via O'Hare International Airport — *the* passageway to Chicago. If most travelers to Chicago are going to share a single experience, that experience is O'Hare. One of the world's busiest airports, O'Hare is often a stopover for both domestic and international travelers (mostly because American and United airlines use O'Hare as a major hub). O'Hare boasts its own police force, zip code, medical center, cemetery, and chapel. Some 68 million people pass through O'Hare annually. If you come to Chicago, you may well do the same. (For info on surviving O'Hare, see Chapter 8.)

But O'Hare isn't the only airport game in town: Don't forget Chicago's smaller airport, Midway International Airport, which has doubled its public spaces to accommodate more travelers. And political debate continues over where and whether to build a third airport. Air service into the Windy City offers a wide range of choices, from major domestic and international carriers to small, no-frills airlines (not that many airlines have an overabundance of frills these days).

Airfares demonstrate capitalism at work — passengers in the same cabin on the same airplane rarely pay the same fare. Rather, they each pay what the market will bear. Business travelers pay for the flexibility to buy their tickets at the last minute, change their itineraries, or get home before the weekend. Passengers who can book their tickets far in advance, stay over Saturday night, or are willing to travel on a Tuesday, Wednesday, or Thursday pay the least, usually a fraction of the full fare. On most flights, even the shortest hops, the full fare can reach $1,000 or more, but a 7-day or 14-day advance-purchase ticket may cost only $200 or $300. Planning ahead pays.

Finding out which airlines fly there

Because O'Hare is one of the country's busiest airports, almost every airline flies through Chicago, many with direct flights. Elk Grove Village, a suburb of Chicago, houses the headquarters of **United Air Lines.** Although this airline giant is going through hard times, it remains one of the largest carriers in the nation and has one of the most extensive offerings of flights from overseas. In fact, O'Hare handles so many international flights that it has its own international terminal (terminal 5). **American, Northwest,** and **Continental** airlines also offer large numbers of flights into both O'Hare and Midway. **Southwest Airlines** and other discount carriers have made extensive investments in facilities at the newly expanded Midway airport. (See the appendix for the toll-free numbers of all these carriers.)

Getting the best deal on your airfare

Competition among the major U.S. airlines is unlike that of any other industry. Every airline offers virtually the same product (basically, a coach seat is always a coach seat), yet prices can vary by hundreds of dollars.

Because Chicago has two airports, O'Hare and Midway, you have more options and chances to lock in a lower fare. Midway is a little closer to downtown Chicago and a slightly cheaper ride by cab or shuttle. Because of varying traffic and road conditions, however, predicting which airport offers a faster ride into the central city or back is difficult. Under optimum conditions, the journey between both airports and the city by car takes around 40 minutes — sometimes less for Midway. But keep in mind that conditions are rarely optimum. During rush hour, the same journey can take one to two hours. Both airports are served by CTA trains, which are oblivious to traffic conditions.

 Compared to O'Hare, Midway is smaller, has fewer restaurants and shops, and is served by fewer airlines. However, you may be able to find a cheaper fare to Midway. Definitely check flights to both airports before buying your ticket.

 Business travelers who need the flexibility to buy their tickets at the last minute and change their itineraries at a moment's notice — and who want to get home before the weekend — pay (or at least their companies pay) the premium rate, known as the *full fare.* For some airlines, if you can book your ticket far in advance, stay over Saturday night, and are willing to travel midweek (Tues, Wed, or Thurs), you can qualify for the least expensive price — usually a fraction of the full fare. On most flights, even the shortest hops within the United States, the full fare is close to $1,000 or more, but a 7- or 14-day advance-purchase ticket may cost less than half of that amount. Obviously, planning ahead pays.

The airlines also periodically hold sales, in which they lower the prices on their most popular routes. These fares have advance-purchase requirements and date-of-travel restrictions, but you can't beat the prices. As you plan your vacation, keep your eyes open for these sales, which tend to take place in seasons of low travel volume. You almost never see a sale around the peak summer vacation months of July and August, or around Thanksgiving or Christmas, when many people fly, regardless of the fare they have to pay.

Consolidators, also known as *bucket shops,* are great sources for international tickets, although they usually can't beat the Internet on fares within North America. Start by looking in Sunday newspaper travel sections; U.S. travelers should focus on the *New York Times, Los Angeles Times,* and *Miami Herald.*

 Bucket-shop tickets are usually nonrefundable or rigged with stiff cancellation penalties, often as high as 50 to 75 percent of the ticket price, and some put you on charter airlines with questionable safety records.

Several reliable consolidators are worldwide and available on the Net. **STA Travel** (☎ 800-781-4040; www.statravel.com), the world's leader in student travel, offers good fares for travelers of all ages. **Flights.com** (☎ 800-872-8800; www.flights.com) has excellent fares worldwide and "local" Web sites in 12 countries. **FlyCheap** (☎ 800-359-2432; www.1800flycheap.com) is owned by package-holiday megalith MyTravel and so has especially good access to fares for sunny destinations. **Air Tickets Direct** (☎ 800-778-3447; www.airticketsdirect.com) is based in Montreal and leverages the currently weak Canadian dollar for low fares.

Booking your flight online

The "big three" online travel agencies, **Expedia** (www.expedia.com), **Travelocity** (www.travelocity.com), and **Orbitz** (www.orbitz.com) sell most of the air tickets bought on the Internet. (Canadian travelers should try www.expedia.ca and www.travelocity.ca; U.K. residents can go for expedia.co.uk and opodo.co.uk.) Each has different business deals with the airlines and may offer different fares on the same flights, so shopping around is wise. Expedia and Travelocity will also send you an **e-mail notification** when a cheap fare becomes available to your favorite destination. Of the smaller travel-agency Web sites, **SideStep** (www.sidestep.com) receives good reviews from users. It purports to "search 140 sites at once," but in reality only beats competitors' fares as often as other sites do.

Great **last-minute deals** are available through free weekly e-mail services provided directly by the airlines. Most of these deals are announced on Tuesday or Wednesday and must be purchased online. Most are only valid for travel that weekend, but some (such as Southwest's) can be booked weeks or months in advance. Sign up for weekly e-mail alerts at airline Web sites or check megasites that compile comprehensive lists of last-minute specials, such as **Smarter Living** (smarterliving.com). For last-minute trips, www.site59.com in the U.S. and www.lastminute.com in Europe often have better deals than the major-label sites.

If you're willing to give up some control over your flight details, use an *opaque fare service* like **Priceline** (www.priceline.com) or **Hotwire** (www.hotwire.com). Both offer rock-bottom prices in exchange for travel on a "mystery airline" at a mysterious time of day, often with a mysterious change of planes en route. The mystery airlines are all major, well-known carriers — and the possibility of being sent from Philadelphia to Chicago via Tampa is remote. But your chances of getting a 6 a.m. or 11 p.m. flight are pretty high. Hotwire tells you flight prices before you buy; Priceline usually has better deals than Hotwire, but you have to play their "name our price" game. ***Note:*** In 2004, Priceline added non-opaque service to its roster. You now have the option to pick exact flights, times, and airlines from a list of offers — or opt to bid on opaque fares as before. Check out *Priceline.com For Dummies* (Wiley) for additional information.

Great last-minute deals are also available directly from the airlines themselves through a free e-mail service called *E-savers*. Each week, the airline sends you a list of discounted flights, usually leaving the upcoming Friday or Saturday and returning the following Monday or Tuesday. You can sign up for all the major airlines at one time by logging on to **Smarter Living** (www.smarterliving.com), or you can go to each individual airline's Web site. Airline sites also offer schedules, flight booking, and information on late-breaking bargains.

Driving to Chicago

Chicago is easier to get to by road for more people than any other city in the nation. Within a 300-mile radius of the heart of the city (or a comfortable one-day drive) lies one of the most densely populated areas of the country. The Windy City also is a major intersection on the interstate highway system. East-west highways I-80, I-88, I-90, and I-94 run through Chicago. The city is connected to north-south interstate routes I-55, I-57, and I-65.

If you're traveling as part of a group, you may save money by driving. However, don't forget to budget the cost of parking, which can run as high as $30 a day in downtown Chicago.

If you plan to drive to Chicago but don't intend to use your car while in the city, consider perimeter parking lots. For bargain perimeter parking, check with the Chicago Transit Authority (CTA). For only $1.50, **CTA's Park and Ride lots,** located near many train-line terminals, allow visitors to stow their cars for up to 24 hours. For long-term parking, CTA's Cumberland lot, ten minutes east of O'Hare, costs $10.75 for 24 hours. (Call ☎ **888-968-7282** for locations and restrictions.)

Also consider parking in a lot located within walking distance of the Loop. **Millennium Park** has four lots. Rates vary, but expect to pay from $10 to $20 for 1 to 24 hours. For the Grant Park North lot, enter on Michigan Avenue at Madison or Randolph streets. For the Millennium Park lot, enter on Columbus Drive at Monroe or Randolph avenues. For the East Monroe Street lot, enter on Columbus Drive at Monroe or Randolph avenues. And for the Grant Park South lot, enter on Michigan Avenue at Van Buren Street.

Traffic on Chicago expressways can be brutal. Avoid arriving or departing during the heart of morning and evening rush hours (about 6:45 to 9:30 a.m. and 3:45 to 6:30 p.m.). All the major arteries, including the Dan Ryan (I-90 and I-94), Edens (I-94), Eisenhower (I-290), Kennedy (I-90), and Stevenson (I-55) expressways, can gridlock. Don't be lured into rush-hour driving by the prospect of *reverse commuting* (coming into town in the afternoon and leaving in the morning). It's a myth. Once upon a time, traffic may have been lighter outbound in the morning and inbound in the evening — but today, that has been negated by the large number of people who live in Chicago and commute to jobs in the suburbs.

Arriving by Other Means

Unlike many cities, Chicago has not been abandoned by the railroad. Thanks to Amtrak, about 50 intercity trains still pull into and out of Union Station (at Adams and Canal streets, just west of the Loop across the Chicago River) on a daily basis. A number of the trains carry the nostalgic names of legendary trains of the past, such as the Lakeshore Limited, the Capitol Limited, the Empire Builder, the California Zephyr, and the Southwest Chief. For example, the City of New Orleans leaves each evening for an overnight trip to the Big Easy via Memphis.

For fares, schedules, and reservations, check with a travel agent or contact Amtrak (☎ **800-872-7245;** www.amtrak.com).

Joining an Escorted Tour

You may be one of the many people who love escorted tours. The tour company takes care of all the details, and tells you what to expect at each leg of your journey. You know your costs up front and, in the case of the tame ones, you don't get many surprises. Escorted tours can take you to the maximum number of sights in the minimum amount of time with the least amount of hassle.

If you decide to go with an escorted tour, I strongly recommend purchasing travel insurance, especially if the tour operator asks you to pay up front. But don't buy insurance from the tour operator! If the tour operator doesn't fulfill its obligation to provide you with the vacation you paid for, there's no reason to think that they'll fulfill their insurance obligations either. Get travel insurance through an independent agency. (I tell you more about the ins and outs of travel insurance in Chapter 7.)

When choosing an escorted tour, along with finding out whether you have to put down a deposit and when final payment is due, ask a few simple questions before you buy:

- ✔ **What is the cancellation policy?** Can they cancel the trip if they don't get enough people? How late can you cancel if you're unable to go? Do you get a refund if you cancel? If they cancel?

- ✔ **How jam-packed is the schedule?** Does the tour schedule try to fit 25 hours into a 24-hour day, or does it give you ample time to relax by the pool or shop? If getting up at 7 a.m. every day and not returning to your hotel until 6 or 7 p.m. at night sounds like a grind, certain escorted tours may not be for you.

- ✔ **How large is the group?** The smaller the group, the less time you spend waiting for people to get on and off the bus. Tour operators may be evasive about this, because they may not know the exact size of the group until everybody has made reservations, but they should be able to give you a rough estimate.

- ✔ **Is there a minimum group size?** Some tours have a minimum group size and may cancel the tour if they don't book enough people. If a quota exists, find out what it is and how close they are to reaching it. Again, tour operators may be evasive in their answers, but the information may help you select a tour that's sure to happen.

- ✔ **What exactly is included?** Don't assume anything. You may have to pay to get yourself to and from the airport. A box lunch may be included in an excursion but drinks may be extra. Beer may be included but not wine. How much flexibility do you have? Can you opt out of certain activities, or does the bus leave once a day, with no exceptions? Are all your meals planned in advance? Can you choose your entree at dinner, or does everybody get the same chicken cutlet?

Depending on your recreational passions, I recommend Online Agency Deals, with a great Web site: www.oladeals.com. You'll be able to search out deals and information on tours and vacation packages from over 3,500 travel companies — just select Chicago as your destination.

If you're a structure-loving traveler, your local travel agent can help you hook up with a guided tour of Chicago. An example is a package available from **City Escapes** that is booked exclusively through travel agencies. At press time, the package included a two-night stay at the Swissôtel or Omni Ambassador and a three-hour tour of the Loop, the lakefront, the South Side, Hyde Park, Michigan Avenue, and the Gold Coast. Total cost was only $274 per person (based on double occupancy) during low season and $339 per person in high season.

Choosing a Package Tour

For lots of destinations, package tours can be a smart way to go. In many cases, a package tour that includes airfare, hotel, and transportation to and from the airport costs less than the hotel alone on a tour you book yourself. That's because packages are sold in bulk to tour operators, who resell them to the public. It's kind of like buying your vacation at a buy-in-bulk store — except the tour operator is the one who buys the 1,000-count box of garbage bags and resells them 10 at a time at a cost that undercuts the local supermarket.

Package tours can vary as much as those garbage bags, too. Some offer a better class of hotels than others; others provide the same hotels for lower prices. Some book flights on scheduled airlines; others sell charters. In some packages, your choice of accommodations and travel days may be limited. Some let you choose between escorted vacations and independent vacations; others allow you to add on just a few excursions or escorted day trips (also at discounted prices) without booking an entirely escorted tour.

To find package tours, check out the travel section of your local Sunday newspaper or the ads in the back of national travel magazines such as *Travel + Leisure, National Geographic Traveler,* and *Condé Nast Traveler.* **Liberty Travel** (☎ 888-271-1584; www.libertytravel.com) is one of the biggest packagers in the Northeast, and usually boasts a full-page ad in Sunday papers.

Another good source of package deals is the airlines themselves. Most major airlines offer air/land packages, including **American Airlines Vacations** (☎ 800-321-2121; www.aavacations.com), **Continental Airlines Vacations** (☎ 800-301-3800; www.covacations.com) **Delta Vacations** (☎ 800-221-6666; www.deltavacations.com), **Southwest Airlines Vacations** (☎ 800-243-8372; www.swavacations.com), and **United Vacations** (☎ 888-854-3899; www.unitedvacations.com). Several big **online travel agencies** — Expedia, Travelocity, Orbitz, Site59, and Lastminute.com — also do a brisk business in packages. If you're unsure about the pedigree of a smaller packager, check with the Better Business Bureau in the city where the company is based, or go online to www.bbb.org. If a packager won't tell you where it's based, don't fly with them.

Package prices vary based on availability, dates, and hotel properties. For example, at press time, American Airlines Vacations offered a high-season rate that included round-trip airfare from Las Vegas and five nights at the upscale Fairmont Hotel for $1,250 per person. A sample package from United Vacations included round-trip airfare from New York and two nights at the Hard Rock Hotel, plus a Chicago City Pass (entrance to six major attractions), round-trip airport/hotel transfer, and a Chicago City Highlights Tour for $1,225 per person during the high season. From New York in low season (Feb), Delta Vacations offered airfare to O'Hare and seven nights at the Chicago Hyatt Hotel for $1,200 per person. Continental Airlines Vacations offered a package from Los Angeles to Chicago in February, with a suburban hotel, for $950 per person. Southwest Airlines Vacations had a package to Chicago from Kansas City in February for the low price of $209 per person, including two nights at the Sheraton Chicago Hotel and Towers.

The **Chicago Office of Tourism** (☎ **877-244-2246;** www.877chicago. com) offers online travel packages to entice visitors into the city. So-called Immersion Weekends have included such packages as "Paint the Town Blues," with two nights at the House of Blues hotel, blues concerts, some drinks, and one dinner. Prices are between $350 and $500 per person. Other packages bundle hotel stays with tickets to hot musicals or art exhibits.

Chapter 6

Catering to Special Travel Needs or Interests

● ●

In This Chapter

▶ Making the most of your family vacation
▶ Traveling as a senior
▶ Finding the best places for travelers with disabilities
▶ Locating resources for gay and lesbian travelers

● ●

*L*ike most big cities, Chicago offers something for everyone, whatever the interest, need, or inclination. This chapter points you toward both national and Chicago-only resources for families, seniors, disabled visitors, and gay and lesbian travelers.

If you have mobility issues, whether you're traveling with kids, a senior, or wheelchair-bound, you'll find that maneuvering around Chicago is pretty manageable. Chicago isn't as congested as New York or as sprawling as Los Angeles. And thanks to a slightly slower pace, Chicago's hustle and bustle isn't so frantic that you have to be on constant alert lest the crowds run over you.

Traveling with the Brood: Advice for Families

If you have enough trouble getting your kids out of the house in the morning, dragging them thousands of miles away may seem like an insurmountable challenge. But family travel can be immensely rewarding, giving you new ways of seeing the world through smaller pairs of eyes.

Familyhostel (☎ 800-733-9753; www.learn.unh.edu/familyhostel) takes the whole family, including kids ages 8 to 15, on moderately priced domestic and international learning vacations. Lectures, field trips, and sightseeing are guided by a team of academics.

You can find good family-oriented vacation advice on the Internet from sites like the **Family Travel Forum** (www.familytravelforum.com), a comprehensive site that offers customized trip planning; **Family Travel**

Network (www.familytravelnetwork.com), an award-winning site that offers travel features, deals, and tips; **Traveling Internationally with Your Kids** (www.travelwithyourkids.com), a comprehensive site that offers customized trip planning; and **Family Travel Files** (www.the familytravelfiles.com), which offers an online magazine and a directory of off-the-beaten-path tours and tour operators for families.

Preparing for your vacation

One of the best ways to get kids excited about an upcoming trip is to involve them in the planning. This gives kids a vested interest in getting the maximum enjoyment from the trip. Start by sharing this book with your kids — go through the attractions listed in Chapters 11 and 13. Next, have your kids list the places they want to visit. Older children can even check out attractions online. Finally, work with your children to create an itinerary that appeals to the whole family. You may want to rent a movie filmed in Chicago, such as *Ferris Bueller's Day Off* or *The Blues Brothers*. In either, you'll see shots of Chicago — the canyons of the Loop, the bridges spanning the Chicago River — all of it scenery the kids will recognize when they arrive.

Before leaving on the trip, try to adjust to a new time zone in advance. Put kids to bed half an hour later each night for a couple of nights if Chicago is west, and you'll gain time. Or, if you're traveling east, put them to bed half an hour earlier.

Go over safety issues with your children before leaving. Make sure to create a plan so children know what to do if they get lost. Put your child's name and some kind of identification inside a jacket.

Traveling to Chicago — and arriving happy and healthy

Want your whole family to arrive in Chicago in a good mood? Follow the steps in this section to improve your plane or car trip.

On the plane

How do you avoid becoming the person everyone hopes won't sit next to them on a plane? Follow these tips for flying with little ones:

- ✓ **Call ahead to order special kids' meals and confirm seating arrangements.** Some airlines offer bassinets for babies traveling in the bulkhead row — parents may prefer the bulkhead row, with the extra room for changing and letting toddlers sit on the floor. Other parents prefer regular seating for the extra under-chair baggage storage.

- ✓ **When you're packing, try not to overpack, but definitely do *not* underpack on necessities.** If you know the number of diapers your child wears, add three in case of emergency. Bring a changing pad in case the tiny restroom has no pull-out changing table.

On the other hand, one coloring book — not five — is sufficient. Two toy cars — not the entire collection of 30 — is all you'll want to carry. Pick one stuffed animal and one blanket. *Remember:* You're not relocating your entire nursery.

✔ **Use a stroller in the airport for nonwalking or barely walking children, and check it at the gate.** The stroller will be waiting for you on the gangway when you deplane.

In the car

Traveling by car presents a whole different set of challenges: those long stretches of open road with the kids asking "Are we there yet?" for the 10,000th time. Here are tips for keeping kids entertained — and adults sane — on the Great American Road Trip:

✔ Pack a cooler with drinks, snacks, fruits, and veggies.

✔ Get out every few hours for air, bathroom breaks, and diaper changes.

✔ Try to stick to a regular feeding schedule and sleeping schedule for babies.

✔ Look at your map for interesting things to visit on the way to your destination.

✔ Prepare to stretch your arm time and time again to reach all the toys and bottles that have fallen out of your children's hands for the tenth time in the last five minutes. A flashlight can help locate those items that roll under the seat.

✔ Use window shades to block the sun.

✔ Bring audiotapes of stories or children's songs. You may even put a small television/VCR/DVD player in the back between the two front seats so the kids can watch movies. Because a kids' video lasts 30 minutes to an hour, it's a great help for long stretches with nothing to do.

✔ Carry a first-aid kit, a box of wipes for clean-ups, a roll of paper towels, extra blankets, plastic bags for motion sickness, a change of clothes, and a cellphone in case of road emergencies.

Choosing sleeps and eats

Your choice of hotel probably isn't only a matter of budget. Choosing a hotel may also depend on the ages of the children who accompany you, and — face it — how well they generally behave. Nothing is more embarrassing to parents, or annoying to other guests who are paying good money for a room, than noisy children running amok through an upscale hotel. Find out if the hotel has a pool (many downtown Chicago hotels don't have one); ask if a video arcade is nearby. Hotels in River North, for example, are near ESPN Zone, a sports-themed attraction with dozens of games (see Chapter 11). Some hotels even offer play areas and kids' programs. Make sure to ask about these services when you call for a reservation.

After you check into your hotel, childproof the room. Remove small and breakable objects from children's reach and check cords. You may also want to plug in a nightlight. Find out from the concierge where to go if you need medical attention or to buy necessities, such as diapers, formula, and medicines.

Chicago is home to many kid-friendly restaurants. There are the obvious choices, such as the **Hard Rock Cafe,** 63 W. Ontario St. at North State Street (☎ 312-943-2252); the **Rainforest Cafe,** 605 N. Clark St. at Ohio Street (☎ 312-787-1501); and '50s-themed **Ed Debevic's,** 640 N. Wells St. at Ontario Street (☎ 312-664-1707). Then you have places such as **Harry Caray's** restaurant with its showcases packed with baseball memorabilia. Youngsters also have fun in the wacky New Orleans–style environment of **Heaven on Seven** on Michigan Avenue; at the original location on Wabash Avenue, kids can skip the exotic gumbo and jambalaya and order a hamburger and chocolate pudding from a luncheon-counter menu. Also along Michigan Avenue, try **Foodlife,** where pizza, burgers, and more await kids in the giant food court, or **Billy Goat Tavern,** the real-life inspiration for the famous *Saturday Night Live* skit that features John Belushi and "Cheeborger, cheeborger, chip, chip. No Coke — Pepsi." (See Chapter 10 for more information on these restaurants.)

For more tips on pleasing pint-size tourists, see Chapter 13.

Finding baby-sitting services

If you want to schedule some adults-only R&R, don't leave finding a babysitter to chance. Make prior arrangements — giving you time to check references — and add to your travel budget the amount that you'll need to cover babysitting. Expect to pay around $14 an hour, with a four-hour minimum. Most agencies require at least 48 hours' notice. For recommendations, check with the concierge or front desk at your hotel. Many hotels maintain lists of reputable babysitting agencies. One of the agencies that many of the top hotels work with is American Childcare Service (☎ 800-240-1820 or 773-248-8100), a state-licensed and insured service that can match you with a sitter. This agency requires that its caregivers undergo background checks, furnish multiple references, and are trained in infant and child CPR.

Making Age Work for You: Advice for Seniors

Mention the fact that you're a senior citizen when you make your travel reservations. Although all the major U.S. airlines except America West have cancelled their senior-discount and coupon-book programs, many hotels still offer discounts for seniors. In most cities, including Chicago, people over the age of 60 qualify for reduced admission to theaters, museums, and other attractions, as well as discounted fares on public transportation. For information on discounts on citywide programs, call the Chicago Park District at ☎ 312-742-7529.

Seniors age 65 and up with a discounted pass get a reduced fare of 85¢ per ride and 15¢ for transfers on Chicago's **public transportation.** Unfortunately, short-term visitors aren't able to take advantage of these discounts, because you must apply for the pass in person and it takes at least a week to obtain one. To obtain the pass, head to the Regional Transit Authority offices at 175 W. Jackson Blvd., second floor (☎ 888-968-7282). Bring a driver's license or passport. Explain that you're from out of town so you can receive the pass within a week (otherwise, processing takes three weeks).

Many of the El (elevated train) stations are difficult to navigate because of stairs or out-of-order escalators. Call the Chicago Transit Authority (CTA) at ☎ 312-836-7000 for a list of El stations that have elevators. If mobility is an issue, you may be better off riding the CTA buses.

Members of **AARP** (formerly known as the American Association of Retired Persons), 601 E St. NW, Washington, DC 20049 (☎ 888-687-2277 or 202-434-2277; www.aarp.org), get discounts on hotels, airfares, and car rentals. AARP offers members a wide range of benefits, including *AARP: The Magazine* and a monthly newsletter. Anyone over 50 can join.

Many reliable agencies and organizations target the 50-plus market. **Elderhostel** (☎ 877-426-8056; www.elderhostel.org) arranges study programs for those aged 55 and over (and a spouse or companion of any age) in Chicago and many other destinations. Most courses last five to seven days, and many include airfare, accommodations in university dormitories or modest inns, meals, and tuition.

Recommended publications offering travel resources and discounts for seniors include: the quarterly magazine *Travel 50 & Beyond* (www.travel50andbeyond.com); *Travel Unlimited: Uncommon Adventures for the Mature Traveler,* by Alison Gardner; *101 Tips for Mature Travelers,* available from Grand Circle Travel (☎ 800-221-2610 or 617-350-7500; www.gct.com); *The 50+ Traveler's Guidebook,* by Anita Williams and Merrimac Dillon; and *Unbelievably Good Deals and Great Adventures That You Absolutely Can't Get Unless You're Over 50* by Joan Rattner Heilman.

Accessing Chicago: Advice for Travelers with Disabilities

Most disabilities shouldn't stop anyone from traveling. More options and resources exist than ever before.

Chicago information and resources

Many Chicago hotels provide special accommodations and services for visitors in wheelchairs, such as ramps and large bathrooms, as well as telecommunications devices for visitors with hearing impairments; inquire when you make your reservation.

Visitors to Chicago find that most attractions are completely accessible. Public museums such as the **Art Institute of Chicago, Adler Planetarium & Astronomy Museum,** and the **Field Museum of Natural History** observe Americans with Disabilities Act (ADA) guidelines, as does the **Sears Tower Skydeck.**

For specific information on facilities for people with disabilities, call or write the **Mayor's Office for People with Disabilities,** 121 N. LaSalle St., Room 1104, Chicago, IL 60602 (☎ **312-744-6673** for voice; 312-744-4780 for TTY). The office is staffed from 8:30 a.m. to 4:30 p.m., Monday through Friday.

Horizons for the Blind, 2 N. Williams St., Crystal Lake, IL 60014 (☎ **815-444-8800**), is a social-service agency that can provide information about local hotels equipped with Braille signage, as well as cultural attractions that offer Braille signage and special tours. The **Illinois Relay Center** enables hearing- and speech-impaired TTY callers to call individuals or businesses without TTYs 24 hours a day. Call ☎ **800-526-0844** (TTY) or 800-526-0857 (voice). The city of Chicago operates a 24-hour information service for hearing-impaired callers with TTY equipment; call ☎ **312-744-8599** or 800-526-0844 (TTY).

Chicago streets and public transit

Pedestrians with disabilities find that downtown Chicago is pretty good about curb cuts and other basics. Unfortunately, though, the Windy City's notoriously unpredictable weather and a challenging public transportation system for those with disabilities (see the next paragraph), often compel Chicagoans and visitors to catch a ride. You can call **Paratransit** (☎ **312-432-7025**) for a description of special services and taxi access programs available in the city.

Despite efforts in recent years to improve its accessibility, Chicago's public transportation system lags behind those of other urban centers in meeting ADA standards. Although the Regional Transit Authority (☎ **847-364-7223;** www.pacebus.com), which operates the city's buses and trains, and Metra (☎ **312-322-6777;** www.metrarail.com), the commuter rail line to the suburbs, claim to be accessible, a trip can be arduous and frustrating. Only one in five buses is equipped with a lift, and fewer than half of all train stations have elevators. Riders with disabilities need to plan public-transit trips carefully. Call the Chicago Transit Authority (☎ **312-836-7000**) for information about accessible bus routes and train stations.

By calling the CTA in advance of their trip, people with disabilities can receive an application for a pass that allows holders to ride buses and trains for half-price. Apply early because passes take about three weeks to process.

Organizations that offer assistance to disabled travelers include

- **MossRehab** (www.mossresourcenet.org): Provides a library of accessible-travel resources online.

- **Society for Accessible Travel and Hospitality (SATH)** (☎ 212-447-7284; www.sath.org; annual membership fees: $45 adults, $30 seniors and students): Offers a wealth of travel resources for all types of disabilities and informed recommendations on destinations, access guides, travel agents, tour operators, vehicle rentals, and companion services.

- **American Foundation for the Blind (AFB)** (☎ 800-232-5463; www.afb.org): A referral resource for the blind or visually impaired that includes information on traveling with Seeing Eye dogs.

For more information specifically targeted to travelers with disabilities, the community Web site **iCan** (www.icanonline.net/channels/travel/index.cfm) has destination guides and several regular columns on accessible travel. Also check out the quarterly magazine **Emerging Horizons** ($14.95 per year, $19.95 outside the U.S.; www.emerging horizons.com); **Twin Peaks Press** (☎ 360-694-2462; http://disabilitybookshop.virtualave.net/blist84.htm), offering travel-related books for travelers with special needs; and *Open World Magazine,* published by SATH (subscription: $13 per year, $21 outside the U.S.).

Following the Rainbow: Resources for Gay and Lesbian Travelers

Chicago has a large gay and lesbian population, supported by numerous resources. The **Gay & Lesbian Chamber of Commerce** (☎ 312-303-3167; www.glchamber.org) is an excellent resource for imparting information about restaurants, bars, and neighborhoods where the gay and lesbian communities gather. The *Windy City Times* and other gay publications are available at many shops and bars in neighborhoods with large gay and lesbian populations.

Among Chicago's gay-friendly neighborhoods are Lakeview, New Town, and Andersonville. Lakeview's main thoroughfare is Belmont, between Broadway and Sheffield. Within Lakeview is a smaller neighborhood known as New Town (or, colloquially, Boys' Town). Andersonville centers around the half-dozen or so blocks of North Clark Street immediately north of Foster Avenue and features the feminist bookstore **Women and Children First**, 5233 N. Clark St. (☎ 773-769-9299).

The **International Gay & Lesbian Travel Association (IGLTA)** (☎ 800-448-8550 or 954-776-2626; www.iglta.org) is the trade association for the gay and lesbian travel industry, and offers an online directory of gay- and lesbian-friendly travel businesses; go to its Web site and click on Members.

Many agencies offer tours and travel itineraries specifically for gay and lesbian travelers. **Above and Beyond Tours** (☎ 800-397-2681; www.abovebeyondtours.com) is the exclusive gay and lesbian tour operator for United Airlines. **Now, Voyager** (☎ 800-255-6951; www.nowvoyager.com) is a well-known San Francisco–based gay-owned and -operated travel service. **Olivia Cruises & Resorts** (☎ 800-631-6277 or 510-655-0364; www.olivia.com) charters entire resorts and ships for exclusive lesbian vacations and offers smaller group experiences for both gay and lesbian travelers.

The following travel guides are available at most travel bookstores and gay and lesbian bookstores, or you can order them from **Giovanni's Room** bookstore, 1145 Pine St., Philadelphia, PA 19107 (☎ 215-923-2960; www.giovannisroom.com): *Frommer's Gay & Lesbian Europe,* an excellent travel resource (www.frommers.com); *Out and About* (☎ 800-929-2268 or 415-644-8044; www.outandabout.com), which offers guidebooks and a newsletter ($20/year; 10 issues) packed with solid information on the global gay and lesbian scene; *Spartacus International Gay Guide* (www.spartacusworld.com/gayguide/) and *Odysseus* (www.odyusa.com), both good, annual English-language guidebooks focused on gay men; the *Damron* guides (www.damron.com), with separate, annual books for gay men and lesbians; and *Gay Travel A to Z: The World of Gay & Lesbian Travel Options at Your Fingertips* by Marianne Ferrari (Ferrari International, Box 35575, Phoenix, AZ 85069), a very good gay and lesbian guidebook series.

Chapter 7

Taking Care of the Remaining Details

· ·

In This Chapter
- Consider whether to rent a car
- Buying travel insurance
- Making dinner and theater reservations
- Packing wisely
- Knowing what to expect at airport security

· ·

*T*he little things mean a lot: having tickets to a great opera or the latest Steppenwolf or Goodman theater production, getting a reservation at that restaurant you've heard so much about, or having the right clothing so you're not constantly freezing or sweating.

Taking care of a few details before you go can save you precious time in Chicago — time otherwise spent waiting in line; trying to get tickets; calling around town; buying the socks, long underwear, or sweater you forgot to bring; and dealing with all the other annoyances that plague the unprepared traveler. This chapter covers everything from buying travel insurance and packing comfortable walking shoes to preparing for airport security.

Renting a Car — Not!

Do you need to rent a car in Chicago? The answer is a qualified "No." A car can be a liability. Parking can be expensive, while street parking and metered parking are scarce. If you drive Chicago's expressways, you'll start to understand why many complain that the road system no longer handles the increased volume of traffic and will be less equipped to do so as time passes. Gridlock is becoming more frequent and intense.

All that said, traffic-wise, Chicago is not as congested as, for example, New York or London. Anyone who has sat fuming in Manhattan's snarled crosstown traffic or on London's ancient and narrow streets may find driving in downtown Chicago a breeze. More often than not, traffic *does* move, even in the heart of the Loop or along the Magnificent Mile. Still, the major arteries in and out of the city usually are jammed during the misnamed *rush hour,* which is more like three hours. All of which brings me to that qualified "No."

A car is not necessary if you plan to stay downtown and confine your touring to the outlying neighborhoods. Public transportation — bus, El (an abbreviation of *elevated*) train, and subway — is fairly comprehensive and reliable. As long as you stick to busy routes during the daytime, you should be safe. (Avoid long rides into unfamiliar areas late at night.) Beyond that, taxis are plentiful and pretty much affordable for short runs. On the other hand, if you want to explore the outlying suburbs (including driving along the scenic lakeshore — see Chapter 14), a car is a must.

Daily costs for a midsize car average about $55, or about $160 per week. For telephone numbers and more rental-car companies with offices in Chicago, see the appendix.

Identifying additional charges

In addition to the daily rental rate, rental-car companies in Chicago charge **18 percent sales tax** and, for rentals at the airport, a **$2.75 daily transaction fee.**

You'll also encounter a few optional charges. The Collision Damage Waiver (CDW), which covers any damage to the car in the event of a collision, is covered by many credit card companies. Check with your credit card company before you go, so you can avoid paying this hefty fee (as much as $20 a day).

The car rental companies also offer additional **liability insurance** (if you harm others in an accident), **personal accident insurance** (if you harm yourself or your passengers), and **personal effects insurance** (if your luggage is stolen from your car). Your insurance policy on your car at home probably covers most of these unlikely occurrences. However, if your own insurance doesn't cover you for rentals or if you don't have auto insurance, definitely consider the additional coverage (ask your car-rental agent for more information). Unless you're toting around the Hope Diamond (and you don't want to leave that in your car trunk anyway), you can probably skip the personal effects insurance, but driving around without liability or personal accident coverage is never a good idea. Even if you're a good driver, other people may not be, and liability claims can be complicated.

Some companies also offer **refueling packages,** in which you pay for your initial full tank of gas up front and can return the car with an empty gas tank. If you reject this option, you pay only for the gas you use, but you have to return the car with a full tank or face charges of $3 to $4 a gallon for any shortfall. In my experience, gas prices in the refueling packages are at the high end, and I always find myself trying to drive the car in on fumes so I don't pay for an extra drop of fuel. So, I prefer to forego the refueling package and always allow plenty of time for refueling en route to the car-rental return. However, if you usually run late and a fueling stop may make you miss your plane, you're a perfect candidate for the fuel-purchase option.

Getting the best deal

Car-rental rates vary even more than airline fares. The price depends on the size of the car, the length of time you keep it, where and when you pick it up and drop it off, where you take it, and a host of other factors. Asking a few key questions may save you hundreds of dollars:

✔ **Ask if the rate is the same for a morning pickup as it is for a pickup at night — these rates can vary.** Weekend rates may be lower than weekday rates. If you're keeping the car five or more days, a weekly rate may be cheaper than the daily rate.

✔ **Ask what the rate would be if you picked up the car from a downtown location rather than at the airport.** Rates sometimes are considerably lower downtown.

✔ **Find out whether age is an issue.** Many car-rental companies add on a fee for drivers under 25, while some don't rent to them at all.

✔ **If you see an advertised price in your local newspaper, ask for that specific rate.** If you don't, you may be charged the standard (higher) rate. Don't forget to mention membership in AAA, AARP, and trade unions. These memberships usually entitle you to discounts ranging from 5 to 30 percent.

✔ **Ask to use your frequent-flier account when booking.** Not only are your favorite (or at least most-used) airlines likely to have sent you discount coupons, but most car rentals add at least 500 miles to your frequent-flier account.

WGN: World's Greatest Newspaper

Tune in to one of Chicago's most popular radio stations, WGN–720 AM, which is owned by the Chicago Tribune Company and has a studio in the showcase window of the Tribune Tower, 435 N. Michigan Ave., just north of the Michigan Avenue Bridge. The company publishes the daily *Chicago Tribune* and is especially proud of the station's call letters — WGN ("World's Greatest Newspaper").

The Tribune Shop (☎ 312-222-3080), on the building's street level, sells reproductions of newspapers with famous headlines — "War Ends," "Bulls Repeat," and the like. Ask for the newspaper issued during the 1948 presidential election with the bold (and incorrect) headline "Dewey Defeats Truman." Democrats especially love this souvenir.

As with other aspects of planning your trip, using the Internet can make comparison shopping for a car rental much easier. You can check rates at most of the major agencies' Web sites. Plus, all the major travel sites — **Frommer's** (www.frommers.com), **Travelocity** (www.travelocity.com), **Expedia** (www.expedia.com), **Orbitz** (www.orbitz.com), and **Smarter Living** (www.smarterliving.com), for example — have search engines that can dig up discounted car-rental rates. Just enter the car size you want, the pickup and return dates, and the location, and the server returns a price. You can even make the reservation online.

Playing It Safe with Travel and Medical Insurance

Three kinds of travel insurance are available: trip-cancellation insurance, medical insurance, and lost-luggage insurance. The cost of travel insurance varies widely, depending on the cost and length of your trip, your age and health, and the type of trip you're taking, but expect to pay between 5 and 8 percent of the vacation itself. Here is my advice on all three:

✔ **Trip-cancellation insurance** helps you get your money back if you have to back out of a trip, if you have to go home early, or if your travel supplier goes bankrupt. Allowed reasons for cancellation can range from sickness to natural disasters. (Insurers usually won't cover vague fears, though, as many travelers discovered who tried to cancel their trips in October 2001 because they were wary of flying.)

A good resource is **"Travel Guard Alerts,"** a list of companies considered high-risk by Travel Guard International (www.travel insured.com). Protect yourself further by paying for the insurance with a credit card — by law, consumers can get their money back on goods and services not received if they report the loss within 60 days after the charge is listed on their credit card statement.

Note: Many tour operators, particularly those offering trips to remote or high-risk areas, include insurance in the cost of the trip or can arrange insurance policies through a partnering provider, a convenient and often cost-effective way for the traveler to obtain insurance. Make sure the tour company is a reputable one, however: Some experts suggest you avoid buying insurance from the tour or cruise company you're traveling with, saying it's better to buy from a third-party insurer than to put all your money in one place.

✔ For domestic travel, buying **medical insurance** for your trip doesn't make sense for most travelers. Most existing health policies cover you if you get sick away from home — but check your policy to be sure.

✔ **Lost-luggage insurance** is not necessary for most travelers. On domestic flights, checked baggage is covered up to $2,500 per ticketed passenger. On international flights (including U.S. portions of international trips), baggage coverage is limited to approximately $9.07 per pound, up to approximately $635 per checked bag. If you plan to check items more valuable than the standard liability, see if your valuables are covered by your homeowner's policy, or get baggage insurance as part of your comprehensive travel-insurance package. Don't buy insurance at the airport; it's usually overpriced. Be sure to take any valuables or irreplaceable items with you in your carry-on luggage, as many valuables (including books, money, and electronics) aren't covered by airline policies.

If your luggage is lost, immediately file a lost-luggage claim at the airport, detailing the luggage contents. For most airlines, you must report delayed, damaged, or lost baggage within four hours of arrival. The airlines are required to deliver luggage, once found, directly to your house or destination free of charge.

For more information, contact one of the following recommended insurers: **Access America** (☎ 866-807-3982; www.accessamerica.com), **Travel Guard International** (☎ 800-826-4919; www.travelguard.com), **Travel Insured International** (☎ 800-243-3174; www.travelinsured.com), or **Travelex Insurance Services** (☎ 888-457-4602; www.travelex-insurance.com).

Staying Healthy When You Travel

Getting sick will ruin your vacation, so I *strongly* advise against it. (Of course, last time I checked, the bugs weren't listening to me any more than they probably listen to you.)

For domestic trips, most reliable health-care plans provide coverage if you get sick away from home. For information on purchasing additional medical insurance for your trip, see the previous section.

Talk to your doctor before leaving on a trip if you have a serious and/or chronic illness. For conditions such as epilepsy, diabetes, or heart problems, wear a **MedicAlert identification tag** (☎ 888-633-4298; www.medicalert.org), which immediately alerts doctors to your condition and gives them access to your records through MedicAlert's 24-hour hotline. The U.S. **Centers for Disease Control and Prevention** (☎ 800-311-3435; www.cdc.gov) provides up-to-date information on health hazards by region or country and offers tips on food safety.

If you're staying in downtown Chicago, the closest hospital will likely be **Northwestern Memorial Hospital,** 251 E. Huron St. (☎ 312-926-2000; www.nmh.org), right off North Michigan Avenue. Its physician referral service is ☎ 312-926-8400. The emergency department (☎ 312-926-5188) is at 250 E. Erie St. near Fairbanks Court.

Packing It Up

The classic packing advice is to start your packing by laying out on your bed everything you think you need. Then get rid of half of it. I hate this advice because I always wind up needing something I left behind. To me, the key is to check out the Weather Channel's Web site (www.weather.com) and see the long-range forecast. Then imagine what you would wear in your own city in that weather, and pack it. Leave room in the suitcase, because you'll undoubtedly buy items while traveling.

If you want to bring only a small bag, you may not be able to leave space for purchases. If that's the case, a good trick is to pack an empty nylon duffel bag. On the way home, you can stuff it with your souvenirs and other loot.

Preparing for sun, rain, and wind

Chicago's famously changeable weather calls for some special packing tips:

✔ **Always pack a sweater when planning to visit Chicago.** Even in summer, you can run into a cool evening by the lake or a theater or restaurant where the air-conditioning reaches polar levels.

✔ **If you're visiting in the winter, be sure to pack some sort of headgear.** You may be concerned about looking unstylish, but believe me, you'll appreciate this advice later. Don't worry about fashion. When temperatures drop in Chicago, no one goes without head covering.

✔ **If you're comfortable wearing shorts, you'll want to pack them for a spring or fall trip, as well as for a summer visit.** Some folks tend to rush the season, and you may see people strolling along the Mag Mile in shorts during a February mild spell.

✔ **Even in summer, a lightweight jacket is always a good idea.** The Windy City can get breezy at any time of year.

Unless you're planning a formal night out, you can leave the high heels and suits at home. Most restaurants, even pricier ones, have become more casual. For men, a dress shirt, a jacket, and a tie will more than suffice for any night out. (In fact, dress pants and a shirt with a sweater are acceptable almost anywhere.) For women, a long skirt with a nice sweater or blouse can work as well.

A few of the top restaurants and clubs (the Pump Room at the Omni Ambassador East Hotel is a notable example) enforce a dress code. If you plan to visit these spots, you need at least one dressy outfit.

Gift shops carry lots of clothes — from cheesy-logo fare to designer-label fashions. They also have raincoats, umbrellas, swimwear, and other weather-related items that you may have forgotten to pack. But be aware that you're likely to pay a premium!

Choosing and packing your suitcase

When choosing your suitcase, think about the kind of traveling you'll be doing. A bag with wheels is handy if you'll be mostly on hard floors but not on uneven surfaces or stairs. A fold-over garment bag helps keep dressy clothes wrinkle-free, but a garment bag may be unnecessary on a casual vacation. Hard-sided luggage protects breakable items better but weighs more than soft-sided bags.

When packing, start with the biggest, hardest items (usually shoes), and then fit smaller items in and around them. Pack breakable items between several layers of clothes, or keep them in your carry-on bag. Put things that could leak — shampoo, sunscreen, moisturizer — in plastic zipper bags, and throw in a few extra plastic bags for dirty laundry. Put identification tags on the inside and outside of your suitcase.

In your carry-on bag, pack anything breakable or irreplaceable, such as your return ticket, passport, expensive jewelry, contact lenses or glasses, and prescription medication. Also consider packing a book or magazines, a personal stereo with headphones, a bottle of water, and a snack in the event that you don't like the airline food. Leave a little space for a sweater or jacket in case the airplane gets cold. See "Keeping Up with Airline Security Measures," later in this chapter, for information on what you can't pack in your carry-on bag.

Staying Connected by Cellphone or E-mail

Just because your cellphone works at home doesn't mean it'll work elsewhere in the country (thanks to our nation's fragmented cellphone system). It's a good bet that your phone will work in major cities, such as Chicago. But take a look at your wireless company's coverage map on its Web site before heading out — T-Mobile, Sprint, and Nextel are particularly weak in rural areas. If you need to stay in touch at a destination where you know your phone won't work, **rent** a phone that does from **InTouch USA** (☎ 800-872-7626; www.intouchglobal.com) or a rental-car location, but beware that you'll pay $1 a minute or more for airtime.

If you're not from the U.S., you'll be appalled at the poor reach of our **GSM (Global System for Mobiles) wireless network,** which is used by much of the rest of the world. Your phone will almost certainly work in Chicago; it may not work in many of Chicago's outlying areas. (To see where GSM phones work in the U.S., check out www.t-mobile.com/coverage/national_popup.asp.) You may or may not be able to send SMS (text messaging) home — something Americans tend not to do anyway, for various cultural and technological reasons. (International budget travelers like to send text messages home because doing so is much cheaper than making international calls.) Assume nothing — call your wireless provider and get the full scoop. In a worst-case scenario, you can always rent a phone; InTouch USA delivers to hotels.

Accessing the Internet away from Home

You have any number of ways to check your e-mail and access the Internet on the road. Of course, using your own laptop — or even a PDA (personal digital assistant) or electronic organizer with a modem — gives you the most flexibility. But even if you don't have a computer, you can still access your e-mail and even your office computer from cybercafes.

Finding a city that *doesn't* have a few cybercafes is difficult. Although there's no definitive directory for cybercafes — these are independent businesses, after all — three places to start looking are at www.cyber captive.com and www.cybercafe.com. Likely neighborhoods to find a nearby cafe are those populated by college students — for example, around the DePaul University campus in the Lincoln Park neighborhood (roughly Halsted Avenue at Belmont Street); in Hyde Park, home to the University of Chicago; and even the streets just west of Michigan Avenue at Chicago Avenue that are home to Loyola University and its law school.

Aside from formal cybercafes, most **youth hostels** nowadays have at least one computer you can get to the Internet on. And most **public libraries** across the world offer Internet access free or for a small charge. Avoid **hotel business centers** unless you're willing to pay exorbitant rates.

Most major airports now have **Internet kiosks** scattered throughout their gates. These kiosks, which you'll also see in shopping malls, hotel lobbies, and tourist information offices around the world, give you basic Web access for a per-minute fee that's usually higher than cybercafe prices. The kiosks' clunkiness and high price mean you should avoid them whenever possible.

To retrieve your e-mail, ask your **Internet service provider (ISP)** if it has a Web-based interface tied to your existing e-mail account. If your ISP doesn't have such an interface, you can use the free **mail2web** service (www.mail2web.com) to view and reply to your home e-mail. For more flexibility, you may want to open a free, Web-based e-mail account with **Yahoo! Mail** (http://mail.yahoo.com). (Microsoft's Hotmail is another popular option, but Hotmail has severe spam problems.) Your home ISP may be able to forward your e-mail to the Web-based account automatically.

If you need to access files on your office computer, look into a service called **GoToMyPC** (www.gotomypc.com). The service provides a Web-based interface for you to access and manipulate a distant PC from anywhere — even a cybercafe — provided your "target" PC is on and has an always-on connection to the Internet. The service offers top-quality security, but if you're worried about hackers, use your own laptop rather than a cybercafe computer to access the GoToMyPC system.

If you're bringing your own computer, the buzzword in computer access to familiarize yourself with is **Wi-Fi** (wireless fidelity), and more and more hotels, cafes, and retailers are signing on as wireless "hotspots" from where you can get high-speed connection without cable wires, networking hardware, or a phone line. You can get a Wi-Fi connection one of several ways. Many laptops sold in the last year have built-in Wi-Fi capability. Mac owners have their own networking technology, Apple AirPort. For those with older computers, a **Wi-Fi card** (around $50) can be plugged into your laptop.

You sign up for wireless access service much as you do cellphone service, through a plan offered by one of several commercial companies that have made wireless service available in airports, hotel lobbies, and coffee shops. **T-Mobile Hotspot** (www.t-mobile.com/hotspot) serves up wireless connections at more than 1,000 Starbucks coffee shops nationwide. **Boingo** (www.boingo.com) and **Wayport** (www.wayport.com) have set up networks in airports and high-class hotel lobbies. IPass providers also give you access to a few hundred wireless hotel-lobby setups. Best of all, you don't need to stay at the Four Seasons to use the hotel's network; just set yourself up on a nice couch in the lobby. The companies' pricing policies can be byzantine, with a variety of monthly, per-connection, and per-minute plans, but in general you pay around $30 a month for limited access — and as more and more companies jump on the wireless bandwagon, prices are likely to get even more competitive.

There are also places that provide **free wireless networks** in cities around the world. To locate the free hotspots in Chicago, go to www. personaltelco.net/index.cgi/WirelessCommunities.

If Wi-Fi is not available, most business-class hotels throughout the world offer dataports for laptop modems, and a few thousand hotels in the U.S. now offer free high-speed Internet access using an Ethernet network cable. You can bring your own cables, but most hotels rent them for around $10. Call your hotel in advance to see what your options are.

In addition, major Internet service providers (ISPs) have **local access numbers** around the world, allowing you to go online by simply placing a local call. Check your ISP's Web site or call its toll-free number and ask how you can use your current account away from home, and how much it will cost. If you're traveling outside the reach of your ISP, the **iPass** network has dial-up numbers in Chicago. You'll have to sign up with an iPass provider, who will then tell you how to set up your computer for Chicago. For a list of iPass providers, go to www.ipass.com and click on "Individual Purchase." One solid provider is **i2roam** (☎ 866-811-6209 or 920-235-0475; www.i2roam.com).

Wherever you go, bring a **connection kit** of the right power and phone adapters, a spare phone cord, and a spare Ethernet network cable — or find out whether your hotel supplies them to guests.

Keeping Up with Airline Security Measures

With the federalization of airport security, security procedures at U.S. airports are more stable and consistent than ever. Generally, you'll be fine if you arrive at the airport **one hour** before a domestic flight and **two hours** before an international flight; if you show up late, tell an airline employee and she'll probably whisk you to the front of the line.

Bring a **current, government-issued photo ID** such as a driver's license or passport. Keep your ID at the ready to show at check-in, the security checkpoint, and sometimes even the gate. (Children under 18 do not need government-issued photo IDs for domestic flights, but they do for international flights to most countries.)

In 2003, the TSA phased out **gate check-in** at all U.S. airports. And **e-tickets** have made paper tickets nearly obsolete. If you have an e-ticket, you can beat the ticket-counter lines by using airport **electronic kiosks** or even **online check-in** from your home computer. Online check-in involves logging on to your airline's Web site, accessing your reservation, and printing out your boarding pass — and the airline may even offer you bonus miles to do so! If you're using a kiosk at the airport, bring the credit card you used to book the ticket or your frequent-flier card. Print out your boarding pass from the kiosk and simply proceed to the security checkpoint with your pass and a photo ID. If you're checking bags or looking to snag an exit-row seat, you'll be able to do so using most airline kiosks. Even the smaller airlines are employing the kiosk system, but always call your airline to make sure these alternatives are available. **Curbside check-in** is also a good way to avoid lines, although a few airlines still ban curbside check-in; call before you go.

Security checkpoint lines are getting shorter than they were during 2001 and 2002, but some doozies remain. If you have trouble standing for long periods of time, tell an airline employee; the airline will provide a wheelchair. Speed up security by **not wearing metal objects** such as big belt buckles. If you have metallic body parts, a note from your doctor can prevent a long chat with the security screeners. Keep in mind that only **ticketed passengers** are allowed past security, except for folks escorting disabled passengers or children.

Federalization has stabilized **what you can carry on** and **what you can't.** The general rule is that sharp things are out, nail clippers are okay, and food and beverages must be passed through the x-ray machine — but that security screeners can't make you drink from your coffee cup. Bring food in your carryon instead of checking it, because explosive-detection machines used on checked luggage have been known to mistake food (especially chocolate, for some reason) for bombs. Travelers in the U.S. are allowed one carry-on bag, plus a "personal item" such as a purse, briefcase, or laptop bag. Carry-on hoarders can stuff all sorts of things into a laptop bag; as long as it has a laptop in it, it's still considered a personal item. The Transportation Security Administration (TSA) has issued a list of restricted items; check its Web site (www.tsa.gov/public/index.jsp) for details.

Airport screeners may decide that your checked luggage needs to be searched by hand. You can now purchase luggage locks that allow screeners to open and relock a checked bag if hand-searching is necessary. Look for Travel Sentry–certified locks at luggage or travel shops and Brookstone stores (you can buy them online at www.brookstone.com). These locks, approved by the TSA, can be opened by luggage inspectors with a special code or key. For more information on the locks, visit www.travelsentry.org. If you use something other than TSA-approved locks, your lock will be cut off your suitcase if a TSA agent needs to hand-search your luggage.

Part III
Settling Into Chicago

The 5th Wave   By Rich Tennant

"I'd give you a hot dog with everything, but I'm out of Fruit Loops."

In this part . . .

*I*t's difficult to get your bearings in a new place: Distances are longer or shorter than they appear on the map, and north, south, east, and west can get mixed up easily. This part is designed to help orient you in the Windy City and give you a lay of the land. When you've gotten acquainted with our neighborhoods, you'll be ready to get the lowdown on Chicago's hotels. I discuss the best options for families, for luxury, for bargain hunters, and more.

Finally, whether you're into tried-and-true restaurants or table-hopping in see-and-be-seen spots, you find a good introduction to Chicago's restaurants in this part. I describe Chicago's best restaurant areas, specialties, and deals, and I offer complete reviews of my favorite places for snacks and meals.

Chapter 8

Arriving and Getting Oriented

● ●

In This Chapter

▶ Traveling from the airport to your hotel

▶ Getting to know the city's layout and neighborhoods

▶ Finding information while you're in Chicago

● ●

*F*inding your way around the Windy City is a breeze. For openers, whenever you spot Lake Michigan dead ahead — the lake is pretty hard to miss — you know you're facing east. In this part of the book, you'll find out how to reach the city from the airports, pick up the finer points of orienting yourself, and get the scoop on Chicago's neighborhoods.

Making Your Way to Your Hotel

Because Chicago is at the hub of the interstate highway system, many visitors arrive by car. In addition, Amtrak serves Chicago relatively well, even in this era of diminished train travel. Nonetheless, Chicago's airports provide most of the city's visitor activity. Each day, several hundred thousand air travelers fly in and out of Chicago.

In the following sections, I give you the scoop on how to get to your hotel no matter how you arrive.

Arriving by plane

Chicago has two major airports, O'Hare and Midway. Despite their combined vast capacity, the city has outgrown them both. For years, the creation of a third airport has been a political football, with plans afoot to locate an airfield in Chicago's far-south suburbs, in neighboring Indiana, and even offshore on a pod in Lake Michigan.

Sometime in the new millennium, Chicago will get that third airport. Until then, the city must struggle with what it has. Although at times frustrating and daunting, O'Hare is fairly user-friendly thanks to a revitalization in the last decade. Over the same period, Midway has gone from a virtually abandoned facility to a frenetically busy airport, which just doubled its public spaces to accommodate the growing number of travelers.

If you fly into O'Hare

Sprawling O'Hare International Airport has the dubious distinction of being one of the world's busiest air-travel hubs. Although traffic at Midway has grown spectacularly over the last decade, O'Hare is by far the city's major airport. In fact, it handles more passengers and aircraft operations than any other airport in the *world*.

Many visitors grumble that they're greeted by unprotected luggage carousels, lines for cabs, grouchy cops, repeated loudspeaker threats to tow illegally parked cars, and tiresome bus rides to rental-car lots deep in the hinterland.

Good things take place at O'Hare, too. A link to Chicago's subway system dodges gridlocked traffic, shuttling you downtown in about 45 minutes for only $1.75. If you prefer a cab (lines are not always long), an airport employee who's in charge of making sure the cab line moves efficiently will pair strangers willing to share rides and cut costs. And should weather unexpectedly lock you in, a pedestrian tunnel means that good food, comfortable accommodations, and an array of services are only a short walk away at the excellent on-site O'Hare Hilton Hotel.

The trek between terminals can be long, but an elevated people-mover system, opened in 1993 as part of $2 billion in improvements, whisks

The time-honored tradition of being stuck at O'Hare

If you find yourself spending significant time at O'Hare, planned or unexpected, check out the visitor services. Information booths are available on the lower levels of Terminals 1, 2, and 3, outside the lower-level customs area, and on the upper level of Terminal 5. (By the way, there's no Terminal 4.) The information booths are open daily from 8:15 a.m. to 8 p.m. Stop by for an airport map, or phone ☎ 773-686-2200 for an extensive menu of airport information.

Travelers with youngsters head for the interactive **Kids on the Fly Children's Museum** in Terminal 2, near the security checkpoint. Hand-on exhibits focus on aviation, travel, and geography.

Some of the Windy City's signature food and drink is available at O'Hare. Pizzeria Uno, Gold Coast Dogs, and Lou Mitchell's Express (a satellite of Chicago's best breakfast spot) are in Terminal 5; Goose Island, the city's best-known microbrewery, operates in Terminal 3.

Early to bed, early to rise

O'Hare Hilton Hotel (☎ 800-445-8667 or 773-686-8000), within the airport, couldn't be more convenient for travelers with early flights. The 858 guest rooms are not only well appointed but also absolutely soundproof, despite being virtually on the runways.

Even if you're not a guest, you can work out at the 10,000-square-foot health club, which has a pool, whirlpool, steam room, and sauna. The fee of $10 a day includes towels, shampoo, conditioner, and hair dryers.

The Hilton is also home to the **Gaslight Club,** an establishment in the Playboy Club genre. **Andiamo** is a full-service restaurant that serves three meals daily and supplies the Hilton's **"Food on the Fly"** program (☎ 773-601-1733). Hot sandwiches and entrees, mostly priced under $10, are a great alternative to airline food.

passengers at 35 mph between the terminals and long-term Parking Lot E. Stations are located at each terminal and at the remote parking lot.

 If you leave O'Hare for another U.S. destination, you often encounter long lines that wind up to the ticket counters like a conga line at a wedding reception. Avoid them with curbside check-in, available for most domestic flights only.

A cab ride downtown costs about $35, including tip. The number for **Yellow Cab** is ☎ 312-829-4222, for **Checker Cab** ☎ 312-243-2537. Airport buses, operated by **Airport Express** (☎ 312-454-7800), cost $23 one-way, $42 round-trip, and stop at most downtown hotels.

 If you're willing to share your taxi from the airport to downtown, you can save almost 50 percent on the fare. Join the queue (if there is one) at the cabstand, and when you reach the head of the line, tell the airport employee that you want to share a ride. In a limousine, a ride for three people runs about $63. Call **My Chauffer Limousine** (☎ 800-762-6888 or 630-920-8888) in advance if this appeals to you.

The **Chicago Transit Authority** (☎ 312-836-7000) subway (called the *El,* short for "elevated" train) is the cheapest and often fastest way downtown, but not necessarily the safest. In 1997, as an economy measure, the CTA eliminated conductors from trains. Many believe this compromises safety. Avoid the subway during quieter times, such as late at night. Rush and daylight hours are safe enough.

To reach the El, follow the signs displayed near baggage-claim areas and in arrival halls. The signs guide you through a series of ped-ways (served by escalators, elevators, and moving walkways) to the CTA blue-line train stop.

Another option for getting into the city is renting a car. Most major car-rental companies have counters at O'Hare, but their lots are remote. You can pick up a shuttle bus outside of the baggage claim area to take you to your rental car.

If you fly into Midway

Midway Airport (☎ **773-838-0600**) almost died in the 1980s, but the addition of flights by ATA and Southwest Airlines revived the facility, which once looked like a strip mall. Today, the airport has undergone a major reconstruction project. A new terminal including restaurants and baggage carousels was built to accommodate the increased traffic.

Midway is actually closer to downtown than O'Hare, and under optimum conditions, the trip from downtown via highways (car, cab, or shuttle bus) can take less than half an hour. But due to traffic, the journey often takes as long as the trip from O'Hare.

Cab rides to Midway are about $5 cheaper than to O'Hare from downtown. Cab sharing from the airport is available, but only if you're going downtown. The airport shuttle van to downtown hotels is cheaper, too, at $18 one-way.

Like O'Hare, most major car-rental companies have counters at Midway, but their lots are remote. Most parking is in remote lots served by shuttle buses, which you can pick up outside of the baggage claim area.

The **CTA** (the El) also serves Midway. The orange-line El trip from Midway is much shorter than the blue-line ride from O'Hare. But the walk from the airport terminal to the subway stop at Midway is long (even without luggage). To get from the terminal to the El, walk from the terminal toward baggage claim, except do *not* take the escalators down to baggage claim. Instead, continue walking up the ramp toward the parking garage. Along the way you'll spot signs marked "trains to city." There is one section of moving sidewalk, but most of the way, you'll have to hoof it.

Arriving by car

All roads lead to Chicago, or so it seems. From the east, I-80 and I-90 cross the northern sector of Illinois. I-90 splits off and turns into Chicago via the Skyway and the Dan Ryan Expressway. From there, I-90 runs through Wisconsin, and beyond as far west as Seattle. Those from the south can enter Chicago on I-55, which winds its way up the Mississippi Valley and enters Chicago from the west, along with the Stevenson Expressway. I-57 originates in southern Illinois and connects in Chicago on the west leg of the Dan Ryan. From the east, I-94 links Detroit and Chicago, and leaves the city heading northwest via the Kennedy expressway.

Arriving by train

Nearly every transcontinental Amtrak route runs through or to Chicago's sprawling Union Station, which is also a hub for Metra commuter train

---

Yes, Virginia, that is a lake

Lake Michigan is 22,300 square miles in size and reaches depths of over 900 feet. The other Great Lakes are Erie, Superior, Ontario, and Huron. Chicago honors each of the lakes with a street on the east-west corridor intersecting the Michigan Avenue shopping district. The U.S.–Canada international boundary runs through all the Great Lakes except Lake Michigan, which lies wholly in U.S. territory.

---

service to the south and southwest suburbs. The cavernous loading and unloading area lies below street level near the heart of the Loop. During the day, you should have no problem hailing a cab curbside. At night, you may want to call for a taxi from inside the station.

North on Canal Street from Union Station is Northwestern Station (now officially called the Ogilvie Transportation Center), the hub of Metra train service to the north and northwest suburbs.

Figuring Out the Neighborhoods

Remember this easy way to keep yourself oriented in Chicago: The lake is always to the east. "The lake," of course, is Lake Michigan, which disappears into the horizon like some huge inland sea. As my friend from London said while staring trancelike at the lake, "You . . . can't . . . see . . . across it."

The Chicago River forms a "Y" that divides the city into three sections: North Side, West Side, and South Side (the east side, of course, is the lake). The Loop, the business and financial center of the city, is located just south of the Chicago River. The main shopping district is North Michigan Avenue, also known as the Magnificent Mile, which stretches north of the Chicago River, not too far west of the lake. On the West Side is Bucktown/Wicker Park, the Randolph Street Market District, and many outlying residential neighborhoods.

As a former part of the Northwest Territories, Chicago is laid out in a grid system, with point zero located at the intersection of State and Madison streets, within the Loop. State Street divides east and west addresses and Madison divides the north and south. Complicating this straightforward layout are a few diagonal streets and streets that end unexpectedly, only to take up again a block or two farther along. Here are some key points to remember:

> ✔ The focal point of the city's numbering system is the intersection of State and Madison streets, in the heart of the Loop. Madison Street runs east-west and is the north-south divider. State Street runs north-south and is the east-west divider.

✔ The Loop is the heart of downtown. Its approximate boundaries are the Chicago River to the north, Congress Street to the south, Halsted Street to the west, and Wabash Avenue to the east.

✔ Numbered streets always run east-west.

✔ All north-south streets have names, not numbers.

✔ The first few streets south of Madison are named for American presidents in the order of their terms: Madison, Monroe, Adams, Jackson, Van Buren, Harrison, Polk, and Taylor.

✔ Streets north of Madison follow a grid system. Division Street, for example, is an east-west street that is approximately 12 blocks north of Madison and is numbered 1200 North. The same grid system applies to north-south streets. For example, Halsted Street, approximately 8 blocks west of State Street, is numbered 800 West.

Chicago is a city of neighborhoods, many with large ethnic populations. Prominent Chicago neighborhoods, from south to north, include

✔ **Chinatown:** Chicago's Chinese enclave is compact, and the main thoroughfares are along short stretches of Cermak Road (also known as 22nd Street) and Wentworth and Archer avenues. Here you find good restaurants, such as **Three Happiness,** 209 W. Cermak Rd. (☎ 312-842-1964), interesting tearooms, and shops.

✔ **The Loop:** Chicago's downtown is named after the elevated train track that loops around the financial district. The main attractions include riding the El and visiting the Mercantile Exchange, where you can watch traders in the pit doing their thing, whatever that is (it has always been beyond me!).

✔ **Near West:** Former warehouses have been converted to living and working space just west of the Kennedy Expressway. The area includes Greektown and Oprah's workplace, Harpo Studios, plus a host of hip restaurants and bars.

✔ **Magnificent Mile:** The northern length of Michigan Avenue is Chicago's version of Fifth Avenue, Oxford Street, and Rodeo Drive. The Mag Mile stretches from the Chicago River to the Oak Street Beach. Anchoring the south end are the distinctive Wrigley Building and Gothic Tribune Towers; at the north end is the Drake Hotel. Highlights include the John Hancock Center Observatory, Millennium Park, Fourth Presbyterian Church, Water Tower Place, Chicago Place Mall, and Westfield North Bridge Mall.

✔ **Streeterville:** Adjoining the Magnificent Mile, Streeterville is a booming neighborhood of trendy restaurants, bars, and tucked-away boutiques and galleries. Streeterville is bounded by Michigan Avenue to the west, Lake Michigan to the east, the Chicago River to the south, and Oak Street to the north.

✔ **River North:** Go gallery hopping and visit the site of some of the city's hippest restaurants and clubs. Some 70 galleries are located in an area dubbed "SuHu" (two of its major east-west streets are Superior and Huron). The neighborhood is bounded by Chicago Avenue to the north, the Chicago River to the west and south, and State Street to the east.

✔ **Near North:** This feast of restaurants, bars, and boutique shops just west and north of the Magnificent Mile includes the famous rows of bars on Rush and Division streets. Great goings-on for going out.

✔ **Gold Coast:** The bastion of Chicago's old money, this beautiful neighborhood has many 19th-century homes and runs along Lake Shore Drive north of Michigan Avenue.

✔ **Bucktown/Wicker Park:** The area is said to be home to the third-largest concentration of artists in the country. In recent years, it has become somewhat gentrified, with waves of hot new restaurants, alternative culture, and loft-dwelling yuppies rolling in. In fact, *Bon Appétit* magazine has recognized Wicker Park as the new mecca for the best neighborhood restaurants in Chicago. The focal point of the neighborhood is the intersection of Milwaukee and North avenues.

✔ **Lincoln Park:** The young and the restless, families just starting out, and anyone else who can afford the high prices inhabit Chicago's most popular neighborhood. On its far eastern edge is the neighborhood's namesake park containing the nation's oldest zoo and two museums. Come to this neighborhood for some of Chicago's most popular bars, restaurants, theater companies, and retail shops.

✔ **Wrigleyville:** Named after Wrigley Field, the neighborhood surrounding the ballpark is filled with "three flats" and "five flats" — apartment buildings with three or five floors of apartments — and sports bars. Many young people just launching their careers in Chicago choose to live here.

✔ **Andersonville:** This formerly Swedish enclave stretches along 3 or 4 blocks of North Clark Street immediately north of Foster Avenue. On Saturdays, a bell-ringer makes his rounds as storekeepers ceremonially sweep sidewalks with corn brooms. Highlights include the Swedish-American Museum, a pair of Scandinavian delis, a Swedish bakery, and two good Swedish restaurants.

✔ **Hyde Park:** Home of the University of Chicago, Hyde Park is an oasis of liberal thinking and intellectualism, hemmed in on all sides by some of Chicago's most crime-ridden neighborhoods. The Museum of Science and Industry is the main attraction, with Rockefeller Chapel at the University of Chicago a close second.

For the locations of these neighborhoods, and many others, see the inside-front cover of this book.

Finding Information After You Arrive

After you're in Chicago, one of the easiest ways to gather information is to visit the **Chicago Office of Tourism** in the Chicago Cultural Center, 78 E. Washington St. (☎ **877-244-2246** or 312-744-2400). It's open weekdays from 10 a.m. to 6 p.m., Saturday from 10 a.m. to 5 p.m., and Sunday from 11 a.m. to 5 p.m. Printed materials, including the *Chicago Visitor's Guide,* are available free. While you're at this historic building, take a free, guided tour and admire the rare marble, mosaics, and Tiffany stained glass. You can also enjoy free entertainment, such as movies, music performances, art exhibitions, and guest speakers. In summer, tours of Chicago's diverse neighborhoods depart from the center.

Another walk-in visitor center operated by the Chicago Office of Tourism is in the historic **Water Tower Pumping Station,** 186 E. Pearson St. (☎ **312-744-8783**). Open daily from 7:30 a.m. to 7 p.m., the tourist office distributes printed materials and is a primary stop for trolley and bus tours. **Hot Tix,** where theatergoers can purchase discounted tickets, is here, too (see Chapter 15).

The **Illinois Marketplace at Navy Pier,** 600 E. Grand Ave. (☎ **312-595-5400**), stays open somewhat late to accommodate visitors to Chicago's most popular tourist attraction. Hours are Monday through Thursday from 10 a.m. to 8 p.m., Friday and Saturday from 10 a.m. to 10 p.m., and Sunday from 10 a.m. to 7 p.m. The marketplace has guidebooks and maps, and sells tickets for Lake Michigan boat rides and dinner cruises that depart from the pier.

Geared to business travelers, the **Chicago Convention and Tourism Bureau** office at McCormick Place on the Lake, 2301 S. Lake Shore Dr. (☎ **312-567-8500**), has information on Chicago's major points of interest. It's open weekdays from 8 a.m. to 5 p.m.

Traveling to the 'burbs on Metra

Metra operates commuter trains on 12 lines between the suburbs and several downtown Chicago terminals. The system is separate from the CTA, with its own fares. Service is frequent during rush hours, and lines run every one to three hours otherwise. Most routes run daily. On some lines, Metra offers heavily discounted weekend passes to encourage leisure travelers to use the system. Trains leave for the suburbs from Union Station (where Amtrak is also based) and Northwestern Station (also known as the Ogilvie Transportation Center) in the Loop. If you're taking a Metra train, make sure to ask from which station your train leaves. For information, contact Metra Passenger Services (☎ **312-322-6777**; www.metrarail.com) during regular business hours or RTA travel information (☎ **312-836-7000**) after hours.

Getting Around Chicago

When in Chicago, do as Chicagoans do and take the train or the bus. Chicago Transit Authority (CTA) subway and elevated trains connect most of the city's key attractions and provide fast, cheap transportation between downtown and O'Hare and Midway airports. Although subject to the same gridlock as automobiles during rush hours, buses are also ideal for getting around.

For tips on sightseeing by public transportation, see Chapter 11.

By the "El" — Chicago's subway

The CTA rail system, also referred to as the *El* (short for "elevated"), has elevated tracks, surface tracks, and underground tracks — often all on the same line. The fare is $1.75, and you need a pass because tokens have been eliminated. All stations sell passes during open hours. There's no central station, but the Loop is the center of the system. Stations are named for the streets where they're located.

For a complete map of Chicago's subway and El lines, see the Cheat Sheet at the front of this book. All the lines are color-coded. The blue line runs between O'Hare and downtown; the orange line runs between Midway and downtown. The main subway and El lines include

- ✔ **Blue line:** Runs west-northwest to O'Hare airport

- ✔ **Brown line:** Zigzags on a north-northwest route

- ✔ **Green line:** Runs along Wabash and Lake streets and travels west-south

- ✔ **Orange line:** Runs southwest and serves Midway Airport

- ✔ **Purple line:** Provides express service north-south to and from Evanston

- ✔ **Red line:** Runs along State Street and heads on a north-south route

Most trains run daily every 5 to 25 minutes through late evening. The red line and blue line run 24 hours. For information, call the CTA at ☎ **312-836-7000** or go to www.yourcta.com.

By bus

CTA buses are a convenient, cheap way to explore downtown Chicago and many of its ethnic neighborhoods. Buses stop about every 2 blocks — look for blue CTA bus-stop signs that list bus numbers and routes. On most routes, buses run every day, every 10 to 20 minutes through late evening. For exact times on various routes, call the **CTA** at ☎ **312-836-7000.**

Sky train: Chicago's El

Watch any Hollywood film or TV series set in Chicago, and chances are they'll feature at least one scene set against our screeching elevated train system, more commonly known as the **El** (witness *The Fugitive, ER,* and others). The trains symbolize Chicago's gritty, "city-that-works" attitude, but they actually began as a cutting-edge technology.

After the Great Fire of 1871, Chicago made a remarkable recovery; within 20 years, the downtown district was swarming with people, streetcars, and horses (but no stop-lights). To help relieve congestion, the city took to the sky, building a system of ele-vated trains 15 feet above all the madness. The first El trains were steam-powered, but by the end of the century, all the lines — run by separate companies — used elec-tricity. In 1895, the three El companies collaborated to build a set of tracks into and around the central business district that all the lines would then share. By 1897, the "Loop" was up and running.

Chicago's El wasn't the nation's first. That honor belongs to New York City, which started running its elevated trains in 1867, 25 years before Chicago. But the New York El has almost disappeared, moving underground and turning into a subway early last century. With 289 miles of track, Chicago has the biggest El in the country and the second-largest public transportation system.

Chicago buses and trains accept dollar bills but do not give change. A ride costs $1.75; a 25¢ transfer is good for two additional rides on any route within a two-hour period. Feed bills into a machine next to the driver, drop coins into a fare box, or insert transfer cards and transit passes into another machine alongside the driver. The fare for children ages 7 to 11 is 85¢, plus 15¢ for a transfer. Children 6 and under ride free.

CTA **visitor passes** are a convenient budget-stretching idea. For $5, a one-day pass offers unlimited rides on CTA buses and trains for 24 hours from the first time you use it. You can also buy passes good for two days ($9), three days ($12), and five days ($18). Passes are sold at visitor centers, Hot Tix booths, select museums, both airports, Union Station, and other locations around town. For advance sales, call ☎ 888-968-7282 or visit the Web site www.yourcta.com.

Be sure to equip yourself with one of the excellent free route maps avail-able at all CTA stations. The maps pinpoint major sightseeing attractions and hotels in relation to bus and train routes. If you're unsure which bus or train runs to your destination, call the **CTA information line** (☎ 312-836-7000). Tell the attendant your point of origin and destination, and he'll give you a route. The line is staffed daily from 5 a.m. to 1 a.m.

CTA buses (routes 1 through 204) run in the city and nearby suburbs. **Pace** buses (☎ 847-364-7223; www.pacebus.com) run throughout the suburbs; connect with the CTA; and accept CTA transfer cards, transit cards, and passes.

By taxi

In areas with plenty of pedestrian traffic, such as the Loop, North Michigan Avenue, and River North, taxis are easy to hail. If you can't find one, head for the nearest major hotel; if the doorman finds one for you, a $1 or $2 tip is in order.

Outside downtown and late at night, cabs are fewer and harder to flag down. To call ahead for a ride, try **Yellow Cab** (☎ 312-820-4222) or **Checker Cab** (☎ 312-243-2537).

Taxi fares are $1.90 for meter start-up, plus $1.60 for each additional mile, $2 for every six minutes of time elapsed, and 50¢ per additional passenger aged 12 to 65. One caveat: In late 2004, taxi drivers and owners petitioned city council for higher fares, so rates may increase by the time you arrive in Chicago.

By car

You don't need a car to explore Chicago. In fact, you're likely better without one. Parking is expensive, street parking is tough to find, and the volume of traffic is at its limit. Who needs the hassle and the expense? After all, public transit is pretty far-reaching. And even better news: Your own two feet are the best way to get up close and check out Chicago from street level.

Taking the free trolley

Want to take a ride on the giant Ferris wheel at Navy Pier and then perhaps head to River North to grab a burger at Rock-N-Roll McDonald's? Forget about parking and take the free trolley shuttle that operates along the Illinois Street–Grand Avenue corridor between Navy Pier and State Street. The trolley runs every 10 to 20 minutes from 10 a.m. to 10 p.m. daily, year-round, making about a dozen stops along the way. The service was started to relieve traffic congestion at Navy Pier.

During the summer, the city of Chicago also operates free trolleys daily between Michigan Avenue and the Museum Campus (site of the Adler Planetarium, the Field Museum of Natural History, and the Shedd Aquarium); the trolleys run only on weekends in the fall and spring.

How to get to McCormick Place Conference Center

BY PUBLIC TRANSPORTATION

Although many trade shows at McCormick Place, 23rd Street and Lake Shore Drive (☎ 312-791-7000; www.mccormickplace.com), arrange transportation from hotels downtown and along North Michigan Avenue, you can also get there from Michigan Avenue by taking the **no. 3 King Drive bus,** which deposits passengers at the foot of McCormick Place's South Building, at 23rd Street and Martin Luther King, Jr., Drive. The no. 3 runs from early morning to about 11 p.m.

You can also take a **Metra Electric** commuter train directly to McCormick Place North. Catch the train in the Loop at the Randolph Street Station at Randolph Street and Michigan Avenue. For more information, call the RTA/CTA Travel Information hot line at ☎ **312-836-7000.**

BY CAR

From the Loop and North Michigan Avenue: Take Lake Shore Drive South and follow the signs to McCormick Place.

From O'Hare Airport: Take the Northwest Tollway (I-90) to the Kennedy/Dan Ryan Expressway (I-94) to the Stevenson Expressway North (I-55). Take the Stevenson Expressway north to Lake Shore Drive, and follow the signs to McCormick Place.

From Midway Airport: Take the Stevenson Expressway (I-55) north to Lake Shore Drive South. Follow the signs to McCormick Place.

PARKING

You'll find two main parking lots, one at 31st Street and Lake Shore Drive, and the other across the street from the South Building, at 2215 S. Prairie Ave.

On foot

You can cover plenty of ground on foot while avoiding gridlock and crowded subway trains. Chicago is a great walking city, with several attractions within relatively short distances, wide sidewalks, and tempting window-shopping — depending on your willpower, maybe that last one's not so good.

Some of my favorite walks are right in the heart of downtown. The Magnificent Mile, for example, is a window-shopper's delight that also offers some architectural gems. On the lakefront, you can stroll past a long string of high-rise apartment buildings on one side and a sandy beach on the other. Just north of downtown, you can walk through the excellent, free Lincoln Park Zoo.

Chicago is as safe as most major cities. Always use common sense. If you don't feel safe, you probably aren't — get into a taxi immediately. Generally safe areas include North Michigan Avenue (and the intersecting streets), Streeterville, River North, Rush Street, Gold Coast, and Lincoln Park. During the day, the Loop is crowded with businesspeople and safe. At night, most of the Loop tends to empty out with the exception of the North Loop Theater District, where plenty of people and cabs still congregate.

Chapter 9

Checking In at Chicago's Best Hotels

. . . .

In This Chapter

▶ Selecting the hotel or bed-and-breakfast that's right for you
▶ Choosing the right neighborhood
▶ Scoping out the best hotels in the city
▶ Knowing your options if you can't get your main pick
▶ Indexing hotels by location and price

. . . .

You may be the kind of traveler who thinks a hotel room is simply a place to sleep and stow your luggage. In that case, you don't need two pools, a half-dozen restaurants and lounges, a glittering grand ballroom, and a health club. Nor do you need to shell out big bucks for the overhead associated with those nonessential extras.

On the other hand, if you enjoy taking full advantage of a hotel's amenities — afternoon tea with harp music, a day at the spa, arcades packed with shops — you can find hotels with those, too. But you usually pay extra for the privilege. You can even enjoy the best of both worlds by staying at a no-frills property and visiting other hotels to enjoy tea and jazz, and to relax with a cocktail by the fountain in a fancy lobby bar with a piano. In Chicago, you can find rooms at both ends of the price and comfort spectrum, and a great many in between.

Because you need a place in Chicago to hang your hat and rest your head, the most important part of planning a trip is nailing down where you're going to stay. Four crucial factors come into play: price, location, roominess, and amenities.

Getting to Know Your Options

When it comes to accommodations, Chicago *does* have something for everyone in terms of style, size, price, and location. You can suit both your personality and your pocketbook.

If you want luxury, you can find it at properties such as the **Four Seasons,** the **Ritz-Carlton,** or the **Peninsula.** If you're interested in combining history and upscale accommodations, look no further than the **Drake** and the venerable **Hotel InterContinental Chicago.**

If you're comfortable with chains — or have a favorite — you can find the **Hilton, Hyatt, Sheraton, Radisson, Embassy Suites, Doubletree Guest Suites,** and others here. Even **Red Roof Inn** and **Comfort Inn** have classy hotels (by those chains' no-frills standards) close to the heart of the Magnificent Mile. If you prefer a suite and want to pay a little less for the space, travel less than 5 miles north to the **City Suites Hotel.**

Music lovers can immerse themselves in the funky atmosphere at the **House of Blues Hotel** in Marina City, or the new **Hard Rock Hotel,** just south of the Chicago River off of Michigan Avenue, a rehab of the famous Carbon and Carbide skyscraper.

For European-style digs, look into accommodations at small boutique hotels, such as the **Whitehall, Raphael,** and **Tremont.** Or try the **Hotel Allegro** and **Hotel Burnham,** stylish hostelries converted from tired old buildings in Chicago's revitalized Loop.

Bed-and-breakfasts

On the surface, Chicago may not seem to have many bed-and-breakfasts (B&Bs). Nonetheless, B&Bs are a viable option for Windy City visitors. Many Chicagoans share their homes by providing B&B accommodations in the European style.

You'll also find a wide range of unhosted B&B accommodations. These consist of a suite or an apartment that you have all to yourself — a home away from home. Sometimes the host is there to greet you and then leaves you with a set of keys and breakfast items in the refrigerator.

One of the best ways to locate either kind of B&B accommodation is through a reservation service, such as **At Home Inn Chicago, Inc.** (☎ **800-375-7084** or 312-640-1050; www.athomeinnchicago.com). This service represents about 50 establishments, all within the city, from the South Loop to the Lakeview neighborhood (with a few farther north). These are a mix of hosted guest rooms in houses and apartments and unhosted accommodations in self-contained apartments. For example, $225 a night gets you a two-bedroom, two-bath condo in a Gold Coast high-rise. For about $155 a night, you can unpack in a studio apartment in the Printers Row neighborhood of the South Loop.

Stand-alone inns are also a nice option. **Windy City Urban Inn** is a Victorian-era B&B in the Lincoln Park area with five rooms in the main house plus three apartments in a carriage house. **The Wheeler Mansion,** an exquisitely restored 1870s Second Empire–style B&B, is just two blocks from McCormick Place and a convenient option for those traveling on business.

Lodgings for families with kids

Families won't want to pick a hotel where peace and quiet are valued commodities and parents find themselves cringing at every sound a child makes. When you have kids in tow, bigger often is better in terms of hotel size. You may want to avoid small boutique hotels, where a certain "hush" pervades the atmosphere, and go for the hustle and bustle of a 2,000-room behemoth such as the Hyatt Regency, where the noise of kids blends right in. If you opt for an all-suites hotel, you'll have an extra room with a separate TV. That may help adults and youngsters better coexist in the relative confinement of a hotel. All-suites hotels typically have kitchens with refrigerators and microwaves (for economizing with a dine-in meal) and a dining area.

Location can also be an important consideration for families traveling with children. Pick a property in River North and you're just steps away from such kid-pleasers as **Rock-N-Roll McDonald's** (see Chapter 10), the **Hard Rock Cafe,** 63 W. Ontario St. at North State Street (☎ **312-943-2252**), and the **Rainforest Café,** 605 N. Clark St. at Ohio Street (☎ **312-787-1501**).

Hotels for travelers with disabilities

Finding wheelchair-accessible accommodations in Chicago can be something of a challenge. Many of the city's storied hotels are old and not designed for guests with disabilities. Many older hotels (such as the **Hotel InterContinental Chicago**) have been renovated to include a small number of wheelchair-accessible guest rooms. The problem is that the tiered floors and sweeping staircases that made these hostelries famous aren't tailored to meet the needs of patrons with mobility impairments. The best bets for travelers with disabilities are the newer hotels, such as the **Courtyard by Marriott.** Unfortunately, accessibility and low cost are not typically found together. Most inexpensive digs don't offer wheelchair-accessible rooms at all. Remember to be explicit about your needs when you make your reservation.

Location, location, location

Chicago's core is relatively compact. If shopping along North Michigan Avenue is the primary objective of your visit, you want to stay at a hotel along or near the **Magnificent Mile.** Then again, if you don't mind a short commute, you could stay in the **North Loop** and walk or take the 151 bus north along Michigan Avenue. Likewise, if you have business in the financial district along South LaSalle Street, a hotel in the **Gold Coast** won't put you too terribly far away. Public transportation is plentiful, and cab rides around the downtown core are relatively swift. Streets don't gridlock as often or intensely as they do in, say, New York or London. However, beware of the bridges: In the summer, traffic can be held up for ten minutes as bridges are raised to allow private yachts egress along the Chicago River.

Finding convenient lodgings in the neighborhood where you spend the bulk of your time is obviously helpful. Having a couple of first-rate restaurants nearby, or a museum or gallery or two, makes sense. To make this easy, I recommend hotels and list the neighborhood where each is located in the following sections; check these locations against the maps to see where the hotel is in relation to the attractions you want to see.

My hotel listings concentrate on the Magnificent Mile, the Gold Coast, the Loop, and Streeterville. Other neighborhoods you may consider include

- **Near North:** Away from the mainstream but near interesting neighborhoods and Lincoln Park.

- **River East:** Fairly close to the Loop and the Magnificent Mile, but River East has a tendency to empty out after dark.

- **River North:** An immensely popular tourist area, with the inevitable sprinkling of tourist traps, but River North also has some lower-priced hotels.

The Magnificent Mile

If your mission is shopping, shops aplenty stretch along North Michigan Avenue from the Michigan Avenue Bridge across the Chicago River and north to Oak Street. This retail bounty includes four high-rise malls, upscale shops along Oak Street just west of Michigan Avenue, and bargain stores. (See Chapter 12 for shopping.) You can also find many of Chicago's priciest hotels, along with a bargain or two.

In a nutshell:

- Chicago's premier shopping is right here.

- Many major bus routes include North Michigan Avenue.

- Convenient access to the numerous boat trips and bus tours that begin at the Michigan Avenue Bridge are available.

But . . .

- You can often find yourself in jostling crowds.

- Traffic can get snarled during evening rush hour.

- Michigan Avenue can be noisy, with horns, sirens, and crews of street musicians banging on garbage cans.

The Gold Coast

This high-rent district is immediately north of the Magnificent Mile. You can find yourself within an easy walk of the lakefront and not too far from prime shopping. Hotels here are near the nightlife of Rush and Division streets.

In a nutshell:

- ✔ The Gold Coast has easy access to Oak Street Beach, lakefront walking, and biking.
- ✔ The location is ideal for sampling nightlife.
- ✔ Leafy streets and handsome brownstones adorn the residential sections of the district.

But . . .

- ✔ Out-of-towners in search of action pack the area around Rush and Division streets.
- ✔ Noisy bars and clubs can be a turnoff.
- ✔ Many of the high-profile restaurants have long waits, even with reservations.

The Loop

The traditional heart of Chicago, its downtown, is home to one of Chicago's most famous thoroughfares — "State Street, that great street." State Street has been through some hard times in recent years. Many big department stores closed, and shoppers fled to the suburbs or stayed on the Magnificent Mile. Chicago has made a commitment to the Loop, and the downtown core is beginning to rebound. New hotels are opening, shops are returning, and a revitalized theater district is drawing evening crowds. Loop hotels, in fierce competition with those north of the river, offer some attractive rates and package deals.

In a nutshell:

- ✔ This area has a good mix of theater, shops, and hotels.
- ✔ The Loop offers an unbeatable location for doing business in the LaSalle Street corridor.
- ✔ The location offers easy access to the Art Institute of Chicago, Chicago Cultural Center, Chicago Mercantile Exchange, State Street, and the best of the city's public art.

But . . .

- ✔ The Loop is still relatively empty after dark — although the scene is no longer comatose as it once was.
- ✔ Despite civic improvements, State Street still looks a bit dowdy in parts.
- ✔ You can expect to be solicited by panhandlers.

Streeterville

A handy location combined with an influx of residents into converted loft spaces and high-rises makes Streeterville a great place to stay. Streeterville contains many good restaurants and faces Lake Michigan. Despite its proximity to high-end real estate, Streeterville offers a number of modestly priced hotel options.

In a nutshell:

- ✔ Streeterville offers an incredibly diverse selection of restaurants to fit a wide range of budgets.
- ✔ The enormously popular Navy Pier is very near.
- ✔ This area is adjacent to the prime shopping of the Magnificent Mile.

But . . .

- ✔ Many of the streets are narrow and easily blocked.
- ✔ Navy Pier can be a zoo, with boisterous crowds and difficult parking that spill into the east side of the neighborhood.
- ✔ Although the neighborhood has become gentrified, a few sleazy pockets remain in its southeast corner.

Finding the Best Room at the Best Rate

Travelers accustomed to spending big bucks for a hotel room the size of a broom closet are in for a pleasant surprise in Chicago. Certainly, the city has glitzy upscale hotels that start at $400 a night. But enough variety also exists to satisfy just about every taste and pocketbook. How do you get the most hotel for your money? This chapter lets you in on the city's best secrets.

Finding the best rate

The *rack rate* is the maximum amount that a hotel charges for a room. The desk clerk will quote the rack rate if you walk in off the street and ask for a room for the night. You sometimes see the rate printed on the fire/emergency exit diagrams posted on the back of hotel-room doors.

Hotels are happy to charge you the rack rate, but you don't have to pay it! Hardly anybody does. Perhaps the best way to avoid paying the rack rate is simple: Just ask for a cheaper or discounted rate. You may be pleasantly surprised. For my tips on beating the rack rate, see the next section.

Price depends on many factors, not the least of which is how you make your reservation. A travel agent may be able to negotiate a better deal with certain hotels than you can get by yourself. (That's because the hotel gives the agent a discount in exchange for steering business toward that hotel.) Reserving a room through the hotel's toll-free number, or the city's (☎ 877-244-2246), may result in a lower rate than if you call the hotel directly. On the other hand, the central reservations number may not know about discounts at specific locations. For example, local franchises may offer a special group rate for a wedding or family reunion but may neglect to tell the central booking line. Your best bet is to call both the local number and the central number and see which one gives you a better deal.

If you're smart, you never have to pay the rack rate. Consider the following when you're searching for a good deal:

- ✔ **All-in-one/inclusive packages:** Packages often include lodging, meals, transportation, sightseeing, or some combination of these. If you were planning to do these things anyway, a package may save you money. Beyond the practical, you might find some fun bonuses, such as shopping vouchers, champagne brunches, and carriage rides. See Chapter 5 for more on package tours.

- ✔ **Family rates:** Deals for families vary from hotel to hotel and from weekday to weekend. Ask what's available, and be sure to find out *exactly* how many kids at what age can stay free.

- ✔ **Weekend rates or packages:** Some business hotels offer discounts to keep volume up during the weekend. Hotels in the heart of the Loop's business district will most likely offer these promotions.

- ✔ **Off-season specials:** Consider visiting during the heart of winter or the tail end of autumn. See the sidebar "When is the off-season?" for more on these deals.

- ✔ **Holiday rates:** If you travel during a holiday, ask if the hotel offers a special rate.

- ✔ **Corporate discounts:** Many hotels, especially branches of the large chains, offer corporate rates. Find out whether these rates apply to you.

- ✔ **Senior and AARP rates:** If you're over 64 (or over 49 and an AARP member), you may be eligible for a senior discount.

- ✔ **Online specials:** See "Surfing the Web for Hotel Deals," later in this chapter, for details on finding hotels at the best price on the Web.

For more ways to cut lodging costs, see Chapter 4.

Surfing the Web for hotel deals

Although the major travel booking sites (Frommer's, Travelocity, Expedia, and Orbitz; see Chapter 5 for details) offer hotel booking, you may be better off using a site devoted primarily to lodging. You can often find properties not listed with more general online travel agencies. A few of the sites worth checking are:

When is the off season?

Chicago is becoming a year-round, seven-days-a-week destination. Still, you can usually find a few good buys from January through March — providing a mega-convention is not swallowing up huge numbers of hotel rooms. In the winter months, the Chicago Office of Tourism Web site (www.877chicago.com) features hotel specials, some as low as $69 per night with some blackout dates and minimum night stays. Most of the more centrally located hotels (but not those in the highest price bracket) may be priced from $99 to $139 per night before taxes. Late fall, when the weather can often be mild and pleasant, is also a time to snare lower room rates, particularly on weekends when the business travelers have left.

✔ **All Hotels on the Web** (www.all-hotels.com): Although the name is something of a misnomer, the site does have tens of thousands of listings throughout the world, including Chicago. Bear in mind that each hotel has paid a small fee ($25 and up) to be included, so the list isn't objective and is more like a book of online brochures.

✔ **hoteldiscount!com** (www.hoteldiscounts.com): This site lists bargain room rates at hotels in more than 50 U.S. and international cities, including Chicago. Because these folks prebook blocks of rooms, you can sometimes reserve rooms at hotels that are otherwise sold out. Select a city and input your dates, and you get a list of the best prices for a selection of hotels. The toll-free number (☎ 800-364-0801) is given on the Web site. Call if you want more options than those hotels that are listed online.

✔ **InnSite** (www.innsite.com): InnSite has B&B listings in all 50 U.S. states. Find an inn at your destination, see pictures of the rooms, and check prices and availability. This extensive directory of B&Bs includes listings only if proprietors submit them; inns don't pay to get listed. The innkeepers write their own descriptions, and many listings link to the inns' own Web sites.

✔ **TravelWeb** (www.travelweb.com): Listing more than 26,000 hotels in 170 countries, TravelWeb focuses mostly on chains (both upper and lower end), and you can book almost 90 percent of these online. TravelWeb's Click-It Weekends, updated each Monday, offers weekend deals at many leading hotel chains.

Reserving the best room

Somebody has to get the best room in the house, and that somebody may as well be you! Here are a few tips for landing a room you'll love:

✔ **Always ask for a corner room.** They're usually larger, quieter, and close to the elevator. Corner rooms often have more windows and light than standard rooms, and they don't always cost more.

> ✔ **Ask if the hotel is renovating.** If it is, request a room away from the renovation work.

> ✔ **Pick your smoking preference.** Many hotels now offer nonsmoking rooms; if smoke bothers you, by all means ask for one.

> ✔ **Inquire about the location of the hotel's restaurants, bars, and discos.** These places can be a source of irritating noise.

If you aren't happy with your room when you arrive, talk to the front-desk staff. If they have another room, they should be happy to accommodate you, within reason.

Arriving without a Reservation

If you show up in Chicago without a reservation, shame on you! But you still have options other than seeking a room at the YMCA or sleeping on a park bench. If you're not successful during the day, call hotels again after 6 p.m., when rooms that are reserved but not secured with a credit card may become available.

When booking a room at the last minute, you can usually negotiate a better rate if you phone (even from around the corner) rather than showing up at the desk with luggage in hand and a look of desperation in your eyes.

Another option is to check with reservation bureaus, which buy up rooms in bulk and resell them. They usually offer sizeable discounts off rack rates. Often, these bureaus are able to find space when other hotels in the city are sold out. So you may luck out with one of the following:

> ✔ **Accommodations Express** (☎ 800-950-4685): Eighty percent of Chicago hotels participate in this service; discounts are 10 to 40 percent off rack rates.

> ✔ **Hotels.com** (☎ 800-96-HOTEL; www.hotels.com): Forty hotels participate; 20 to 50 percent off rack rates.

> ✔ **Hot Rooms** (☎ 800-468-3500; www.hotrooms.com): This Chicago-based service is the best source for discounted rooms at all of Chicago's best hotels.

> ✔ **Quikbook** (☎ 800-789-9887; www.quikbook.com): Twenty hotels participate; 10 to 40 percent off rack rates.

Chicago's Best Hotels

Chicago has been on a hotel-building binge. Lest you think I exaggerate, 21 new properties have opened their doors in the downtown area since 1998, adding 6,400 new rooms. Existing hotels have also polished themselves up in an effort to keep up with the Joneses. Some 14 hotels finished renovations in the last few years. (See the sidebar "New or improved Chicago hotels" later in this chapter for a list of properties.)

What does this mean to the intrepid traveler — other than construction cranes on the horizon and scaffolding on the streets? In the past, conventioneers told tales of sleeping on cots in hotel hallways because there was literally no room at the inn. Now travelers have more lodging options than ever before. Increased competition means wiggle room on prices is more likely, too.

When a major convention is in town, look out. Even with all the construction going on, getting a room can be difficult, so book early. To find out if an upcoming convention coincides with the dates you plan to visit Chicago, call the **Chicago Convention & Tourism Bureau** at ☎ **312-567-8500,** or check its Web site at www.choosechicago.com (click on "For Meeting Planners").

Each hotel listing in this chapter includes a price rating between one and four dollar signs. The number of dollar signs reflects the average *rack rate* (the maximum rate a hotel charges for a room) for a standard double room for one night, excluding taxes. The more dollar signs under the name, the more you pay. Table 9-1 has the breakdown.

Table 9-1	Key to Hotel Dollar Signs	
Dollar Sign(s)	**Price Range**	**What to Expect**
$	Less than $125	These accommodations are relatively simple and inexpensive. Rooms will likely be small, and televisions are not necessarily provided. Parking is not provided but rather catch-as-you-can on the street.
$$	$126–$200	A bit classier, these midrange accommodations offer more room, more extras (such as irons, hair dryers, or a microwave), and a more convenient location than the preceding category.
$$$	$201–$300	Higher-class still, these accommodations begin to look plush. Think chocolates on your pillow, a classy restaurant, underground parking garages, maybe even expansive views of the water.
$$$$	$301 and up	These top-rated accommodations come with luxury amenities such as valet parking, on-premise spas, and in-room hot tubs and CD players — but you pay through the nose for 'em.

Central Chicago Accommodations

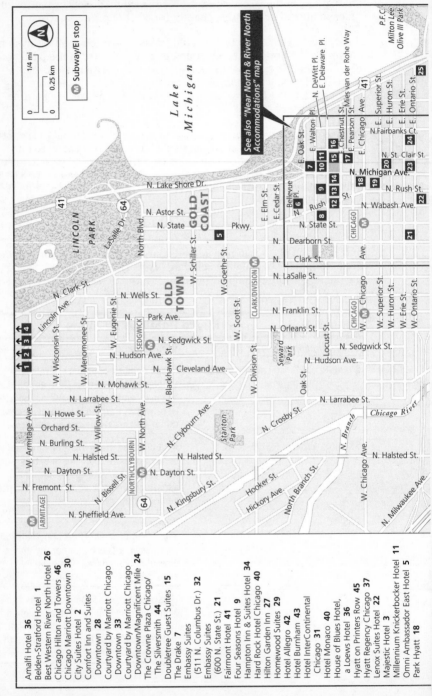

N

0   1/4 mi
0   0.25 km

Ⓜ Subway/El stop

See also "Near North & River North Accommodations" map

Lake Michigan

P.F.C.
Milton Lee
Olive III Park

N. DeWitt Pl.
E. Delaware Pl.
N. Oak St.
E. Walton Pl.
E. Chestnut St.
Mies van der Rohe Way
E. Pearson St.
E. Chicago Ave.
E. Superior St.
E. Huron St.
E. Erie St.
E. Ontario St.
N. Fairbanks Ct.
N. St. Clair St.
N. Michigan Ave.
N. Rush St.
N. Wabash Ave.
Bellevue
Rush St.
N.
N. State St.
CHICAGO Ⓜ
Dearborn St.
Clark St.
Ave.

N. Lake Shore Dr.
N. Astor St.
N. State
GOLD COAST
Pkwy.
E. Elm St.
E. Cedar St.
W. Schiller St.
N. Goethe St.
W.
N.
Dearborn St.
Clark St.
N. LaSalle St.
CLARK/DIVISION Ⓜ

LINCOLN PARK

41
64
LaSalle Dr.
North Blvd.
N. Clark St.
Lincoln Ave.
N. Wells St.
N. Eugenie St.
OLD TOWN
SEDGWICK Ⓜ
N. Park Ave.
N. Sedgwick St.
N. Hudson Ave.
W. Scott St.
W. Division St.
N. Franklin St.
N. Orleans St.
Locust St.
W. Chicago
CHICAGO Ⓜ
W. Superior St.
W. Huron St.
W. Erie St.
W. Ontario St.

N. Wisconsin St.
N. Menomonee St.
W. Eugenie St.
W. Menomonee St.
N. Blackhawk St.
N. Sedgwick St.
Seward Park
N. Hudson Ave.
N. Mohawk St.
N. Cleveland Ave.
N. Larrabee St.
N. Larrabee St.
N. Sedgwick St.
N. Howe St.
Orchard St.
N. Burling St.
W. Willow St.
W. North Ave.
N. Clybourn Ave.
Stanton Park
N. Crosby St.
Oak St.
Chicago River
N. Branch
N. Chicago Ave.
N. Halsted St.

N. Halsted St.
N. Dayton St.
N. Fremont St.
N. Bissell St.
NORTH/CLYBOURN Ⓜ
64
N. Dayton St.
N. Kingsbury St.
Hooker St.
Hickory Ave.
North Branch St.
W. Chicago Ave.
N. Milwaukee Ave.
ARMITAGE Ⓜ
N. Sheffield Ave.

1 2 3 4

1 2 3 4

5
6
7
8
9
10
11
12
13
14
15
16
17
18
19
20
21
22
23
24
25

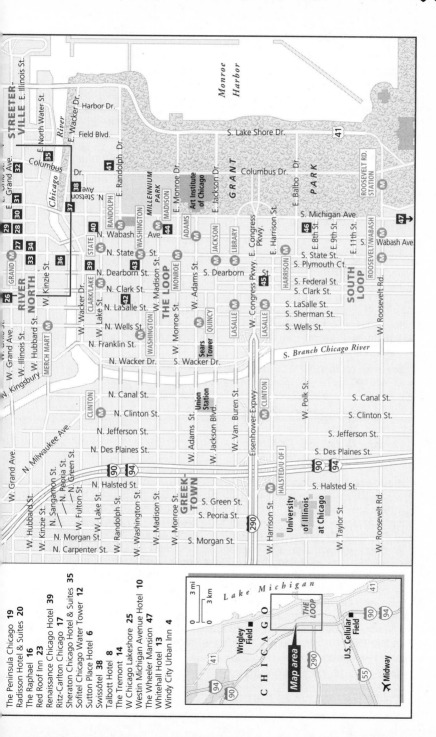

The Kid Friendly icon designates hotels that are especially good for families. These hotels may offer play areas, kids' menus in the restaurants, or swimming pools, and all have an open (not stuffy) atmosphere that makes families feel at ease. (Nothing stresses a parent more than Junior knocking over a multi-thousand-dollar Chinese vase in the lobby, right?) Bear in mind that every hotel in town accommodates children's needs; a listing without this icon does not mean "kid unfriendly." Most properties allow kids to stay free with their parents, but the cut-off age varies. Always ask when you're booking.

For locations of my recommended hotels, see the "Central Chicago Accommodations" and "Near North and River North Accommodations" maps in this chapter.

Belden-Stratford Hotel
$$$ Lincoln Park

This north-side hotel is one of Chicago's best-kept lodging secrets. This gracious apartment building offers 25 hotel rooms. The rooms are large, the doorman greets you as if you were a resident, and one of Chicago's finest French restaurants, **Ambria** (see Chapter 10), is located off the lobby. If you prefer a neighborhood atmosphere and doing as the natives do, this is the place for you. Be sure to ask for a room with a view of Lincoln Park, so you can watch runners pass and couples stroll as you sip your coffee in the morning.

See map p. 98. 2300 N. Lincoln Park West (just north of Fullerton Avenue). ☎ *800-800-6261 or 773-281-2900. CTA: Bus no. 151 stops at Fullerton in Lincoln Park; walk west to the hotel. Parking: Valet (with in-out privileges) $25. Rack rates: $209–$299 double. AE, DC, DISC, MC, V.*

Chicago Hilton and Towers
$–$$$$ South Loop

Big is not necessarily a bad thing in a hotel. Sprawling over several city blocks, this massive hotel, with 1,545 rooms, is a virtual city within a city. Public areas abound with shops, bars, restaurants, and artwork. Rooms feature cherry-wood furnishings and feel spacious, thanks to high ceilings. Many rooms have two bathrooms — a bonus for families with kids. A club level in the tower provides a higher degree of pampering and has its own check-in. Kitty O'Shea's pub recruits chefs, bartenders, and wait staff under an Irish government exchange program. Buckingham's, the hotel's fine-dining restaurant, specializes in steaks and is known for an outstanding selection of single-malt Scotch. This hotel is ideally located for sightseers — across from Grant Park, 5 blocks south of the Art Institute of Chicago and Millennium Park, and a 20-minute walk from the Field Museum of Natural History, John G. Shedd Aquarium, and Adler Planetarium & Astronomy Museum.

See map p. 98. 720 S. Michigan Ave. (at Balbo Drive). ☎ *800-HILTONS or 312-922-4400.* www.chicagohilton.com. *CTA: Buses stop in front of the hotel; red* *line to Harrison/State. Parking: Valet $32, self-parking $29. Rack rates: $124–$324 double. AE, DC, DISC, MC, V.*

Chicago Marriott Downtown
$$ Magnificent Mile

You can't go wrong at the Marriott, located in the heart of the Magnificent Mile near the new North Bridge shopping and entertainment complex. Exceptionally fine rooms of above-average size are more than comfortable. Concierge floors are available for a bit more money. An indoor pool and sun deck, health club, and basketball courts round out the amenities. Although large, at 1,192 rooms, you feel at home here. And you can go play at nearby ESPN Zone and shop 'til you drop at Nordstrom in the adjacent Westfield North Bridge Mall.

See map p. 98. 540 N. Michigan Ave. (at Grand Avenue). ☎ *800-228-9290 or 312-836-0100.* www.marriotthotels.com. *CTA: Buses stop in front of the hotel. Parking: Valet (with in-out privileges) $34. Rack rates: $220 double. AE, DC, DISC, MC, V.*

Courtyard by Marriott Chicago Downtown
$$–$$$ River North

This chain offers good deals in the heart of River North, one of Chicago's flashiest tourist areas. Here you're just a short walk from the shops of Michigan Avenue, the Loop, and River North's main strip, and the free trolley to Navy Pier stops nearby. The newly renovated rooms have large desks and two-line phones with high-speed Internet access, granite vanities and sofas (some with pull-out beds). Coffee and newspapers (included in the room rate) are available in the lobby, and the hotel has an exercise room, pool, and sun deck. The 30 East Cafe & Lounge offers a breakfast buffet, lunch and dinner and room service. Another bonus, you're close to numerous restaurants, the legendary jazz club Andy's (see Chapter 16), and a number of galleries and antiques shops.

See map p. 98. 30 E. Hubbard St. (at State Street). ☎ *800-321-2211 or 312-329-2500. CTA: Red line El to Grand (at State Street), then walk 2 blocks south. Parking: Valet (with in-out privileges) $33; self-parking $20.50. Rack rates: $169–$229 double. AE, DC, DISC, MC, V.*

Beware the one-armed man

Movie fans who stay at the Chicago Hilton and Towers should keep their eyes peeled for the one-armed man. Numerous scenes for the movie *The Fugitive* were filmed in the hotel and its Conrad Hilton Suite. For those who really want to stay in style, the 5,000-square-foot suite comes with its own butler, maid, limousine service, and helipad — and goes for about $5,000 a night. In addition to Harrison Ford, other celebs who have stayed in the city's most luxurious suite include Presidents Reagan, Bush Sr., and Clinton, as well as John Travolta.

New or improved Chicago hotels

More than 11 hotels have been built in Chicago since 1998, and one more is scheduled for completion in 2005 (that's the construction site of Baymont Inn & Suites, at the intersection of Rush and Ontario). Standouts among the new kids on the block include **Peninsula Hotel** and **Sofitel Chicago Water Tower** (for details, see the reviews in this chapter). Recently opened properties include the conveniently located **Comfort Inn and Suites Downtown,** 15 E. Ohio St., River North (☎ **312-894-0900**), and the large **Embassy Suites,** 511 N. Columbus Dr., Streeterville (☎ **312-836-5900**). Other newly constructed hotels include

✔ **Amalfi Hotel,** 10 W. Kinzie St., completed in 2004

✔ **Hard Rock Hotel,** 230 N. Michigan Ave., completed in 2004

✔ **Courtyard by Marriott,** 165 E. Ontario St., completed in 2003

Several hotels have also spiffed up their accommodations. If you're booking one of the following properties, ask for one of its recently renovated rooms: **DoubleTree Guest Suites,** the **Drake Hotel, Embassy Suites** (600 N. State St., River North), **Fairmont Hotel, Hotel Inter-Continental Chicago,** and the **Whitehall Hotel.** (For details, see the listings in this chapter.)

Courtyard by Marriott Chicago Downtown/Magnificent Mile
$$–$$$ **Magnificent Mile**

This confusingly named (it's easy to get it mixed up with its River North counterpart) but brand-new hotel sits in a prime location just a half-block east of Michigan Avenue. You'll pay a little more to stay at this hotel than the Courtyard in River North, and that's partly due to the location, and partly due to the room size, which tends to be a little larger here. Double rooms offer two queen beds — a nice change from the standard two double beds — and king suites make this a comfortable choice for families. Add to that the lovely swimming pool on the tenth floor and a large fitness room with great views, and you just may want to up the ante and stay here. The lobby décor is Art Deco, and the room décor is pretty standard, but everything is clean and new. An on-site American cafe, Viand Bar & Kitchen, is kid-friendly and also provides room service. And when you need a pick-me-up, you can visit the Starbucks in the lobby.

See map p. 98. 165 E. Ontario St. (just east of Michigan Avenue). ☎ 312-573-0800. www.marriott.com. *CTA: Red line to Grand (at State Street). Parking: Valet (with in-out privileges) $35; self-parking $35, no in-out privileges. Rack rates: $249 double, $309 king suite. AE, DC, DISC, MC, V.*

Near North and River North Accommodations

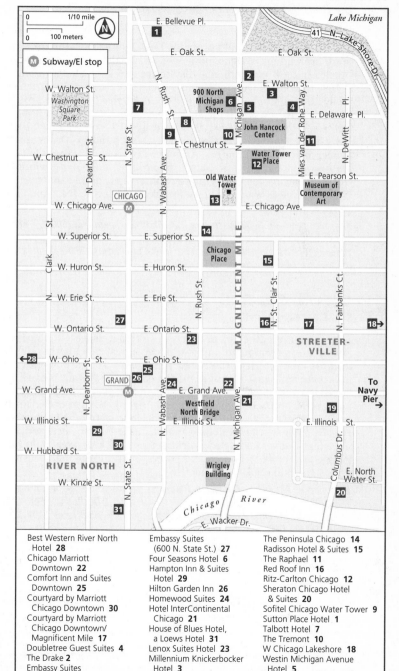

Best Western River North
  Hotel **28**
Chicago Marriott
  Downtown **22**
Comfort Inn and Suites
  Downtown **25**
Courtyard by Marriott
  Chicago Downtown **30**
Courtyard by Marriott
  Chicago Downtown/
  Magnificent Mile **17**
Doubletree Guest Suites **4**
The Drake **2**
Embassy Suites
  (511 N. Columbus Dr.) **19**

Embassy Suites
  (600 N. State St.) **27**
Four Seasons Hotel **6**
Hampton Inn & Suites
  Hotel **29**
Hilton Garden Inn **26**
Homewood Suites **24**
Hotel InterContinental
  Chicago **21**
House of Blues Hotel,
  a Loews Hotel **31**
Lenox Suites Hotel **23**
Millennium Knickerbocker
  Hotel **3**
Park Hyatt **13**

The Peninsula Chicago **14**
Radisson Hotel & Suites **15**
The Raphael **11**
Red Roof Inn **16**
Ritz-Carlton Chicago **12**
Sheraton Chicago Hotel
  & Suites **20**
Sofitel Chicago Water Tower **9**
Sutton Place Hotel **1**
Talbott Hotel **7**
The Tremont **10**
W Chicago Lakeshore **18**
Westin Michigan Avenue
  Hotel **5**
Whitehall Hotel **8**

The Crowne Plaza Chicago/The Silversmith
$$$–$$$$ Loop

Frank Lloyd Wright would probably be delighted with this smart hotel — there are enough Wright influences to satisfy even his enormous ego. Opened in 1998 as a hotel, the distinctive dark-green building was created in 1897 to house silversmiths and jewelers. A National Historic Landmark today, the building contains eight floors of guest units (143 rooms), and no two rooms on any floor are alike. Rooms are decorated in Arts and Crafts and Prairie School style, with original 12-foot ceilings, 10-foot windows draped in velvety curtains, and red-oak furniture. Desks are designed to accommodate computers. Armoires contain built-in televisions, refrigerators, and CD players. Many rooms have cushioned window seats. Oversize bathrooms have granite countertops and tile-and-granite floors. Thrifty travelers with families may ask about the suites, which are a bargain compared to those in other downtown hotels.

See map p. 98. 10 S. Wabash Ave. (at Madison Street). ☎ *800-227-6963 or 312-372-7696. CTA: Orange, brown, or green line El to Madison/Wabash, or red line to Washington/State. Parking: Valet (with in-out privileges) $28. Rack rates: $149–$279 double; from $289 suites. AE, DC, DISC, MC, V.*

DoubleTree Guest Suites
$$–$$$$ Streeterville

A step up in elegance from other all-suite hotels, the DoubleTree Guest Suites offers comfort in one of Chicago's best neighborhoods. A casual attitude characterizes the hotel, which is tucked into an elegant street in Streeterville just a couple blocks east of Michigan Avenue, near the Drake. Here you get a warm, inviting, immaculate room, plus a separate living room and bedroom and a deluxe bathroom. Surrounded in glass, the pool deck on the 30th floor is a great place to watch the fireworks at Navy Pier. Families will feel welcome at Mrs. Park's Tavern, an American bistro. The small but very adequate workout room will keep you fit after that Mrs. Park's meal. You'll find fresh flowers in the lobby and freshly baked chocolate-chip cookies at check-in.

See map p. 98. 198 E. Delaware Place (at Mies van der Rohe Street). ☎ *800-222-8733 or 312-664-1100.* www.doubletree.com. *CTA: Red line El to Chicago (at State Street). Parking: Valet (with in-out privileges) $34. Rack rates: $109–$309 double suite. AE, DC, DISC, MC, V.*

The Drake
$$$$ Magnificent Mile

The Drake is civilization at its finest. Although now a link in the Hilton chain, this grande dame of Chicago hotels still displays gracious style and boundless charm. Rooms have high ceilings, polished woodwork, marble bathrooms, and every amenity you'd expect, from terry robes to fresh fruit and Swiss chocolates at turndown. Elevators even have velvet seats. Coffee lounges on each floor offer lake views. Besides being a great place to stay, the Drake is a great place to play. A shopping arcade is ideal for browsing. And dining spots include the Cape Cod Room, a Chicago institution for seafood since 1933. The Coq d'Or piano bar (see Chapter 16) is known for well-made, 4-ounce martinis. In the Palm Court, you can enjoy afternoon tea around a marble fountain with a harpist accompanying your finger-sandwich eating. A jazz group plays on Saturdays.

See map p. 98. 140 E. Walton Place (at Michigan Avenue). ☎ *800-553-7253 or 312-787-2200.* www.thedrakehotel.com. *CTA: Buses stop on Michigan Avenue, ½ block west. Red line El to Chicago/State. Parking: Valet (with in-out privileges) $32. Rack rates: $255–$295 double. AE, DC, DISC, MC, V.*

Embassy Suites
$$–$$$$ River North

The spacious units at this all-suites hotel, with a huge atrium and gushing waterfall, offer plenty of room for kids and adults. Youngsters enjoy in-room Nintendo games and the proximity to Gino's Pizza, the Hard Rock Cafe, Rainforest Cafe, and other kid-friendly, high-profile dining spots. Parents like the extras that make a stay easy on the pocketbook, such as cooked-to-order breakfasts free every morning, and evening cocktails. Suites have well-equipped kitchens and television sets in both the living room and bedroom. Papagus Taverna, a faux Greek restaurant, is on the street level. You may also check out the recent addition of another Embassy Suites at 511 N. Columbus Dr., Streeterville (☎ **312-836-5900**), conveniently located near Navy Pier and Michigan Avenue.

See map p. 98. 600 N. State St. (at West Ohio Street). ☎ *800-362-2779 or 312-943-3800.* www.embassysuites.com. *CTA: Red line El to Grand (at State Street). Parking: Valet (with in-out privileges) $34. Rack rates: $199–$259 king suite; $269–299 double suite. Rates include full breakfast and evening cocktails. AE, DC, DISC, MC, V.*

Fairmont Hotel
$$$–$$$$ River East

Businessmen frequent the Fairmont for its location, a few blocks north of the Loop, and the exceptionally large rooms. Your room may have a dressing room, walk-in closet, and marble bathroom with a separate shower, enclosed toilet, telephone, and mini-TV. Rooms are no more than four

---

You're in good company at the Coq d'Or

Marilyn Monroe, Joe DiMaggio, Jack Benny, and Vince Lombardi carved their initials into the tiny wooden bar of the Coq d'Or. Management once announced plans to replace the bar, causing such a furor among patrons that it was left in place. Introduce yourself to manager Patrick Bredin, another Drake institution, and take time for a bowl of signature Bookbinder's red snapper soup or oysters at the raw bar.

doors away from an elevator. One unit on each of the 37 floors is accessible to travelers with disabilities. Public spaces, clad with marble, are decked out with fine artwork and arrangements of fresh flowers. In the lobby lounge, waiters in tails serve afternoon tea. The new Aria Ristorante, with its American and culturally inspired cuisine, is a welcome addition. An underground walkway leads fitness buffs to "Mount Chicago," a 110-foot-high climbing wall in the well-equipped Lakeshore Athletic Club — hotel guests can use the facilities for a fee.

See map p. 98. 200 N. Columbus Dr. (at Lake Street). ☎ *800-526-2008 or 312-565-8000.* www.fairmont.com. *CTA: Buses stop on Michigan Avenue, 2 blocks west; brown, orange, or green line El to Randolph. Parking: Valet (with in-out privileges) $30. Rack rates: $129–$389 double. AE, DC, DISC, MC, V.*

Four Seasons Hotel
$$$$ **Magnificent Mile**

In many cities, the local Four Seasons hotel is the best. In Chicago, the Four Seasons Hotel is considered to be one of the best hotels in the world. Spacious guest rooms are packed with extras and served by twice-daily maid service (including delivery of a carafe of water at turndown). Italian marble, crystal, intricate woodwork, and plush carpeting lavishly appoint the hotel's attractive public areas. Chandeliers are as common as light bulbs are at Motel 6. Connected to the hotel are the 70 shops of 900 North Michigan Avenue, the Magnificent Mile's most upscale mall, otherwise known as the Bloomingdale's mall. Still, you may never venture beyond the hotel's seventh-floor lobby, which holds the Seasons lounge and restaurant. The lounge offers afternoon tea and views of the Magnificent Mile. The restaurant features cutting-edge American cuisine. The hotel's clublike bar, just off the lobby, accommodates cigar smokers. The health spa holds a pool, huge whirlpool, sun deck, and outdoor jogging track.

See map p. 98. 120 E. Delaware Place (at Michigan Avenue). ☎ *800-332-3442 or 312-280-8800.* www.fourseasons.com. *CTA: Buses stop on Michigan Avenue, ½ block east; red line El stops at Chicago/State. Parking: Valet (with in–out privileges) $36; self $26. Rack rates: $435–$535 double. AE, DC, DISC, MC, V.*

Hampton Inn & Suites Hotel
$–$$ **River North**

Conveniently located near the Merchandise Mart and Michigan Avenue shops, the Hampton Inn brings welcome relief to the escalating hotel prices in trendy River North. The hotel has a combination of guest rooms, two-room suites, and studios. The residential, warm atmosphere of the hotel puts you close to tourist hot spots, such as the Rainforest Cafe, Rock-N-Roll McDonald's, and the Hard Rock Cafe. A second-floor skywalk also connects the hotel to a branch of Ruth's Chris Steak House. Children under 18 and third and fourth guests are free. You get a minicourse in Chicago history with a great display of photographs and architectural artifacts.

See map p. 98. 33 W. Illinois St. (at Dearborn Street). ☎ *800-426-7866 or 312-832-0330.* www.hamptoninn.com. *CTA: Buses stop at the corner of Grand and State* *streets; red line El to Grand (at State Street). Parking: Valet (with in-out privileges) $32. Rack rates: $129–$179 double. AE, DC, DISC, MC, V.*

Hard Rock Hotel Chicago
$$$ Loop

The good news: This hotel is not located on top of the super-touristy hard Rock Cafe, which is located about a mile away in River North. In fact, the hotel is a relatively restrained rehab of one of the city's historic sky-scrapers, the 40-story Carbide and Carbon Building. As expected, the theme here is music: pop tunes echo through the lobby, TV monitors show videos, and glass cases display pop-star memorabilia. If your kids are in the age range that considers wearing a Hard Rock T-shirt from exotic locales a badge of honor, they may well get a kick from a stay here. But for the grown-ups in your crowd, the mix of old and new can be somewhat jar-ring. The black-and-gray lobby feels like a nightclub, while the marble-and-gold-trimmed elevator bank still says "high-rise office building." Don't expect too much rock-star attitude; to date, the Hard Rock appears to be populated by youngish business travelers and families. The guest rooms are neutral in décor with modern furnishings. The building's larger-than-average windows let in plenty of natural light. The Hard Rock rooms on the corners of each floor are larger than the standard double rooms and feature chaise lounges for stretching out. Families should inquire about the suites, located in the tower at the top of the building, which come in various one- and two-bedroom configurations.

The hotel's restaurant, China Bar & Grill, serves up Asian fusion cuisine in a high-energy setting, and the street-level bar, open 'til 4 a.m., features live music and DJs most nights. Despite its efforts to become a Chicago hip-ster hangout, the place still has the feel of a hotel bar. The hotel is actively courting rock bands who come through town on tour, but my guess is that U2 will be hard-pressed to exchange their ultraluxury digs at the Park Hyatt for the Hard Rock.

See map p. 98. 230 N. Michigan Ave. (at Lake Street). ☎ *877-762-5468 or 312-345-1000. Fax: 312-345-1012.* www.hardrockhotelchicago.com. *CTA: El red line or blue line to Lake. Parking: Valet (with in–out privileges) $35. Rack rates: $169–$239 double; from $1,500 suite. Kids under 12 stay free in parent's room. AE, DC, DISC, MC, V.*

Hotel Allegro
$$ Loop

Located across the street from City Hall and in the North Loop theater district, the 483-room Hotel Allegro is splashy, fun, and a great value. Formerly the Bismarck Hotel, the place first opened in 1894 and was rebuilt in 1926 and again in 2000, the most recent date pioneering the redesign of old hotels into updated boutique offerings. Warm, vibrant colors and bold patterns dominate the public spaces and smallish guest rooms. (Don't be surprised if your room is painted a perky pink-grapefruit color.) Suites have nice amenities, including terry robes, VCRs, and two-person Jacuzzi tubs. You also get melon-and-magenta bedspreads and green throw pillows sprinkled with gold stars. Whirlpools are installed in 31 suites. Guests gather each evening for complimentary wine served around a polished, black grand piano and limestone fireplace. 312 Chicago restaurant, a colorful extension of the hotel, serves an Italian-American menu.

See map p. 98. 171 W. Randolph St. (at LaSalle Street). ☎ *800-643-1500 or 312-236-0123.* www.allegrochicago.com. *CTA: Buses stop along LaSalle Street; all El lines stop at Washington. Parking: Valet (with in-out privileges) $30. Rack rates: $149–$299 double. Rates include complimentary evening wine. AE, DC, DISC, MC, V.*

Hotel Burnham
$$$ Loop

Back in 1999, in one of the city's best restorations in years, the Kimpton Group of San Francisco transformed one of the world's first skyscrapers, D. H. Burnham's Reliance Building (1891), into a superhip boutique hotel. (Thanks to the same group for creating Hotel Allegro and Hotel Monaco — both listed in this chapter.) In the heart of the Loop, just across from Marshall Field's department store, the hotel has 103 rooms and 19 suites — average in size, below average in price. Visitors marvel at huge guest-room windows that stretch from floor to ceiling. Ask for a high, corner room overlooking Marshall Field's. The playful Café Atwood, which serves eclectic American cuisine on the ground floor, allows you to simultaneously dine and admire the restored terrazzo floors and Carrara wainscoting.

See map p. 98. 1 W. Washington St. (at State Street). ☎ *866-690-1986 or 312-782-1111.* www.burnhamhotel.com. *CTA: Buses stop on State Street; red line El to Washington/State. Parking: Valet (with in-out privileges) $29. Rack rates: $149–$299 double. AE, DISC, MC, V.*

Hotel InterContinental Chicago
$$$$ Magnificent Mile

Installed in two adjoining buildings at the foot of the Magnificent Mile, this hotel is both eccentric and lovable. The hotel's south tower was built in 1929 as the Medinah Athletic Club, a luxury men's club, and recently updated. Climbing to the eighth floor in the south tower, visitors are swept through a mélange of architectural styles, from classic Italian renaissance to French Louis XVI, from medieval England to Spain and Mesopotamia. Flourishes include hand-stenciled ceilings, marble columns, brass inlays, and beautiful tapestries and artwork. Service is smooth, and rooms are elegant and intimate. Each unit at this 814-room luxury property comes with thick terry robes, a coffeemaker, a refrigerator, a desk, and three dual-line phones. Rooms in the older tower are more classic in style; rooms in the north tower are modern and more standard. The hotel's restaurant, Zest, is the only street-level restaurant on Michigan Avenue, so grab a table by the window and enjoy the people-watching.

See map p. 98. 505 N. Michigan Ave. (at Grand Avenue). ☎ *800-327-0200 or 312-944-4100.* www.intercontinental.com. *CTA: Buses stop in front of the hotel; red line El to Grand/State. Parking: Valet (with in–out privileges) $35. Rack rates: $249–$359 double. AE, DC, DISC, MC, V.*

Hotel Monaco
$$$ **North Loop**

Rooms at this vibrant makeover of the dowdy Oxford House come complete with a pet. A goldfish in a bowl will be delivered on request and may be kept for the duration of the stay. Gimmicks aside, this sleek hotel, offering 192 guest rooms (including 22 suites, each with a two-person whirlpool), is distinguished by its rich décor. Guest rooms are furnished with mahogany writing desks, Art Deco armoires, and lipstick-red quilted headboards. Amenities include coffeemakers and robes. Each evening, guests enjoy complimentary wine around a limestone fireplace, the centerpiece of Monaco's jewel-box lobby. The registration desk is whimsically modeled after a classic steamer trunk, and the adjoining restaurant, South Water Kitchen, includes a 30-foot-long exhibition kitchen on its lower level. Hotel guests as well as local office workers laud the restaurant's American comfort food, including big butcher-block sandwiches, macaroni and cheese, and chicken pot pies.

See map p. 98. 225 N. Wabash Ave. (at Wacker Drive). ☎ *800-397-7661 or 312-960-8500.* www.monaco-chicago.com. *CTA: Buses stop at State and Wacker; brown, orange, or green line El to Randolph/Wabash or red line to Washington/State. Parking: Valet (with in-out privileges) $28. Rack rates: $139–$299 double. Rates include complimentary evening wine. AE, DC, DISC, MC, V.*

House of Blues Hotel, a Loews Hotel
$$–$$$ **North Loop**

Located in the distinctive Marina Towers complex alongside the Chicago River, the House of Blues Hotel is part of what's become an entertainment mecca. The House of Blues music club, plus steakhouse Smith & Wollensky, wine bar Bin 36, Crunch Health & Fitness Center, and a marina with boat rentals, make this an all-in-one experience. The eclectic décor of the hotel, part of the Loews Hotel group, combines Gothic, Moroccan, East Indian, and New Orleans styles. It's the place to stay if you want your hotel to be an experience, not just a place to sleep. Hall monitors show

Touring Tarzan's old haunt

Even if you don't stay at the Hotel Inter-Continental Chicago, stop by for a fascinating free architectural tour. Guests and nonguests can take a 30-minute tape-recorded, self-guided walking tour narrated by WGN radio personality Roy Leonard. Leave a driver's license or other identification as security and get a loaner Walkman. Discover the beautiful Venetian-style, junior Olympic-size pool, where Olympic gold medalist and screen actor Tarzan Johnny Weismuller trained and pioneer bodybuilder Charles Atlas coached the wealthy. Mobster Al Capone threw a huge poolside party here, but only for an episode of *The Untouchables* TV series. Nonguests may use the pool and a state-of-the-art health club for $15 per visit. Changing rooms, saunas, showers, and toiletries are provided.

live concerts from the House of Blues club. Upon check-in, guests receive a complimentary music CD. Technology-friendly rooms provide television Internet access, as well as interesting furniture (much of which is painted blue) and fabulous Southern folk art.

See map p. 98. 333 N. Dearborn St. (at the river). ☎ *800-235-6397 or 312-245-0333.* www.loewshotels.com. *CTA: Buses stop at the corner of State Street and Wacker Drive, then walk 1½ blocks north, 1 block west; red line El goes to Grand/State. Parking: Valet (with in-out privileges) $28. Rack rates: $139–$349 double. AE, DC, DISC, MC, V.*

Hyatt on Printers Row
$$$ South Loop

History meets high-tech at this comfortable hotel. Surrounded by loft apartments in a fashionable area — known as Printers' Row thanks to the presence of former printing plants — this 161-room hotel fuses the 1896 Morton Salt Building with a century-old printing plant. The location is a comfortable walk from the Art Institute of Chicago, Grant Park, Sears Tower, Harold Washington Library, and the city's financial district. Guest rooms feature Frank Lloyd Wright–style geometric designs as well as stylish black lacquer furniture and heavy tapestry spreads. While old-world European in flavor, this hotel offers amenities such as VCRs, computer workstations, two telephones per room, and TVs. Adjoining the hotel is the acclaimed Prairie restaurant, which serves innovative Midwestern cuisine.

See map p. 98. 500 S. Dearborn St. (at Congress Parkway). ☎ *800-233-1234 or 312-986-1234.* www.hyatt.com. *CTA: Buses stop at South State Street, across from the Washington Library, then walk 1 block west; brown line El to Library/Van Buren or red line to Harrison/State. Parking: Valet $32; self $20 in nearby lots (no in-out privileges). Rack rates: $215–$279 double. AE, DC, DISC, MC, V.*

Hyatt Regency Chicago
$$–$$$$ River East

This sprawling hotel with more than 2,019 rooms is as impersonal as Union Station, bustling with a steady stream of travelers. For the same reason, the hotel is family-friendly — parents don't need to worry unduly about kids acting, well, like kids. With all the hustle and bustle, kids blend right into the general commotion of the place. With its emphasis on conventions and business meetings, the hotel offers in-room conveniences such as desk, fax, and Internet hookups. Beefs: Guest rooms are distributed over two high-rise towers and can be a long hike from the front desk; sound-proofing in some rooms is not all it could be. Bonuses: Food is available through 24-hour room service and at a half-dozen restaurants and cafes, which include Big's, an aptly named gigantic brasserie and bar offering 87 brands of single-malt Scotch, 46 kinds of cognac, 115 Armagnacs, and 164 varieties of liqueurs and cordials.

See map p. 98. 151 E. Wacker Dr. (at North Upper Michigan Avenue). ☎ *800-233-1234 or 312-565-1234.* www.hyatt.com. *CTA: Buses stop at the corner of Wacker Drive and Michigan Avenue, 1 block west. Parking: Valet (with in-out privileges) $36. Rack rates: $180–$330 double. AE, DC, DISC, MC, V.*

Omni Ambassador East Hotel
$$$ Gold Coast

Traditionalists breathed a sigh of relief when a major renovation in the late 1990s left this hotel and its famous restaurant, the Pump Room, vastly improved but basically unaltered. Opened in 1926, the 285-room hotel, in a leafy residential neighborhood just 2 blocks west of Lake Michigan's famed beaches, features custom furnishings and marble bathrooms. Rooms are clean and tidy. Standard rooms have two-line phones and minibars, and the 54 suites, each with a separate bedroom, two bathrooms, a small kitchen, and a dining room, include 13 ultraplush "celebrity" units named after famous former guests. Most extravagant is the Presidential Suite, which boasts a canopied terrace and marble fireplace. On the tiny floor alongside the Pump Room bar, guests can dance to live entertainment.

See map p. 98. 1301 N. State Parkway (2 blocks north of Division Street). ☎ *800-843-6664 or 312-787-7200.* www.omnihotels.com. *CTA: Buses stop on North Lake Shore Drive, 2 blocks east; red line El goes to Clark/Division. Parking: Valet (with in-out privileges) $34. Rack rates: $160–$200 double. AE, DC, DISC, MC, V.*

Park Hyatt
$$$$ Magnificent Mile

How stunning is this hotel? Stunning enough that Chicago's Pritzker family, owners of the international Hyatt hotel chain, moved in when it first opened several years ago. Part hotel, part condominium building, the 67-story building is a showpiece of the high-end Park Hyatt line, occupying one of the most desirable spots on North Michigan Avenue overlooking Water Tower Square. The décor is sleek and contemporary, and you'll know immediately that you're in Chicago by the elegant black-and-white photographs of the city in each guest room. Relaxing is easy in the 7,000-square-foot pool and spa facility. Guest rooms are oversized. Not as traditionally flowery as the Four Seasons or the Ritz-Carlton, the Park Hyatt has a more masculine style of elegance — not unlike the Giorgio Armani designs you can buy in the boutique on the ground level. The hotel caters to individual business travelers seeking out the ultimate in personalized service and amenities. What might you expect? Sony flat-screen televisions, DVD and CD players, a BRNO desk chair and an Eames chair designed by Ludwig Mies van der Rohe and Charles Eames, and four — count 'em — four two-line phones.

See map p. 98. 800 N. Michigan Ave. (at Chicago Avenue). ☎ *800-233-1234 or 312-335-1234.* www.parkchicago.hyatt.com. *CTA: Buses stop on Michigan Avenue in front of Water Tower Place; red line El to Chicago/State. Parking: Valet (with in-out privileges) $36. Rack rates: $375–$425 double. AE, DC, DISC, MC, V.*

The Peninsula Chicago
$$$$ Magnificent Mile

The Peninsula breezed into town a few years ago and has been giving the luxury hotel market a run for its money ever since. Service here is practically a religion, followed by the in-room technology, which rivals any hotel in the world. The 339 spacious rooms feature marble bathrooms with a separate shower and tub, hands-free phones, and high-tech entertainment systems. A small silver "command station" by every bed allows guests to control the lights, curtains, and room temperature without getting out from under the covers. The 20-story hotel tower above the Tiffany and Co. boutique on Michigan Avenue is topped by a 3,500-square-foot suite with its own outdoor terrace. According to its promoters, the hotel's mixture of Eastern graciousness (the headquarters are in Hong Kong) and Midwestern hospitality sets it apart — a claim I can second.

See map p. 99. 108 E. Superior St. (at Michigan Avenue). ☎ *866-288-8889 or 312-337-2888.* www.peninsula.com. *CTA: Buses stop along Michigan Avenue; red line El to Chicago/State. Parking: Valet (in-out privileges) $36. Rack rates: $450 double. AE, DC, MC, V.*

The Raphael
$$–$$$ Streeterville

This European-flavored boutique hotel, with only 172 rooms and suites, is well known for more than just hospitality. Rooms and suites, done in Mediterranean style, are spacious and have big picture windows. The 16-story brick building, which fits in comfortably with its chic residential neighbors, occupies a prime location just steps from Water Tower Place and North Michigan Avenue. The rooms may be a bit frayed around the edges, but the hotel represents a good value for the location. Suite prices, as low as $130 in the winter months, compare favorably with what you may spend on a standard room at one of the neighboring glitzy properties on or near the Mag Mile. Guests enjoy complimentary coffee in the lobby and access to a nearby health club at discounted rates.

See map p. 99. 201 E. Delaware Place (at North Mies Van Der Rohe Way). ☎ *800-821-5343 or 312-943-5000.* www.raphaelchicago.com. *CTA: Buses stop on Michigan Avenue in front of Water Tower Place. Parking: Valet (with in-out privileges) $38. Rack rates: $109–$219 double. AE, DC, DISC, MC, V.*

Red Roof Inn
$ Streeterville

When Motel 6 converted the historic French-owned Hotel Richmont in the 1990s, this became *the* budget hotel in the pricey Streeterville neighborhood. Red Roof Inn then acquired the property and completed another renovation. This is your best bet for the lowest-priced lodgings near the normally pricey Magnificent Mile area. Rooms and amenities match the budget prices, but who cares, if you're spending most of your time out on the town? On the ground floor, hungry travelers can enjoy Coco Pazzo, a charming sidewalk cafe with excellent Italian fare at prices that won't eat up all that money you saved on lodgings.

See map p. 99. 162 E. Ontario St. (at St. Clair). ☎ *800-733-7663 or 312-787-3580.* www.redroof.com. *CTA: Buses stop on Michigan Avenue, 1 block west; red line El to Grand, then walk 2 blocks north and 4 blocks east. Parking: Valet (no in-out privileges) $18. Rack rates: $86–$102 double. AE, DC, DISC, MC, V.*

Renaissance Chicago Hotel
$$–$$$$ North Loop

Returning guests claim that the Renaissance Chicago — which has retained a strong following (mostly business travelers, who are the hotel's bread and butter) through several name changes — is the most comfortable hotel in the city. The 553-room, 27-story luxury hotel built by Stouffer in 1991 features bay windows that offer priceless views of the river and city. Comfortable-but-simple guest rooms are tastefully decorated in dark woods, with rich draperies and fabrics and plush carpeting. Four club floors offer even more comfortable lodgings (in extra-large rooms), a battery of business amenities, plus rates that include concierge service, a private lounge, breakfast, and evening hors d'oeuvres. The hotel has a small indoor pool and health club on the fourth floor, with a new spa room that's been added to provide massage services. Stop in the Lobby Court for evening cocktails and live jazz or piano music. Theatergoers should inquire about packages that include performances in the nearby North Loop theater district.

See map p. 99. 1 W. Wacker Dr. (at State Street). ☎ *800-468-3571 or 312-372-7200.* www.renaissancehotels.com. *CTA: Buses stop at State and Wacker; brown line El to State/Lake or red line to Washington/State. Parking: Valet (with in-out privileges) $34. Rack rates: $159–$259. AE, DC, DISC, MC, V.*

Ritz-Carlton Chicago
$$$$ Magnificent Mile

Yes, that *was* Oprah heading into the hotel dining room. You may also find Mayor Richard Daley holding a power dinner, or Christie Hefner, Playboy Enterprises CEO. This celebrity magnet, known for its open and airy setting, is super-luxurious yet large enough, with 435 rooms, to provide anonymity. Guest rooms have handsome cherry-wood furnishings and marble bathrooms; suites are ultraplush, with glass French doors separating bedroom and living room. Standard amenities include king-size beds, hair dryers, robes, and double-line phones. The Ritz forms part of the Water Tower complex, in the heart of the Magnificent Mile. You can find shoppers taking a respite — perhaps with afternoon tea or an evening aperitif — in the hotel's atrium lobby. Sunday brunch is one of the best in town and includes a separate buffet for kids. Don't miss the *gravlax* (cured salmon, a Scandinavian delicacy). Despite its upscale ambience, the size and bustle make this hotel a place where parents can feel comfortable with kids.

See map p. 99. 160 E. Pearson St. (½ block east of North Michigan Avenue, connected to Water Tower Place). ☎ *800-621-6906 or 312-266-1000.* www.four seasons.com. *CTA: Buses stop in front of Water Tower Place; red line El to Chicago/State. Parking: Valet (with in-out privileges) $36. Rack rates: $395–$535 double. AE, DC, DISC, MC, V.*

Sheraton Chicago Hotel & Suites
$$–$$$$ **Streeterville**

This is a big hotel, but somehow it doesn't feel impersonal. The huge lobby has a friendly piano bar and windows overlooking an esplanade along the Chicago River. Rooms are sizable and comfortable, featuring a sitting area with loveseat and chair. Many of the 1,209 rooms in this 34-story hotel offer spectacular views of Lake Michigan. Guests in the 110 club-level rooms pay extra for such amenities as robes and access to a club room that serves breakfast and cocktails (included in the room rate). Guests include a large percentage of convention-goers, taking advantage of the property's 120,000 square feet of meeting and convention space. A standout among the hotel's five restaurants and lounges is Don Shula's Steakhouse, serving excellent steaks and chops.

See map p. 99. 301 E. North Water St. (at North Columbus Drive). ☎ *800-325-3535 or 312-464-1000.* www.sheraton.com. *CTA: Buses stop on Michigan Avenue, 3 blocks west. Parking: Valet (with in-out privileges) $34. Rack rates: $129–$329 double. AE, DC, DISC, MC, V.*

Sofitel Chicago Water Tower
$$$–$$$$ **Magnificent Mile**

Another recent addition to Chicago's crowded luxury hotel scene, the Sofitel aims to impress by drawing on the city's tradition of great architecture. French designer Pierre-Yves Rochon created a building that's impossible to pass without taking a second look: a soaring, triangular tower with a glass and aluminum facade that sparkles in the sun. If you're looking for clubby exclusivity, this won't be your scene, but fans of abundant natural light will be able to get their fix here (weather permitting, of course). The guest rooms feature contemporary décor with natural beechwood walls and chrome hardware for a modern touch. All the rooms enjoy good views of the city (but the privacy-conscious will want to stay on the upper floors, where they won't be on display to surrounding apartment buildings). The standard doubles are fairly compact, but thanks to large picture windows, the spaces don't feel cramped. The sleek bathrooms are relatively spacious, and the amenities are top-notch.

See map p. 99. 20 E. Chestnut St. (at Wabash Street). ☎ *800-763-4835 or 312-324-4000.* www.sofitel.com. *CTA: Buses stop on Michigan Avenue, 1 block east; red line El to Chicago/State. Parking: Valet (no in-out privileges) $35. Rack rate: $199–$459 double; $499–$599 suite. AE, DC, DISC, MC, V.*

The Sutton Place Hotel
$$$–$$$$ Gold Coast

Here's an oasis of quiet sophistication off noisy, raucous Rush Street. Housed in a striking 1980s-built geometric granite-and-glass-skinned building (which has won awards for architecture and interior design), the 246-room deluxe hotel offers entertainment gadgetry and high-tech conveniences. Rooms were renovated in 2003. Each guest room has a stereo TV and VCR (with movie rentals available 24 hours a day), a stereo receiver with a compact disc player (and an in-room selection of CDs), a fully stocked minibar, three telephones (one with a speakerphone), and a dedicated fax or computer hookup. Among 40 luxurious suites are some with balconies, terraces, and sweeping city-and-lake views. You can work out in the fitness suite, or borrow step boxes and a Reebok step video to take back to your room. Whiskey Bar & Grill, owned by Rande Gerber (yeah, he's the guy married to Cindy Crawford), fills with beautiful people and has outdoor seating that overlooks the bustle of Rush Street, where more beautiful people drink and dine.

See map p. 99. 21 E. Bellevue Place (at Rush Street). ☎ *800-606-8188 or 312-266-2100.* www.suttonplace.com. *CTA: Buses stop on North Lake Shore Drive, 1 block east; red line El to Clark/Division. Parking: Valet (with in-out privileges) $37. Rack rates: $189–$330 double. AE, DC, DISC, MC, V.*

Talbott Hotel
$$$ Magnificent Mile

One of the hidden gems of the bustling Michigan Avenue shopping corridor, the Talbott Hotel combines the charm of an English inn with a location that's hard to beat. Just off the lobby, you'll find a cozy sitting room where you can curl up in a leather armchair by the fireplace. A bar area and sidewalk cafe with first-rate people-watching were added recently. You won't find extensive hotel facilities here, but the cozy atmosphere makes for a bed-and-breakfast feel without the sometimes-too-personal bed-and-breakfast intrusions (is the hotels boasts a complimentary continental breakfast, too). But the real surprise is the rooms: Many are exceptionally large, and all are available at very competitive prices. Suites and the hotel's executive king rooms entice with Jacuzzi tubs, and all suites have separate sitting areas with sofa beds and dining tables.

Time waits for no one

Kids are fascinated by the interactive sculpture at Columbus Drive and Illinois Street, near the Sheraton Chicago Hotel & Suites. This giant horizontal clock is 70 feet in diameter. The raised granite numerals that serve as benches are swept clean every 59 minutes by the relentless minute hand.

See map p. 99. 20 E. Delaware St. (between Rush and State streets). ☎ *800-825-2688 or 312-944-4970.* www.talbotthotel.com. *CTA: Buses stop on Michigan Avenue, ½ block east; red line El to Chicago/State. Parking: Self-parking $21. Rack rates: $149–$289 double. AE, DC, DISC, MC, V.*

The Tremont
$$$ Magnificent Mile

If you're looking for a small, romantic European-style hotel, the Tremont has great appeal. The building feels more like a secluded bed-and-breakfast than a hotel right off the busiest shopping street in the city. The cozy lobby with a fireplace sets the mood from the start. In the guest rooms, the tasteful furnishings, plush terry robes, vases of fresh flowers, and marble bathrooms invite lounging. Rooms aren't spacious, but they are cheery, with yellow walls and large windows (ask for a room facing Delaware Street if you crave natural light — rooms in other parts of the hotel look into neighboring buildings). With its bright colors and solicitous service, The Tremont is one of the city's best picks for a romantic getaway. Guests who call room service are connected to Mike Ditka's Restaurant, the boisterous New Orleans–style eatery on the premises where football and cigars reign. Check out the fabulous Chicago Bears memorabilia on the upstairs walls.

See map p. 99. 100 E. Chestnut St. (1 block west of Michigan Avenue). ☎ *800-621-8133 or 312-751-1900.* www.tremontchicago.com. *CTA: Buses stop on Michigan Avenue, 1 block east; red line El to Chicago/State. Parking: Valet (no in-out privileges) $34. Rack rates: $119–$279 double. AE, DC, DISC, MC, V.*

Westin Michigan Avenue Hotel
$$$$ Magnificent Mile

Kudos to the Westin for sprucing up this ideally located hotel, fronting Michigan Avenue at the corner of Delaware Place, right across the street from the 900 North Michigan mall. For years, this fairly average hotel just offered potential. Now, with the opening of the Grill, a restaurant that has won rave reviews, the hotel has risen to being more than just average — and based on its stellar location alone, you may want to consider it. Ask for a tower lake-view room, which is larger than standard and features upgraded bathrooms and turndown service.

See map p. 99. 909 N. Michigan Ave. (at Delaware Place). ☎ *800-937-8461 or 312-943-7200.* www.westinmichiganave.com. *CTA: Buses stop on Michigan Avenue. Parking: Valet (with in-out privileges) $35. Rack rates: $145–$329 double. AE, DC, DISC, MC, V.*

Whitehall Hotel
$$$ Magnificent Mile

European style and ambience abound in this hideaway hotel tucked into a side street off Michigan Avenue. This landmark, 221-room hotel offers stylish, comfortable accommodations with mahogany furnishings, includ-ing armoires and Chippendale desks. Rooms come with three multi-line telephones (with fax and Internet capability), Crabtree & Evelyn toi-letries, terry robes, and a daily newspaper. Among the eight luxury suites, appointed in 18th-century English style with Asian touches, are two with outdoor terraces and knockout skyline views. Because this is an older property, expect narrow hallways and small bathrooms. The fully equipped fitness center supplies exercise bikes for in-room use. At press time, the hotel restaurant was renamed Fornetto Mei (little oven), and planned to serve Italian and Asian fare. The restaurant's new centerpiece is its wood-burning pizza oven, located in the restaurant's atrium over-looking Delaware Street. Molive, an American bistro, serves reasonably priced lunch fare and a dinner menu with Californian, Mediterranean, and Asian accents. Off the small, paneled lobby are a piano bar and a tea room, which serves British-style afternoon tea.

See map p. 99 105 E. Delaware Place (just west of Michigan Avenue). ☎ *800-948-4255 or 312-944-6300.* www.slh.com/whitehall. *CTA: Buses stop on Michigan Avenue, ½ block east; red line El to Chicago/State. Parking: Valet (with in-out privi-leges) $31. Rack rates: $179–$279 double. AE, DC, DISC, MC, V.*

Runner-Up Hotels

Best Western River North Hotel
$–$$ River North

This former motor lodge may surprise you with its attractive interior, which bears little resemblance to most of its Best Western brethren. Offering moderately priced lodging within easy walking distance of one of the busiest nightlife and restaurant zones of the city, it's worth check-ing out.

See map p. 98. 125 W. Ohio St. (at LaSalle Street). ☎ *800-528-1234 or 312-467-0800.* www.rivernorthhotel.com. *CTA: Red line El to Grand/State. Parking: Free park-ing for guests (one car per room). Rack rates: $105–$149 double. AE, DC, DISC, MC, V.*

City Suites Hotel
$–$$ Near North

This affordable 45-unit hotel offers suites with sleeper sofas, armchairs, and desks. The upside? An unusual level of amenities for a modestly priced hotel, including plush robes and complimentary continental breakfast. The downside? Most rooms can be fairly noisy, as some face the street, and some face the El tracks. Bring your earplugs to ensure a good night's sleep.

See map p. 98. 933 W. Belmont Ave. (at Sheffield Avenue). ☎ *800-248-9108 or 773-404-3400.* www.cityinns.com. *CTA: Red line El to Belmont. Parking: Adjacent lot (with in-out privileges) $18. Rack rates: $99–$169 double. AE, DC, DISC, MC, V.*

Comfort Inn and Suites Downtown
$ **River North**

Fans of budget chains should check out the deal at the Comfort Inn and Suites Downtown. This historic building is newly renovated, with an Art Deco lobby. The hotel offers a free continental breakfast and a great location, and easy access to Navy Pier and the Magnificent Mile. At these prices, you can't expect a pool, but you can find a fitness room with a whirlpool and sauna.

See map p. 98. 15 E. Ohio St. (just east of Michigan Avenue) ☎ *312-894-0900. CTA: Red-line El to Grand/State. Parking: Valet (with in-out privileges) $21. Rack rates: $129–189 double AE, DC, DISC, MC, V.*

Hilton Garden Inn
$$$ **River North**

In an enviable location which places it near the ESPN Zone, a Virgin Megastore, and Nordstrom's mall, this location will please most families traveling with young ones.

See map p. 98. 10 E. Grand Ave. (at State Street). ☎ *800-445-8667 or 312-595-0000.* www.hilton.com. *CTA: Red line El to Grand/State. Parking: Valet (with in-out privileges) $34; self parking (with no in-out privileges) $20. Rack rates: $169–309 double. AE, DC, DISC, MC, V.*

Homewood Suites
$$$ **River North**

An excellent choice for families, this hotel is located near the North Bridge development, just west of Michigan Avenue. This simple-yet-comfy hotel offers 233 one-bedroom suites, each with a full kitchen, and will make you feel right at home.

See map p. 98. 40 E. Grand Ave. (at Wabash Street). ☎ *800-225-5466 or 312-644-2222.* www.homewood-suites.com. *CTA: Red line El to State/Grand. Parking: Valet (with in-out privileges) $32. Rack rates: $99–$249 double. AE, DC, DISC, MC, V.*

Lenox Suites Hotel
$$ **Magnificent Mile**

Although this hotel is a little dowdy by Michigan Avenue standards, shoppers love its location, only 1 block west of the shopping mecca.

See map p. 98. 616 N. Rush St. ☎ *800-44-LENOX or 312-337-1000.* www.lenox suites.com. *CTA: Buses stop on Michigan Avenue, 1 block east; red line El to Grand (at State Street), then walk 3 blocks east. Parking: Valet (with in-out privileges) $34. Rack rates: $99–$199 double. AE, DC, DISC, MC, V.*

Majestic Hotel
$$ Near North

This 52-room hostelry in a leafy residential neighborhood near Wrigleyville was recently renovated and has the ambience of an English inn, with larger suites including butler's pantries with a microwave, refrigerator, and wet bar.

See map p. 98. 528 W. Brompton St. (at Lake Shore Drive). ☎ *800-727-5108 or 773-404-3499.* www.cityinns.com. *CTA: Buses stop on Marine Drive, ½ block east; red line El to Addison, walk several blocks east to Lake Shore Drive and 1 block south. Parking: Self-parking in nearby garage (with no in-out privileges) $19. Rack rates: $99–$179 double. Rates include continental breakfast. AE, DC, DISC, MC, V.*

Millennium Knickerbocker Hotel
$$$ Streeterville

This member of the Millennium chain has made big strides in sprucing up its 305 rooms and does offer good value and a superb location.

See map p. 98. 163 E. Walton St. (just east of Michigan Avenue). ☎ *800-621-8140 or 312-751-8100.* www.milleniumhotels.com. *CTA: Buses stop on Michigan Avenue, ½ block west; red line El to Chicago/State. Parking: Valet (with in-out privileges) $35; self-parking $24. Rack rates: $129–$299 double. AE, DC, DISC, MC, V.*

Radisson Hotel & Suites
$$–$$$$ Streeterville

One rare feature of this recently renovated hotel is a rooftop, outdoor swimming pool — a kid-pleaser. The sleeping rooms, which start on the 14th floor, also have great views.

See map p. 99. 160 E. Huron St. (just east of Michigan Avenue). ☎ *800-333-3333 or 312-787-2900.* www.radisson.com. *CTA: Buses serving many routes stop on Michigan Avenue, ½ block west. Parking: Valet (with in-out privileges) $35. Rack rates: $149–$399 double. AE, DC, DISC, MC, V.*

Swissôtel
$$$–$$$$ River East

The focus here is on the business traveler, but you'd be surprised at the generous weekend deals on offer. Spacious guest rooms feature superior views created by this hotel's modernistic, triangular glass design.

See map p. 99. 323 E. Wacker Dr. (at Columbus Drive). ☎ *888-737-9477 or 312-565-0565.* www.swissotel.com. *CTA: Buses stop at Wacker Drive and Michigan Avenue, 3 blocks west; brown, orange, or green line El to Randolph. Parking: Valet (with in-out privileges) $35. Rack rates: $159–$409 double. AE, DC, DISC, MC, V.*

W Chicago Lakeshore
$$$–$$$$ **Streeterville**

If access to outdoor activities — the lakefront bike and running path, Lake Michigan swimming and beaches, and Navy Pier — is a priority, here's your spot. The only hotel situated on the lakefront, this boutique hotel tries hard to achieve hipness.

See map p. 99. 644 N. Lake Shore Dr. (at Ontario Street). ☎ *877-946-8357 or 312-943-9200.* www.whotels.com. *CTA: Red line to Grand/State. Parking: Valet (with in-out privileges) $36. Rack rates: $229–$429 double. AE, DC, DISC, MC, V.*

Index of Accommodations by Neighborhood

Gold Coast
Omni Ambassador East Hotel ($$$)
The Sutton Place Hotel ($$$–$$$$)

Loop
Chicago Hilton and Towers ($–$$$$)
The Crowne Plaza Chicago/The Silversmith ($$$–$$$$)
Hard Rock Hotel Chicago ($$$)
Hotel Allegro ($$)
Hotel Burnham ($$$)
Hotel Monaco ($$$)
House of Blues Hotel ($$–$$$)
Hyatt on Printers Row ($$$)
Renaissance Chicago Hotel ($$–$$$$)

Magnificent Mile
Chicago Marriott Downtown ($$)
Courtyard by Marriott Chicago Downtown/Magnificent Mile $$–$$$)
The Drake ($$$$)
Four Seasons Hotel ($$$$)
Hotel Inter-Continental Chicago ($$$$)
Lenox Suites Hotel ($$)
Park Hyatt ($$$$)
The Peninsula Chicago ($$$$)
Ritz-Carlton Chicago ($$$$)
Sofitel Chicago Water Tower ($$$–$$$$)
Talbott Hotel ($$$)
The Tremont ($$$)
Westin Michigan Avenue Hotel ($$$$)
Whitehall Hotel ($$$)

Near North/Lincoln Park
Belden-Stratford Hotel ($$$)
City Suites Hotel ($–$$)
Majestic Hotel ($$)

River East
Fairmont Hotel ($$$–$$$$)
Hyatt Regency Chicago ($$–$$$$)
Swissôtel ($$$–$$$$)

River North
Best Western River North Hotel ($–$$)
Comfort Inn and Suites Downtown ($)
Courtyard by Marriott Chicago Downtown ($$–$$$)
Embassy Suites ($$–$$$$)
Hampton Inn & Suites Hotel ($–$$)
Hilton Garden Inn ($$$)
Homewood Suites ($$$)

Streeterville
DoubleTree Guest Suites ($$–$$$$)
Embassy Suites ($$)
Millennium Knickerbocker Hotel ($$$)
Radisson Hotel & Suites ($$–$$$$)
The Raphael ($$–$$$)
Red Roof Inn ($)
Sheraton Chicago Hotel & Suites ($$–$$$$)
W Chicago Lakeshore ($$$–$$$$)

Index of Accommodations by Price

$$$$

Chicago Hilton and Towers (South Loop)

The Crowne Plaza Chicago/The Silversmith (Loop)

DoubleTree Guest Suites (Streeterville)

The Drake (Magnificent Mile)

Embassy Suites (River North, Streeterville)

Fairmont Hotel (River East)

Four Seasons Hotel (Magnificent Mile)

Hotel Inter-Continential Chicago (Magnificent Mile)

Hyatt Regency Chicago (East River)

Park Hyatt (Magnificent Mile)

The Peninsula Chicago (Magnificent Mile)

Radisson Hotel & Suites (Streeterville)

Renaissance Chicago Hotel (North Loop)

Ritz-Carlton Chicago (Magnificent Mile)

Sheraton Chicago Hotel & Suites (Streeterville)

Sofitel Chicago Water Tower (Magnificent Mile)

The Sutton Place Hotel (Gold Coast)

Swissôtel (River East)

Westin Michigan Avenue Hotel (Magnificent Mile)

$$$

Belden-Stratford Hotel (Lincoln Park)

Chicago Hilton and Towers (South Loop)

Courtyard by Marriott Chicago Downtown (River North)

Courtyard by Marriott Chicago Downtown/Magnificent Mile (Magnificent Mile)

The Crowne Plaza Chicago/The Silversmith (Loop)

DoubleTree Guest Suites (Streeterville)

Embassy Suites (River North, Streeterville)

Fairmont Hotel (River East)

Hard Rock Hotel Chicago (Loop)

Hilton Garden Inn (River North)

Homewood Suites (River North)

Hotel Burnham (Loop)

Hotel Monaco (North Loop)

House of Blues Hotel (North Loop)

Hyatt on Printers Row (South Loop)

Hyatt Regency Chicago (River East)

Millennium Knickerbocker Hotel (Streeterville)

Omni Ambassador East Hotel (Gold Coast)

Radisson Hotel & Suites (Streeterville)

The Raphael (Streeterville)

Renaissance Chicago Hotel (North Loop)

Sheraton Chicago Hotel & Suites (Streeterville)

Sofitel Chicago Water Tower (Magnificent Mile)

The Sutton Place Hotel (Gold Coast)

Swissôtel (River East)

Talbott Hotel (Magnificent Mile)

The Tremont (Magnificent Mile)

W Chicago Lakeshore (Streeterville)

Whitehall Hotel (Magnificent Mile)

$$

Best Western River North Hotel (River North)

Chicago Hilton and Towers (South Loop)

Chicago Marriott Downtown (Magnificent Mile)

City Suites Hotel (Near North)

Courtyard by Marriott Chicago Downtown (River North)

Courtyard by Marriott Chicago Downtown/Magnificent Mile (Magnificent Mile)

DoubleTree Guest Suites (Streeterville)

Embassy Suites (River North, Streeterville)

Hampton Inn & Suites Hotel (River North)

Hotel Allegro (Loop)

House of Blues Hotel (North Loop)
Hyatt Regency Chicago (East River)
Lenox Suites Hotel (Magnificent Mile)
Majestic Hotel (Near North)
Radisson Hotel & Suites (Streeterville)
The Raphael (Streeterville)
Renaissance Chicago Hotel (North Loop)
Sheraton Chicago Hotel & Suites (Streeterville)

$
Best Western River North Hotel (River North)
Chicago Hilton and Towers (South Loop)
City Suites Hotel (Near North)
Comfort Inn and Suites Downtown (River North)
Hampton Inn & Suites Hotel (River North)
Red Roof Inn (Streeterville)

Chapter 10

Dining and Snacking in Chicago

. . . .

In This Chapter

▶ Discovering what's new and what's hot
▶ Sampling Chicago's culinary favorites for dining and snacking
▶ Eating your way around the globe: Ethnic cuisine
▶ Getting the lowdown on some of Chicago's best restaurants
▶ Looking for a rush: Coffee and tea

. . . .

Chicago is no longer the meat-and-potatoes place that it was back when the Chicago stockyards and packing houses fed the nation. Today, dining in Chicago is as sophisticated as dining in New York, San Francisco, and other cosmopolitan cities.

But don't worry about missing out on the classics: Chicago still offers the famous deep-dish pizza that was invented here in the 1940s. **Gino's East** and other Chicago pizzerias continue to draw big crowds. (See Chapter 2 for more information.) And Chicago is still the place for steak. Historically, Chicago's highest grossing restaurant has been **Gibson's Steakhouse,** a clubby, dark-wood den of cigars, fine red wine, and gargantuan steaks. Many other Chicago restaurants famously serve up juicy cuts of beef — see the "Chicago's steak joints" sidebar for a list of the best.

But Chicago is much more than pizza and steak You can find everything from elegant foodie meccas like **Charlie Trotter's** to basement-level dives like **Billy Goat Tavern.** Ethnic options abound: Mexican food doesn't get any better than **Frontera Grill,** where the museum-quality Mexican art completes an atmosphere that matches the level of the cuisine. And a bit off the beaten path, farther north, **Arun's** offers exquisite Thai food and desserts so beautiful they'll bring tears to your eyes.

Getting the Dish on the Local Scene

The most recent trend in Chicago dining is a movement toward fascinating mixes of cuisines and cultures — and the result is truly wonderful, brand-new flavor and taste. A leading example is **SushiSamba Rio,** which takes its inspiration from the Japanese immigrants who moved to Peru and Brazil in the early 20th-century, eventually creating a cuisine that mixed their native Asian dishes with South American ingredients.

The second trend spreading like wildfire among Chicago foodies is small plates. Two restaurants are standouts in this regard. Vegetarians and veggie lovers alike will delight in the twist on fine dining served up at **Green Zebra.** The restaurant features "small plates" of veggie specialties, such as fennel risotto cake with a syrah reduction, and Hawaiian heart of palm with kaffir lime and Thai basil chili. Another hot new spot featuring small plates is **Avec,** which is garnering kudos from foodies nationwide.

On the other end of the dining spectrum, industry analysts have noted an increase in consumers' appetites for quick and casual eateries where you order food at a counter and sit down, like the local **Potbelly's** and **Corner Bakery.** Such places provide convenient and fairly healthy meals — very healthy, when compared to traditional fast food — and are especially popular for lunch.

Many hotels are handing over restaurant operations to independent restaurateurs — often celebrity chefs. In many cases, the new restaurants provide room service, too. A couple of notable examples include **Mike Ditka's Restaurant** in the Tremont Hotel and the **Atwood Cafe** in the Hotel Burnham.

Chicago restaurants reflect the neighborhoods in which they're located. In the **Loop,** restaurants cater to an expense-account business crowd. Around the **Magnificent Mile,** you find plenty of outdoor dining where stylish people go to see and be seen. In the burgeoning **Randolph Street Market District,** a former warehouse and market area where Oprah's Harpo Studios and many design and production companies make their home, a whole row of hip new restaurants has popped up. **River North,** the gallery district, is where you find the city's largest concentration of dining spots. In **Lincoln Park** and on the **North Side,** you find locals hanging out at their neighborhood favorites, which tend to change less frequently.

One Chicago neighborhood stands out for some of the hottest dining in the country: the **Bucktown/Wicker Park** neighborhood, home to a large concentration of artists, boasts eclectic fare and restaurants with cutting-edge décor. The area's offerings range from eclectic, small cafes along Milwaukee Avenue to the high-end hot spots **Mod** and **Spring.**

To get your bearings in terms of Chicago's neighborhoods, see Chapter 8. See "Tasting Chicago's ethnic eats," later in this chapter, for a dining guide to some of Chicago's many ethnic neighborhoods.

Making reservations

Do you want reservations at the city's hottest restaurant? Or perhaps you want to find out what blues musicians are in Chicago during your visit? This section can help you plan ahead for your night on the town.

If your ideal evening includes dinner at the trendiest restaurant followed by seeing an award-winning play, you must make reservations in advance of your trip. Call popular restaurants two to three weeks in advance for weekend reservations. For plays, you may need to purchase tickets a few months in advance.

Some restaurants are so popular with walk-in diners that they choose not to accept reservations. To avoid a long wait, plan an early or late lunch (say, 11:30 a.m. or 1:30 p.m.) or an early or late dinner (before 7 p.m. or after 9:30 p.m.). Exceptions at dinner include restaurants close to theaters, where you can usually get a table easily around 8 p.m., after the crowds have left to make the curtain.

In Chicago, you can usually get a table at most restaurants with only a day or two of notice — sometimes even with a same-day phone call. In cases where I recommend reservations, I do urge that you take the few minutes to make them — especially for dinner. If you arrive without reservations during the dinner rush at Chicago's most popular restaurants, you may find yourself cooling your heels for at least an hour. And, speaking of cool, that's the reception you'll get from the harried hostess.

Dressing to dine

As "Casual Day" has taken hold in corporate America, restaurant dress codes, too, have become more casual. With a few exceptions — the **Pump Room** is a notable one — Chicago restaurant dress codes are relaxed, and many top spots allow jeans and sports shirts. If a man wears a tie and a woman a cocktail dress, you may feel slightly overdressed in all but the most formal Chicago restaurants. (Still, I feel more comfortable being slightly overdressed than slightly underdressed.) In most places,

Time-savers

Busy, diner-type restaurants (with booths, tables, and counter seats) usually don't take reservations. If you're willing to take a seat at the counter, you can often be seated immediately. The counter is not as intimate or private as a table, of course, but it's a good option if you're pressed for time. This strategy usually works, for example, at **Lou Mitchell's,** the Loop's most popular breakfast spot, which often has long lines.

women can feel comfortable in black pants, a sweater, and boots; men, in dress pants and a sweater. In the summertime, a sundress with cardigan and sandals for women and khakis and golf shirt for men should suffice in most places. If you're concerned, call ahead and ask if the restaurant has a dress code.

Smoking — or not

Unlike New York and California, Chicago still allows smoking in restaurants, but there has been a recent movement toward a smoking ban. At the time of publication, city ordinances require that all restaurants provide nonsmoking sections. How comfortable and effective they are for nonsmokers depends on the ventilation and the distance between designated smoking and nonsmoking areas. Sometimes nonsmoking sections are in a separate room, away from smokers; often the sections adjoin.

Finding other restaurant sources

What follows are the best print and online sources for entertainment and events information:

- ✔ **Centerstage Chicago** (www.centerstage.net/chicago) offers an online menu of music, food, dancing, theater, art, and bars.

- ✔ *Chicago Magazine* (☎ 312-222-8999; www.chicagomag.com), the premier city magazine, covers lifestyles, culture, theater, Chicago gossip, and other entertainment, and is a reliable source of restaurant reviews.

- ✔ The free *Chicago Reader* (☎ 312-828-0350; www.chicago reader.com) is a hippie-era alternative newspaper that has gone mainstream — mostly. Published on Thursday and distributed in the city's restaurants, cafes, and bookstores, the *Reader* contains Chicago's most comprehensive entertainment listings and reviews, covering a wide range of tastes and lifestyles.

- ✔ *Weekend,* the Friday entertainment section of the *Chicago Sun-Times* (☎ 312-321-3000; www.suntimes.com), is packed with listings. Most famous are the movie reviews by critic Roger Ebert; the restaurant review section is also good.

- ✔ The *Chicago Tribune* (☎ 312-222-3232; www.chicagotribune.com) publishes a weekend tabloid insert, *Friday,* that's full of listings and reviews. The section is known for excellent restaurant reviews.

- ✔ The *Daily Herald* (☎ 847-427-4300; www.dailyherald.com), published in suburban Arlington Heights and distributed throughout the city, has a fat weekend entertainment section, *Time Out!,* published on Friday.

- ✔ **North Shore** (www.northshoremag.com) covers Chicago's northern suburbs and might be of interest if you are planning to spend time there, or want to ogle the homes in the city's priciest suburbs.

✔ **Metromix** (www.metromix.com), sponsored by the *Chicago Tribune,* is a great site for keeping abreast of new restaurants, clubs, bars, and shows.

✔ Gritty *New City* (www.newcitychicago.com) strives to be what the *Chicago Reader* once was. Published on Thursday, its pages are full of the offbeat and the irreverent.

✔ *Where Chicago* is stocked in most hotel rooms and lobbies, and lists some of the city's dining, entertainment, and shopping destinations.

Tasting Chicago's ethnic eats

A patchwork of ethnic diversity, stitched from cuisines from around the globe, distinguishes Chicago's dining scene. Looking for the cuisine of Cuba or China? Of Japan or Jamaica? Of Laos or Lithuania? You'll find them all and many more in the Windy City, where sending your taste buds on a multinational culinary adventure is easy.

Italian, Chicago-style

At the south end of the Loop, Taylor Street is as Italian as spaghetti and meatballs. Here in Chicago's own "Little Italy" (which, sadly, is shrinking due to encroaching urban renewal), the neighborhood wears its ethnicity boldly.

Check out the red-white-and-green décor of **Mario's Italian Lemonade,** at 1068 W. Taylor St. (no phone). Pans of rich pizza bread, crusty loaves, and amaretto cookies fill the air with wonderful smells at **Scafuri Bakery,** 1337 W. Taylor St. (☎ 312-733-8881). And stores still sell imported olive oil, sausages, cheeses, and wines. You may even run into Italian-American celebrities like Tony Bennett dining at old neighborhood favorites, such as the **Rosebud,** 1500 W. Taylor St., near Ashland Avenue (☎ 312-942-1117). And, as in the old days in this neighborhood, black-shawl-draped elderly women gossip on stoops, and men in cloth caps linger over strong coffee.

To market, to market

One of Chicago's hottest new areas, the **Randolph Street Market District,** sprouted among the cabbages and turnips of the produce market of West Randolph Street. The neighborhood is about a $6 cab ride from the Mag Mile. The young and the beautiful flock to this "urban chic" neighborhood, with such restaurants as **Marché,** 833 W. Randolph St. (☎ 312-226-8399); **Blue Point Oyster Bar,** 741 W. Randolph St. (☎ 312-207-1222); **Red Light,** 820 W. Randolph St. (☎ 312-733-8880); and **Vivo,** 838 W. Randolph St. (☎ 312-733-3379).

Italian restaurants, old and new, are sprinkled throughout the city. A Loop landmark for more than 70 years, **Italian Village,** 71 W. Monroe St. at Dearborn Street (☎ 312-332-7005), is three restaurants in one and a favorite for pre- and post-theater dining. Stylish **Coco Pazzo,** 300 W. Hubbard St. (☎ 312-836-0900), features the cooking of Tuscany. Just off the Magnificent Mile, **Bice Ristorante** (see listing later in this chapter) offers top food and great people-watching from a sidewalk dining area.

When Jay Leno brings his *Tonight Show* to Chicago, he often heads for **Mr. Beef on Orleans**, 666 N. Orleans St., between Erie and Huron streets (☎ 312-337-8500) for an Italian beef or sausage sandwich. Don't miss this Chicago favorite — juicy beef or spicy grilled sausage served on a chewy roll and dressed with sweet or hot peppers.

Although the famed Maxwell Street market has relocated, you can still buy trademark pork-chop sandwiches along **Halsted Street.** Other don't-miss Chicago treats include double cheeseburgers at **Billy Goat Tavern,** 430 N. Michigan Ave. (☎ 312-222-1525); all-beef Vienna hot dogs and fries smothered in cheddar cheese at **Gold Coast Dogs,** 159 N. Wabash, at Randolph Street (☎ 312-917-1677); and ribs at **Twin Anchors** (see listing later in this chapter). Suburban outposts include **Robinson's No. 1 Ribs** in Oak Park and **Hecky's Barbecue** in Evanston.

It's all Greek to me

Long tables and family-style dining reign in Greektown, which is a popular destination for large groups. Greektown, which received a facelift in 1996 around the time of the Democratic Convention in Chicago, occupies a few blocks of Halsted Street north of Jackson Boulevard and offers a zesty mix of Greek restaurants, nightclubs, and grocery stores. Greektown restaurants serve such Mediterranean staples as Greek salad, *saganaki* (flaming cheese), and *baklava* (a dessert made with thin layers of pastry, nuts, and honey), as well as the ubiquitous gyro plate or sandwich. One of the area's most attractive restaurants is **Pegasus,** 130 S. Halsted St. (☎ 312-226-3377), where a rooftop garden offers a panoramic view of the Chicago skyline. Another favorite of mine is **Santorini,** 800 W. Adams St. (☎ 312-829-8820) — although most of the restaurants in the neighborhood offer the same lively atmosphere and similar fare.

Best of the wurst

Good German fellowship (known as *gemutlichkeit*) flows — along with mounds of plump sausages — at several German restaurants. One of the most centrally located is the Loop's **Berghoff,** 17 W. Adams St. (☎ 312-427-3170), with its own brews on tap (and its own root beer, for those not imbibing).

The largest concentration of German food and culture is found in the Lincoln Square neighborhood, accessible via the brown-line El (at the Western Avenue stop). Business is often transacted in German at **Meyer's Delicatessen,** 4750 N. Lincoln Ave. (☎ 773-561-3377), and the **Merz Apothecary,** 4716 N. Lincoln Ave. (☎ 773-989-0900), with its fragrant

European herbs and toiletries. The **Chicago Brauhaus,** 4732 N. Lincoln Ave. (☎ 773-784-4444), resembles a Munich beer hall and offers schnitzel, smoked pork loin, *Koenigsberger klopse* (meatballs in caper sauce), and other German specialties.

Dim sum and then some

Chicago's Chinatown is located about 20 blocks south of the Loop and about 2 long blocks west of the McCormick Place convention complex. Some 50 restaurants, plus bakeries, markets, and import houses, are strung along a few blocks of Cermak Road and Wentworth Avenue. Perennially popular restaurants include **Three Happiness,** 209 W. Cermak Rd. (☎ 312-842-1964) and 2130 S. Wentworth Ave. (☎ 312-791-1228), known for its bountiful dim sum cart, and **Emperor's Choice,** 2238 S. Wentworth Ave. (☎ 312-225-8800), which serves superior seafood. Elsewhere in the city, head for River North to try the satay bar at **Ben Pao,** 52 W. Illinois St. at Dearborn Street (☎ 312-222-1888).

Thai one on

Thai restaurants are to Chicago what Chinese restaurants are to many other American cities: ubiquitous, affordable, and perfect for a quick meal that offers a taste of the exotic. If you've never tried Thai, Chicago is a great place to start. Good introductory dishes are pad thai noodles topped with minced peanuts, or the coconut-based mild yellow curry.

Arun's (see listing later in this chapter) is one of the city's reigning gourmet interpreters of Thai cuisine, but you can find many other low-key places where entrees don't go much beyond $10. A staple of the River North dining scene is the bright and airy **Star of Siam,** 11 E. Illinois St. at North State Street (☎ 312-670-0100). **Amarit,** 1 E. Delaware Place at State Street (☎ 312-649-0500), a few blocks off the Magnificent Mile, consistently delivers top-quality noodles, curries, and Thai iced tea, even if the décor runs toward the shabby. The North Side's **Thai Classic,** 3332 N. Clark St. at Roscoe Street (☎ 773-404-2000), near Wrigley Field, offers an excellent all-you-can-eat buffet on weekends, if you want to try a taste of everything.

Samplings from around the world

A Vietnamese enclave known as Little Saigon centers on Argyle Street and North Sheridan Road, about a 20-minute cab ride north of downtown. You find a number of restaurants here that feature **Vietnamese** and **Laotian** specialties, as well as markets offering Oriental vegetables, exotic spices, and hand-painted teapots. Even the El station on Argyle sports a red, pagoda-style roof.

Go just to the east and a bit north of Little Saigon to find Andersonville, a formerly **Scandinavian** neighborhood with eateries such as **Svea Restaurant,** 5236 N. Clark St. (☎ 773-275-7738) and **Ann Sather** (see listing later in this chapter). They serve traditional pea soup, potato sausage, Swedish meatballs, and Swedish pancakes with tart lingonberries. Check out the Swedish American Museum Center, a pair of Scandinavian delis, and the **Swedish Bakery,** 5348 N. Clark St. (☎ 773-561-8919) — a must-visit if you're in the area. This is the reigning star of bakeries in Chicago, in my humble opinion, and you don't have to be Swedish to love it (although their wide array of Swedish Christmas cookies are to die for). Middle Eastern food is also becoming popular in the area, with several excellent bakeries and restaurants.

Other major enclaves in Chicago that offer ethnic cuisine include a **Lithuanian** area around Marquette Park on the southwest side; a concentration of **Indian** shops and restaurants along Devon Avenue; and **Ukrainian Village** (on the West Side, near Chicago Avenue and Oakley Boulevard), where you find borscht and cabbage rolls. Sections of North Milwaukee Avenue are "Main Street" for Chicago's huge **Polish** population (the second-largest urban concentration after Warsaw's), with storefront restaurants such as **Red Apple Restaurant,** 3123 N. Milwaukee Ave. at Central Park Avenue (☎ 773-588-5781).

Trimming the Fat from Your Budget

Chicago is a great food town — but you're not here just to eat. You'll probably want some cash left over for other activities. In that case, it's time to investigate cheap eats.

I have two sure bets for bargain hunters. First, try eating at some of Chicago's many ethnic restaurants. Two people can enjoy a hearty Thai meal for about $30, including beer to wash down the spicy peanut sauce. Second, eat your big meal at lunch. Many restaurants serve dinner only, but the ones that open at midday (or even for breakfast) offer great values at lunch.

Other strategies: Split an appetizer or dessert. Skip the alcohol or enjoy a before- or after-dinner drink from your private (and cheaper) stash in your room. If possible, skip beverages altogether — those $2 Diet Cokes can really add up. Order the fixed-price menu (not available everywhere but always a good deal). Have a meal on the go for lunch and save your cash for a big night out.

Tips about tipping and taxes

How much should you tip? Throughout the United States, the standard tip is 15 percent of the total before tax is added; 20 percent is considered a generous tip. If you prefer, you can strike a reasonable compromise by figuring 15 percent of the total, tax included. Chicago's food tax is substantial. Restaurants levy an 8.75 percent state tax, plus a 1 percent city tax. I find it easiest to double the tax, leaving that amount for the tip.

A server who rattles off daily specials without prices may be busy or forgetful — or may be counting on your reluctance to look cheap in front of your friends or family. Always ask, and no $23 plate of noodles (true story) will ever sneak up on you.

To help you budget, each listing in this chapter includes a price range for main courses and a dollar-sign rating. The ratings represent the price of an appetizer, entrée, and nonalcoholic beverage — but not tax or tip — and correspond with the following ranges:

Table 10-1	Key to Restaurant Dollar Signs
Dollar Sign(s)	*Price Range*
$	$20 or less
$$	$21–$35
$$$	$36–$45
$$$$	$45–$60
$$$$$	$61 and over

Use the dollar-sign ratings to get a rough idea of how much you're likely to spend on a meal, but don't rely only on them. Certainly, you can get $$ meals at $$$ restaurants — and vice versa — depending on what you order. Remember, too, that many restaurants offer specials and fixed-price meals that the dollar signs don't reflect.

You can use the indexes at the end of this chapter to help you choose restaurants by neighborhood, cuisine, or price. The maps in this chapter show the locations of restaurants recommended here.

Chicago's Best Restaurants

Ambria
$$$$ Lincoln Park   FRENCH

Ambria is one of Chicago's finest restaurants, and one of the longest-running, at 20 years and counting. Housed in the stately Belden-Stratford Hotel (now mostly condominiums), across the street from the Lincoln Park Zoo, Chicago's classical French restaurant consistently maintains a high standard. You find deals being brokered and couples celebrating anniversaries in the wood-paneled, clublike atmosphere. Service is exemplary, from the charming hostess who makes you feel comfortable in the upscale French atmosphere to the professional waitstaff. The food, from roasted rack of lamb to medallions of New Zealand venison, is superb. Ask for a soufflé for dessert when you order your main course (so they have time to prepare this light-as-air French classic).

Central Chicago Dining

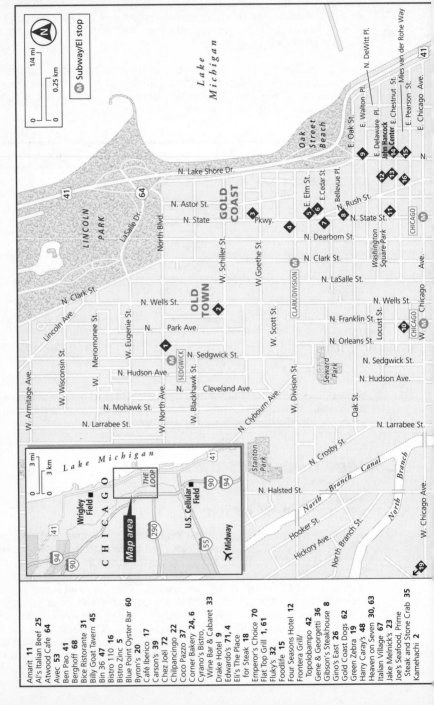

Amarit **11**
Al's Italian Beef **25**
Atwood Cafe **64**
Avec **53**
Ben Pao **41**
Berghoff **68**
Bice Ristorante **31**
Billy Goat Tavern **45**
Bin 36 **47**
Bistro 110 **16**
Bistro Zinc **5**
Blue Point Oyster Bar **60**
Byron's **20**
Cafe Iberico **17**
Carson's **39**
Chez Joël **72**
Chilpancingo **22**
Coco Pazzo **37**
Corner Bakery **24, 6**
Cyrano's Bistro,
  Wine Bar & Cabaret **33**
Drake Hotel **9**
Edwardo's **71, 4**
Eli's The Place
  for Steak **18**
Emperor's Choice **70**
Flat Top Grill **1, 61**
Fluky's **32**
Foodlife **15**
Four Seasons Hotel **12**
Frontera Grill/
  Topolobampo **42**
Gene & Georgetti **36**
Gibson's Steakhouse **8**
Gino's East **26**
Gold Coast Dogs **62**
Green Zebra **19**
Harry Caray's **48**
Heaven on Seven **30, 63**
Italian Village **67**
Jake Melnick's **23**
Joe's Seafood, Prime
  Steak and Stone Crab **35**
Kamehachi **49**

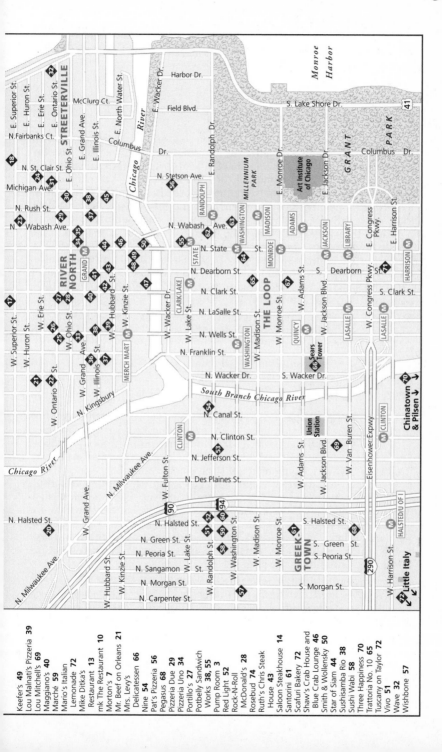

Keefer's **49**
Lou Malnati's Pizzeria **39**
Lou Mitchell's **69**
Maggiano's **40**
Marché **59**
Mario's Italian
  Lemonade **72**
Mike Ditka's
  Restaurant **13**
mk The Restaurant **10**
Morton's **7**
Mr. Beef on Orleans **21**
Mrs. Levy's
  Delicatessen **66**
Nine **54**
Pat's Pizzeria **56**
Pegasus **68**
Pizzeria Due **29**
Pizzeria Uno **34**
Portillo's **27**
Potbelly Sandwich
  Works **38, 55**
Pump Room **3**
Red Light **52**
Rock-N-Roll
McDonald's **28**
Rosebud **74**
Ruth's Chris Steak
  House **43**
Saloon Steakhouse **14**
Santorini **61**
Scafuri Bakery **72**
Shaw's Crab House and
  Blue Crab Lounge **46**
Smith & Wollensky **50**
Star of Siam **44**
Sushisamba Rio **38**
Sushi Wabi **58**
Three Happiness **70**
Trattoria No. 10 **65**
Tuscany on Taylor **72**
Vivo **51**
Wave **32**
Wishbone **57**

See map p. 136. 2300 Lincoln Park West (at Belden Avenue). ☎ 773-472-5959. CTA: Bus no. 151 to Belden Avenue. Reservations recommended. Main courses: $25–$36; fixed-price meals $65–$75. AE, DC, DISC, MC, V. Open: Mon–Fri 6–10 p.m., Sat 5–10:30 p.m.

Ann Sather
$ North Side   SCANDINAVIAN

Gooey, buttery-soft homemade cinnamon rolls are reason enough to visit this mecca of Swedish delights. So are thin Swedish pancakes with lingonberry sauce, and maybe a side of mild Swedish potato sausage. This popular breakfast spot is especially busy on weekends — you may have to wait, but lines move quickly. (Get there before 11 a.m. for the fastest service). Hearty, inexpensive lunches include chopped beefsteak, roast pork loin, and meatballs. Ann Sather's is bright and cheerful, decorated with paintings from a Swedish fairy tale. A sister restaurant is located in the Swedish enclave of Andersonville, at 5207 N. Clark (☎ 773-271-6677). Several other branches serve only breakfast and lunch: a restaurant in Wicker Park, at 1448 N. Milwaukee Ave. (☎ 773-394-1812), and smaller cafes in Lakeview, at 3411 N. Broadway (☎ 773-305-0024) and 3416 N. Southport Ave. (☎ 773-404-4475).

See map p. 136. 929 W. Belmont Ave. (by North Sheffield Avenue). ☎ 773-348-2378. CTA: Red-line El to Belmont. Reservations not accepted. Main courses: $7–$12. AE, DISC, MC, V. Open: Daily 7 a.m.–9 p.m.

Arun's
$$$$$ North Side   THAI

Stunningly beautiful Thai food and an ever-changing chef's menu make this the best Thai restaurant in the city. For my money, Arun's may be the best Thai restaurant in the country. Tucked away in a far-northwest neighborhood, the restaurant's unassuming exterior cloaks a spectacular interior. It offers a fixed-price-only menu of twelve courses for $85 — expensive, but worth it. On any given night, you may sample hot-and-sour shrimp soup, three-flavored red snapper, or garlic prawns. Even classic dishes become unforgettable here: Courses of various delicate dumplings are accented with edible, carved dough flowers. And the desserts, including the scrumptious sticky rice with papaya, are tiny works of art. If you take public transportation here, you might want to splurge on a cab home, as buses run sporadically late at night.

See map p. 136. 4156 N. Kedzie (at Irving Park Road). ☎ 773-539-1909. CTA: Blue-line El to Irving Park Road, then transfer to eastbound bus no. 80; or brown-line El to Irving Park, then transfer to westbound bus no. 80. Reservations required with credit card. Main courses: 12-course chef's menu $85 per person. AE, DC, DISC, MC, V. Open: Tues–Sun 5–10 p.m.

Atwood Cafe
$$ Loop ECLECTIC

Colorful and offbeat, this stylish eatery in the Hotel Burnham is eclectic and fun and serves up a fresh take on American comfort food. This fanciful and romantic spot is filled with nooks and crannies and sofa-like seats. Soaring windows allow you to take in the bustle of State Street from the comfort of your own table. Don't miss the mussels in a garlicky tomato sauce with crusty, grilled homemade bread, and for dessert, you can't go wrong with the banana-and-white-chocolate bread pudding. The bar is small, so you're allowed to take drinks and sit in cozy chairs around the fireplace in the hotel lobby.

See map p. 132. 1 W. Washington St. (at State Street). ☎ *312-368-1900. CTA: Bus no. 151 to Washington and Michigan, then walk west; or red-line El to Washington/ State. Reservations recommended. Main courses: $18–$26; three-course prix fixe $38. AE, DISC, MC, V. Open: Breakfast Mon–Fri 7–10 a.m., Sat 8–10 a.m., Sun brunch 8 a.m.–3 p.m.; lunch Mon–Sat 11:30 a.m.–3:45 p.m.; dinner Sun–Thurs 5–10 p.m., Fri–Sat 5–11 p.m.*

Avec
$$–$$$ Randolph Street Market District ECLECTIC

No, you aren't walking into a sauna: The wood-paneled walls and long benches for communal dining are part of the experience at this hot new restaurant, the latest from the owners of Blackbird, the restaurant right next door that's been a happening spot for years. Avec is all about small plates and matching wines. And speaking of wine, it's served carafe-style, a real value, because you get about a glass and a half of wine for the price of one glass. Specialties cooked in the woodburning oven include charcuterie (such as homemade chorizo and salami dishes), and a wide range of small salads rounds out the menu.

See map p. 132. 615 W. Randolph St. (by North Jefferson Street). ☎ *312-377-2002. It's recommended that you take a cab here, about a $6 ride from the Loop. Reservations recommended. Main courses: $15–$25. AE, DC, MC, V. Open: Sun 3:30–10 p.m.; Mon–Thurs 3:30 p.m. to midnight; Fri–Sat 3:30 p.m.–1a.m.*

Bice Ristorante
$$–$$$ Streeterville ITALIAN

This sleek, flashy restaurant just east of Michigan Avenue serves homemade pasta and other Northern Italian fare. It's often busy, but the bar is stylish and pleasant enough to rest your weary feet after a long day of shopping or touring. Many prefer to sit outside, where you can watch passersby.

See map p. 132. 158 E. Ontario St. (by North Michigan Avenue). ☎ *312-664-1474. CTA: Bus no. 151 to Ontario Street and Michigan Avenue, then walk 1 block west. Reservations recommended. Main courses: $15–$25. AE, DC, MC, V. Open: Sun–Thurs 11:30 a.m.–10:30 p.m., Fri–Sat 11:30 a.m.–11:30 p.m.*

Lincoln Park and Wrigleyville Dining

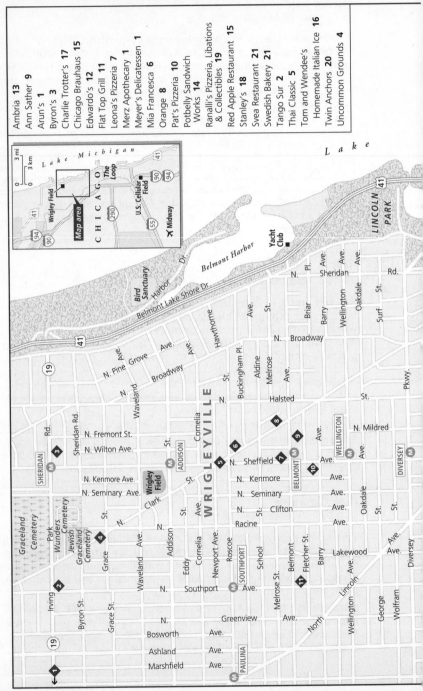

Ambria **13**
Ann Sather **9**
Arun's **1**
Byron's **3**
Charlie Trotter's **17**
Chicago Brauhaus **15**
Edwardo's **12**
Flat Top Grill **11**
Leona's Pizzeria **7**
Merz Apothecary **1**
Meyer's Delicatessen **1**
Mia Francesca **6**
Orange **8**
Pat's Pizzeria **10**
Potbelly Sandwich Works **14**
Ranalli's Pizzeria, Libations & Collectibles **19**
Red Apple Restaurant **15**
Stanley's **18**
Svea Restaurant **21**
Swedish Bakery **21**
Tango Sur **2**
Thai Classic **5**
Tom and Wendee's Homemade Italian Ice **16**
Twin Anchors **20**
Uncommon Grounds **4**

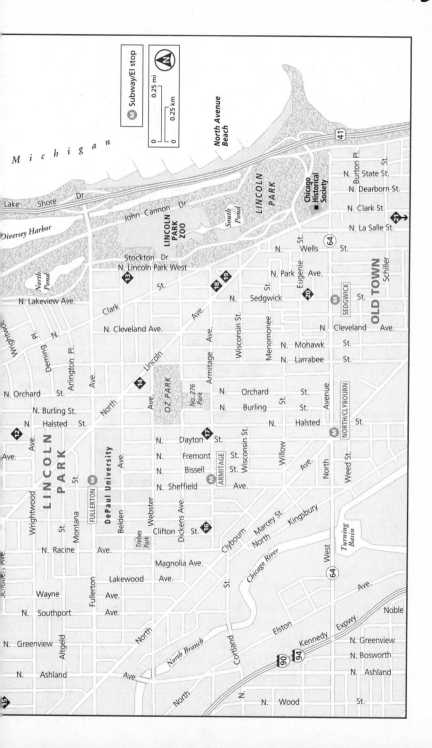

Bin 36
$$–$$$ **North Loop**   **AMERICAN**

It's all about wine at this bistro, located in a lofty, airy space in the Marina Towers complex, right across from the House of Blues music venue. This place is so wine-centric that the menu even recommends which red or white would best complement each offering. Ordering glasses of wines from certain regions or of specific varietals will bring out the wine expert in you. (A *flight* is two to three small glasses of different wines served together.) And the food, enlivened with Californian and Mediterranean accents, is yummy enough to make sure you don't drink on an empty stomach. In the tavern, you can sit at the bar and snack to your heart's delight on small plates such as shiitake spring rolls, steamed mussels, and homemade pâtés. Book a table in the Cellar for a full dinner menu that includes seafood, seared venison, and braised pork shank.

See map p. 132. 339 N. Dearborn St. (by West Kinzie Street). ☎ *312-755-9463.* www.bin36.com. *CTA: Bus no. 22 to Kinzie Street; red-line El to Grand/State. Reservations recommended. Main courses: $18–$26. AE, DC, DISC, MC, V. Open: Mon–Thurs 11 a.m. to midnight, Fri 11 a.m.–1:30 a.m., Sat noon to 1:30 a.m., Sun noon to 10 p.m.*

Bistro 110
$$ **Magnificent Mile**   **AMERICAN**

A neighborhood crowd gathers at Bistro 110 for its changing weekly specials, posted on a chalkboard on one wall of the restaurant. (You can also check the blackboard for the weather forecast and other local news.) This is the perfect spot to get a grilled piece of fish, steak, or roasted veggie platter, and the place has become so well-known for its roasted garlic with crunchy French bread that the restaurant gives each table a card with the recipe to take home. Because it's a neighborhood crowd, the atmosphere is relaxed and kid-friendly. Sunday brunch with a New Orleans–inspired menu and a live jazz band is a popular ritual; get there early — or be prepared for a long wait.

See map p. 132. 110 E. Pearson St. (just west of Michigan Avenue). ☎ *312-266-3110.* www.levyrestaurants.com. *CTA: Red-line El to Chicago/State; bus no. 151 to Water Tower. Reservations recommended. Main courses: $13–$28. AE, DC, DISC, MC, V. Open: Mon–Wed 11:30 a.m.–10 p.m., Thurs–Sat 11:30 a.m.–11 a.m., Sun 10 a.m.–10 p.m.*

Bistro Zinc
$$ **Gold Coast**   **BISTRO**

The curving zinc bar, where you find hard-boiled eggs on offer for customers and bottles of French liqueur, such as Chartreuse, is the most striking feature of this French bistro, which also has a traditional tile floor. The atmosphere is energetic, the serving staff upbeat. Salade frisée, salade niçoise, skate fish, and escargot are some of the specialties.

See map p. 132. 1131 N. State St. (near Rush Street). ☎ *312-337-1131. CTA: Red-line El to Clark/Division; bus no. 36 to State and Rush streets. Main courses: $13–$19.*

AE, DC, MC, V. Open: Mon–Thurs 11:30 a.m.–10 p.m., Fri 11:30 a.m.–11 p.m., Sat 10 a.m.–11 p.m., Sun 10 a.m.–9 p.m.

Café Absinthe
$$$ Bucktown/Wicker Park   ECLECTIC

Café Absinthe doesn't look like much from the outside (in fact, you enter from the alleyway), but the romantic interior is the perfect place to linger over a meal with a date. Be prepared for trendy types soaking in the moody atmosphere while jazz plays in the background. Draperies divide the tables, creating privacy for a tête-à-tête. Food is interesting and changes seasonally. Appetizers may include grilled ostrich fillet with confit onion, fresh figs and mandarin oranges, or brie cooked en croute with hazelnuts, blackberry preserves, and spiced strawberries. Main courses run the gamut from wasabi-seared tuna with oriental vegetable rolls to Pernod-glazed rack of lamb with macadamia-nut couscous. Dessert is as exotic as the rest of the meal; if it's available, try the tea-scented crème brûlée, or go ultra-decadent with the chocolate-and-hazelnut mousse served in a martini glass.

See map p. ###. 1954 W. North Ave. (by North Damen Avenue). ☎ 773-278-4488. Reservations recommended. CTA: Blue-line El to Damen. Main courses: $17–$27. AE, DC, DISC, MC, V. Open: Sun–Thurs 5:30–10 p.m., Fri–Sat 5:30–11 p.m.

Café Iberico
$ River North   SPANISH

Sure, this place is loud. And boisterous. And crowded. But the food is fresh, authentic, and inexpensive. It's a longtime local favorite for singles in their 20s and 30s, making it a good group destination. You may try going in the off-hours, such as very late at night (after 10 p.m.) or early (at 4 p.m., after a day of shopping or touring). After you give your name to the hostess, head to the bar to order a pitcher of sangria, and join in the fun. Tapas (appetizer-size portions perfect for sharing) include baked goat cheese, grilled octopus, and tortilla española. In a town where many restaurant kitchens close by 10 p.m., this place is one of Chicago's most reliable and popular spots for a late-night dinner.

See map p. 132. 739 N. LaSalle St. (between Chicago Avenue and Superior Street). ☎ 312-573-1510. Reservations accepted during the week for parties of six or more. CTA: Red-line El to Chicago/State; bus No. 156 to Chicago Avenue. Main courses: $8–$13; tapas $2–$7. DC, DISC, MC, V. Open: Mon–Thurs 11 a.m.–11 p.m., Fri 11 a.m.–1:30 a.m., Sat noon to 1:30 a.m., Sun noon to 11 p.m.

Carson's
$$ River North   BARBECUE

A true Chicago institution, Carson's calls itself "The Place for Ribs," and, boy, is it ever. The barbecue sauce is sweet and tangy, and the ribs are meaty. Included in the $20 price for a full slab of ribs are coleslaw and one of four types of potatoes (the most decadent are au gratin), plus right-out-of-the-oven rolls. For dinner there's often a wait, but don't despair. In the bar area, you'll find a heaping mound of some of the best chopped liver around and plenty of cocktail rye to go with it. When you're seated at your table, tie on your plastic bib — and indulge. In case you don't eat ribs, Carson's also barbecues chicken, salmon, and pork chops, and the restaurant's steaks aren't bad. But ribs are the house specialty, so make sure that at least someone in your group orders them. (The waitstaff will be shocked if you don't.) If by some remarkable feat you have room left after dinner, the candy-bar sundaes are a scrumptious finale to the meal. Carson's popularity has led to something of a factory mentality among management, which evidently feels the need to herd 'em in and out, but the servers are responsive to requests not to be hurried through the meal.

See map p. 132. 612 N. Wells St. (at Ontario Street). ☎ *312-280-9200. Reservations accepted for groups of six or more. CTA: Red-line El to Grand. Main courses $8.95–$30. AE, DC, DISC, MC, V. Open: Mon–Thurs 11 a.m.–11 p.m.; Fri 11 a.m.–12:30 a.m.; Sat noon to 12:30 a.m.; Sun noon to 11p.m. Closed Thanksgiving (fourth Thurs in Nov).*

Charlie Trotter's
$$$$$ Lincoln Park   NOUVELLE

Welcome to Chicago's foodie mecca. Located in a 1908-built brownstone, Charlie Trotter's is a destination, not just a restaurant. The food outshines even the restaurant's setting. Highly stylized items and lush ingredients make for complex dishes that are innovative, improvisational, and harmonious. The grand menu assortment ($110) changes daily, and a vegetable menu is $90. Those are your only two choices, so don't expect to order à la carte. The coveted table in the kitchen allows for the best viewing and must be booked well in advance. Be prepared to make this your entire evening's activity, because meals here can take up to three hours. Naturally, you'll find an extensive wine list and a sommelier to help you match wines with each course.

For a taste of Trotter's gourmet fare on a smaller scale, stop by **Trotter's To Go,** his takeout store in Lincoln Park, located at 1337 W. Fullerton Ave. (☎ **773-868-6510**).

See map p. 136. 816 W. Armitage Ave. (near Halsted Street). ☎ *773-248-6228.* www.charlietrotters.com. *Reservations required. Jackets required, ties requested. CTA: Brown-line El to Armitage. Fixed-price dinners: $90 and $110. AE, DC, DISC, MC, V. Open: Tues–Sat 6–10 p.m.*

Chez Joël
$$ Little Italy   BISTRO

Cozy and romantic, this tiny piece of France in Little Italy is well worth the trip. A pretty garden adjoining the dining room is a wonderful setting in the summer. Main courses may include fish specials, *steak frites* (skirt steak with french fries), braised lamb shank, and *coq au vin* (chicken in red-wine sauce with vegetables).

Bucktown/Wicker Park Dining and Nightlife

DINING ◆

Café Absinthe **10**
Jane's **6**
Le Bouchon **4**
Margie's Candies **2**
Mas **18**
Meritage Café & Wine Bar **3**
Mirai Sushi **15**
MOD **9**
Soju **11**
Spring **8**

NIGHTLIFE ●

Artful Dodger **7**
Double Door **12**
Empty Bottle **14**
Fireside Bowl **1**
Holiday Club **13**
Lava Lounge **17**
Lemmings **5**
Rainbo Club **16**

Ⓜ Subway/El stop

See map p. 132. 1119 W. Taylor St. (by South Aberdeen Street). ☎ *312-226-6479. Reservations recommended. CTA: Blue-line El to Polk. Main courses: $12–$22. AE, DC, DISC, MC, V. Open: Mon–Thurs 11 a.m.–3 p.m. and 5–10 p.m.; Fri 11 a.m.–3 p.m. and 5–11 p.m., Sat 5–11 p.m., Sun 4:30–10 p.m.*

Chilpancingo
$$ River North MEXICAN

Restaurants like this have made Chicago a center of modern Mexican cooking. In this loftlike space, named after the capital of Mexico's Guerrero state and enlivened with colorful Mexican folk art and masks, you indulge in starters such as ceviche on tortilla triangles and jalapeno peppers stuffed with pork and served with black-bean sauce. The standouts on the regional Mexican menu are the mole sauces, which are made with 25 ingredients, resulting in a dark, complex sauce served over chicken. Salmon, rack of lamb, tuna, and squid are all featured on the menu, which goes well beyond your typical enchilada and burrito fare. After your meal, don't miss the Café Maya Xtabentun (ask your server for the correct pronunciation!). The coffee is flavored with Kahlua and a Mayan liqueur, and lit by the server before pouring it into your glass. A less expensive way to sample the fare here is the Sunday brunch, served from 10:30 a.m. to 2:30 p.m.

See map p. 132. 358 W. Ontario St. (west of Orleans). ☎ *312-266-9525.* www. chilpancingorestaurant.com. *Reservations recommended on weekends. CTA: Brown-line El to Chicago. Main courses: $15–$25. AE, DC, DISC, MC, V. Open: Mon–Thurs 11:30 a.m.–2:30 p.m. and 5–10 p.m.; Fri–Sat 11:30 a.m.–2:30 p.m. and 5–11 p.m.; Sun 10:30 a.m.–2:30 p.m. and 5–10 p.m.*

Cyrano's Bistro, Wine Bar & Cabaret
$$ River North BISTRO

This charming restaurant has yellow walls, gilt mirrors, and French posters — after a glass of wine, you just may think you're in Southwest France. In fact, Bergerac, France, happens to be the hometown of this lovely restaurant's chef, and also the hometown of Cyrano de Bergerac, for whom the restaurant is named. For $26.95, you can have a three-course fixed-price feast that may include ratatouille, coq au vin, and a bread pudding with chocolate sauce. A three-course lunch special for $20 is a real deal. A live cabaret is presented Wednesday to Saturday nights, so expect a $10 cover charge and two-drink minimum those nights, or pay the $35 for an all-inclusive dinner and cabaret package.

See map p. 132. 546 N. Wells St. (between Ohio Street and Grand Avenue). ☎ *312-467-0546. CTA: Brown-line El to Merchandise Mart. Reservations highly recommended. Main courses: $9–$25. AE, DC, DISC, MC, V. Open: Mon–Fri 11:30 a.m.–2:30 p.m. and 5:30–10:30 p.m., Sat 5:30–10:30 p.m.*

Flat Top Grill
$ Old Town/North Side/Randolph St. Market District   ASIAN

This create-your-own stir-fry restaurant often has lines, but never fear, they move quickly. If you've never assembled your own stir-fry dish, you may want to follow the suggested recipes on the giant blackboards. Choose from over 70 ingredients including rice, noodles, seafood, chicken, beef, sauces, and veggies — for one low price. And remember, the price includes multiple visits to the food line. If at first you don't succeed, try, try again. Kids love to create their own dishes, and the price is definitely right if you have a few wee ones in tow: a kid's stir-fry is $5. Flat Top Grill has three Chicago locations, each with different hours.
www.flattopgrill.com. *Main courses (one price): Lunch $9; dinner $12. AE, DC, DISC, MC, V.*

See map p. 132. 319 W. North Ave. ☎ *312-787-7676. CTA: Bus no. 76 to North Avenue. Reservations not accepted. Open: Mon–Thurs 5–10 p.m., Fri–Sat 11:30 a.m.–11 p.m., Sun 11:30 a.m.–10 p.m.*

See map p. 132. 1000 W. Washington Blvd. ☎ *312-829-4800. The neighborhood is a $5 cab ride from downtown. Reservations accepted. Open: Mon–Thurs 11 a.m.–10 p.m., Fri 11 a.m.–11 p.m., Sat noon to 11 p.m., Sun noon to 9 p.m.*

See map p. 136. 3200 N. Southport Ave. ☎ *773-665-8100. CTA: Brown-line El to Southport. Reservations accepted. Open: Sun–Thurs 11:30 a.m. to 10 p.m., Fri–Sat 11:30 a.m.–11 p.m.*

Frontera Grill and Topolobampo
$$–$$$$ River North   MEXICAN

Owners Rick and Deann Bayless travel extensively throughout Mexico, gathering authentic regional recipes for what is arguably one of America's best Mexican restaurants, containing two dining options. Topolobampo is more upscale, and you can order off its menu at its more casual sister eatery, Frontera Grill. Both are housed in the same building. Try the signature *tacos al carbon* (the precursor of Americanized fajitas) or chili-marinated stuffed quail with smoky red beans, enchiladas, browned potatoes, and tangy cabbage. The signature appetizer at Frontera is the *sopes surtidos,* corn "boats" filled with chicken in red mole sauce, or black beans with homemade chorizo, and more. At Topolobampo, you'll find white tablecloths and more upscale ingredients and presentation. Because Frontera only accepts reservations for parties of five to ten, do as the locals do after putting their names on the list: Order a few margaritas in the lively bar area, decorated with terra-cotta tile and rustic wooden tables and bar stools.

See map p. 132. 445 N. Clark St. (between Illinois and Hubbard streets). ☎ *312-661-1434.* www.fronterakitchens.com. *Reservations required at Topolobampo for parties of one to eight, reservations accepted at Frontera Grill only for groups of five to ten. CTA: Red-line El to Grand at State Street. Main courses:*

Frontera Grill $15–$21, Topolobampo $20–$29 (chef's five-course tasting menu). AE, DC, DISC, MC, V. Open: Frontera Grill: Tues–Thurs 11:30 a.m.–2:30 p.m. and 5–10 p.m., Fri 11:30 a.m.–2:30 p.m. and 5–11 p.m., Sat 10:30 a.m.–2:30 p.m. and 5–11 p.m. Topolobampo: Tues 11:45 a.m.–2 p.m. and 5:30–9:30 p.m., Wed–Thurs 11:30 a.m.–2 p.m. and 5:30–9:30 p.m., Fri 11:30 a.m.–2 p.m. and 5:30–10:30 p.m., Sat 5:30–10:30 p.m.

Gibson's Steakhouse
$$$$ Gold Coast STEAKHOUSE

Chicagoans come here to see and be seen, and the food isn't bad either. Photos of celebs decorate the Art Deco–style rooms. The bar has its own life, where the who's who of the city mingle and mix. Everything is larger than life, from the patrons to the martinis, which come in 10-ounce glasses. Entrees are also giant-size, and well-aged steaks are the star of the show. With such ample portions, Gibson's is ideal for a group interested in sharing dishes. (The turtle pie alone could probably serve eight!) This is one of Chicago's most popular restaurants, so call well in advance for reservations. If you aren't up for a big meal, you can also order from the bar menu.

See map p. 132. 1028 N. Rush St. (at Bellevue Place). ☎ 312-266-8999. www. gibsonssteakhouse.com. CTA: Red-line El to Clark/Division. Reservations recommended. Main courses: $22–$35. AE, DC, DISC, MC, V. Open: Daily 11:30 a.m. to midnight; bar open later.

Gino's East
$ River North PIZZA

Chicago's famous pizzeria serves up deep-dish pizzas in the classic style at the block-long location in the former Planet Hollywood site. Patrons are welcome to scrawl on the graffiti-covered walls and furniture, making this

---

Chicago's steak joints

Since the days of the stockyards, Chicago has been known for its beef. The stockyards are long gone, but the steakhouses remain. The most profitable restaurant in Chicago is **Gibson's Steakhouse,** where the drinks are as big as the beef (see the listing in this chapter). **Morton's,** 1050 N. State St. (☎ 312-266-4820), a Chicago original with branches nationwide (and with other Chicago area locations), is considered by some to be the city's best steakhouse. Other local favorites include the **Saloon Steakhouse** (see the listing in this chapter); **Eli's The Place for Steak,** 215 E. Chicago Ave. (☎ 312-642-1393), which is also the place for cheesecake; and **Gene & Georgetti,** 500 N. Franklin St. (☎ 312-527-3718). National chains with branches in Chicago include **Ruth's Chris Steak House,** 431 N. Dearborn St. (☎ 312-321-2725), and **Smith & Wollensky,** 318 N. State St. (☎ 312-670-9900). And finally, another entry into the local steak market is **Keefer's,** 20 W. Kinzie St. (☎ 312-467-9525), which works in a few French touches.

a favorite among kids. Most people consider Gino's the quintessential Chicago deep-dish pizza. It's so filling that, for many diners, one piece is sufficient for a meal — and a small cheese pizza is plenty for two. Three or more pieces is enough to send you into cholesterol overdrive. Specialties include the supreme, with layers of cheese, sausage, onions, green pepper, and mushrooms; and the vegetarian, with cheese, onions, peppers, asparagus, summer squash, zucchini, and eggplant.

See map p. 132. 633 N. Wells St. (between Ontario and Erie streets). ☎ *312-943-1124. CTA: Brown-line El to Chicago. Reservations not accepted. Main courses: Deep-dish pizza $8–$20. AE, DC, DISC, MC, V. Open: Mon–Thurs 11 a.m.–9 p.m., Fri–Sat 11 a.m. to midnight, Sun noon to 9 p.m.*

Green Zebra
$$$ **River North**   **VEGETARIAN**

The latest offering from the chef who won raves at Spring (see review later in this chapter), this new restaurant on the western fringes of River North is attracting attention for its "small plates" approach, featuring veggie delights. Try the fennel risotto cake with a syrah reduction, and the Hawaiian heart of palm with kaffir lime and Thai basil chili. And count on ordering two mini-portions if you want to fill up. This vegetarian doesn't come cheap, but it's a much-needed haven for vegetarians with sophisticated tastes.

See map p. 132. 1460 W. Chicago Ave (at Greenview Street). ☎ *312-243-7100. Reservations recommended. CTA: Bus no. 66 or take a cab. Main courses: $7–$14. AE, DC, DISC, MC, V. Open: Mon–Tues 5–10 p.m., Wed–Thurs 5:30–10 p.m., Fri–Sat 5:30–11 p.m., Sun 5–9 p.m.*

Harry Caray's
$$–$$$ **River North**   **ITALIAN/STEAKHOUSE**

Holy cow! One of Chicago's most flamboyant eateries is larger than life, like its namesake, legendary baseball broadcaster, the late Harry Caray. From the huge baseball bat outside to showcases filled with uniforms, helmets, cards, and photographs, this is Valhalla for those who follow America's favorite pastime. (Have you ever hurled a baseball from a pitcher's mound to home plate? To get an idea of the distance, take a look at the bar at Harry Caray's restaurant. It measures 60 feet, 6 inches, the exact distance from hill to plate.) The food is pretty good, too — steaks, chops, pasta with red sauce, and such Italian basics as chicken Vesuvio, cheese ravioli, and calamari. The bar offers homemade thick-cut potato chips that can be addictive. Be careful not to ruin your appetite!

See map p. 132. 33 W. Kinzie St. (at Dearborn Street). ☎ *312-828-0966. Reservations accepted. CTA: Brown-line El to Merchandise Mart, or red-line El to Grand at State Street. Main courses: $11–$33. AE, DC, DISC, MC, V. Open: Mon–Thurs 11:30 a.m.–2:30 p.m. and 5–10:30 p.m.; Fri–Sat 11:30 a.m.–2:30 p.m. and 5–11 p.m.; Sun noon to 4p.m. (lunch bar only) and 4–10 p.m.*

Heaven on Seven
$$ Loop and Magnificent Mile   CAJUN

Tucked away on the seventh floor of the Garland Building, you can find what may well be the best Cajun and Creole cooking north of New Orleans. Don't miss the acclaimed gumbo, po' boy sandwiches (try the oyster and soft-shell crab versions), hoppin' John (black-eyed peas), and spicy jambalaya. Sweet-potato pie and bread pudding are top desserts, or try the coffee, which comes with chicory, after your meal. This original location opens one night a month for dinner. The restaurant has two additional locations: a trendy location on the Magnificent Mile at **600 N. Michigan Ave.,** at Rush and Ohio streets (☎ 312-280-7774); and a Wrigleyville location at **3478 N. Clark St.** Unlike the original location, both new locations accept credit cards and reservations and are open for dinner.

See map p. 132. 111 N. Wabash Ave. (at Washington Street). ☎ *312-263-6443. CTA: Orange-, brown-, or green-line El to Madison/Wabash, then walk 1 block north. Reservations not accepted. Main courses: $8–$11. No credit cards. Open: Mon–Fri 8:30 a.m.–5 p.m., Sat 10 a.m.–3 p.m., third Fri of each month 5:30–9 p.m.*

Jake Melnick's
$–$$ Magnificent Mile   AMERICAN

This warm and inviting restaurant offers a good approximation of a northern Wisconsin lodge and supper club. A screened-in porch area is pleasant in summer, and the fireplaces and big booths are comfy in winter. Food is substantial and homey. The menu features chopped salads, hamburgers, and sandwiches, as well as home-cooked specialties like barbequed ribs and fish 'n' chips. For dessert, try the chocolate-chip cookie skillet sundae. The relaxed atmosphere, large crowd (where young ones blend in easily), and comfort food make this a good place to take the kids for a night out.

See map p. 132. 41 E. Superior St. (at Wabash Avenue). ☎ *312-266-0400. Reservations accepted. CTA: Red-line El to Chicago/State; bus no. 151 to Superior Street, then 1 block east. Main courses: $10–$15. AE, DC, DISC, MC, V. Open: Mon–Wed 11:30 a.m. to midnight, Thurs–Sat 11:30 a.m.–2 a.m., Sun 11 a.m.–11 p.m.*

Jane's
$$ Bucktown/Wicker Park   ECLECTIC

Jane's is a neighborhood charmer that's managed to keep an off-the-beaten-track feel. Casual and chic, the restaurant is located in an old house that was gutted, so it's open to the roof. The walls are decorated with ever-changing work by local artists. In the winter, soft yellow light makes the place cozy; in the summer, you can sit outside at sidewalk tables. Bucktown residents pack the place, so you usually wind up squeezing into the bar area to wait. But the experience is worth it. Try Jane's version of salade niçoise, with grilled ahi tuna. Pan-roasted grouper and goat cheese and stuffed chicken breast are also favorites.

See map p. 141. 1655 W. Cortland St. (1 block west of Ashland Avenue). ☎ *773-862-5263. CTA: Blue-line El to Damen Avenue, then walk 3 blocks north on Damen, 4 blocks east* *on Cortland. Reservations available on a limited basis. Main courses: $9–$20. AE, MC, V. Open: Mon–Thurs 5–10 p.m., Fri 5–11 p.m., Sat 11 a.m.–11 p.m., Sun 11 a.m.–10 p.m.*

Joe's Seafood, Prime Steak and Stone Crab
$$–$$$ Magnificent Mile SEAFOOD/STEAKHOUSE

Here's a little piece of Miami Beach transplanted to the North Bridge area. If you've never sampled stone crab, this outpost of famed Joe's Stone Crab of Miami Beach is just the thing. The crab claws are flown in from Florida and cracked perfectly so as to preserve the delectable meat. (**Note:** The claws are served cold.) Sides include creamed spinach and hash browns. The Key lime pie is the best I've ever had — and believe me, I've tasted many. If you get hooked, never fear: You can order stone crabs from Joe's over the Web and they'll arrive via Fed Ex the next day, packed in dry ice.

See map p. 132. 60 E. Grand Ave. (at the corner of Grand and Rush, behind the Marriott Hotel). ☎ *312-379-5637.* www.leye.com. *CTA: Red-line El to State/Grand. Reservations recommended and available on a limited basis. Main courses: $15–$50 (depends on market price). AE, DC, DISC, MC, V. Open: Mon–Thurs 11:30 a.m.–10 p.m., Fri–Sat 11:30 a.m.–11 p.m., Sun 4–9 p.m.*

Kamehachi
$$ Old Town JAPANESE/SUSHI

When my sushi-loving friends and I debate the merits of Chicago sushi spots, we always come back to Kamehachi. The place is constantly filled with a good-looking crowd, and the sushi is fresh. In the fast-changing restaurant world, Kamehachi's record is impressive. This family-owned restaurant has been going strong since 1967, when it opened as Chicago's first sushi bar. If you have a group, call ahead and book the tatami room, where you can make plenty of noise and linger over dinner. Otherwise, ask for a table upstairs where you can watch the Old Town crowd swirl by. A second location is centrally located just off the Magnificent Mile at 240 E. Ontario St.

See map p. 132. 1400 N. Wells St. (at Schiller Street). ☎ *312-664-3663.* www.kamehachi.com. *Reservations recommended. CTA: Bus no. 22 to Clark and North Avenue, walk west to Wells Street and south to Schiller. Main courses: $8–$15. AE, DC, DISC, MC, V. Open: Mon–Thurs 11:30 a.m.–2 p.m. and 5 p.m. to midnight, Fri–Sat 11:30–2 p.m. and 5 p.m.–1:30 a.m., Sun 4:30–11:30 p.m.*

Le Bouchon
$$ Bucktown/Wicker Park BISTRO

This idyllic, tin-ceilinged French bistro packs them in for classics like escargot, French onion soup, rabbit, herb-roasted chicken, country pâté, and steak frites. Many come just for the house specialty, roast duck for two bathed in Grand Marnier–orange marmalade sauce. If you're guessing that the fare is on the heavy, rich side, you're right. Located in a tiny storefront, the tables are closely packed, meaning that the atmosphere is intimate and, after your fellow diners get a glass or two of wine in them, boisterous as well. Some people find it cozy and others feel it's claustrophobic. You probably can already guess where you stand! The desserts are outstanding, including one of the best crème brûlées in Chicago. Prices here are more than reasonable, so even with reservations, you may be in for a long wait: Be prepared to have a drink at the (small) bar.

See map p. 141. 1958 N. Damen Ave. (by Armitage Avenue). ☎ *773-862-6600.* www.lebouchonofchicago.com. *Reservations recommended. CTA: Blue-line El to Damen. Main courses: $13–$15. AE, DC, DISC, MC, V. Open: Mon–Thurs 5:30– 11 p.m., Fri–Sat 5 p.m. to midnight.*

Lou Mitchell's
$ Loop AMERICAN

Plan to eat at least one breakfast at this South Loop diner, a Chicago tradition since 1923. It's a longtime favorite, known for airy omelets and other egg dishes served in sizzling skillets. You double your pleasure (and cholesterol) with Mitchell's use of double-yolk eggs. Pancakes and waffles are good, too. Orders come with thick slabs of toasted Greek bread and homemade marmalade. The wait can be long, especially on weekends, but it can be shorter if you're willing to take a counter seat. The restaurant has a tradition of handing out boxes of Milk Duds to female patrons — and doughnut holes for everyone waiting.

See map p. 133. 565 W. Jackson Blvd. (at Jefferson Street). ☎ *312-939-3111. CTA: Blue-line El to Clinton Street, then walk 2 blocks north and 1 block west. Reservations not accepted. Breakfast dishes: $5–$12. No credit cards. Open: Mon–Sat 5:30 a.m.– 3 p.m., Sun 7 a.m.–3 p.m.*

Maggiano's
$$ River North ITALIAN

A great pick for large groups, Maggiano's is a shrine to family-style Italian dining. Like many of its fellow Lettuce Entertain You restaurants, Maggiano's feels a bit contrived, with traditional Italian red-checkered tablecloths and old family portraits (which family, we'll never know), designed to create the feel of Little Italy throughout the nine separate dining rooms. Still, heaping plates of pasta meant to be shared make Maggiano's a good choice for a large or budget-conscious family (and who isn't?). In fact, everything on the menu is super-sized. Steaks are all more than a pound, and most pasta dishes weigh in over 25 ounces. You're expected to share dishes, pass things around, and try a little bit of everything. The menu is vast and features Italian pasta classics such as chicken and spinach manicotti, eggplant parmesan and meat or marinara lasagna, plus chicken, veal, steaks, chops, and seafood. Try the Prime New York Steak al Forno, Gorgonzola, a strip steak served with caramelized onions and melted gorgonzola cheese. There's no kids' menu, but the kitchen will accommodate with smaller portions. Downstairs, there's a banquet room that accommodates parties of 20 to 200. On holidays, Maggiano's has live music.

See map p. 133. 516 N. Clark St. (by West Grand Avenue). ☎ *312-644-7700. CTA: Brown-line El to Merchandise Mart; red-line El to Grand; bus no. 65 or 22. Main courses: $11–$33. AE, DC, DISC, MC, V. Open: Mon–Thurs 11:30 a.m.–10 p.m., Fri–Sat 11:30 a.m.–11 p.m., Sun noon to 10 p.m.*

Mas
$$$ Bucktown/Wicker Park   LATIN AMERICAN

Urban, cozy, and dark, Mas is almost always packed with faithful regulars who come for the Latin cocktails and modern takes on Central and South American cuisine. Appetizers (called *primeros*) include a succulent ceviche of the day, such as blue marlin marinated in rum and vanilla. Entrees worth the wait include chile-cured pork tenderloin over smoky white beans, and traditional Brazilian shrimp and chicken stew with coconut broth and black beans. Out-of-the-ordinary desserts include lightly fried pound cake with fresh plum compote. The wine list emphasizes selections from Spain, Argentina, and Chile. At the bar, try a Brazilian caipirinha, made with sugar, lime, and a Brazilian brandy made from sugar cane.

See map p. 141. 1670 W. Division St. (by Pauline Street). ☎ *773-276-8700.* www.mas restaurant.com. *CTA: Blue-line El to Damen. Reservations recommended. Main courses: $17–$27. AE, DC, MC, V. Open: Mon–Thurs 5:30–10:30 p.m., Fri–Sat 5:30–11 p.m.*

Meritage Café & Wine Bar
$$$ Bucktown/Wicker Park   AMERICAN

The romantic, bring-the-outdoors-indoors atmosphere is the draw at this neighborhood restaurant. The front room features a long wood bar and tin ceilings; this is the place to sit if you want the feel of a hip wine bar. The patio, however, is the best place to enjoy a meal: It's covered and heated in the winter, making for the unusual indoor-outdoor feel. My favorites here always include seafood, whether it's ahi tuna or seared scallops that are out of this world. Wild game is another specialty here, including grilled ostrich and venison. An apple-caramel Dutch pancake and chocolate mousse cake are among the most comforting, feel-good desserts you'll have anywhere. The West Coast–oriented wine list is heavy on Bordeaux blends, with more than 20 wines by the glass.

See map p. 141. 2118 N. Damen Ave. (at Charleston Street). ☎ *773-235-6434.* www. meritagecafe.com. *CTA: Blue-line El to Damen. Reservations recommended. Main courses: $16–$28. AE, DC, MC, V. Open: Mon–Thurs 5:30–10 p.m., Fri–Sat 5:30– 11 p.m., Sun 11 a.m.–2 p.m. and 5–9 p.m.*

Mia Francesca
$$ North Side/Little Italy/Andersonville   ITALIAN

This place is crowded, noisy, overly warm — and people love it. Thanks to the generous helpings of pasta at reasonable prices, the place is packed night in and night out with neighborhood singles and couples on dates. Call for reservations or you'll be in for a long wait. The menu changes weekly and might include thin-crust pizza appetizers; four-cheese ravioli; linguine with seafood; and farfalle with ham, peas, and wild mushrooms. Given its popularity, numerous locations have sprouted up in Chicago and the suburbs. The two other locations in the city are **Francesca's Bryn Mawr** in the Andersonville neighborhood, 1039 W. Bryn Mawr (☎ 773-506-9261), and **Francesca's on Taylor,** 1400 W. Taylor St. (☎ 312-829-2828).

See map p. 136. 3311 N. Clark St. (just north of Belmont Avenue). ☎ *773-281-3310.* www.miafrancesca.com. *CTA: Red-line El to Belmont. Reservations recommended. Main courses: $10–$23. AE, MC, V. Open: Sun–Thurs 5–10:30 p.m., Fri–Sat 5–11 p.m.*

Mike Ditka's Restaurant
$$–$$$ Magnificent Mile STEAKHOUSE

For many Chicago football diehards, the glory days of former Coach Mike Ditka are still alive and well. From the football memorabilia to the cigar smoking in the upstairs lounge, this place is all Ditka, all the time. Local celebs and a sleek crowd gather here, bathed in amber light and tucked into dark-wood, leather banquettes. Televisions in the bar allow you to drink Scotch and watch the Bears while praying for "Da Coach" to come home to Chicago and help the Bears rise from the ashes. Food here is many notches above sports-bar fare. A hamburger here, one of the city's best, can feed two. Or, go for the "fullback-size" filet mignon with spinach and homemade onion rings, or "Da Pork Chop," surrounded by warm cinnamon apples and a green-peppercorn sauce. And keep your eyes open, because Da Coach himself does make regular appearances.

See map p. 133. 100 E. Chestnut St. (in the Tremont Hotel, between Michigan and Rush avenues). ☎ *312-587-8989.* www.mikeditkaschicago.com. *CTA: Red-line El to Chicago/State; bus no. 151 to Water Tower. Reservations accepted. Main courses: $15–$30. AE, DC, DISC, MC, V. Open: Mon–Thurs 11 a.m.–10 p.m., Fri 11 a.m.–11 p.m., Sat 10 a.m.–11 p.m., Sun 10 a.m.–10 p.m.*

Mirai Sushi
$$$ Bucktown/Wicker Park JAPANESE/SUSHI

Mirai (meaning "the future") surfs atop the crest of Chicago's sushi tsunami. Blending a serious devotion to sushi and sake with a youthful and funky ambience, Mirai is one hot destination for cold, raw fish; other Japanese fare is available as well. The futuristic second-floor sake lounge is the hippest place in town to slurp down sushi, chilled sakes, and "red ones," the house cocktail of vodka with passion fruit, lime, and cranberry juices. The bright, smoke-free main-floor dining room offers a comparatively traditional environment. Fish is flown in daily for the sushi bar, where several chefs work hard at crafting everything from beginner's sushi (California roll) to escalating classifications of tuna, five types of salmon and a half-dozen varieties of fresh oysters. Even the sake menu will expand your horizons, with about a dozen different selections.

See map p. 141. 2020 W. Division St. (at North Damen Avenue). ☎ *773-862-8500. CTA: Blue-line El to Division. Reservations recommended. Sushi: $1.75–$4 per piece. AE, DC, DISC, MC, V. Open: Sun–Wed 5–10 p.m., Thurs–Sat 5–11 p.m. Upstairs lounge open until 2 a.m.*

mk
$$$ River North   AMERICAN

This restaurant draws a chic, mixed-age crowd and is considered one of the best American restaurants in town, although you may gripe about the prices. Start with lobster soup with cumin, carrots, and Granny Smith apples, or fresh goat cheese ravioli with tomatoes and rosemary. mk specializes in creative combinations, such as sautéed whitefish and Maine lobster with sweet corn, mushrooms, and a light cream sauce. Don't miss the sweet seasonal masterpieces, from homemade ice creams to playful adaptations of classic fruit desserts. The One Banana, Two Banana plate (banana brioche pudding, banana sherbet, and banana coffee cake topped with butterscotch and hot fudge) is worth every calorie.

See map p. 133. 868 N. Franklin St. (1 block north of Chicago Avenue). ☎ *312-482-9179.* www.mkchicago.com. *CTA: Brown-line El to Chicago/Franklin. Reservations recommended. Main courses: $24–$38. Menu dégustation: $58. AE, DC, MC, V. Open: Sun–Thurs 5:30–10 p.m.; Fri–Sat 5:30–11 p.m.*

MOD
$$$ Bucktown/Wicker Park   AMERICAN

MOD's main draw is its postindustrial, MTV-style décor: circular, recycled foam banquettes covered in clear vinyl, egg-shaped chairs, inflatable lamps, and a floor made from recycled tires. See it to believe it. The menu, which offers some globally influenced selections, is a little more down-to-earth, with an emphasis on organic ingredients. First courses include hand-chopped spicy tuna on ice with crispy lentil pappadams. The salads are equally intriguing: melon with feta cheese and olive oil, for instance. Entrees include a crispy duck confit with grilled nectarines and a rosemary broth, and clams with grilled fennel sausage, roasted tomato, little ear pasta, and olive oil. The mascarpone "mac and cheese" is a signature side dish. Desserts include a toasted hazelnut napoleon with vanilla-bean-scented raspberries and Frangelico mousse. Call far in advance for a table. And don't forget to wear your designer leather.

See map p. 141. 1520 N. Damen Ave. (1 block south of North Avenue). ☎ *773-252-1500. CTA: Blue-line El to Damen. Reservations recommended. Main courses: $16–$27. AE, DC, DISC, MC, V. Open: Mon–Thurs 5:30–10:30 p.m., Fri–Sat 5:30–11:30 p.m., Sun 10 a.m.–2:30 p.m. and 5:30–10 p.m.*

Nine
$$$–$$$$ Loop   SEAFOOD/STEAKHOUSE

Less hip than it was a few years ago, when Chicago's trendsetters flocked here in droves, Nine still features such crowd-pleasers as plasma TV screens in the seductive lounge and the boys' restroom, a circular "ice bar" just for champagne and caviar, and an upstairs Ghost Lounge, whose signature drink is a glow-in-the-dark Midori martini. The icy, metallic look of mirrored tiles and stainless steel is warmed with the use of ash wood in the décor. And the food is based on straightforward favorites of steak and seafood. You find grouper, ahi tuna, a 22-ounce veal porterhouse, and filet mignon on the menu — most with an interesting twist. (The grouper, for example, is served with bacon, escarole, and beans in a Cabernet reduction.)

See map p. 133. 440 W. Randolph St. (at North Canal Street). ☎ *312-575-9900. CTA: Bus no. 125 or 129 to Randolph and Canal. Reservations recommended. Main courses: $15–$33. AE, DC, MC, V. Open: Mon–Thurs 11:30 a.m.–2 p.m. and 5:30–10 p.m., Fri 11:30 a.m.–2p.m. and 5 p.m. to midnight, Sat 5 p.m. to midnight. Ghost Bar: Thurs–Fri 9 p.m.–2 a.m., Sat 9 p.m.–3 a.m.*

Orange
$$ North Side   AMERICAN

The brunch here will last you until at least dinner. In fact, breakfast, lunch, and multiple combinations of the two is all that this place serves. On weekends, the wait starts as soon as the door opens and doesn't let up until about 1:30 p.m. And with creative variations on traditional breakfast favorites, it's not hard to see why. The pan-seared cut oatmeal with dried fruit compote and apple cider–brown sugar syrup tastes more like pie than Quaker Oats. You'll find a different theme each week (such as apples) for the pancake "flight" — four silver-dollar-sized stacks of buttermilk pancakes served in a slightly different way. And, no, that isn't your mother's hash, unless she uses Guinness-braised brisket and butternut squash. Other favorites include the puff pastry and fruit smoothies blended with whatever juices you request. A second location rests in the South Loop at 75 W. Harrison St. (☎ **312-447-1000**).

See map p. 136. 3231 N. Clark St. (north of Belmont Avenue). ☎ *773-549-4400. CTA: Red-line El to Belmont. Reservations not accepted. Main courses: $5–$12. DISC, MC, V. Open: Tues–Sun 8 a.m.–3 p.m.*

Pump Room
$$$ Gold Coast   FRENCH

Chicago's most iconic restaurant was once the bastion of stars whose appearance in Booth One would guarantee a photo in the newspaper the next morning. Today, the Pump Room is slightly less star-filled — but the room has been restored to its former glory, in the original cobalt-blue-and-gold décor. Service is now provided by a well-trained crew, and the food is classic American dishes with a sophisticated twist. Appetizers include a simple beef tartare or a caviar plate, or a "flight" of different foie gras preparations. Entrees also provide some creative twists on old classics, including Maine lobster with apple-tarragon puree, or lamb loin with a mint pesto crust. There's a live band and dancing every Friday and Saturday night from 8 p.m. to midnight.

The Pump Room has a dress code — and it's enforced. Men must wear jackets after 4 p.m., and no jeans are allowed.

See map p. 133. 1301 N. State Parkway (in the Omni Ambassador East Hotel). ☎ *312-266-0360. CTA: Bus no. 151 to Goethe Street; red-line El to Division Street, walk 2 blocks east to State, then 2 blocks north. Reservations required. Main courses: $23–$36. AE, DC, DISC, MC, V. Open: Mon–Thurs 7 a.m.–2 p.m. and 6–10 p.m., Fri–Sat 7 a.m.–2 p.m. and 6 p.m. to midnight, Sun 10:30 a.m.–2 p.m. and 6–10 p.m.*

Saloon Steakhouse
$$–$$$ Streeterville STEAKHOUSE

The Saloon Steakhouse is all that a steakhouse should be. It has a warm, cheery look and is usually filled with happy, animated carnivores attacking high-quality cuts of flavorful beef. You can't go wrong with steaks, suitably marbled and dry-aged, but many regulars go for the 16-ounce bone-in filet mignon prepared in the restaurant's smoker. Be sure to try a side of bacon-scallion mashed potatoes.

See map p. 133. 200 E. Chestnut St. (at Mies van der Rohe Way). ☎ *312-280-5454. CTA: Bus no. 151 to Chestnut, then walk 1 block west. Reservations recommended. Main courses: $13–$35. AE, DC, DISC, MC, V. Open: Mon–Thurs 11:30 a.m.–10 p.m., Fri 11:30 a.m.–11 p.m., Sat 4–11 p.m., Sun 4–10 p.m.*

Shaw's Crab House and Blue Crab Lounge
$$ River North SEAFOOD

You'd swear you stepped into a 1940s-era restaurant on the Atlantic Coast when you enter Shaw's. The busy dining room has a lively feel, and the extensive menu should suit all tastes. The appetizers alone run the gamut from popcorn shrimp and fried calamari to exotic sushi combinations. Fresh seafood is the specialty, with fried smelt, sautéed sea scallops, and grilled fish among the fare. The adjoining Blue Crab Lounge offers an excellent raw bar and jazz or blues — although some of us are entertained simply by watching the shuckers do their thing.

See map p. 133. 21 E. Hubbard St. (between State Street and Wabash Avenue). ☎ *312-527-2722. www.shawscrabhouse.com/chicago. CTA: Red-line El to State/Grand. Reservations accepted for the main dining room. Main courses: $14–$31. AE, DC, DISC, MC, V. Open: Mon–Thurs 11:30 a.m.–2 p.m. and 5:30–10 p.m., Fri 11:30 a.m.–2 p.m. and 5–11 p.m., Sat 5–11 p.m., Sun 5–10 p.m.*

Soju
$$ Bucktown/Wicker Park KOREAN

Until Soju opened, it was difficult to find authentic Korean food outside of certain Korean neighborhoods on the North Side of the city. This restaurant, therefore, is a welcome addition, offering tasty Korean fare in a casual, urban setting — a step above neighborhood ethnic dining, and priced accordingly. The menu is slightly Americanized, with a few basic sushi offerings, and is broken down into American-style courses. The kimchi-rice flour pancakes are served with a soy-and-sesame dipping sauce, and the suun-dubu, a spicy soft tofu casserole, is not to be missed. The signature house chicken entree is sauced with *soju,* a vodka-like Korean liquor, and the classic *bibimbop,* a mixture of rice and vegetables, can be ordered with beef, chicken, or tofu.

See map p. 141. 1745 W. North Ave. (by N. Wood Street). ☎ *773-782-9000.* www. sojuchicago.com. *CTA: Blue-line El to Damen. Reservations for large parties only. Main courses: $11–$15. AE, DC, DISC, MC, V. Open: Mon–Thurs 6–10 p.m., Fri–Sat 6–11 p.m.*

Spring
$$$ Bucktown/Wicker Park   AMERICAN

This former Russian bathhouse has been transformed into an oasis of Zen calm. This restaurant attracted national attention when it opened, and it still attracts foodies. Diners step down into a dining room hidden from the street, then sink into banquettes that zigzag across the center of the room. The menu emphasizes seafood and pan-Asian preparations. Appetizers include an aromatic lemon grass–red curry broth with rice noodles, and sea scallop and potato ravioli with sautéed mushrooms and truffle essence. Most of the entrees are seafood based: New Zealand snapper with lemon couscous and fennel salad is one example. Desserts tend to go the Asian route, although the coconut brûlée with warm pineapple puts a whole new twist on rice pudding.

See map p. 141. 2039 W. North Ave. (at Milwaukee Avenue). ☎ *773-395-7100.* www.springrestaurant.net. *CTA: Blue-line El to Damen. Reservations recommended. Main courses $16–$25. AE, DC, DISC, MC, V. Open: Tues–Thurs 5:30–10 p.m., Fri–Sat 5:30–11 p.m., Sun 5:30–9 p.m.*

Stanley's
$ Lincoln Park   AMERICAN

Here's a great neighborhood bar and restaurant that stands in the heart of Lincoln Park, the epicenter of the young and the restless, but which also welcomes families. Stanley's front room is a bar with several booths, tall tables with old chrome-and-leather bar stools, satellite- and cable-fed TVs, and a jukebox. The adjacent dining room is an abrupt leap into the family den, decorated with photos, quilts, bowling trophies, and children's drawings. This popular family spot has a special kids' menu with corn dogs and PB&J. On Saturday and Sunday there's an all-you-can-eat brunch buffet, featuring make-your-own omelets, build-your-own-Belgian waffles, home-fried potatoes, fried chicken, and mashed potatoes for $11. Daily specials are posted on the chalkboard out front.

See map p. 136. 1970 N. Lincoln Ave.(by North Sedgwick Street). ☎ *312-642-0007. CTA: Bus no. 11 or 73 to Armitage. Main courses: $8–$15; kids' menu $4. Mon and Tues 5 p.m.–2 a.m.; Wed–Fri 11:30 a.m.–2 a.m.; Sat 11 a.m.–3 a.m.; Sun 11 a.m.–2a.m.*

Sushisamba Rio
$$$ River North   LATIN AMERICAN/SUSHI

Latin American ceviche combined with sushi seems an odd juxtaposition, but it works surprising well at this new restaurant, which is based on a Peruvian and Brazilian culinary tradition that was created when Japanese immigrants moved there in the early 20th century. The dramatic dining room has become a fashionable scene, and tables are scattered on different levels, some in a sunken red "conversation pit," others up on a balcony along one wall. Beaded curtains hang from the ceiling and bathrooms are set in a bamboo-filled garden. But after admiring the scenery, what will you eat? Try one of the creative "samba rolls," which combine the traditional sticky-rice-and-seaweed wrapping with unexpected fillings. The El Topo, a mix of salmon, jalapeno pepper, fresh melted mozzarella, and crispy onions, is delicious; also worth trying is the Samba Rio roll, with guava-glazed short ribs and sweet pepper. More straightforward is the Surf & Turf, here interpreted as seared rare tuna and a tender beef filet on a bed of carrot-and-ginger puree.

See map p. 133. 504 N. Wells St. (by West Illinois Street). ☎ *312-595-2300.* www. sushisamba.com. *Reservations recommended. Main courses: $8–$17 lunch, $12–$29 dinner. AE, DC, DISC, MC, V. Open: Sun–Tues 11:45 a.m.–11 p.m., Wed 11:45 a.m. to midnight, Thurs–Fri 11:45 a.m.–1 a.m., Sat 11:45 a.m.–2 a.m.*

Sushi Wabi
$$ Randolph Street Market District   JAPANESE/SUSHI

The minimal-chic décor is industrial and raw, and the lighting is dark and seductive at one of Chicago's hippest sushi restaurants, which attracts the young and the restless. You'll be rewarded for getting a table here with interesting sashimi and sushi, plus maki rolls like the "dragon" — rolled eel and avocado with tempura shrimp as the dragon's head and tail. Desserts are excellent and put green tea and red-bean ice cream to new and creative uses. If you don't make a reservation, be prepared to wait. While you're cooling your heels, try a martini with a ginger-stuffed olive or one of a large variety of chilled sakes.

To get here, take a taxi — about a $5 ride from the Loop.

See map p. 133. 842 W. Randolph St. (by North Green Street). ☎ *312-563-1224.* www. sushiwabi.com. *Reservations recommended. Main courses: $10–$24. AE, DC, DISC, MC, V. Open: Mon–Fri 11:30 a.m.–2 p.m. and 5 p.m. to midnight, Sat 5 p.m. to midnight, Sun 5–11 p.m.*

Tango Sur
$ North Side   ARGENTINE

This upbeat storefront restaurant, located in one of my favorite neighborhoods, often has lines outside for the mouth-watering Argentine barbecue. Tango music provides the backdrop for the imported Argentine beef, mixed grill of short ribs, sweetbreads, chorizo, and *morcilla* (blood sausage) with *chimichurri* (parsley, garlic, and olive oil). Empanadas are a specialty. Be forewarned: If you want a drink, it's BYOB. Afterwards, head down the block to Cullen's for a drink, or catch a movie at Chicago's most charming old-time theater, the Music Box (see Chapter 15), where an organist plays before the show.

See map p. 136. 3763 N. Southport (south of Irving Park Road). ☎ *773-477-5466. CTA: Brown-line El to Belmont, then walk north. Reservations not accepted. Main courses: $4.29–$18. AE, DC, DISC, MC, V. Open: Mon–Thurs 5–10:30 p.m., Sat 5:30–11 p.m., Sun noon to 11:30 p.m.*

Trattoria No. 10
$$ Loop ITALIAN

This ideal pre-theater spot is located underground on Dearborn Street and is a favorite with Chicagoans who work in the Loop. Even though it's underground, the place has a Tuscan feel, with dimly lit rooms and a warm, orangey glow. Ceramic floor tiles and gracefully arched ceilings complement the décor. The real bargain here is the wonderful (and cheap) after-work buffet ($12 all-you-can-eat with a $6 drink minimum). In the dining room, pasta reigns. Ravioli (try the butternut squash version, topped with walnut sauce) is supreme, as is the farfalle with duck confit, asparagus, caramelized onions, and pine nuts.

See map p. 133. 10 N. Dearborn St. (between Madison and Washington streets). ☎ *312-984-1718. CTA: Red- or blue-line El to Dearborn. Reservations recommended. Main courses: $14–$27. AE, DC, DISC, MC, V. Open: Mon–Thurs 11:30 a.m.–2 p.m. and 5:30–9 p.m., Fri 11:30 a.m.–2 p.m. and 5:30–10 p.m., Sat 5:30–10 p.m.*

Tuscany on Taylor
$$ Little Italy ITALIAN

This restaurant is the real thing, one of the most reliable restaurants in Little Italy, with green-checkered tablecloths and waiters who wax poetic over pasta. Family-owned Tuscany features large portions of Tuscan pastas and specializes in Tuscan sausage dishes and anything cooked on the wood-burning grill. Some of the meals are so rich you won't need dessert. By the end of your dinner, you'll feel like part of the family. Other Tuscan fare includes pizzas, veal, chicken, and a risotto of the day. A second location is across from Wrigley Field at 3700 N. Clark (☎ 773-404-7700).

See map p. 133. 1014 W. Taylor St. (between Racine Avenue and Halsted Street). ☎ *312-829-1990.* www.stefanirestaurants.com. *CTA: Blue-line El to Polk. Reservations recommended. Main courses: $10–$28. AE, DC, DISC, MC, V. Open: Lunch Mon–Fri 11 a.m.–3:30 p.m.; dinner Mon–Thurs 5–11 p.m., Fri–Sat 5 p.m. to midnight, Sun 4–9:30 p.m.*

Twin Anchors
$ Old Town   BARBECUE

Although it keeps classy company in a neighborhood of elegant brown-stones, this eatery is strictly a rib joint. Done in dark mahogany and serv-iceable Formica, Twin Anchors has been around since the days when the Untouchables battled to clean up the city. Sinatra was an occasional patron, and you find Ol' Blue Eyes featured prominently on the walls and the jukebox. Meaty slabs of slow-cooked baby back ribs are fall-off-the-bone tender (go for the zesty sauce). You can also get steaks and chicken — but ribs are what keep people coming back. For dessert, there's a daily cheesecake selection. On the weekends, prepare for a long wait.

See map p. 136 1655 N. Sedgwick St. (1 block north of North Avenue). ☎ *312-266-1616.* www.twinanchorsribs.com. *CTA: Brown-line El to Sedgwick. Reservations not accepted. Main courses: $9.95–$20. AE, DC, DISC, MC, V. Open: Mon–Thurs 5–11 p.m., Fri 5 p.m. to midnight, Sat noon to midnight, Sun noon to 10:30 p.m.*

Vivo
$$–$$$ Randolph Street Market District   ITALIAN

In 1991, this restaurant was a pioneer, constructed in an old warehouse in the produce market just west of the Loop. Today, the Market District has become one of the city's dining hot spots, with restaurants scattered among the onions and tomatoes. The glitterati still gather at Vivo, which remains hip *and* affordable. The daily spread of antipasti is always worth sampling. You can't go wrong with the rigatoni or the roasted lamb chops, served with sautéed garlic spinach. Pastas include a black linguine with crabmeat or a daily homemade ravioli selection. For dessert, try the excellent

---

Worth the trip

If you have a car in Chicago, these restaurants are worth a trip to the suburbs. All are within 30 to 60 minutes of downtown.

- ✔ **Phil Smidt's,** Hammond, Indiana (☎ 219-659-0025): Just across the Chicago Skyway (close to the Indiana gambling boats), you find great all-you-can-eat perch dinners followed by tart gooseberry pie. Closed on Monday.

- ✔ **White Fence Farm,** Lemont, Illinois (☎ 630-739-1720): Here you find the best fried chicken north of the Mason-Dixon line, served with all the fixings.

- ✔ **Robinson's No. 1 Ribs,** Oak Park, Illinois (☎ 708-383-8452): Backyard Chef Charlie Robinson parlayed a win in the late Mike Royko's first annual rib cook-off into this large and extremely popular venue. The restaurant serves smoky ribs and a secret sauce made with 17 herbs and spices.

- ✔ **Hecky's Barbecue,** Evanston, Illinois (☎ 847-492-1182): Head north to this rib joint, which also smokes hot pork links, chicken, and turkey drumsticks.

double-chocolate cake with espresso sauce — and with this dose of caffeine, be prepared to stay awake well into the evening! Vivo's most requested seating is a solitary table poised atop an old elevator shaft. Celebrities and the romantically inclined tend to sit here. Call well in advance to reserve this special place.

To get here, take a taxi — about a $5 ride from the Loop.

See map p. 133. 838 W. Randolph Ave. (at Halsted St.). ☎ *312-733-3379.* www. vivo-chicago.com. *Reservations recommended. Main courses: $13–$26. AE, DC, MC, V. Open: Mon–Wed 11:30 a.m.–2:30 p.m. and 5–10:30 p.m., Thurs 11:30 a.m.–2:30 p.m. and 5–11 p.m., Fri 11:30 a.m.–2:30 p.m. and 5 p.m. to midnight, Sat 5 p.m. to midnight, Sun 5–10 p.m.*

Wave
$$–$$$ Streeterville   AMERICAN/ECLECTIC

Located in the W Hotel Lakeshore, this has been called Chicago's hippest hotel dining room. The sophisticated and cool furnishings are topped off by a red canopy that crests like a wave overhead. Wave's Ice Bar is a see-and-be-seen hangout with a fresh spin on cocktails. (Case in point: Try the Linie aquavit on the rocks with orange syrup and pink peppercorns). Most of Wave's entrees, which include plenty of fish, are prepared with Mediterranean accents. Favorites include the toasted fennel seed New York strip steak and whole fish.

See map p. 133. 644 N. Lake Shore Dr. (at East Ontario Street). ☎ *312-255-4460. CTA: Bus no. 151 to Ontario Street, then walk east to Lake Shore Drive. Reservations recommended. Main courses: $17–$29. AE, DC, DISC, MC, V. Open: Sun–Thurs 6:30 a.m.–10 p.m., Fri–Sat 6:30 a.m.–11 p.m.*

Wishbone
$ Randolph St. Market District/North Side   CAJUN/SOUTHERN

Primitive art decorates this bright, open restaurant that's always bustling. It's one of the few restaurants in Chicago that draws a highly diverse crowd, from Harpo Studios employees (Oprah is headquartered just around the corner) to families, suits, and creative types. The breakfast is outstanding — try the salmon cakes. Dinner offerings may include pan-fried chicken, jambalaya, or chicken étoufée. For dessert, the tart Key lime pie is a stand out. If you're looking for a place to eat on the North Side, check out the Wishbone location in the Lakeview neighborhood at 3300 N. Lincoln, just north of Belmont (☎ 773-549-2663).

To get there, take a taxi — about a $5 ride from the Loop.

See map p. 133. 1001 W. Washington St. (at Morgan Street). ☎ *312-850-2663. Reservations accepted, except for weekend brunch. Main courses: $5.25–$9.50 breakfast and lunch, $6.95–$14 dinner. AE, DC, DISC, MC, V. Open: Mon 7 a.m.–3 p.m., Tues–Fri 7 a.m.–3 p.m. and 5–9 p.m., Sat 8 a.m.–3 p.m. and 5–10 p.m., Sun 8 a.m.–3 p.m.*

Dining and Snacking on the Go

Being a tourist can really take it out of you. Sometimes all you want is to rest your aching feet and reenergize with a quick snack. Unlike New York, Chicago doesn't have battalions of pushcart food vendors (thankfully — their absence keeps the sidewalks clear and cuts down on greasy smells). But this city does have great portable food and quick eats. Maybe you've burned off your lunch more quickly than expected. Or maybe you have only an hour to squeeze in a meal before a show. You're in luck: Chicago's got what you want.

Carnivore favorites

Local carnivore favorites include Italian beef and Italian sausage sandwiches. My favorite spot for these specialties is **Mr. Beef on Orleans,** 666 N. Orleans St., between Erie and Huron streets (☎ **312-337-8500**). This hole-in-the-wall eatery has a counter up front and seating at picnic benches in the rear. When Jim Belushi and Jay Leno are in Chicago, they stop by, as do local media celebs. There are two main decisions to make: whether you want an Italian beef (juicy, thinly sliced, piled high) or an Italian sausage (charbroiled and spicy), and whether you want toppings of hot or sweet peppers. Each sandwich is packed into a chewy roll. If you can't decide, order a combo.

Another good choice is **Al's Italian Beef,** with its two branches at 169 W. Ontario St. at Wells Street (☎ **312-943-3222**) and 1079 W. Taylor St., between Aberdeen and Carpenter in Little Italy (☎ **312-226-4017**).

Refreshing Italian ice

If you're going the low-fat route (or even if you aren't), you'll enjoy **Mario's Italian Lemonade** in Little Italy, 1068 W. Taylor St. (no phone). From May to late October, the stand sells refreshing Italian ice — cups of shaved ice doused with syrup (traditional lemon flavor and a variety of others). **Tom and Wendee's Italian Ice,** 1136 W. Armitage Ave. at Clifton Street, Lincoln Park (☎ **773-327-2885**) sells a version made with fresh fruit rather than syrup.

Chicago treats

Deep-dish pizza may be Chicago's culinary claim to fame, but the city has also added to the national waistline in other ways. Twinkies and Wonder Bread were invented here; Chicago businessman James L. Kraft created the first processed cheese; and Oscar Mayer got his start as a butcher in the Old Town neighborhood.

World-famous Chicago hot dogs

"Hot dogs" in Chicago mean Vienna All-Beef franks served with mustard, green relish, chopped onion, sliced tomato, hot peppers, and celery salt. Ketchup is another option, though purists don't use it. Several popular chains sell these delicious dogs. One of these is **Gold Coast Dogs,** 159 N. Wabash Ave., at Randolph Street (☎ 312-917-1677). Gold Coast Dogs is a place where you can grab your food and run, or join the crowd in the restaurant. Get a Vienna hot dog and top it with the works, Chicago-style. Finish off your meal with a thick shake in chocolate, vanilla, or strawberry. It's open Monday to Friday from 10 a.m. to 8 p.m., Saturday 10 a.m. to 6 p.m., and Sunday 10 a.m. to 6 p.m.

Fluky's, in the Westfield North Bridge mall at 520 N. Michigan Ave. (☎ 312-245-0702), is part of a local chain that has been serving great hot dogs since the Depression. **Portillo's,** 100 W. Ontario St. (☎ 312-587-8930), is another local chain that specializes in hot dogs but also serves excellent pastas and salads. **Byron's** serves Vienna All-Beef hot dogs at three locations: 1017 W. Irving Park Rd. (☎ 773-281-7474), 1701 W. Lawrence (☎ 773-271-0900), and 680 N. Halsted St. (☎ 312-738-0968).

Fast food with big flavors

Chicagoans in the know head for **Potbelly Sandwich Works.** The made-to-order grilled sub sandwiches on warm, crusty homemade bread can be loaded up with all sorts of meats, cheeses, and veggies. The shakes are fantastic, too. Yes, there's even a potbellied stove inside and all sorts of Old West–type memorabilia. From the original at 2264 N. Lincoln Ave., between Belden and Webster (☎ 773-528-1405), the franchise has grown to ten locations in Chicago, including 190 N. State St. at Lake Street in the Loop (☎ 312-683-1234) and 520 N. Michigan Ave, in the Westfield North Bridge shopping center (☎ 312-664-1008), which are convenient to the Loop and the Magnificent Mile.

Also in the Loop (in the Sears Tower, to be exact) is **Mrs. Levy's Delicatessen,** a retro deli that displays signed photographs of famous patrons. Staples such as knishes, blintzes, and soups are made daily from scratch. Sandwiches are piled high and include such standards as corned beef, beef brisket, and pastrami; soup choices include sweet-and-sour

I scream, you scream . . .

Worth the trip is **Margie's Candies**, 1960 N. Western Ave. at Armitage Avenue (☎ 773-384-1035), a classic ice-cream parlor that makes its own hot fudge, butterscotch, and caramel. The place is frozen in time; from the looks of it, time froze in the 1940s (the place has been in existence since 1921). Margie's serves sundaes in giant dishes shaped like conch shells.

cabbage, chicken matzo ball, and mushroom barley. You can find Mrs. Levy's on the mezzanine level of the Sears Tower, 233 S. Wacker Dr. (☎ **312-993-0530**).

Corner Bakery offers cafeteria-style dining and sandwiches, soups, salads, pastas, and pizzas. (Plus, check out the bakery items — hard to resist!) Over a dozen locations are spread around the downtown area. Two of the larger ones are located at 676 N. St. Clair at Erie Street (☎ **312-266-2570**) and 1121 N. State St. near Cedar Street (☎ **312-787-1969**).

Foodlife, located on the mezzanine level of Water Tower Place, at 835 N. Michigan Ave. (☎ **312-335-3663**), takes the concept of "food court" to a higher level. Here you find many healthy alternatives to fast food. A dozen or so kiosks offer everything from barbecued chicken to Asian stir-fry, from pizza to low-fat Caesar salad. A hostess will seat you and give you an electronic card, and then it's up to you to stroll around and select whatever food suits your fancy (each purchase is recorded on your card, and you pay on the way out).

If you're a TV fan, you've probably heard the phrase "Cheeborger, cheeborger, chip, chip. No Coke — Pepsi," made famous by John Belushi's crabby Greek short-order cook on *Saturday Night Live.* Chicago's **Billy Goat Tavern,** 430 N. Michigan Ave. (☎ **312-222-1525**), served as the inspiration for Belushi's character. The Billy Goat is a hangout for newspaper writers from the nearby Tribune and Sun-Times buildings. Come on down (it's below street level) for a beer and a burger; you'll get a real Chicago experience.

I would be remiss in writing about Chicago if I omitted McDonald's (because the company headquarters is in suburban Oak Brook). One of the chain's most profitable franchises, the **Rock-N-Roll McDonald's,** 600 N. Clark St. at Ohio Street (☎ **312-867-0455**), was torn down in July 2004. A new and improved flagship store opened in the same location in April 2005.

World-famous pizza

Chicago has three pizza styles: Chicago-style, also known as deep-dish, which is thick-crusted and often demands a knife and fork; stuffed, which is similar to a pie, with a crust on both top and bottom; and thin-crust. Many pizzerias serve both deep-dish and thin, and some make all three kinds.

Three of Chicago's best gourmet deep-dish restaurants are **Pizzeria Uno,** 29 E. Ohio St. at Wabash Avenue (☎ **312-321-1000**); **Pizzeria Due,** 619 N. Wabash Ave. at Ontario Street (☎ **312-943-2400**); and **Gino's East** (see earlier in this chapter).

In River North, **Lou Malnati's Pizzeria,** 439 N. Wells St. (☎ **312-828-9800**), bakes both deep-dish and thin-crust pizza and even has a low-fat-cheese option.

Edwardo's is a local pizza chain that serves all three varieties, but with a wheat crust and all-natural ingredients (spinach pizza is the specialty here); locations are in the Gold Coast at 1212 N. Dearborn St. at Division Street (☎ 312-337-4490), in the South Loop at 521 S. Dearborn St. (☎ 312-939-3366), and in Lincoln Park at 2662 N. Halsted St. (☎ 773-871-3400). Not far from Lincoln Park Zoo is **Ranalli's Pizzeria, Libations & Collectibles,** 1925 N. Lincoln Ave. (☎ 312-642-4700), with its terrific open-air patio and extensive selection of beers.

In Wrigleyville, just off Belmont Avenue, are **Leona's Pizzeria,** 3215 N. Sheffield Ave. (☎ 773-327-8861), and **Pat's Pizzeria,** 3114 N. Sheffield Ave. (☎ 773-248-0168), both of which serve all three kinds of pizza. Leona's also has a location in Little Italy at 1419 W. Taylor St. (☎ 312-850-2222), and Pat's has one downtown in the Athletic Club Illinois Center at 211 N. Stetson Ave. (☎ 312-946-0220).

Tea or coffee

If you're shopping on the Magnificent Mile and feel like having an elegant afternoon tea complete with finger sandwiches, scones, and pastries, go to the Palm Court at the **Drake,** 140 E. Walton Place (☎ 312-787-2200), or the sunny Seasons Lounge of the **Four Seasons Hotel,** 120 E. Delaware Place (☎ 312-280-8800). A fine afternoon tea is also served at the Greenhouse at the **Ritz-Carlton,** 160 E. Pearson St. (☎ 312-266-1000), in the 12th-floor lobby above the Water Tower Place mall.

On the North Side, you can head to one of my favorite coffee shops, **Uncommon Grounds,** 1214 W. Grace St. at Clark Street (☎ 773-929-3680), which serves up fine breakfasts and sandwiches, plus wine and beer. In fact, a good portion of this book was written there, so you know you can hang out for hours without anyone bothering you!

Index of Establishments by Neighborhood

Andersonville
Ann Sather (Breakfast and Scandinavian, $)
Francesca's on Taylor (Italian, $$)
Mia Francesca (Italian, $$)
Swedish Bakery (Sweets, $)
Svea Restaurant (Scandinavian, $)

Bucktown/Wicker Park
Café Absinthe (Eclectic, $$$)
Jane's (Eclectic, $$)
Le Bouchon (Bistro, $$)
Margie's Candies (Sweets, $)
Mas (Latin American, $$$)

Meritage Café and Wine Bar (American, $$$)
Mirai Sushi (Japanese/Sushi, $$$)
MOD (American, $$$)
Soju (Korean, $$)
Spring (American, $$$)

Chinatown
Emperor's Choice (Chinese, $$)
Three Happiness (Chinese, $$)

Gold Coast
Bistro Zinc (Bistro, $$)
Corner Bakery (American, $)

Edwardo's (Pizza, $)
Gibson's Steakhouse (Steakhouse, $$$$)
Pump Room (French, $$$)

Greektown
Pegasus (Greek, $$)
Santorini (Greek, $$)

Lincoln Park
Ambria (French, $$$$)
Charlie Trotter's (Nouvelle, $$$$$)
Edwardo's (Pizza, $)
Potbelly Sandwich Works (Cajun, $)
Ranalli's Pizzeria, Libations &
Collectibles (Pizza, $)
Stanley's (American, $)
Thai Classic (Thai, $$)
Tom and Wendee's Italian Ice
(Sweets, $)

Lincoln Square
Chicago Brahaus (German, $$)
Meyer's Delicatessen (German, $$)
Merz Apothecary (German, $$)

Little Italy
Al's Italian Beef (Steakhouse, $)
Chez Joël (Bistro, $$)
Francesca's on Taylor (Italian, $$)
Mia Francesca (Italian, $$)
Mario's Italian Lemonade (Sweets, $)
Rosebud (Italian, $$)
Scafuri Bakery (Sweets, $)
Tuscany on Taylor (Italian, $$)

Loop
Atwood Café (Eclectic, $$)
Berghoff (German, $$)
Bin 36 (American, $$–$$$)
Edwardo's (Pizza, $)
Gold Coast Dogs (American, $)
Heaven on Seven (Cajun, $$)
Italian Village (Italian, $$)
Lou Mitchell's (American, $)
Mrs. Levy's Delicatessen (American, $)

Potbelly Sandwich Works (Cajun, $)
Nine (Seafood/Steakhouse, $$$–$$$$)
Trattoria No. 10 (Italian, $$)

Logan Square
Red Apple Restaurant (Eclectic, $)

Magnificent Mile
Amarit (Thai, $$)
Billy Goat Tavern (American, $)
Bistro 110 (American, $$)
Corner Bakery (Breakfast, $)
Drake (Eclectic, $$)
Fluky's (American, $)
Foodlife (American, $)
Four Season Hotel (Eclectic, $$)
Heaven on Seven (Cajun, $$)
Jake Melnick's (American, $–$$)
Joe's Seafood, Prime Steak and Stone
Crab (Seafood/Steakhouse, $$–$$$)
Mike Ditka's Restaurant (Steakhouse,
$$–$$$)
Ritz-Carlton (Eclectic, $$)

North Side
Ann Sather (Breakfast and
Scandinavian, $)
Arun's (Thai, $$$$$)
Flat Top Grill (Asian, $)
Mia Francesca (Italian, $$)
Orange (American, $$)
Tango Sur (Argentine, $)
Uncommon Grounds (Eclectic, $)
Wishbone (Cajun/Southern, $)

Old Town
Flat Top Grill (Asian, $)
Kamehachi (Japanese/Sushi, $$)
Twin Anchors (Barbecue, $)

Randolph Street Market District
Avec (Eclectic, $$–$$$)
Flat Top Grill (Asian, $)
Sushi Wabi (Japanese/Sushi, $$)
Vivo (Italian, $$–$$$)
Wishbone (Cajun/Southern, $)

River North

Al's Italian Beef (Steakhouse, $)
Ben Pao (Chinese, $$)
Byron's (American, $)
Café Iberico (Spanish, $)
Carson's (Barbecue, $$)
Chilpancingo (Mexican, $$)
Coco Pazzo (Italian, $$$)
Cyrano's Bistro, Wine Bar & Cabaret (Bistro, $$)
Frontera Grill and Topolobampo (Mexican, $$–$$$$)
Gene & Georgetti (Steakhouse, $$)
Gino's East (Pizza, $)
Green Zebra (Vegetarian, $$$)
Harry Caray's (Italian/Steakhouse, $$–$$$)
Keefer's (Steakhouse, $$$)
Lou Malnati's Pizzeria (Pizza, $)
Maggiano's (Italian, $$)
mk (American, $$$)
Mr. Beef on Orleans (Steakhouses, $)
Pizzeria Due (Pizza, $)
Pizzeria Uno (Pizza, $)
Portillo's (American, $)

Potbelly Sandwich Works (Cajun, $)
Rock-N-Roll McDonald's (American, $)
Ruth's Chris Steak House (Steakhouse, $$$)
Shaw's Crab House and Blue Crab Lounge (Seafood, $$)
Smith & Wollensky (Steakhouse, $$$)
Star of Siam (Thai, $$)
Sushisamba Rio (Latin American/Sushi, $$$)

Streeterville

Bice Ristorante (Italian, $$–$$$)
Eli's The Place for Steak (Steakhouse, $$–$$$)
Morton's (Steakhouse, $$$)
Saloon Steakhouse (Steakhouse, $$–$$$)
Wave (American/Eclectic, $$–$$$)

Wrigleyville

Byron's (American, $)
Leona's Pizzeria (Pizza, $)
Pat's Pizzeria (Pizza, $)

Index of Establishments by Cuisine

American

Billy Goat Tavern (Magnificent Mile, $)
Bin 36 (Loop, $$–$$$)
Bistro 110 (Magnificent Mile, $$)
Byron's (River North and Wrigleyville, $)
Fluky's (Magnificent Mile, $)
Foodlife (Magnificent Mile, $)
Gold Coast Dogs (Loop, $)
Jake Melnick's (Magnificent Mile, $–$$)
Lou Mitchell's (Loop, $)
Meritage Café and Wine Bar (Bucktown/Wicker Park, $$$)
mk (River North, $$$)
MOD (Bucktown/Wicker Park, $$$)
Mrs. Levy's Delicatessen (Loop, $)
Orange (North Side, $$)
Portillo's (River North, $)
Rock-N-Roll McDonald's (River North, $)

Spring (Bucktown/Wicker Park, $$$)
Stanley's (Lincoln Park, $)
Wave (Streeterville, $$–$$$)

Argentine

Tango Sur (North Side, $)

Asian

Flat Top Grill (Old Town, North Side, and Randolph Street Market District, $)

Barbecue

Carson's (River North, $$)
Twin Anchors (Old Town, $)

Bistro

Bistro Zinc (Gold Coast, $$)
Chez Joël (Little Italy, $$)

Cyrano's Bistro, Wine Bar & Cabaret (River North, $$)
Le Bouchon (Bucktown/Wicker Park, $$)

Breakfast

Ann Sather (Andersonville and North Side, $)
Corner Bakery (Magnificent Mile and Gold Coast, $)
Lou Mitchell's (Loop, $)
Orange (North Side, $)
Wishbone (North Side and Randolph Street Market District, $)

Cajun/Creole/Southern

Heaven on Seven (Loop and Magnificent Mile, $$)
Potbelly Sandwich Works (Lincoln Park, Loop, and River North $)
Wishbone (North Side and Randolph Street Market District, $)

Chinese

Ben Pao (River North, $$)
Emperor's Choice (Chinatown, $$)
Three Happiness (Chinatown, $$)

Eclectic

Atwood Café (Loop, $$)
Avec (Randolph Street Market District, $$-$$$)
Drake (Magnificent Mile, $$)
Café Absinthe (Bucktown/Wicker Park, $$$)
Four Seasons Hotel (Magnificent Mile, $$)
Jane's (Bucktown/Wicker Park, $$)
Red Apple Restaurant (Logan Square, $)
Ritz-Carlton (Magnificent Mile, $$)
Uncommon Grounds (North Side, $)
Wave (Streeterville, $$-$$$)

French

Ambria (Lincoln Park, $$$$)
Pump Room (Gold Coast, $$$)

German

Berghoff (Loop, $$)
Chicago Brauhaus (Lincoln Square, $$)
Meyer's Delicatessen (Lincoln Square, $$)
Merz Apothecary (Lincoln Square, $$)

Greek

Pegasus (Greektown, $$)
Santorini (Greektown, $$)

Italian

Bice Ristorante (Streeterville, $$-$$$)
Coco Pazzo (River North, $$$)
Francesca's on Taylor (Little Italy, $$)
Harry Caray's (River North, $$-$$$)
Italian Village (Loop, $$)
Maggiano's (North Side, $$)
Mia Francesca (North Side, Little Italy, Andersonville, $$)
Rosebud (Little Italy, $$)
Trattoria No. 10 (Loop, $$)
Tuscany on Taylor (Little Italy, $$)
Vivo (Randolph Street Market District, $$-$$$)

Japanese/Sushi

Kamehachi (Old Town, $$)
Mirai Sushi (Bucktown/Wicker Park, $$$)
Sushi Wabi (Randolph Street Market District, $$)
Sushisamba Rio (River North, $$$)

Korean

Soju (Bucktown/Wicker Park, $$)

Latin American

Mas (Bucktown/Wicker Park, $$$)
Sushisamba Rio (River North, $$$)

Mexican

Chilpancingo (River North, $$)
Frontera Grill and Topolobampo (River North, $$-$$$$)

Nouvelle
Charlie Trotter's (Lincoln Park, $$$$$)

Pizza
Edwardo's (Gold Coast, Loop, Lincoln Park, $)
Gino's East (River North, $)
Leona's Pizzeria (Wrigleyville, $)
Lou Malnati's Pizzeria (River North, $)
Pat's Pizzeria (Wrigleyville, $)
Pizzeria Due (River North, $)
Pizzeria Uno (River North, $)
Ranalli's Pizzeria, Libations and Collectibles (Lincoln Park, $)

Scandinavian
Ann Sather (Andersonville and North Side, $)
Svea Restaurant (Andersonville, $)

Seafood
Joe's Seafood, Prime Steak and Stone Crab (Magnificent Mile, $$–$$$)
Nine (Loop, $$$–$$$$)
Shaw's Crab House and Blue Crab Lounge (River North, $$)

Spanish
Café Iberico (River North, $)

Steakhouses
Al's Italian Beef (River North and Little Italy, $)
Eli's The Place for Steak (Streeterville, $$–$$$)

Gene & Georgetti (River North, $$)
Gibson's Steakhouse (Gold Coast, $$$$)
Harry Caray's (River North, $$–$$$)
Joe's Seafood, Prime Steak and Stone Crab (Magnificent Mile, $$–$$$)
Keefer's (River North, $$$)
Mike Ditka's Restaurant (Magnificent Mile, $$–$$$)
Morton's (Streeterville, $$$)
Mr. Beef on Orleans (River North, $)
Nine (Loop, $$$–$$$$)
Ruth's Chris Steak House (River North, $$$)
Saloon Steakhouse (Streeterville, $$–$$$)
Smith & Wollensky (River North, $$$)

Sweets
Mario's Italian Lemonade (Little Italy, $)
Margie's Candies (Bucktown/Wicker Park, $)
Scafuri Bakery (Little Italy, $)
Swedish Bakery (Andersonville, $)
Tom and Wendee's Italian Ice (Lincoln Park, $)

Thai
Amarit (Magnificent Mile, $$)
Arun's (North Side, $$$$$)
Star of Siam (River North, $$$)
Thai Classic (Lincoln Park, $$)

Vegetarian
Green Zebra (River North, $$$)

Index of Establishments by Price

$
Al's Italian Beef (Steakhouses, River North and Little Italy)
Ann Sather (Scandinavian and Breakfast, Andersonville and North Side)
Billy Goat Tavern (American, Magnificent Mile)

Byron's (American, River North and Wrigleyville)
Café Iberico (Spanish, River North)
Corner Bakery (Breakfast, Magnificent Mile and Gold Coast)
Edwardo's (Pizza, Gold Coast, Loop, and Lincoln Park)

Flat Top Grill (Asian, Old Town, North Side, and Randolph Street Market District)

Fluky's (American, Magnificent Mile)

Foodlife (Eclectic, Magnificent Mile)

Gino's East (Pizza, River North)

Gold Coast Dogs (American, Loop)

Jake Melnick's (American, Magnificent Mile)

Leona's Pizzeria (Pizza, Wrigleyville)

Lou Manalti's Pizzeria (Pizza, River North)

Lou Mitchell's (American, Loop)

Margie's Candies (Sweets, Bucktown/Wicker Park)

Mario's Italian Lemonade (Sweets, Little Italy)

Mr. Beef on Orleans (Steakhouses, River North)

Mrs. Levy's Delicatessen (American, Loop)

Pat's Pizzeria (Pizza, Wrigleyville)

Pizzeria Due (Pizza, River North)

Pizzeria Uno (Pizza, River North)

Portillo's (American, River North)

Potbelly Sandwich Works (Cajun, Lincoln Park, Loop, and River North)

Ranalli's Pizzeria, Libations and Collectibles (Pizza, River North)

Red Apple Restaurant (Eclectic, Logan Square)

Rock-N-Roll McDonald's (American, River North)

Scafuri Bakery (Sweets, Little Italy)

Stanley's (American, Lincoln Park)

Svea Restaurant (Scandinavian, Andersonville)

Swedish Bakery (Sweets, Andersonville)

Tango Sur (Argentine, North Side)

Tom and Wendee's Italian Ice (Sweets, Lincoln Park)

Twin Anchors (Barbecue, Old Town)

Uncommon Grounds (Eclectic, $)

Wishbone (Cajun/Southern, North Side and Randolph Street Market District)

$$

Amarit (Thai, Magnificent Mile)

Atwood Cafe (Eclectic, Loop)

Avec (Eclectic, Randolph Street Market District)

Berghoff (German, Loop)

Bice Ristorante (Italian, Streeterville)

Bin 36 (American, Loop)

Bistro 110 (American, Magnificent Mile)

Bistro Zinc (Bistro, Gold Coast)

Carson's (Barbecue, River North)

Chez Joël (Bistro, Little Italy)

Chicago Brauhaus (German, Lincoln Square)

Chilpancingo (Mexican, River North)

Cyrano's Bistro, Wine Bar & Cabaret (Bistro, River North)

Drake (Eclectic, Magnificent Mile)

Eli's the Place for Steak (Steakhouse, Streeterville)

Four Seasons (Eclectic, Magnificent Mile)

Francesca's on Taylor (Italian, Little Italy)

Frontera Grill and Topolobampo (Mexican, River North)

Gene & Georgetti (Steakhouse, River North)

Harry Caray's (Italian/Steakhouse, River North)

Heaven on Seven (Cajun, Loop and Magnificent Mile)

Italian Village (Italian, Loop)

Jake Melnick's (American, Magnificent Mile)

Jane's (Eclectic, Bucktown/Wicker Park)

Joe's Seafood, Prime Steak and Stone Crab (Seafood/Steakhouse, Magnificent Mile)

Kamehachi (Japanese/Sushi, Old Town)

Le Bouchon (Bistro, Bucktown/Wicker Park)

Maggiano's (Italian, River North)

Merz Apothecary (German, Lincoln Square)

Meyer's Delicatessen (German, Lincoln Square)

Mia Francesca (Italian, North Side, Little Italy and Andersonville)

Mike Ditka's Restaurant (Steakhouse, Magnificent Mile)

Orange (American, North Side)

Pegasus (Greek, Greektown)

Ritz-Carlton (Eclectic, Magnificent Mile)

Saloon Steakhouse (Steakhouse, Streeterville)

Santorini (Greek, Greektown)

Shaw's Crab House and Blue Crab Lounge (Seafood, River North)

Soju (Korean, Bucktown/Wicker Park)

Star of Siam (Thai, River North)

Sushi Wabi (Japanese/Sushi, Randolph Street Market District)

Thai Classic (Thai, Lincoln Park)

Trattoria No. 10 (Italian, Loop)

Tuscany on Taylor (Italian, Little Italy)

Vivo (Italian, Randolph Street Market District)

Wave (American, Streeterville)

$$$

Avec (Eclectic, Randolph Street Market District)

Bice Ristorante (Italian, Streeterville)

Bin 36 (American, Loop)

Café Absinthe (Eclectic, Bucktown/Wicker Park)

Coco Pazzo (Italian, River North)

Eli's the Place for Steak (Steakhouse, Streeterville)

Frontera Grill and Topolobampo (Mexican, River North)

Green Zebra (Vegetarian, River North)

Harry Caray's (Italian/Steakhouse, River North)

Joe's Seafood, Prime Steak and Stone Crab (Seafood/Steakhouse, Magnificent Mile)

Keefer's (Steakhouse, River North)

Mas (Latin American, Bucktown/Wicker Park)

Meritage Café and Wine Bar (American, Bucktown/Wicker Park)

Mike Ditka's Restaurant (Steakhouse, Magnificent Mile)

Mirai Sushi (Japanese/Sushi, Bucktown/Wicker Park)

mk (American, River North)

MOD (American, Bucktown/Wicker Park)

Morton's (Steakhouse, Streeterville)

Nine (Seafood/Steakhouse, Loop)

Pump Room (French, Gold Coast)

Ruth's Chris Steak House (Steakhouse, River North)

Saloon Steakhouse (Steakhouse, Streeterville)

Smith & Wollensky (Steakhouse, River North)

Spring (American, Bucktown/Wicker Park)

Sushisamba Rio (Latin American/Sushi, River North)

Vivo (Italian, Randolph Street Market District)

Wave (American, Streeterville)

$$$$

Ambria (French, Lincoln Park)

Frontera Grill and Topolobampo (Mexican, River North)

Gibson's Steakhouse (Steakhouse, Gold Coast)

Nine (Seafood/Steakhouse, Loop)

$$$$$

Arun's (Thai, North Side)

Charlie Trotter's (Nouvelle, Lincoln Park)

Part IV
Exploring Chicago

The 5th Wave   By Rich Tennant

©RICHTENNANT

SIGNED $40.00

SIGNED ORIG. $70.00

AUTHEN. $40

NOT SIGNED $20.00

LS 3

"We do offer an authentic William 'The Refrigerator' Perry football jersey for sale, we just don't have a wall large enough to display it on."

In this part . . .

*W*hether you want to make your own itinerary or follow my ready-made suggestions, this part will help you peruse Chicago's sights. I cover Chicago's main attractions, and others that are worth a stop if you have the time and energy. I've created itineraries based on the length of your stay — what should you do if you have one day, or two, or three? — and special interests. And what would travel be without a little souvenir hunting? In this part, you'll find a complete guide to shopping, from Michigan Avenue's glittering boutiques to off-the-beaten-track vintage shops. Finally, I provide five day trips for those who have the time and inclination to venture beyond Chicago.

Chapter 11

Discovering Chicago's Best Attractions

In This Chapter

▶ Discovering museums for fans of art and science
▶ Exploring the parks and lakefront
▶ Entertaining athletes and fans
▶ Orienting yourself with a sightseeing tour
▶ Sailing smoothly on boat tours

Chicago is a sophisticated city with diverse attractions including museums with world-famous collections; outstanding buildings by internationally known architects; miles of running and biking paths along the lakefront; and, of course, major sports venues such as Wrigley Field, the friendly confines of the Chicago Cubs. Best of all for visitors, the majority of the top attractions are in or near downtown, all accessible by public transportation.

In this chapter, I describe the city's most popular attractions. See the map in this chapter for locations, unless noted otherwise.

Chicago's Top Sights

Adler Planetarium & Astronomy Museum
Museum Campus (near the Loop)

The first planetarium in the Western Hemisphere launched itself into the new millennium with a facelift and an addition that wraps itself around the 1920-built planetarium like a high-tech glass visor. And high-tech it is: Sky Pavilion includes four exhibition galleries, including the world's first StarRider virtual-reality theater, which propels visitors on an exhilarating voyage of discovery into the infinity of space. Visitors participate in the journey by operating controls in the armrests of their seats. **Galileo's,** the

Taking advantage of free museum days

The city's major museums all have free admission days. Schedule your visits correctly, and you can save some dollars while immersing yourself in the best culture Chicago has to offer.

✔ **Monday:** Adler Planetarium (Sept–Feb, except the last two weeks of Dec), Museum of Science and Industry (Sept–Feb, except the last two weeks of Dec), Shedd Aquarium (Sept–Feb, except the last two weeks of Dec; Oceanarium admission extra)

✔ **Tuesday:** Adler Planetarium (Sept–Feb, except the last two weeks of Dec), Art Institute of Chicago, Field Museum of Natural History (Sept–Feb, except the last two weeks of Dec), International Museum of Surgical Science, Museum of Contemporary Art (5–8 p.m. only), Museum of Science and Industry (Sept–Feb, except the last two weeks of Dec), Shedd Aquarium (Sept–Feb, except the last two weeks of Dec; Oceanarium admission extra)

✔ **Thursday:** Chicago Children's Museum (5–8 p.m. only)

✔ **Friday:** Spertus Museum

✔ **Sunday:** DuSable Museum of African-American History (see Chapter 17)

✔ **Always free:** Chicago Cultural Center, Garfield Park Conservatory, David and Alfred Smart Museum of Art, Jane Addams Hull House Museum, Lincoln Park Conservatory, Lincoln Park Zoo, Martin D'Arcy Gallery of Art, Mexican Fine Arts Museum, Museum of Contemporary Photography, Newberry Library

pavilion's cafe, offers stunning views of Chicago's skyline and a wide selection of salads, soups, and sandwiches. On the first Friday of every month, visitors can view dramatic close-ups of the moon, the planets, and distant galaxies through a closed-circuit monitor connected to the planetarium's Doane Observatory telescope. It's definitely worth a visit, especially if you have kids and want to check out the mind-blowing StarRider Theater. Allow at least two hours at the Adler, or combine a visit with a day at the Museum Campus (see the "Mixing fish, fossils, and outer space: The Museum Campus" sidebar, in this chapter).

See map p. 174. 1300 S. Lake Shore Dr. ☎ *312-922-7827.* www.adlerplanetarium. org. *CTA: Red-line El to Roosevelt; bus no. 12 or 146 to planetarium entrance. Admission (including one show): $13 adults, $12 seniors and $11 children 4–17, free for children under 4. Free admission Mon and Tues Sept–Feb only (except for the last two weeks in Dec). Open: Mon–Fri 9:30 a.m.–4:30 p.m., Sat–Sun 9 a.m.–4:30 p.m.; first Fri of every month until 10 p.m.; open until 6 p.m. daily Memorial Day–Labor Day. StarRider Theater and Sky Shows at numerous times throughout the day; call for current times.*

Art Institute of Chicago
Near the Loop

Chicago's pride and joy is a warm, welcoming museum, a world-class institution that never seems stuffy. (You can get an idea of the museum's sense of whimsy during the holidays when the famous lion sculptures that guard its entrance sport Santa hats.) A diverse museum like New York's Metropolitan Museum of Art and Paris's Louvre, the Art Institute has several different departments, each with its own exhibition space and impressive collection. Highlights include well-known works such as *Sunday Afternoon on the Island of the Grande Jatte,* by Georges Seurat; *Paris Street: Rainy Day,* by Gustave Caillebotte; and two icons of American isolation, Edward Hopper's *Nighthawks* and Grant Wood's *American Gothic.*

The size and scope of the Art Institute's collections can be overwhelming. First-timers do well to take a Collection Highlight Tour (2 p.m. Sat, Sun, and Tues). The tour is free and lasts about an hour, concentrating on a few major works. A highlight tour for kids runs on some Saturdays, and the **Kraft Education Center** on the lower level offers fun seek-and-find programs for children and interactive exhibits. If you're touring on your own, don't miss the outstanding **French Impressionist** collection, with one of the world's largest collections of Monet paintings) and the **Thorne Miniature Rooms** — 68 dollhouse-like chambers that chronicle decorative arts through the centuries. Watch for major touring shows, for which reservations are usually required. The bustling gift shop is a great place to shop for jewelry, glassware, books, and quality reproductions. Reserve at least two hours for the museum and try to visit during off times, such as weekdays, early mornings, or late afternoons.

Mixing fish, fossils, and outer space: The Museum Campus

The Museum Campus is a 1990s creation that brings together three great Chicago institutions — the Field Museum of Natural History, John G. Shedd Aquarium, and Adler Planetarium & Astronomy Museum. Previously divided by the northbound lanes of Lake Shore Drive, the area was much like the center grounds of the Indy 500 racetrack — without professional drivers. Today, the Drive has been moved west of Soldier Field, and you can stroll from the Field Museum to the Shedd Aquarium and the Planetarium without fear of being struck by a speeding auto. A new pedestrian underpass makes the campus a 15-minute walk east from the Roosevelt El stops or a longer (but enjoyable) stroll through Grant Park and along the lakefront from the Loop. If you're not up for a walk, bus no. 146 runs from North Michigan Avenue and State Street in the Loop. Parking isn't bad because the museums have access to the lots around Soldier Field, but be aware that no public parking is available during Chicago Bears football games in the fall; Bears fans get first dibs on all surrounding parking spaces. Check out www.museumcampus.org for driving directions and information on parking and public transportation.

Central Chicago Attractions

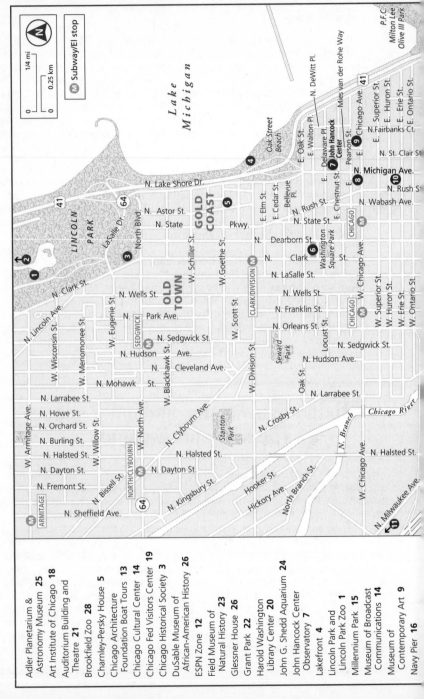

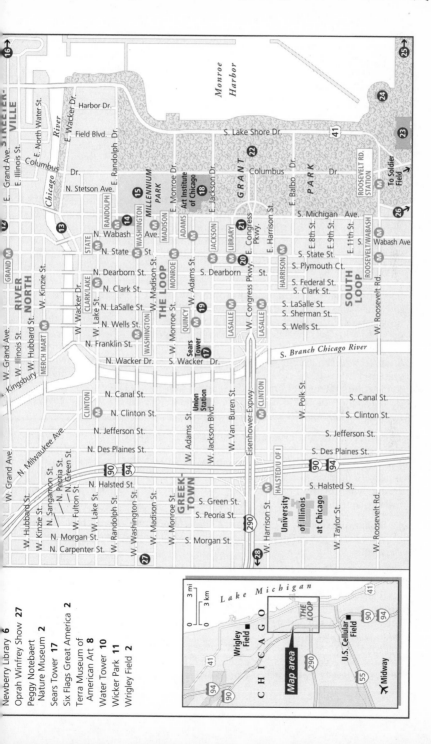

See map p. 174. 111 S. Michigan Ave. ☎ *312-443-3600.* www.artic.edu. *CTA: Green-, brown-, purple-, or orange-line El to Adams, or red-line El to Monroe or Jackson, then walk 1 block east; bus no. 3, 4, 60, 145, 147, or 151 to Monroe and South Michigan Avenue. Admission (suggested): $10 adults; $6 seniors, students, and children. Free admission Tues. Open: Mon and Wed–Fri 10:30 a.m.–4:30 p.m., Tues 10:30 a.m.– 8 p.m., Sat–Sun 10 a.m.–5 p.m. Closed Thanksgiving (fourth Thurs in Nov) and Dec 25.*

Chicago ArchiCenter and Chicago Architecture Foundation Boat Tours
Near the Loop

Chicago is the first city of architecture, and a quick swing through the ArchiCenter, followed by a Chicago Architecture Foundation (CAF) boat tour, is the best way to survey the city's architectural highlights. The ArchiCenter is run by the Foundation and is conveniently located across the street from the Art Institute. Exhibits include a scale model of downtown Chicago, profiles of the people and buildings that shaped the city's look, and a searchable database with pictures and information on many of Chicago's best-known skyscrapers. "Architecture ambassadors" are on hand to provide information on tours run by the Foundation. The most popular tour is a one-and-a-half-hour "Architecture River Cruise" along the north and south branches of the Chicago River. You see 50 or so buildings, including the Gothic 1925 Tribune Tower, designed by a New York architect who won a contest; Marina City, home of Bob Newhart on *The Bob Newhart Show* (if you remember back that far); Sears Tower; and NBC Tower, constructed in wedding-cake style in homage to the city's old zoning codes mandating that sunlight must reach down to the street. Lecturers generally do a good job of making the cruise enjoyable for visitors with all levels of architectural knowledge.

The boat tours are extremely popular, so purchase tickets in advance through **Ticketmaster,** or avoid the service charge and buy your tickets at the ArchiCenter at 224 S. Michigan Ave., at Hot Tix at the WaterWorks Visitor Center on Michigan Avenue, or from the boat launch on the southeast corner of Michigan Avenue and Wacker Drive (look for the blue awning marking the stairway entrance).

CAF also offers architecture tours year-round by foot and bus. Call the number in the following paragraph or check the very thorough Web site for details.

See map p. 174. Chicago ArchiCenter: 224 S. Michigan Ave. ☎ *312-922-3432.* www.architecture.org. *Free admission. Exhibits open daily 9:30 a.m.–4 p.m., shop and tour desk open Mon–Sat 9 a.m.–6:30 p.m. CTA: Brown-, green-, purple-, or orange-line to Adams, or red-line to Jackson. Chicago Architecture Foundation boat tours: Tour boats depart from the Michigan Avenue Bridge.* ☎ *312-922-8687 (for information only).* www.architecture.org. *Tickets must be purchased in advance or through Ticketmaster (*☎ *312-902-1500;* www.ticketmaster.com*). CTA: Brown-, green-, orange-, or purple-line El to State/Lake, then walk 1 block north to Wacker and 1 block east to Michigan Avenue Bridge; bus no. 151 to Wacker and*

Michigan. Tickets: Fri–Sat and holidays, $25, Mon–Thurs $23. Boat tours: May 1–Nov 20. Call or check Web site, because times change.

Chicago Cultural Center
Near the Loop

The cultural center offers a storehouse of not-too-heavy culture and plenty of pure fun — for free. Built in 1897 as the city's library, the building exhibits the Beaux Arts style that became popular here after the 1893 World's Columbian Exposition on the city's South Side. But it's what's inside that will knock your socks off. Free tours guide visitors up a sweeping staircase of white Italian marble to admire what is, for my money, the most stunning interior in Chicago. You discover rare marble; fine hardwood; stained glass; polished brass; and mosaics of Favrile glass, colored stone, and mother-of-pearl inlaid in white marble. At the top of the grand staircase is a Tiffany dome, believed to be the world's largest. The grand setting hosts an array of art exhibitions, concerts, films, lectures, and other special events, many of them free. A longstanding tradition is the Dame Myra Hess Memorial classical concert every Wednesday in the Preston Bradley Hall. Allow about an hour to visit the cultural center.

See map p. 174. 78 E. Washington St. ☎ 312-744-6630 or 312-346-3278 for weekly events. www.cityofchicago.org/exploringchicago. *CTA: Brown-, green-, orange-, or purple-line El to Randolph, then walk ½ block east, or red-line El to Washington/State; bus no. 3, 4, 20, 56, 145, 146, 147, 151, or 157 to Randolph and Michigan. Admission: Free. Open: Mon–Thurs 10 a.m.–7 p.m., Fri 10 a.m.–6 p.m., Sat 10 a.m.–5 p.m., Sun 11 a.m.–5 p.m.*

Chicago Fed Visitors Center
Loop

The Visitors Center at the Federal Reserve Bank of Chicago is a quick stop-off if you're touring the Loop. More than just the standard history-of-banking displays, the center has kid-friendly features such as a giant cube that holds a million dollars, and an exhibit that lets you try detecting counterfeit bills. And there's even a section that enables visitors to pretend to wield the power of Alan Greenspan for a moment, showing how changes in interest rates affect the economy. Free guided tours are offered weekdays at 1 p.m. Allow 30 minutes for the tour.

See map p. 174. 230 S. LaSalle St. (at Quincy Street). ☎ 312-322-2400. www.chicagofed.org. *CTA: Brown-line El to Quincy/Wells; bus no. 134, 135, 156. Admission: Free. Open: Mon–Fri 9 a.m.–4:15 p.m., except federal holidays.*

Field Museum of Natural History
Museum Campus (near the Loop)

As a place of pure fun, the Field Museum is pretty hard to beat. Kids absolutely love this museum for its wide-open spaces, giant dinos, and hands-on exhibits. Come to see Sue, the largest T. rex fossil ever unearthed, but stay to explore gleaming gems, giant stuffed elephants, mummies, and Native American artifacts. Visitors can climb into a life-size Egyptian tomb, step into the sun-drenched desert, and visit an ancient Egyptian marketplace. Take time to explore the African continent, visiting a royal Cameroon palace, witnessing some of the great savanna wildlife, and traveling across the Sahara and back to Nigeria. You can "travel" to America by ship and feel what it may have been like for Africans taken against their will and sold into slavery. The museum also has its own McDonald's on the lower level. While you're downstairs, plug a dollar bill into one of the old-fashioned wax-molding machines and watch as a red T. rex or green brontosaurus comes to life in front of your eyes. Kids get a real thrill out of taking home their very own Field Museum dinosaur! Allow at least a half a day here.

See map p. 174. Roosevelt Road and Lake Shore Drive. ☎ *312-922-9410.* www.fieldmuseum.org. *CTA: Bus no. 6, 10, 12, 130, or 146 to museum entrance. Admission: $10 adults, $7 seniors and students, $5 children 3–11. Free for teachers, armed-forces personnel in uniform, and children 2 and under. Free admission Mon and Tues mid-Sept–Feb (except the last two weeks in Dec). Open: Daily 9 a.m.–5 p.m. Open Thurs to 8 p.m. mid-Aug. Closed Jan 1 and Dec 25.*

Frank Lloyd Wright Home and Studio
Suburban Oak Park

World-famous architect Frank Lloyd Wright made his first home and studio in Oak Park, a suburb just west of Chicago. Wright lived and worked here for 20 of his most productive years. During this time, he experimented with and perfected what became known as the Prairie School style of architecture. His home and studio were built in 1889 as a cottage that came to house the 22-year-old architect, his new bride, and a growing family. You can glimpse Wright's genius on a guided tour (the only way to see the place), as guides show how the house became the architect's showcase and laboratory. You may not agree with his controversial lifestyle (he left his wife to live with a client's wife in Wisconsin), but you have to admire a man who became the single most important influence on American architecture. While you're in Oak Park, you can check out **Unity Temple,** Wright's masterpiece for the Unitarian Church, and take a walking tour to

More museums, less $$$

If you're planning on visiting lots of Chicago museums, you should invest in a CityPass, a prepaid ticket that gets you into the biggest attractions (Art Institute, Field Museum of Natural History, Shedd Aquarium, Adler Planetarium, Museum of Science and Industry, and Hancock Observatory). The cost is $49 for adults and $39 for children, which is about 50 percent cheaper than paying all the attractions' individual admission fees. You can buy a CityPass at any of these six attractions, or purchase one online at www.citypass.net before you arrive in Chicago.

view the exteriors of homes throughout the neighborhood that were built by Wright. (See Chapter 14 for a complete Oak Park itinerary.) Plan on a full day to visit the home and studio and tour the surrounding neighborhood.

951 Chicago Ave., Oak Park (10 miles west of downtown Chicago). ☎ *708-848-1976.* www.wrightplus.org. *CTA: Green-line El to Harlem, then walk 4 blocks north on Harlem Avenue and 3 blocks east on Chicago Avenue. Admission: $9 adults, $7 seniors and children 7–18, free for children under 7. Combined admission for home and studio tour and guided or self-guided historic district tour: $15 adults, $11 seniors and children 7–18, free for children under 7. Admission to home and studio is by guided tour only; tours depart Gingko Tree Bookshop Mon–Fri 11 a.m., 1 p.m., 3 p.m.; Sat–Sun every 20 minutes 11 a.m.–3:30 p.m. Facilities for people with disabilities are limited; please call in advance.*

Grant Park
Near the Loop

During the summer, festivals reign in Grant Park, the Loop's front lawn overlooking Lake Michigan. **Blues Fest, Jazz Fest, Gospel Fest,** and the ever-popular **Taste of Chicago** food free-for-all take place here. (For details on when and where festivals take place, see Chapter 3.) But Grant Park also offers quieter pleasures — all of them free.

For picnic supplies, head to the **Corner Bakery** (see Chapter 10) on the corner of Jackson Boulevard and Michigan Avenue, across the street from the Art Institute.

This 319-acre swath of greenery wedged between South Michigan Avenue and the lakeshore is not contiguous parkland but a patchwork of greenery dissected by city streets. Chief among the park's charms is **Buckingham Fountain** — twice as big as the Latona Basin at Versailles, after which it was modeled. Built in 1927 of Georgia pink marble, the baroque fountain delights park strollers with a computer-orchestrated symphony of dancing water. (If you ever watched *Married with Children* on television, you've seen the fountain spurt during the show's introduction.) After dark between Memorial Day and Labor Day, colored lights play on the splashing water.

See map p. 174. From East Randolph Drive to East Roosevelt Road, and Michigan Avenue to Lake Michigan. CTA: All El stops in the Loop along State and Wabash; bus no. 3, 4, 6, 60, 146, or 151 along Michigan Avenue, Randolph Street, or Roosevelt Road.

John G. Shedd Aquarium
Museum Campus (near the Loop)

The world's largest indoor aquarium is a spectacular draw, especially the **Oceanarium,** which re-creates a Pacific Northwest coastal environment. The wall of windows revealing Lake Michigan just beyond the Oceanarium's windows creates the optical illusion of an expanse of sea. You can follow a winding nature trail and watch dolphins, sea otters, and harbor seals. The most popular animals are three female Beluga whales, remarkably cute creatures whose humped heads and natural "smiles" make them seem human.

It's impossible to miss the 90,000-gallon **circular tank** in the aquarium's central rotunda. Divers doing the feedings describe animals and their environment via underwater microphones. Watch for a hawksbill sea turtle named Hawkeye who has been here 20 years, and keep an eye out for the very scary moray eel. Don't miss the **penguin colony** in a separate exhibit that approximates the Falkland Islands in the southern sea off Argentina. **Seahorse Symphony** presents the world's largest collection of seahorses and their relatives. An **Amazon riverbank** exhibit is not to be missed, and features an array of piranhas, birds, sloths, insects, snakes, catfish, stingrays, iguanas, and caimans. The newest signature exhibit is **Wild Reef — Sharks at Shedd,** a series of 26 interconnected habitats that house a Philippine coral reef patrolled by sharks and other predators (they even swim over your head at certain spots). Allow three hours to visit the Shedd.

See map p. 174. 1200 S. Lake Shore Dr. ☎ *312-939-2438.* www.sheddaquarium.org. *CTA: Bus no. 6, 10, 12, 130, or 146 to aquarium entrance. Admission: All-Access Pass (to all exhibits) $21 adults, $15 seniors and children 3–11. Admission to aquarium and either Oceanarium or Wild Reef: $17 adults, $13 seniors and children 3–11; aquarium only $8 adults, $6 children and seniors. Free admission to aquarium Mon and Tues, Oct–Feb (except the last two weeks in Dec) Oceanarium tickets are limited and available on a first-come, first-served basis. Purchase tickets in advance through Ticketmaster (*☎ *312-902-1500;* www.ticketmaster.com*) or by calling* ☎ *312-559-0200. Open: Mon–Fri 9 a.m.–5 p.m. (until 6 p.m. Memorial Day–Labor Day), Sat–Sun and some holidays 9 a.m.–6 p.m. Last entrance into Oceanarium is 15 minutes before closing. Closed Jan 1 and Dec 25.*

John Hancock Center Observatory
Magnificent Mile

A location right on the Magnificent Mile means the John Hancock Center offers an up-close-and-personal view of the city from its observatory on the 94th floor. Okay, so visits to "Big John" are not as popular as the Sears Tower Skydeck, but for my money, the view is more interesting and the location can't be beat. The view looking north over the Gold Coast and Lincoln Park is fantastic, with the curving lakefront, beaches, and high-rises disappearing in a line toward the suburbs. Looking west, you get an interesting view of the congested Mag Mile, which twinkles with lights on any evening, but especially during the holidays. (The observatory doesn't close until 11 p.m.!) On a clear day, you can see about 65 miles and part of three states surrounding this corner of Illinois — Michigan, Indiana, and Wisconsin. A refurbishment in 1997 added some new gadgets, such as talking telescopes. A high-speed elevator, presumably the fastest in the world, whisks passengers to the observatory in 40 seconds — kids love the ride. Allow one hour.

The **Signature Room** on the 95th floor, a sleek restaurant with adjoining lounge, allows you to take in views with a drink in hand. (Ladies, make sure to visit the restroom — it has the best view in the restaurant.) If the line for the observatory is too long, head here. You'll pay the cost of a drink rather than admission — about the same price.

See map p. 174. 94th floor of the John Hancock Center, 875 N. Michigan Ave.
☎ *888-875-8439 or 312-751-3681.* www.hancock-observatory.com. *CTA: Red-line El to Chicago/State, walk 3 blocks east, then 3 blocks north; bus no. 151 to Michigan Avenue and Delaware Place. Admission: $9.50 adults, $7.50 seniors, $6 children 5–12, free for children under 5 and military personnel in uniform or with active-duty cards. Open: Daily 9 a.m.–11 p.m.*

Lakefront

Walk, run, bike, skate, or just sit and watch the world go by at Chicago's lakefront, the city's number-one free attraction, lined with paths and beaches. The best-known beach is **Oak Street Beach,** the location of which at the northern tip of the Magnificent Mile creates some interesting sights as sun worshippers wearing flip-flops and carrying coolers make their way up Michigan Avenue. For some seclusion, try **Ohio Street Beach,** an intimate sliver of sand in tiny Olive Park, just north of Navy Pier. With buoys marking a 1-mile course, Ohio Street Beach is also the place for serious open-water swimming (see "Especially for active types," later in this chapter). Beaches are officially open and staffed by lifeguards from Memorial Day to Labor Day until 9:30 p.m. Contact the Chicago Park District (☎ 312-742-7529) for more information on the beaches.

To rent bikes or in-line skates, go to **Bike Chicago** (see "Especially for active types," later in this chapter) at North Avenue Beach, Millennium Park, or Navy Pier. For picnic supplies, head to **Bockwinkel's** (☎ 312-482-9900), a grocery store in the basement of the Chicago Place mall, at Superior Street and Michigan Avenue.

The most popular beach in Chicago is **North Avenue Beach,** about 6 blocks north of Oak Street, which has developed into a volleyball hot spot and recently rebuilt its landmark steamship-shaped beach houses and added an outdoor gym. This is where Lincoln Park singles come to play, check each other out, and fly by on bikes and in-line skates.

Because Lake Shore Drive runs between the lake and the city, access to the lakefront is somewhat limited. Near the Magnificent Mile, you find pedestrian tunnels to the lakefront at the corner of Oak Street and Michigan Avenue, at Chicago Avenue and Lake Shore Drive, and at Grand Avenue and Lake Shore Drive near Navy Pier. On the near North Side, you find access under and over Lake Shore Drive at North Avenue, from the Lincoln Park Zoo, and at Fullerton Avenue.

See map p. 174. CTA: To Oak Street Beach, red-line El to Division, walk east to the lake; to Oak Street and North Avenue beaches, bus no. 151 along Lake Shore Drive; to Ohio Street Beach, bus no. 29, 56, 65, or 66 to Navy Pier.

Lincoln Park and Lincoln Park Zoo
Lincoln Park

Lincoln Park is the city's largest park. Straight and narrow, Lincoln Park begins at North Avenue and follows the shoreline of Lake Michigan for several miles. Within its elongated 1,200 acres are bathing **beaches** (see the preceding listing for the lakefront); the **Chicago Historical Society** and the **Peggy Notebaert Nature Museum** (see "Especially for serious museum buffs," later in this chapter); the **Lincoln Park Conservancy** with its lovely botanical gardens; a **driving range, golf course,** and **tennis courts** near Diversey Avenue; and miles of paths for walking and running.

The park's free **Lincoln Park Zoo,** 2200 N. Cannon Dr. (☎ **312-742-2000;** www.lpzoo.com), is convenient, compact (35 acres), and charming. The nation's oldest, founded in 1868, the zoo is home to more than 200 species. Among the standard zoo exhibits, the seal and sea lion feedings are popular, as are the Children's Zoo and its nursery. One of the joys of visiting the Farm-in-the-Zoo is watching young urbanites meet cows, pigs, horses, chicks, and goats for the first time. The popular lowland gorillas, who have delivered a record-setting number of babies in captivity, have a newly rebuilt home in the **Great Ape House,** where you can watch the families interact. Another popular spot is the Sea Lion Pool, located in the center of the zoo and home to harbor seals, gray seals, and California sea lions. An underwater viewing area spans 70 feet. Look for special seasonal events, such as caroling to the animals in December and concerts in summer, when you can stroll among the great cats with a glass of chardonnay in hand. The zoo grounds are open from 8 a.m. to 6 p.m.; the buildings are open from 10 a.m. to 5 p.m. Allow two to three hours.

When hunger strikes, head to **Cafe Brauer,** 2021 Stockton Dr. near Armitage Avenue in the park (☎ **312-742-2400**). Here you find fast food and an ice-cream parlor, plus **paddleboat rentals** at the edge of the South Pond. For more upscale dining, try the **North Pond Café,** 2610 Cannon Dr., south of Diversey Parkway in the park (☎ **773-477-5845**), serving American specialties in a Prairie School–style setting.

Free lunchtime entertainment under the Picasso

While you're in the Loop, stop by the Picasso sculpture in Daley Plaza at the Richard J. Daley Center any weekday at noon, where a free show awaits. Offerings, which include music, dance, and other performing arts, are popular with Loop workers, who often come here with their brown-bag lunches. As the days grow colder, performances move indoors to the lobby.

Daley Center is between North Dearborn, North Clark, West Randolph, and West Washington streets. For "Under the Picasso" information, call ☎ **312-346-3278,** the Department of Cultural Affairs' cultural programming hotline. To get to Daley Plaza, take the brown-, green-, orange-, or purple-line El to Clark, walk 1 block south on Clark, and then walk ½ block east on Randolph. Or take bus no. 22, 24, or 42 to the corner of Randolph and Clark streets.

See map p. 174. Lincoln Park runs from North Avenue to Ardmore Avenue along the lakefront. CTA: Bus no. 151 runs the length of the park.

Millennium Park

At the north end of Grant Park along Michigan Avenue is the city's newest urban showpiece. The architectural highlight of the park is the Frank Gehry–designed Pritzker Music Pavilion, home of the free summer music concerts performed by the Grant Park Symphony Orchestra. Another popular attraction is the huge elliptical sculpture by British artist Anish Kapoor, officially named *Cloudgate,* his first public work in the U.S. But you'll soon be affectionately calling it the "Bean" like most Chicagoans. I dare you to stand with your toes in the water at the Crown Fountain, surveying the spectacular cityscape of South Michigan Avenue, and not feel an irrepressible urge to uproot your family and move into a condo in downtown Chicago. The park is a strikingly beautiful success, and thank goodness Chicago's donors and government saw fit to overspend the budget by leaps and bounds and go far beyond the deadline for opening to ensure a place like this. It's really an example of what a modern park can be.

Compare Millennium Park's interactive fountain with the grande dame of Chicago fountains, Buckingham Fountain (just to the south in Grant Park), which is lovely but untouchable, and you'll see how far we've come. Even the sculpture is interactive — the "Bean" by Anish Kapoor is essentially a gigantic 3-D mirror. Kids and adults are equally attracted to its reflective surface and house-of-mirrors qualities. The Crown Fountain is another favorite, with its two 50-foot glass-brick towers, facing each other across a black granite plaza, with water cascading down their sides. Faces of Chicagoans are projected through the glass blocks and change at regular intervals — and watch out, because water spews from their mouths when you least expect it. It's public art with a sense of humor. The Jay Pritzker Pavilion, with its Frank Gehry–designed band shell, is a sight to behold, and the BP Pedestrian Bridge, also designed by Gehry, curves and winds its way over Columbus Drive, providing changing views of the cityscape as you walk. Gardens of native plants are just beginning to flourish, and by the next edition of this book, you'll surely feel that you're walking through a Midwestern prairie as you stroll the Lurie Garden, with 250 varieties of native perennial plants. All in all, this is a must-see, must-experience park.

You can lunch at the Park Grill (☎ **312-521-7275;** www.parkgrill chicago.com; open daily 11 a.m.–10:30 p.m.), an eatery overlooking the McCormick Tribune Plaza ice-skating rink. Next door to the grill, Park Café offers takeout salads and sandwiches. Parking is easy too, with plentiful underground lots at the bargain rate of $10, the best deal in the city.

See map p. 174. Michigan Avenue, from Randolph Drive on the north to Monroe Drive on the south, and west to Columbus Drive. ☎ *312-742-1168.* www.millennium park.org. *CTA: Blue-line El to Washington; red-line El to Lake; brown-, green-, orange-, or purple-line to Randolph. Admission: Free. Open: 6 a.m.–11 p.m. daily.*

Museum of Science and Industry
Hyde Park

Would you like to step aboard a captured **World War II U-boat** or a retired **727 United Airlines** jetliner? Perhaps you'd like to travel deep into a replica of a Southern Illinois **coal mine?** Or concentrate on the story of space exploration at the **Henry Crown Space Center?** Little girls — some boys, too! — love **Colleen Moore's Fairy Castle,** a lavishly decorated miniature palace, while most younger children (up to age 10) enjoy the **Idea Factory,** where they can explore scientific principles. A massive model train exhibit called **The Great Train Story** and **All Aboard the Silver Streak,** a refurbished Burlington Pioneer Zephyr train with onboard interactive exhibits should please most kids. This huge interactive museum (there are 2,000 exhibits!) is so full of wonders that you may not know where to start. One thing is for sure: Don't try to see everything in one shot, but concentrate on the attractions that have the most appeal to you. If you have Internet access, visit the museum's Web site to scope out the options and check the schedule for the **OMNIMAX Theater,** for which you may need advance tickets. When hunger strikes, you can head to one of the museum's five restaurants, including a kid-pleasing **Pizza Hut** and an ice-cream parlor.

57th Street and Lake Shore Drive. ☎ *800-468-6674.* www.msichicago.org. *CTA: Bus no. 6, 10, 35, 151, or 156 to museum entrance. Open: Mon–Sat 9:30 a.m.–4 p.m., Sun 11 a.m.–4 p.m. (until 5:30 p.m. daily Memorial Day–Labor Day). Admission: $9 adults, $7.50 seniors, $5 children 3–11, free for children under 3. Free admission Mon and Tues mid-Sept–Nov and Jan–Feb. Combination museum and OMNIMAX Theater: $15 adults, $12.50 seniors, $10 children 3–11, free for children under 3 on an adult's lap.*

Navy Pier
East of Streeterville

Jutting three-quarters of a mile into Lake Michigan, Navy Pier was built in 1916 as a shipping and recreational facility. Today, with its 50 acres of parks, gardens, shops, restaurants, and attractions, Navy Pier is Chicago's number-one tourist attraction. And rightfully so: This is the best place for dining outside or strolling along the water and taking in stunning views of the city.

Kids love the **IMAX theater** (☎ 312-595-5629); the small **ice-skating rink;** and the mammoth **Ferris wheel,** with cars that look like red french-fry boxes (the sponsor is McDonald's). The wonderful **Chicago Children's Museum** (☎ 312-527-1000) has areas especially for preschoolers as well as for older children, and several permanent exhibits that allow kids a maximum of hands-on fun.

The pier also hosts periodic art shows, outdoor sculpture exhibits, and more. Plus, the **Chicago Shakespeare Theater** (see Chapter 15) makes its home here, and several boat tours — from speedboats to tall ships — depart from the pier's south side (see "Seeing Chicago by Guided Tour" later in this chapter). Summer is one long party at the pier, with fireworks Wednesday and Saturday evenings.

The pier has nine restaurants and a food court. **Bubba Gump Shrimp Co.** (☎ **312-252-4867**) re-creates the down-home atmosphere of the movie *Forrest Gump*. A more elegant alternative is **RIVA** (☎ **312-644-7482**), specializing in fresh seafood, steaks, and pasta, and which has a fabulous view of Chicago's skyline.

The pier has its downsides, including massive weekend crowds and limited parking. Try to come during the week or at least on Sunday (Saturday can be a zoo). To avoid the parking issue, take the free trolley service between Navy Pier and State Street along Grand Avenue and Illinois Street. Trolley hours are 10 a.m. to 9 p.m. Sunday to Thursday, 10 a.m. to midnight on Friday, and 10 a.m. to 11 p.m. on Saturday. Trolleys run about every 20 minutes, and pickup points are indicated by the "Navy Pier Trolley Stop" signs along the route.

See map p. 174. 600 E. Grand Ave. (on the lakefront). ☎ *800-595-7437 or 312-595-7437.* www.navypier.com. *CTA: Bus no. 29, 65, 66, 120, or 121. Admission: Free. Open: Summer Sun–Thurs 10 a.m.–10 p.m.; Fri–Sat 10 a.m. to midnight; fall through spring Mon–Sat 10 a.m.–10 p.m., Sun 10 a.m.–7 p.m. Parking: Rates start at $11 for the first hour and go up to $19 for up to 8 hours. However, lots fill up quickly.*

Oprah Winfrey Show
Randolph Street Market District

Are you in touch with your spirit? If not, you'd better hightail it over to the Harpo Studios for the *Oprah Winfrey Show*. With a little persistence, you too can be a part of the show's taping. Considered the world's largest cult by detractors, and must-see television by followers, the show is taped Tuesday through Thursday at 8 a.m. and noon. You can get tickets by calling ☎ **312-591-9222** (persistence required!). Call at least four weeks in advance. Even if you don't love Oprah, watching her producers work like a well-oiled machine and seeing Oprah turn on the charm when the cameras roll gives you great insight into how television works. The studio is surprisingly small and intimate, and Oprah answers questions and talks with the audience during commercial breaks, which are taken even though the show isn't live. After the show, head over to **Wishbone** (see Chapter 10), a Harpo Studios favorite hangout, for Southern-style cooking.

See map p. 174. 1058 W. Washington Blvd. ☎ *312-591-9222 (Mon–Fri 9 a.m.–5 p.m.).* www.oprah.com. *$7 cab ride from the Loop. Reservations can be made generally only one month in advance. Ticket price: Free. Tapings take place Sept–early Dec and Jan–early June Tues–Thurs 8 a.m. and noon.*

Sears Tower
Loop

The Sears Tower is a good place to orient yourself to the city and beyond, as it provides a panorama of Chicago and the Midwest. On a clear day, you can see about 65 miles and four states (including Illinois). Visitors rocket to the top in a high-speed elevator that goes from ground to the 103rd floor in 70 seconds. Built in 1973 and long the world's tallest building, the Sears Tower had to surrender its title to a building in Malaysia with longer decorative spires. Allow one to two hours, depending on the length of the line (arrive in the late afternoon to avoid the worst of the crowds).

In my opinion, you get a better bird's-eye view of Chicago at the John Hancock Center Observatory, which overlooks more interesting neighborhoods and architecture and is more centrally located — the Sears Tower sits in the west Loop, which becomes a dead zone on weekends.

See map p. 175. 233 S. Wacker Dr. (enter on Jackson Boulevard). ☎ *800-759-3325 or 312-875-9696.* www.the-skydeck.com. *CTA: Bus no. 1, 7, 126, 146, 151, or 156 to Jackson Boulevard; brown-, purple-, or orange-line El to Quincy or red- or blue-line El to Jackson. Admission: $9 adults, $7.75 seniors, $6.75 children 3–12. Open: Daily May–Sept 10 a.m.–10 p.m., Oct–Apr 10 a.m.–8 p.m. The last ticket is sold 30 minutes before closing.*

Wrigley Field
Wrigleyville

Nothing makes you feel more optimistic than opening day at Wrigley Field. Sure, you may be wearing long underwear and earmuffs, but that doesn't deter Cubs fans, for whom hope springs eternal. Wrigley Field is an almost-perfect ballpark, from its ivy-covered outfield walls to the hand-operated scoreboard. Attend a day game, buy a hot dog, a beer, and a box of Crackerjacks and the whole afternoon runs about $40 a person. Because Wrigley is small, just about every seat is decent, but the coveted outfield seats get more sun — significant if a tan is more important to you than the game. Call in advance for tickets; although the Cubs lose plenty of games every year, tickets can be difficult to obtain.

See map p. 175. 1060 W. Addison St. ☎ *800-843-2827 for tickets.* www.cubs.com. *CTA: Red-line El to Addison; bus no. 22 to Addison. Wrigley Field box office: Mon–Fri 9 a.m.–6 p.m., Sat 9 a.m.–4 p.m., and during games.*

Finding More Cool Things to See and Do

Beyond the city's major attractions, Chicago has plenty to offer visitors with special interests — whether you're an amateur architectural historian or you just have kids in tow. The following suggestions should keep your diverse tastes and needs satisfied.

Especially for kids

Chicago offers loads of activities for pint-size and teenage tourists. For the major attractions with kid appeal — **Adler Planetarium & Astronomy Museum, Art Institute of Chicago, Field Museum of Natural History, John G. Shedd Aquarium, John Hancock Center Observatory, Lincoln Park** and **Lincoln Park Zoo, Museum of Science and Industry, Navy Pier,** and **Sears Tower** — see "Chicago's Top Sights," earlier in this chapter.

For kid-friendly sightseeing tours, particularly **MetroDucks Tours** and **Seadog,** see "Seeing Chicago by Guided Tour," later in this chapter. For ideas on restaurants, see Chapter 9, and for itinerary suggestions, see Chapter 13.

Brookfield Zoo
Suburban Brookfield

The Chicago area's largest zoo is spread over 216 acres with 2,700 animals in residence. Observe giraffes, snow leopards, Siberian tigers, green sea turtles, baboons, and more. **Habitat Africa!** is a multiple-ecosystem exhibit, almost 30 acres in size. All the animals live in naturalistic environments that allow them to live side-by-side with other inhabitants of their regions. The **Seven Seas** show featuring dolphins is a perennial hit with kids. One of the newest exhibits is **The Living Coast,** which explores the western coast of Chile and Peru and includes everything from a tank of plate-size moon jellies to a rocky shore where Humboldt penguins swim. If you plan to visit on a weekend, make sure to buy tickets to the dolphin show several hours in advance because it always sells out. The **Hamill Family Play Zoo** is a wonderful stop for kids, a place where they can pet animals, build habitats, learn how to plant a garden, and play animal dress-up. There's a separate admission fee — $3 adults, $2 children — for the Play Zoo.

See map p. 174. First Avenue and 31st Street in Brookfield. ☎ *708-485-0263.* www. brookfieldzoo.org. *CTA: Bus no. 304 or 311. By car: Take the Stevenson (I-55) and Eisenhower (I-290) expressways 14 miles west of the Loop; parking is $8. Admission: $8 adults, $4 seniors and children 3–11. Free admission Tues and Thurs, Oct–Mar. Open: Daily Memorial Day–Labor Day, 9:30 a.m.–6 p.m.; fall through spring daily 10 a.m.–5 p.m.*

ESPN Zone
Near the Magnificent Mile

This sports-themed entertainment and dining complex is a hit with teenagers. Inside you find the Studio Grill, designed with replicas of studio sets from the network's shows; the Screening Room, a sports pub with a 16-foot screen and TV monitors; radio sets carrying broadcasts of games; and the Sports Arena, a gaming area with interactive and competitive attractions. You even find a mini basketball court where parents can play with their kids.

See map p. 174. 43 E. Ohio St. ☎ *312-644-3776. CTA: Red-line El to Grand; bus no. 22 or 36. Admission: Free, but games cost extra. Open: Mon–Thurs 11:30 a.m. to midnight, Fri 11:30 a.m.–1 a.m., Sat 11 a.m.–1 a.m., Sun 11:30 a.m.–11:30 p.m.*

Peggy Notebaert Nature Museum
Lincoln Park

This museum (also known as the Nature Museum of the Chicago Academy of Sciences) focuses on human activities and the environment. Interactive exhibits include the **Children's Gallery,** where kids can check out a beaver lodge from the inside or climb around in a model, ground-level squirrel town. The highlight by far is the **Butterfly Haven,** where 25 Midwestern species, along with butterflies and moths from around the world, carry on their life cycles in a greenhouse environment. **Water Lab,** a model river system, highlights the uses and abuses of a waterway traveling from a rural to an urban environment. In summertime, stop by the sunny Butterfly Café to enjoy an early-morning coffee and muffin with joggers and other locals.

See map p. 175. 2430 N. Cannon Dr. (off Fullerton Parkway). ☎ *773-755-5100.* www. chias.org. *CTA: Bus no. 146 or 151. Admission: $7 adults, $5 seniors and students, $4 children 3–12, free for children under 3. Free admission Thurs. Open: Mon–Fri 9 a.m.–4:30 p.m., Sat–Sun 10 a.m.–5 p.m. Closed Jan 1, Thanksgiving (fourth Thurs in Nov), and Dec 25.*

Six Flags Great America
Suburban Gurnee

If your kids have thrill-seeking personalities, head for this major theme/amusement park located in the northern suburbs, about a 45-minute drive from Chicago. The park has more than 100 rides and attractions and is a favorite with roller-coaster fans. You find a whopping ten roller coasters, including the nausea-inducing Déjà Vu, where riders fly forward and backward over a twisting, looping, inverted steel track, and Superman, where you speed along hanging headfirst. Other don't-miss rides for the strong of stomach include the Iron Wolf, where you do corkscrew turns and 360-degree loops while standing up, and the American Eagle, a classic wooden coaster. Teenagers have a ball here, but so do little ones: The Looney Tunes National Park is full of kiddie rides with cartoon themes. Six Flags also has live shows, IMAX movies, and restaurants. If you take the trouble to get here, allow a full day.

See map p. 175. I-94 at Route 132 East. ☎ *847-249-4636.* www.sixflags.com. *Admission (including unlimited rides, shows, and attractions): $41.99 adults, $29.99 seniors and children under 54 inches tall, free for children 3 and under. Parking: $10. Open: Daily May 10 a.m.–7 p.m., June–Aug 10 a.m.–10 p.m., weekends only in Sept 10 a.m.–7 p.m. Take I-94 or I-294 to Route 132 (Grand Avenue).*

Especially for architecture lovers

Chicago has so many great buildings — by such notable architects as Frank Lloyd Wright, Louis Sullivan, and Ludwig Mies van der Rohe — that architecture buffs will be in heaven.

Also see the listings for the **Chicago Architecture Foundation Boat Tours, Chicago Cultural Center,** and **Frank Lloyd Wright Home and Studio** earlier in this chapter. Building buffs may also want to visit the **Sears Tower** or the **John Hancock Center** (earlier in this chapter) or the **Harold Washington Library Center** (later in this chapter). See "Seeing Chicago by Guided Tour," later in this chapter, for information on architecture tours.

Auditorium Building and Theatre
Loop

A truly grand theater with historic landmark status, the Auditorium is worth a visit to experience late-19th-century Chicago opulence. Designed and built in 1889 by Louis Sullivan and Dankmar Adler, the Auditorium was a wonder of the world: the heaviest (110,000 tons) and most massive modern edifice on earth, the most fireproof building ever constructed, and the tallest in Chicago. It was also the first large-scale building to be electrically lighted, and its theater was the first in the country to install air-conditioning.

Today, the 4,000-seat auditorium is a venue for touring Broadway shows, and the office building is the home of Roosevelt University. Tours are available but must be arranged in advance.

See map p. 174. 50 E. Congress Parkway (at Michigan Avenue). ☎ *312-922-2110.* www.auditoriumtheatre.org. *CTA: Brown-, green-, orange-, or purple-line El to Library/Van Buren or red-line El to Jackson; bus no. 145, 147, or 151. For ticket reservations or box office information, call Ticketmaster at* ☎ *312-902-1500. Call* ☎ *312-431-2354 to arrange a one-hour tour. Tour tickets: $5 adults, $3 seniors and students.*

Charnley-Persky House
Gold Coast

Architecture junkies may want to visit this modest Gold Coast mansion, designed by Frank Lloyd Wright in 1891 while working in the office of Louis Sullivan. Elements of the design can be traced to both architects — Sullivan's famous organic ornamentation decorates the fireplaces while the layout around the home's hearth is pure Wright. A stop here makes a nice highlight to a walking tour of the surrounding neighborhood. Visits to the house, now the home of the Society of Architectural Historians, are by guided tour only; enter the house by the south gate. Tours last approximately 45 minutes.

See map p. 174. 1365 N. Astor St. ☎ *312-915-0105.* www.charnleyhouse.org. *CTA: Bus no. 11, 22, 36, or 151 to Inner Lakeshore Drive and Goethe Street, then walk 2 blocks west. Tours: $5 adults, $3.50 seniors and students, free for children; free for all on Wed. Tour times: Wed noon, Sat 10 a.m. and 1 p.m. Extended tour of home and Astor Place area on Saturday for $10. Call ahead for information.*

Glessner House
South of the Loop

Prairie Avenue, south of the Loop, was the city's first "Gold Coast," and its most famous address is Glessner House, a must-see for anyone interested in architectural history. The only surviving Chicago building designed by Boston architect Henry Hobson Richardson, the house represented a dramatic shift from traditional Victorian architecture upon its completion in 1886. The imposing granite exterior gives the home a forbidding air, but step inside and you discover a welcoming, cozy retreat filled with Arts and Crafts furnishings. Visits to the house are by guided tour only, and are first-come, first-served.

See map p. 174. 1800 S. Prairie Ave. ☎ 312-326-1480. www.glessnerhouse.org. *CTA: Bus no. 1, 3, or 4 from Michigan Avenue at Jackson Boulevard, get off at 18th Street. Tickets: $10 adults, $9 seniors and students, $5 children 5–12. Tours: Wed–Sun 1, 2, and 3 p.m. Closed major holidays.*

Water Tower
Magnificent Mile

One of Chicago's best-known landmarks dominates the Magnificent Mile like a gleaming fairy-tale castle. However, its original purpose is decidedly un-fairy-tale-like. The tower was designed to conceal an ugly, 138-foot-high standpipe used in connection with pumping water from Lake Michigan. Many thought the structure itself even more unsightly — Oscar Wilde described it as "a castellated monstrosity with pepper boxes stuck all over it." But Chicagoans have come to be proud of their talisman, one of the few buildings to survive the Great Fire of 1871. (Its companion pumping station, across the street, was another.) The tower has been spruced up and is surrounded by lawns and park benches. Lights illuminate the tower at night, and street musicians often play in the surrounding park.

See map p. 174. 800 N. Michigan Ave. ☎ 312-440-3165. CTA: Red-line El to Chicago/ State; bus no. 125, 145, 146, 147, or 151 to Michigan and Chicago avenues. Open: Mon–Sat 10 a.m.–7 p.m., Sun noon to 6 p.m.

Wicker Park

If you hit just one outlying neighborhood, Wicker Park, with its Victorian homes and 19th-century buildings first built by Polish immigrants, is the place to go. Not long ago, this was a tough neighborhood whose "mean streets" served as a model for author Nelson Algren in novels such as *The Man With the Golden Arm*. Wicker Park is now being gentrified — its many large homes are being remodeled, and restaurants and boutiques are opening. **Chicago Neighborhood Tours** (☎ 312-742-1190 for information; www.chgocitytours.com) offers an excursion that explores Wicker Park. Sights include art galleries, the distinctive **Flatiron Building,** 1569–79 N. Milwaukee Ave. at North Avenue, an office building designed in 1929 by Holabird & Root that now houses galleries and artist studios. The tour also passes **Holy Trinity Russian Orthodox Cathedral,** 1121 N. Leavitt St., designed in 1899 by Louis Sullivan and constructed with a donation from Czar Nicholas II.

Strong evidence does remain of Wicker Park's Polish past and present. Coexisting with chic coffee bars and galleries are the shops, eateries, and churches that serve the Polish community. Many Poles still live in Wicker Park — sometimes referred to as Chicago's "Ethnic Gold Coast." The **Polish Museum of America,** 984 N. Milwaukee Ave. (☎ 773-384-3352), features an extensive exhibit about Ignacy Jan Paderewsky, a Polish

Renaissance Man who was a world-class pianist, composer, and prime minister of Poland.

See map p. 174. Bordered by John F. Kennedy Expressway and Western, Chicago, and Fullerton avenues. CTA: Blue-line El to Damen or Division; bus no. 56, 70, or 72 along Milwaukee Avenue.

Especially for romantics

Don't be fooled by the sports-town image: Chicago can be just as romantic as the next city. When the stars rise on a warm summer evening, few cities can match its seductive lake breezes and city lights.

You can always go to an expensive restaurant to find a romantic setting, but why not try something a bit more creative? Here are some of my favorites:

✔ On a starry night, head to **Navy Pier** (see Chapter 11), where you can take a spin on the Ferris wheel or just stroll along the water and gaze at the city's lights.

✔ Pack up your picnic supplies and candelabra for a classy night under the stars at the **Ravinia Music Festival** (see Chapter 15) in suburban Highland Park.

 ✔ You can enjoy the moon, music, and munchies closer to downtown during free concerts in Millennium Park's Pritzer Bandshell by the **Grant Park Symphony and Chorus** (see Chapter 15).

✔ What could be more romantic than spending the day on a sailboat? You can rent a boat from the **Chicago Sailing Club** in Belmont Harbor. See the next section for details.

 ✔ The McKinlock Court Garden Restaurant (☎ 312-443-3600), tucked away in the center of the **Art Institute of Chicago** (see listing in this chapter), is the spot for free jazz — as well as good quiche, wine, cheesecake, and cappuccino. The outdoor cafe surrounds the soothing Triton fountain. On Tuesday evenings during warm-weather months, jazz aficionados sit outside among the flowers and trees and listen to live music. Museum admission is free on Tuesdays; the restaurant has an $8-per-person minimum.

Taking love to new heights

Navy Pier's 148-foot-high Ferris wheel, which opened in 1995, quickly became a Chicago landmark. The ride was modeled after the very first Ferris wheel, which was built for Chicago's 1893 World's Columbian Exposition. Only weeks after the new Ferris wheel opened, a man and woman were married on it. You don't have to get married to enjoy the ride: A seven-and-a-half-minute ride costs $5 (bride or groom not included), and the views are spectacular.

Especially for active types

From biking to climbing to skating, Chicago presents loads of opportunities for indoor and outdoor adventures. If you're traveling with a teenager, one of these activities may be just the thing to combat teen boredom — no doubt the result of too many hours spent touring museums with the family.

- ✔ **Biking:** Chicago boasts 18 miles of paved lakefront paths. **Bike Chicago** rents bicycles during the warm months at Navy Pier (☎ 312-595-9600) and North Avenue Beach (☎ 773-327-2706), and year-round at Millennium Park (☎ 888-245-3929). Rates are $8.75 an hour, $30 for a half-day (four hours) or $34 a day. If you make a reservation during the summer, you can join a free, two-hour, 6-mile sightseeing tour led by a guide. Bike Chicago also rents in-line skates. Call ahead for times.

  Both the Chicago Park District (☎ 312-742-7529) and the Chicagoland Bicycle Federation (☎ 312-427-3325; www.chibikefed.org) offer free maps that detail biking routes.

- ✔ **Climbing:** Waiting to challenge climbers at the **Lakeshore Athletic Club,** 211 N. Stetson, 1 block east of North Michigan Avenue at Lake Street (☎ 312-616-9000), is "Mount Chicago," billed as the "world's highest indoor climbing wall." Rising 110 dizzying feet, the man-made wall offers a climbing adventure even to those who lack previous experience. Climbers must take an orientation and safety class and wear a protective body harness. The cost is $35 for first-time climbers; return visitors pay $20.

- ✔ **Fishing:** Want to do battle with a scrappy coho salmon, or tie into a tackle-testing, arm-aching, 20-plus-pound Chinook? Salmon fishing has been big on Lake Michigan since Pacific species were introduced in the 1970s. The **Chicago Sportfishing Association** (☎ 312-922-1100) can help you find a charter in Burnham Harbor and Diversey Harbor, most of which cost about $395 for five hours.

- ✔ **Golfing:** To warm up your swing in the spring, head to the **Diversey Driving Range,** 141 W. Diversey Parkway (☎ 312-742-7929), in Lincoln Park just north of Diversey Harbor. This two-level range attracts all levels, and the price is certainly right — $10.50 for a bucket of 50 balls. The Chicago Park District runs six golf courses in the city; one of the most popular is the nine-hole **Sydney Marovitz Course,** 3600 N. Lake Shore Dr., at Waveland Avenue; many Chicagoans refer to it simply as Waveland. Thanks to its picturesque lakefront location, it's always full on the weekends, so make a reservation well in advance. This course, and other city-run courses, is open mid-April through November. For information on greens fees, locations, and hours, call the Chicago Park District golf office (☎ 312-245-0909; www.cpdgolf.com).

- **The Green at Grant Park,** an 18-hole putting course in Grant Park, boasts spectacular views of the city. For information on greens fees, locations, and hours, call ☎ 312-642-7888 or visit www.thegreen online.com.

- **Ice-skating:** Whether you're a graceful glider or merely a stumbler, you can ice-skate (weather permitting) in the heart of Chicago's Loop at **McCormick-Tribune Ice Rink,** 55 N. Michigan Ave. (☎ 312-742-5222). Located in Millennium Park on the north end of Grant Park, the 16,000-square-foot rink is open from late November through March. Admission is free, and skate rentals cost $5. There's also a relatively small rink at Navy Pier, 600 E. Grand Ave. (☎ 312-595-7437).

- **Sailing:** The **Chicago Sailing Club** in Belmont Harbor (☎ 773-871-7245; www.chicagosailingclub.com) rents J-22 and J-30 boats from 9 a.m. to sunset, weather permitting, May through October. A J-22 holds four adults, and a J-30 accommodates six. Rates range from $35 to $90 an hour or from $305 to $520 a day, depending on boat size. The services of a skipper are extra; if you choose not to hire a skipper, you must prove your sailing skills (a small evaluation fee is charged). Reservations are essential.

- **Swimming:** The lakefront is open for swimming until 9:30 p.m. from Memorial Day to Labor Day in areas watched over by lifeguards (no swimming off the rocks, please). A good place to swim is Ohio Street Beach, located near Navy Pier. The Chicago Triathalon Club marks a course here each summer with a buoy at both the ¼- and ½-mile distance. This popular swimming route follows the shoreline in a straight line and is fairly shallow. For more information, contact the Chicago Park District (☎ 312-742-7529).

- **Walking or running:** The paved lakefront path is perfect for walking or running. See the "Walking in Chicago" sidebar in this chapter for my recommended route.

Especially for sports fans

Chicago's pro sports teams tend to be underachievers. The **Cubs** haven't played in a World Series since 1945, and the **White Sox** have been excluded from baseball's fall classic since 1959. Not since the glory days of 1961 have the **Blackhawks** hoisted hockey's Stanley Cup. The **Bears** won their one and only Super Bowl after the 1985–1986 season. The **Bulls** were the exception. During the Jordan years, they took six NBA championships. But with Michael gone, the Bulls are mired at the bottom of the league.

The general lack of success doesn't deter hard-core fans, but it does keep away fair-weather followers. That means tickets are generally available, although Cubs and Bears tickets are a little tougher to obtain than the others, especially for key matchups.

Walking in Chicago

Chicago is a great city for stretching your legs. If you stay downtown, take a stroll along **Michigan Avenue** from Oak Street to the Chicago River. Although the walk can be enjoyable at any hour, I recommend the morning, before the crowds descend.

If the day is pleasant and you have a bit more energy, head to the **lakefront path,** a popular destination for locals. You can access the lakefront at the intersection of Oak Street and Michigan Avenue. (If it's daytime and busy in the area, use the pedestrian tunnel. Do not use the tunnel at night or very early in the morning.) After you're on the lakefront path at Oak Street Beach, head south. You'll go around a bend and see two stunning glass apartment buildings designed by Mies van der Rohe to your right. Keep heading south. You may see swimmers (in wetsuits during much of the year) swimming alongside you in the water. When you reach the black Lakefront Tower (the only high-rise to the east of Lake Shore Drive), head east to **Navy Pier.** Walk or run along the south side of the pier all the way to the end and back. You can return to Michigan Avenue along the same route or use the pedestrian underpass beneath Lake Shore Drive at Chicago Avenue. (Again, don't use the underpass at night or very early in the morning.) After you emerge from the tunnel, walk due west to Michigan Avenue. Navy Pier is ¾ mile in length. The run (or walk) from Oak Street adds just over 2 miles.

What follows is a guide to Chicago's professional sports teams:

- ✔ **Chicago Bears: Soldier Field,** Lake Shore Drive and 16th Street (www.chicagobears.com), is home of the Chicago Bears. The classic colonnade was retained in a recent renovation, but football fans will recognize little else. A giant addition looks like a spaceship was crammed awkwardly on top of the venerable old stadium. But the "Monsters of the Midway" will continue to battle wind, snow, and fog, in addition to their opponents — the revamped stadium still doesn't have a dome. For Bears tickets, call ☎ 847-615-2327. Bus no. 146 travels to the stadium.

- ✔ **Chicago Blackhawks:** The Chicago Blackhawks (www.chicago blackhawks.com) have a devoted, passionate following of fans who work themselves into a frenzy with the first note of "The Star-Spangled Banner." The 'Hawks play at the **United Center,** 1901 W. Madison St., west of the Loop, which they share with the Chicago Bulls. For hockey tickets, call Ticketmaster at ☎ 312-559-1212.

- ✔ **Chicago Bulls:** The Bulls play at the **United Center,** 1901 W. Madison St., a facility that they share with the Blackhawks. The life-size bronze statue of Michael Jordan at the stadium entrance pretty much sums up the recent success of pro sports in Chicago. For Bulls tickets, go to the Web site www.nba.com/bulls or call ☎ 800-462-2849. Bus no. 20 travels from the Loop to the United Center.

✔ **Chicago Cubs:** See the listing for **Wrigley Field** earlier in this chapter.

✔ **Chicago White Sox:** This south-side baseball club has a reputation for attracting "blue-collar" fans (compared to the Cubs' "white-collar" supporters). The toughest ticket in town is the Sox-Cubs matchup. The White Sox (www.whitesox.mlb.com) play in **U.S. Cellular Field** (formerly called Comiskey Park), 333 W. 35th St. For Sox tickets, call Ticketmaster at ☎ **866-769-4263** or visit the park's box office. To get to the ballpark by the El, take the red line to Sox/35th Street.

Especially for serious museum buffs

After you hit the major Chicago institutions — the **Art Institute of Chicago,** the **Museum of Science and Industry,** and the offerings of the **Museum Campus** (see "Chicago's Top Sights," earlier in this chapter for details on all of these) — museum fans still have more options.

Chicago Historical Society
Lincoln Park

In a state that dubs itself "the Land of Lincoln," you'd expect to see a wealth of memorabilia relating to the 16th president. This museum doesn't disappoint. The powerful exhibit "A House Divided: America in the Age of Lincoln" uses video, audio, and memorabilia to capture the era and its problems, including slavery and the destruction created by the Civil War. Displays include Lincoln's deathbed and the table at which generals Robert E. Lee and Ulysses S. Grant signed the surrender at Appomattox. Other exhibits deal with pioneer life, the Great Chicago Fire, and the city's ethnicity. In the Hands-On History Gallery, families can visit a fur-trading post, play old-time radio sound effects, and view the contents of early mail-order catalogs. In 2005, the museum will undergo major upgrades and renovations, and although it will remain open, you'll want to call in advance or see the Web site to check the status of any exhibits.

See map p. 174. 1601 N. Clark St. at North Avenue. ☎ *312-642-4600.* www.chicago history.org. *CTA: Bus no. 11, 22, 36, or 151 to Inner Lakeshore Drive and North Avenue. Admission: $5 adults, $3 seniors and students 12–23, $1 children 6–12 years, free for children under 6. Free admission Mon. Open: Mon–Sat 9:30 a.m.–4:30 p.m., Sun noon to 5 p.m.*

DuSable Museum of African-American History
South Side

The pride and the pain of African Americans is chronicled in the museum named for Jean Baptiste Point du Sable, born of a French father and a black mother. The affluent, well-educated du Sable became Chicago's first permanent settler when he established a trading post in 1779. Exhibits portray the degradations and cruelty of slavery and the hope of the civil rights movement. Offering a mix of art and history, the museum displays significant works by African-American artists and celebrates African Americans' exploits in the armed forces. It also documents lynchings, Ku Klux Klan activities, and demeaning products (such as *Little Black Sambo* books).

See map p. 174. Washington Park, 740 E. 56th Place. ☎ *773-947-0600.* www. dusablemuseum.org. *CTA: Metra electric train to 57th Street and Lake Park Avenue, then a short cab ride. Admission: $3 adults, $2 seniors and students, $1 children 6–12, free for children under 6. Free admission Sun. Open: Mon–Sat 10 a.m.–5 p.m., Sun noon to 5 p.m. Closed Jan 1, Thanksgiving (fourth Thurs of Nov), and Dec 25.*

Museum of Broadcast Communications
River North

This museum, formerly housed in the basement of the Chicago Cultural Center, closed its doors in 2004, and plans to reopen in 2006 in a new, 50,000-square-foot home on State Street at Kinzie Avenue. The Museum of Broadcast Communications claims to be one of only three broadcast museums in the nation. Its new home will include expanded archives and exhibit galleries, seminars and public events, a radio and television studio, a gift shop, and a cafe. Stay tuned for more, as they say in the business.

See map p. 174. 400 N. State St. at Kinzie, Suite 240. ☎ *312-245-8200.* www. mbcnet.org.

Museum of Contemporary Art
Magnificent Mile

The nation's largest contemporary art museum opened in 1996 to mixed reviews. Set between the lake and the Water Tower on a piece of prime real estate, the building feels a bit inaccessible, with a daunting set of stairs leading to the entrance. The interior, however, is light and vibrant. The museum highlights works dating back to 1945, including work by Alexander Calder, Sol LeWitt, Donald Judd, and Bruce Nauman — plus Andy Warhol and Jeff Koons. You may want to take the free daily tour or rent an audio tour for insights into the often-challenging exhibits. You'll find wonderful cultural programming here, including "Stories on Stage," with Chicago actors reading classic and contemporary short stories. It's great fun.

See map p. 174. 220 E. Chicago Ave., just east of Michigan Avenue. ☎ *312-280-2660.* www.mcachicago.org. *CTA: Red-line El to Chicago/State; bus no. 3, 10, 11, 66, 125, 145, 146, or 152. Admission: $10 adults, $6 seniors and students, free children 12 and under. Free admission Tues 5–8 p.m. Open: Tues 10 a.m.–8 p.m., Wed–Sun 10 a.m.–5 p.m.*

Oriental Institute Museum
Hyde Park

Don't be misled by the name, which predates the term *Middle East.* At this location at the midpoint of the University of Chicago campus, you'll find mummies, Persian kings' gold jewelry, a fragment of the Dead Sea Scrolls, and Tutankhamen's tomb. This user-friendly, free museum contains one of the world's largest collections of Near Eastern art, including a massive statue of the boy-king, Tutankhamen. The museum is divided into the Egyptian Gallery, Mesopotamian Gallery, and Persian Gallery. So if you're interested in ancient Egypt, Syria, Palestine, Iran, Iraq, Turkey, and other Middle Eastern countries, come here to discover amazing artifacts — and don't miss the 40-ton Assyrian winged bull.

1155 E. 58th St. at University Avenue. ☎ *773-702-9514.* www-oi.uchicago.edu. *CTA: Bus no. 6 or Metra electric train to 57th Street and Lake Park Avenue. Admission: Free; suggested donation $5 adults, $2 children. Open: Tues and Thurs–Sat 10 a.m.–4 p.m., Wed 10 a.m.–8:30 p.m., Sun noon to 4 p.m.*

Especially for book lovers

Bibliophiles find plenty to keep them entertained in Chicago. Book collectors and readers alike may want to schedule their visit around the **Printers Row Book Fair,** which takes place in June (see Chapter 3).

Harold Washington Library Center
Loop

Chicago's first African-American mayor was a charismatic leader, and this handsome library is a fitting tribute. A permanent exhibition chronicles the life of the popular mayor, who died in 1987 during his second term. The political memorabilia includes a button collection; one reads "Honkies for Harold," symbolizing his universal appeal. Artworks by African-American artists fill the ten-story interior. The ninth floor contains the sun-dappled winter garden, a good spot for study and contemplation, and the stylish **Beyond Words Café.** A children's library offers puppet shows and other activities. On the ground floor, **Second Hand Prose** sells (for pennies) books retired from circulation.

The library offers free one-hour guided tours of its art and architecture. Tours depart daily at 2 p.m.

See map p. 174. 400 S. State St. ☎ *312-747-4300.* www.chipublib.org. *CTA: Purple-, brown-, or orange-line El; bus no. 2, 6, 10, 11, 29, 36, 44, 62, 99, 146, or 164 to State and Van Buren. Admission: Free. Open: Mon–Thurs 9 a.m.–7 p.m., Fri–Sat 9 a.m.–5 p.m., Sun 1–5 p.m.*

Newberry Library
Near the Magnificent Mile

This attractive five-story granite building houses a noncirculating research library with rare books and manuscripts (including Shakespeare's First Folio and Jefferson's copy of *The Federalist Papers*). The library is a major destination for genealogists — the genealogy holdings are available to the public for free if you're over age 16 and have a photo ID. Public exhibitions display many of the library's books and maps. Programs include concerts, lectures, children's story hours, and a holiday bazaar in early December.

Free one-hour tours are available on Thursday at 3 p.m. and on Saturday at 10:30 a.m.

See map p. 175. 60 W. Walton St. at Dearborn Parkway. ☎ *312-943-9090 or 312-255-3700 for programs.* www.newberry.org. *CTA: Red-line El to Chicago/State; bus no. 22, 36, 125, 145, 146, or 151 to Chestnut and Dearborn streets. Admission: Free. Open: Reading room Tues–Thurs 10 a.m.–6 p.m., Fri 9 a.m.–5 p.m.*

Especially for movie lovers

Tired of sightseeing? Is the weather too hot or rainy to be outside? Seek shelter in the comforts of a movie theater. For locations and movie listings for Chicago's many multiplexes, pick up a copy of the *Chicago Tribune* or *Chicago Sun-Times.*

If you're in the mood for something different (no doubt you can go to a multiplex in your hometown), visit one of these movie houses that cater to cinema buffs with truly original programming:

✔ **Facets Multi-Media,** 1517 W. Fullerton Ave. (☎ **773-281-9075;** www. facets.org; CTA: Red- or brown-line El to Fullerton), is for the diehard cinematic thrill-seeker. This nonprofit center screens independent films and videos from around the world. Facets also hosts the Children's Film Festival (Oct–Nov) and the Chicago Latino Film Festival (Apr–May).

✔ The **Gene Siskel Film Center,** 164 N. State St. (☎ **312-846-2600;** www.siskelfilmcenter.org; CTA: Red-line El to Washington or brown-line El to Randolph), named after the well-known *Chicago Tribune* film critic who died in 1999, is part of the School of the Art Institute of Chicago. The center hosts an eclectic selection of film series in two theaters, including lectures and discussions with filmmakers. The Film Center often shows foreign films that are not released commercially in the United States.

✔ The **Music Box Theatre** on the far North Side is a classic movie house with a big screen and a house organist; see Chapter 15 for details.

Chicago's colorful politics

Read the newspapers or listen to the news, and you get a glimpse into Chicago's ward politics and political machine ("vote early and often" was a phrase coined in the Windy City), as well as the not-so-complimentary nicknames that Chicago gives its politicians. Corrupt Alderman "Bathhouse" John Coughlin earned his nickname because he formerly labored in a public bathhouse. Snippy Mayor Jane Byrne was known as "Attila the Hen" and "Crazy Jane." Slick-tongued, deal-making Alderman Edward Vrodolyak was known as "Fast Eddie." Not-so-slick-tongued Mayor Eugene Sawyer was dubbed "Mayor Mumbles." Mayor Anton Cermak was labeled "Pushcart Tony" because of his former job as a teamster.

If you're a fan of the oldies, you have two interesting options, both free:

✔ **Chicago Cultural Center,** 78 E. Washington St., near the Loop (☎ 312-744-6630), screens classics such as *Casablanca* on Tuesday evenings.

✔ The **Oriental Institute Museum** (☎ 773-702-9507; see listing earlier in this chapter) in Hyde Park screens such flicks as *Cleopatra,* the 1934 Cecil B. DeMille epic starring Claudette Colbert, on Sundays.

For inexpensive seats to Hollywood's more-recent offerings, check out one of these second-run movie theaters:

✔ **3 Penny Cinema,** 2424 N. Lincoln Ave. (☎ 773-525-3449; CTA: Red- or brown-line El to Fullerton/Lincoln)

✔ **Davis Theaters,** 4614 N. Lincoln Ave. (☎ 773-784-0893; CTA: Brown-line El to Western)

✔ **Village North,** 6746 N. Sheridan Rd. (☎ 773-764-9100; CTA: Bus no. 147 or 151 to the door)

✔ **Village South,** 1548 N. Clark St. (☎ 312-642-2403; CTA: Bus no. 135 or 136 to LaSalle and North, walk 1 block east)

Seeing Chicago by Guided Tour

While you already have a friend to show you around Chicago (this book!), I won't be offended if you want an in-person guided tour. A good guide can escort you around the city and its neighborhoods, pointing out the sights and giving you special insights.

Just the basics: Orientation tours

Take a tour as soon as you arrive. You can take a basic sightseeing tour on a motor coach, van, double-decker bus, open trolley, or boat. Even if you did your homework and have read this book cover to cover, there's nothing like seeing the city firsthand. Suddenly, the geography you tried to fix in your mind makes sense. Attractions and sights you read about come to life. It's like the difference between viewing a movie in black-and-white and viewing it in color.

One popular spot for picking up a land or water tour is at the Michigan Avenue Bridge (over the Chicago River at East Wacker Drive). Other land tours take off from the intersection of Pearson Street and Michigan Avenue (near the Water Tower).

One word of caution about guided tours: Don't regard everything you hear as fact. Narrators are known to take liberties with the truth and are apt to spread a rumor or two. They also read from a script that is usually

Insider tours — for free!

Want to see the city from a native's point of view? Chicago Greeter, a new program run by the Chicago Office of Tourism, matches tourists with local Chicagoans who serve as volunteer guides. Visitors can request a specific neighborhood or theme (everything from Polish heritage sites to Chicago movie locations), and a greeter gives a free, two- to four-hour tour. Greeters won't escort groups of more than six people, but kids of all ages are welcome (bringing newborns on the tours, however, is discouraged). When you call, be sure to specify that you'll be using a stroller, so your guide can plan accordingly for accessing public transportation. Popular family tours include Lincoln Park Zoo and the Shedd Aquarium. Specific requests for tours should be made at least a week in advance, but "InstaGreeters" are also available on a first-come, first-served basis at the Chicago Cultural Center, 77 E. Randolph St., Friday through Sunday. For details, call ☎ **312-744-8000** or visit www.chicagogreeter.com.

memorized — the 10,000th repetition may be dull. Treat these tours as what they are: basic sightseeing and orientation — here's the Water Tower, there's the Sears Tower, here's Lake Michigan.

Any of the following companies can give you a good overview of the city:

- ✔ **American Sightseeing Tours** (☎ **312-251-3100**): This company offers ten different bus excursions that include basic orientation, neighborhood, nightlife, and architectural tours. Tours run two to five and a half hours and cost $20 to $40. The $40 tour includes admission to the Sears Tower Skydeck.

- ✔ **Chicago Trolley Company** (☎ **773-648-5000**): Breezy trolleys provide one-and-a-half-hour narrated tours of the major sites and also offer all-day on-and-off privileges. In inclement weather, vehicles are enclosed and heated. Trolleys run every 20 minutes or so, depending on the seasonal demand. The fare is $20 for adults, $17 for seniors, and $10 for children 3 to 11. Tours run daily 9 a.m. to 9 p.m. (until 6:30 p.m. Apr–Oct).

- ✔ **Gray Line Tours** (☎ **312-251-3107**; www.grayline.com): You'll find the granddaddy of tour companies in every major city, including Chicago. Gray Line offers a range of bus excursions, including four-hour *Inside Chicago* tour packages, which cost $28 for adults and $14 for children 5 to 12.

- ✔ **MetroDucks Tours** (☎ **800-298-1506**; www.metroducks.com): These amphibious transports go on land and water — originally they were designed to bring troops and supplies ashore during World War II. You'll start with a one-hour land tour of the Loop, Michigan Avenue, Grant Park, and the Museum Campus. Next, your duck rolls into the water — kids love the change from car to boat — and transports you on a 30-minute tour of Chicago from the lake. Tickets are $20 for adults, $18 for seniors and active military personnel, $10 for children 4 to 12, and $1 for children 3 and under. Tours run daily from 10 a.m. to 4 p.m.

Water, water everywhere: Boat tours

A variety of excursion boats travel the Lake Michigan shoreline and three branches of the Chicago River. The boats offer sightseeing by day, and dining and dancing at night. Primary boarding spots are along the Chicago River between North Michigan and Wabash avenues; Ogden Slip, at the east end of East Illinois Street next to River East Plaza; and Navy Pier.

You may be surprised at this advice from an off-the-beaten-path aficionado, but here goes: Get thee on that boat. Chicagoans know the absolute best way to get the lay of the land is by water. You save oodles of time. Instead of wandering around (like a tourist, I must add), you can maneuver with something resembling confidence and get a taste of Chicago's beautiful lakefront from a unique perspective.

Do-it-yourself sightseeing

A cheap way to tour the city is by hopping aboard one of Chicago's El trains or buses. You can take you own tour for the cost of subway or bus fare — $1.75, plus 25¢ for a transfer (good for a return trip if you use it within two hours). Here are some of the city's best sightseeing routes (for information on public transportation, see Chapter 8):

✔ **Brown-line El** (trip duration 20 minutes; daily): Ride from the Loop to Belmont Station. You get a bird's-eye view of downtown, gentrified loft districts, and a number of historic neighborhoods. Start at the big El station at Clark and Lake streets and get on the northbound train.

✔ **No. 151 Sheridan bus** (trip duration 30 minutes; daily): Pick up the 151 downtown on Michigan Avenue (the bus stops every 2 blocks on the avenue) and ride it north to Belmont. You cover Lake Shore Drive and Lincoln Park. If you take the bus south, you travel State Street and wind up at Union Station.

✔ **No. 146 Marine-Michigan bus** (trip duration 20 minutes; daily): This express bus allows you to take in North Michigan Avenue, State Street, and the Museum Campus. Pick up the bus on Sheridan and Diversey going south. (You can also pick up the 146 along Michigan Avenue, although it has fewer stops than the 151.) You see the Harold Washington Library, the Art Institute of Chicago, the Chicago Cultural Center, and the landmark Water Tower.

✔ **No. 10 Museum of Science and Industry bus** (trip duration 35 minutes; weekends year-round, daily in summer and winter holiday season): From North Michigan Avenue at the Water Tower (the stop is in front of Borders on Michigan Avenue across from Water Tower Place), ride south to the Museum Campus. You see Grant Park, the Art Institute of Chicago, the University of Chicago, and Chinatown.

For most sightseeing boats, the season runs from early May through late October. Tours typically last 90 minutes, but shorter and longer trips are available. Most operate on a set schedule, and reservations are advisable during prime times, such as weekends and holidays in the middle of summer. At other times, walking on is possible.

The following tour companies offer great ways to see the city from the water (also see **MetroDucks Tours** and **Chicago Architecture Foundation Boat Tours** earlier in this chapter):

- ✔ **Mercury Chicago's Skyline Cruiseline** (☎ 312-332-1353) offers river and lake cruises departing from the southeast corner of the Michigan Avenue Bridge (Michigan Avenue at Wacker Drive). The daily sightseeing tour along the Chicago River and Lake Michigan takes one and a half hours. The fare is $17 for adults, $10 for children under 11. Architectural tours along the river are offered on *Chicago's First Lady*. This one-and-a-half-hour tour costs $23 Monday through Friday and $25 on weekends. Tickets are available through Ticketmaster (☎ 312-902-1500). Daylong weekend excursions along the National Heritage Corridor, the river route connecting Chicago and the Mississippi River, cost $69. Cruises operate daily from the end of April through the end of October.

- ✔ **Mystic Blue Cruises** (☎ 877-299-7783; www.mysticbluecruises. com) offers a casual dinner cruise with a DJ, TV monitors playing music videos, and spirited dancing. You may run into a bachelor or bachelorette party. Food is served buffet-style. The fare is $28 to $61, depending on the time of day, and cruises run year-round.

- ✔ *Seadog* (☎ 888-636-7737; www.seadogcruises.com) combines sightseeing and thrills. Expect to get wet as the distinctive yellow speedboat knifes through the waters of Lake Michigan and kicks up a 15-foot-high spray. The 149-seat *Seadog* can reach speeds of more than 50 knots and offers exciting 30-minute rides along the lakefront. Board at Navy Pier. Tickets are $17 for adults, $10 for children ages 3 to 11. Cruises operate May 1 through September 30.

- ✔ *Spirit of Chicago* (☎ 866-211-3804; www.spiritcruises.com) and *Odyssey II* (☎ 888-957-2322;www.odysseycruises.com), a pair of sleek motor yachts, offer luxury cruises. They include lunch, brunch, or dinner, and a romantic moonlight cruise with bubbly and dancing. The 600-passenger *Spirit of Chicago* and the 800-passenger *Odyssey II* depart from Navy Pier. Tickets run from $37 to over $100.

- ✔ The *Tall Ship Windy* (☎ 312-595-5555) is for those who enjoy listening to the slap of sails as they plow through the waves of Lake Michigan. The 148-foot, four-masted schooner offers 90-minute daytime and evening cruises. Passengers help raise and trim sails and take turns at the ship's wheel. Adults ride for $25, seniors and children under 12 ride for $15. Call for sailing times.

✔ **Wendella Sightseeing Boats** (☎ 312-337-1446; www.wendella boats.com) has operated cruises on the Chicago River and Lake Michigan since 1935. Guides identify the skyscrapers, which are brilliantly lit at night. Guided lake and river tours run one, one and a half, and two hours. Tickets are $18 for adults, $16 for seniors, and $9 for children ages 3 to 11. The boats run daily from April through October.

Beyond the basics: Architectural and cultural tours

Chicago is a living textbook of architectural styles, and the high-quality tours offered by the **Chicago Architecture Foundation** (☎ 312-922-8687; www.architecture.org) provide an excellent introduction. More than 50 tours are offered — by bus, train, boat, and bicycle, as well as on foot. For more on their most popular tour, the "Architecture River Cruise" along the north and south branches of the Chicago River, see the listing under "Chicago's Top Sights," earlier in this chapter. Other perennial favorite tours are the "Rise of the Skyscraper" and "On and About North Michigan Avenue" walking tours, and the "Chicago Architecture Highlights by Bus" trip. The bus tour, which covers a number of high-impact historical districts, departs at 9:30 a.m. every Saturday, some Wednesdays and some Sundays from 224 S. Michigan Ave.; the tour lasts over three hours and costs $35 ($32 for students and seniors).

The **Chicago Department of Cultural Affairs** offers audio walking tours in the Loop. Pick up the headset that includes a tape at the Shop at the Cultural Center, 78 E. Washington (☎ 312-742-0079). The 90-minute tape, narrated by local broadcast journalist Bill Kurtis, provides visitors with an overview of downtown's skyscrapers, public spaces, and sculptures. The tour package costs $5 (with a $50 returnable deposit, cash or credit card) and includes rental of a tape player and a map and booklet of the downtown area.

By horse and carriage

Noble Horse (☎ 312-266-7878), which maintains the largest fleet of antique horse carriages in the city, is stationed around the old Water Tower Square, at the northwest corner of Chicago and Michigan avenues. Each of the drivers, outfitted in black tie and top hat, has his or her variation on the basic Magnificent Mile itinerary. (You can also do tours of the lakefront, river, Lincoln Park, and Buckingham Fountain.) The charge is $30 for each half-hour for up to four people. The coaches run year-round, with convertible coaches in the warm months and enclosed carriages furnished with wool blankets on bone-chilling nights. You'll find several other carriage operators, all of whom pick up riders in the vicinity.

The **Chicago Historical Society** offers daylong and half-day bus tours year-round that cover unique themes or aspects of the metropolitan area's history. Led by historians and scholars, they take place in the city and surrounding areas. Tours are different every year and are usually related to exhibits at the Historical Society's museum; call the Historical Society (☎ **312-642-4600**) for updates. Prices are $60 per person for full-day tours (10 a.m.–4 p.m.), including lunch; and $30 for half-day tours (1–5 p.m.). Tours depart from the museum, at Clark Street and North Avenue.

Meet the locals: Neighborhood tours

Chicago Neighborhood Tours (☎ 312-742-1190; www.chgocitytours.com) offers half-day, narrated, bus excursions to about a dozen diverse communities throughout the city, and you'll be accompanied by local greeters. Tours are divided into three categories: Neighborhood Tours, Special Interest Tours (focusing on the Great Chicago Fire, for example), and Cultural Historian's Choice Tours, led by the cultural historian for the Chicago Department of Cultural Affairs, who takes visitors to some offbeat gems.

These tours are a wonderful way to see landmarks, cultural centers, and museums. Tours also explore shopping centers and allow you to taste local cuisine. For example, the Chinatown/Pilsen tour includes a guided walking tour of Chinatown led by Chinese American Service League representatives, with a stop for refreshments at a Chinese bakery. Then there's a visit, reception, and shopping at the Mexican Fine Arts Center Museum, and a guided bus tour of the Pilsen neighborhood that takes in murals by local artists. Another tour includes the Bronzeville neighborhood on the South Side, a view of Chicago's Jewish neighborhoods.

Tours depart from the **Chicago Cultural Center,** 77 E. Randolph St., at 10 a.m. on Saturdays and last approximately four to five hours. Call first, because the tours don't run on major holidays and generally don't run during the month of January. Advance purchase is recommended. Neighborhood tours include refreshments and are $30 for adults; $20 for seniors and students; Special Interest tours include lunch and are $50 for adults and $45 for seniors/students; Cultural Historian's Choice tours include refreshments and are $35.

Gangsters and ghosts: Specialty tours

Untouchable Tours (☎ 773-881-1195 — ask for Bugsy; www.gangstertour.com) are led by Da Boys and their molls. Suitably costumed guides — the men in snap-brimmed fedoras, the women in flapper outfits — brandish machine guns and pistols. Two-hour tours visit Prohibition-era gangster hangouts and hit spots (such as the Biograph Theatre, where John Dillinger met his end, and the site of the St. Valentine's Day massacre). The fare is $24 for adults and $18 for children under age 16. Tours depart from the corner of Clark and Ohio streets and run

Monday through Wednesday at 10 a.m.; Thursday at 10 a.m. and 1 p.m.; Friday at 10 a.m., 1p.m., and 7:30 p.m.; Saturday at 10 a.m., 1 p.m., and 5 p.m.; and Sunday at 10 a.m. and 1 p.m.

Focusing on the supernatural and paranormal, the **Tour of Haunted and Legendary Places** (☎ **708-499-0300;** www.ghosttours.com) visits graveyards, haunted houses, and other ghostly places, led by Richard Crowe, who bills himself as a "professional ghost hunter." Crowe does know his stuff, so you'll get some informative history lessons along the way. A four-hour narrated bus tour costs $35 per person and departs from Goose Island Restaurant at 1800 N. Clybourn Ave.; a two-hour supernatural boat excursion in the summer is $24 per person and leaves from the Mercury boat dock at Michigan Avenue and Wacker Drive. Reservations are required for each tour. Crowe's tours are especially popular around Halloween, so book well in advance.

Chapter 12

Shopping the Local Stores

· ·

In This Chapter

▶ Checking out the local shopping scene
▶ Exploring the best shopping neighborhoods

· ·

C hicago is a shopping mecca. Why do you think the Magnificent Mile is called "magnificent"? Not because of the sightseeing, believe me. On Michigan Avenue, the stores are the thing.

Everything from Hermes scarves to LEGO building blocks can be purchased on or around Michigan Avenue. As you stroll the length of the Magnificent Mile, you'll find that locating the department stores and four high-rise shopping malls is no problem. But for those who want to discover Chicago's boutiques and specialty stores, in this chapter I point you in the right direction. (Even within the downtown mall complexes, you may miss some of the smaller stores that make Chicago a great shopping destination.) I also explore other neighborhoods that offer boutique shopping.

Surveying the Scene

Stores traditionally stay open latest on Thursday night, until 8 p.m. or so. Department stores stay open until about 7 p.m. all other nights except Sundays, when they open around 11 a.m. and close around 6 p.m. Smaller stores close by 5 p.m. or 6 p.m.

The biggest **sales** of the year take place in January when retailers slash prices on winter clothing to make room for spring offerings. This is the best time to shop (if you didn't blow all your bucks over the holidays!), especially because Chicago's **sales tax** is high at 8.75 percent. Ouch.

Checking Out the Big Names

Chicago's homegrown department store is Marshall Field's (yes, the Field Museum is named after the merchant). Trademarks are the dark-green shopping bags, Frango mints, and the window displays of the State

Street store. Here's info on Marshall Field's, as well as the many other department stores that await you:

- ✔ **Bloomingdale's,** 900 North Michigan Ave. (☎ **312-440-4460;** www.bloomingdales.com): New York City's beloved Bloomie's opened its first Midwestern outpost in Chicago. The six-level store includes a section devoted to Bloomingdale's logo merchandise. That same year, all the home furnishings were moved to a new location in the former Medinah Temple, a historic building at 600 North Wabash Ave. (☎ **312-324-7500**).

- ✔ **Carson Pirie Scott,** 1 South State St. (☎ **312-641-7000**): Stunning architecture by Louis Sullivan (one of Frank Lloyd Wright's mentors) makes this century-old department store easy on the eyes. The exterior incorporates intricate ornamental iron filigree. The store is also easier on your pocketbook than nearby Marshall Field's and carries slightly lower-end merchandise as well.

- ✔ **Lord & Taylor,** 835 North Michigan Ave. (☎ **312-787-7400;** www.lordandtaylor.com): The multilevel department store anchors Water Tower Place (along with a Marshall Field's branch). It's known for its conservative, "all-American" style.

- ✔ **Marshall Field's,** 111 North State St. (☎ **312-781-1000;** www.fields.com): Chicago traditions include meeting under the Field's clock and viewing the animated holiday window displays at the 1852-built store. Another custom is afternoon tea in the gracious Walnut Room (which, during the holidays, is home to a giant Christmas tree and another tradition, "breakfast with Santa"). The chain's flagship store also offers 73 acres of shopping. A smaller branch is located in Water Tower Place (☎ **312-335-7700**).

- ✔ **Neiman Marcus,** 737 North Michigan Ave. (☎ **312-642-5900;** www.neimanmarcus.com): Texas's favorite department store has top merchandise and prices to match. If you're in town in late January, the "Last Call" sale is one of the city's best. The fourth-floor epicure shop specializes in pâté, caviar, and other delicacies.

- ✔ **Nordstrom,** Westfield North Bridge Mall, 520 North Michigan Ave. (☎ **312-379-4300;** www.nordstrom.com): The newest department store addition to the Magnificent Mile, Nordstrom anchors a mall that has attracted traffic to the south end of Michigan Avenue. Why go to Nordstrom? Shoes. On the weekends, you'll have to take a number, and an employee with a microphone walks around the huge department calling out the next number to be served. Despite the microphone, the service is renowned.

- ✔ **Saks Fifth Avenue,** Chicago Place, 700 North Michigan Ave. (☎ **312-944-6500;** www.saks.com): High-priced designer fashions are what this seven-story department store is all about. Visit the beautiful jewelry department on the first floor, or shop for makeup and the city's best selection of Jo Malone scents, lotions, and other beauty products.

Going to Market

When the temperature rises, retail vendors hit the streets. This section guides you to the best of the summer markets and art fairs.

Farmers' markets

From mid-May to late October, Chicago's downtown plazas and neighborhoods come alive (literally) with fruits, vegetables, flowers, and food from farms outside the city and even out-of-state. Markets in residential neighborhoods, such as the **gourmet market** at Lincoln Park High School, 2001 North Orchard St., usually take place on Saturdays. The farmers' markets that are held downtown — including those listed in this section — take place during the week. Schedules may vary, so contact the **Mayor's Office of Special Events** (☎ 312-744-3315) for more information. Downtown markets include

✔ **Daley Plaza,** 55 West Randolph St., on Thursdays

✔ **Federal Plaza,** Adams Street and Jackson Boulevard, on Tuesdays

✔ **Park at Jackson and Wacker,** across from the Sears Tower, on Thursdays

✔ **Prudential Plaza,** 130 East Randolph St., every other Tuesday

Art fairs

Chicago hosts a festival in one of its parks or neighborhoods practically every weekend in the summer. Many of the best are focused around art. Artists from all over the country apply to be accepted into these four juried art fairs:

✔ **Around the Coyote,** at the intersection of Damen, North, and Milwaukee avenues (☎ 773-342-6777; www.aroundthecoyote.org): This art festival, held the second weekend in September, showcases the talent of local artists in Wicker Park and Bucktown. The entrance fee entitles you to enter not only local art galleries but also many artists' homes and studios for a look behind the scenes.

✔ **Bucktown Arts Fest,** near Fullerton and Western avenues (☎ 312-409-8305; www.bucktownartsfest.com): This most recent addition to the art-fair circuit is staged in a comfortable park setting. Don't forget your sunscreen or hat, however, because it's typically pretty steamy the last weekend in August.

✔ **57th Street Art Fair,** 57th Street in downtown Hyde Park (☎ 773-493-3247; www.57thstreetartfair.org): This long-standing fair is a natural outgrowth of the intellectual and artsy enclave on Chicago's South Side. Much less crowded than the Old Town Art Fair the weekend before, this fair on the third weekend in June makes for a more comfortable, if less social, art-viewing experience.

✔ **Old Town Art Fair,** Lincoln Avenue and Wisconsin Street (☎ 312-337-1938): The most high-end of Chicago's art-fair offerings boasts art prices to match. It kicks off the art-fair season the second weekend in June. Go early or late in the day to avoid unbearable midday crowds. Be careful not to accidentally pay entrance into the other nearby festivals that take advantage of the art fair's draw, unless you're more interested in drinking beer and hearing bands than seeing art. (See Chapter 3 for more details.)

Street fairs

Although not in the same league as the art fairs in the preceding section, almost every neighborhood festival includes booths with vendors selling jewelry, bohemian clothing, sunglasses, African drums, and even massages. In this city that loves to eat, you also find a healthy helping of food vendors offering a variety of ethnic cuisines. See Chapter 3 for a list of the most popular festivals. You can also contact the **Mayor's Office of Special Events** (☎ 312-744-3315) for a festival calendar.

Discovering the Best Shopping Neighborhoods

In this section, I describe Chicago's best stores, organized by neighborhood.

Magnificent Mile and environs

This high-priced stretch of real estate on Michigan Avenue reaches from Oak Street to the Chicago River. You find high-visibility names, from Cartier to Kenneth Cole, Filene's Basement to Ralph Lauren, Gucci to Nike. For the locations of stores in the vicinity of the Magnificent Mile, see the "Magnificent Mile Shopping" map in this chapter. Standout shops include

✔ **Active Endeavors,** 45 East Grand Ave. (☎ 312-822-0600; www.activeendeavors.com): Gear for outdoor pursuits, from hiking to biking to skiing. Fun casual clothes, too. Located in the Westfield North Bridge mall, on the street level facing Grand Avenue.

✔ **American Girl Place,** 111 East Chicago Ave. (☎ 877-247-5223; www.americangirl.com): The "in" place for the preteen set. You can never collect enough American Girl dolls . . . and then you need to add to their extensive wardrobe and accessories. This three-story, 37,500-square-foot store lures in millions of shoppers each year. In order to avoid disappointing the American girl in your life, I strongly advise that you call ahead about a month in advance to secure lunch in the chic cafe or to catch a performance of *The American Girls Revue,* performed five days a week in a 150-seat theater.

✔ **Ann Taylor,** 600 North Michigan Ave. (☎ 312-587-8301; www.anntaylor.com): The Chicago flagship store for this seller of women's casual and career clothing, accessories, and shoes, including petite and regular sizes.

✔ **Anthropologie,** 1120 North State St. (☎ 312-255-1848; www. anthropologie.com): Ethereal and funky clothing combines with household decorating items in this beautiful store. Great for gifts.

✔ **The Apple Store,** 679 North Michigan Ave. (☎ 312-981-4104; www. store.apple.com): The four-story mecca for all technological gadgets beginning with *i:* iPod, iMac, and more.

✔ **Aveda,** 875 North Michigan Ave., in the plaza of the John Hancock Center Observatory (☎ 312-664-0417; www.aveda.com): The Minnesota company creates all-natural scents, lotions, hair-care products, and makeup. Come here and breathe in the aromatherapy.

✔ **Banana Republic,** 744 North Michigan Ave. (☎ 312-642-0020; www. bananarepublic.com): The Gap's stylish sibling has a megastore on Michigan Avenue and a smaller shop in Water Tower Place. This store has great going-out clothes and clothing to blend in with the city folk.

✔ **Barnes & Noble,** 1130 N. State St. (☎ 312-280-8155; www.bn.com): Tucked into Rush Street, this two-level store offers a cafe on the street level, perfect for watching the parade of shoppers as you peruse a book. There's another store in Lincoln Park, 1 block west of Clark Street (☎ 773-871-9004), and one at 1441 W. Webster Avenue at Clybourn Avenue (☎ 773-871-3610).

✔ **Borders,** 830 North Michigan Ave. (☎ 312-573-0564; www.borders. com): This enormously popular and well-trafficked bookstore has a cafe that overlooks Michigan Avenue as well as the standard assortment of books, CDs, and videos. On the main floor is a section of books on Chicago. Downstairs, you find a colorful selection of writing accessories, including notebooks and pens.

✔ **Brooks Brothers,** 713 North Michigan Ave. (☎ 312-915-0060; www. brooksbrothers.com): The East Coast preppy haven is still *the* place for men's shirts. (They look good on women, too.)

✔ **Burberry's Ltd.,** 633 North Michigan Ave. (☎ 312-787-2500; www. burberry.com): Formerly traditional, newly hip. This is the place to pick up that kilt you've wanted for years.

✔ **Cartier,** 630 North Michigan Ave. (☎ 312-266-7440; www.cartier. com): Jewels, jewels, jewels. Need we say more? The window displays alone cause sidewalk traffic jams.

✔ **Chalet Wine & Cheese Shop,** 40 East Delaware Place (☎ 312-787-8555): Wine, liquor, beer, a wonderful cheese counter, pâté, crackers, and anything else to make a romantic picnic or party with friends.

✔ **Crate & Barrel,** 646 North Michigan Ave. (☎ 312-787-5900; www. crateandbarrel.com): Stylish home furnishings and housewares in a three-floor store that's fun to browse.

✔ **Diesel,** 923 North Rush St. (☎ 312-255-0157; www.diesel.com): Cutting-edge industrial-style fashion. And, of course, great jeans.

Magnificent Mile Shopping

Resting at Crate & Barrel

Need a quick break during your shopping spree? The overstuffed couches on the third and fourth floors of Crate & Barrel practically beg to be tested out — and there are always at least a few weary shoppers slumped against the piles of pillows. Go ahead and rest awhile; the store's staff won't bug you. Make sure you stop by the terrace on the fourth floor for a bird's-eye view of bustling Michigan Avenue and enjoy a moment of contemplation before rejoining the hordes below.

✔ **Eddie Bauer,** 600 North Michigan Ave. (☎ **312-951-5888;** www.eddiebauer.com): The preppy East Coast clothier has great casual styles and offers dress-casual clothing, too. Furniture and house-hold furnishings are upstairs.

✔ **Filene's Basement,** 830 North Michigan Ave. (☎ **312-482-8918;** www.filenesbasement.com): This bargain "basement" with name-brand clothing for less occupies the upper floors of a flashy Mag Mile building.

✔ **Georg Jensen,** 959 North Michigan Ave. (☎ **312-642-9160;** www.georgjensen.com): Scandinavian design in jewelry, silver, and other household items. Housed in the Drake Hotel.

✔ **H & M,** 840 North Michigan Ave. (☎ **312-640-0060;** www.hm.com): Cheap and chic clothing from a European style-setting chain.

✔ **L'Appetito,** 875 North Michigan Ave. (☎ **312-337-0691**): An Italian grocery located in the lower level of the John Hancock Center Observatory that carries a wide selection of cheeses, sausages, and cold cuts.

✔ **Material Possessions,** 704 North Wabash St. (☎ **312-280-4885**): Unusual table settings including pottery and glass.

✔ **Niketown,** 669 North Michigan Ave. (☎ **312-642-6363;** www.niketown.com): The United Center (see Chapter 11) isn't the only house that Michael Jordan built. This three-level store, virtually a shrine to Chicago's favorite son, is the place to buy the shoes that will help you increase your hang time. You can also practice free throws and view a collection of MJ's shoes.

✔ **Original Levi's Store,** 600 North Michigan Ave. (☎ **312-642-9613;** www.levi.com): If you can't find a pair of jeans here, you won't find a pair anywhere. Or let the staff measure you and send you a pair of custom-made jeans.

✔ **Polo Ralph Lauren,** 750 North Michigan Ave. (☎ **312-280-1655;** www.polo.com): Ralph Lauren has built a giant Polo palace where you can revel in his look. A small Italian restaurant named, appropriately, RL (and decorated in Ralph's style, of course), is attached to the palace on Chicago Avenue.

✔ **Pottery Barn,** 734 North Michigan Ave. (☎ 312-587-9602; www. potterybarn.com): Boasts everything you need to decorate your home, plus furniture.

✔ **Salvatore Ferragamo,** 645 North Michigan Ave. (☎ 312-397-0464; www.ferragamo.com): Upscale Italian fashions ranging from shoes and handbags to tailored suits for men and women.

✔ **Tiffany & Co.,** 730 North Michigan Ave. (☎ 312-944-7500; www. tiffany.com): This is the home of the little blue box; you can get your engagement ring on the first floor and register for wedding gifts upstairs. Affordable silver jewelry can be had for about $100.

✔ **Timberland,** 543 North Michigan Ave. (☎ 312-494-0171; www. timberland.com): Boots and clothing for treks to the north woods (or to Starbucks).

✔ **Urban Outfitters,** 933 North Rush St. (☎ 312-640-1919; www.urbn. com): Fun, funky, and offbeat clothing and accessories, from bean-bag chairs to glittery nail polish.

Malls on the Magnificent Mile

North Michigan Avenue's four shopping malls are also places for a fast snack, a good meal, or a movie. The descriptions in this section are for locations from north to south.

900 North Michigan

This indoor mall doesn't have a name, but most locals call it the "Bloomingdale's Building," after the anchor store. Along with about 70 shops are some good restaurants on the fifth and sixth floors, including **Baisi Thai** and **Tucci Bennuch** (Tuscan). On the main floor of the marble-clad atrium, a branch of the celebrated **Corner Bakery** sells coffee, crusty bread, rolls, and pastries; on the lower level is the stylish Mario Tricoci Salon and Day Spa (highly recommended). The Four Seasons Hotel is also in this building; to get there through the mall, go to the sixth floor and walk west to the Four Seasons elevator bank. Stores in this mall include

✔ **Charles David** (☎ 312-944-9013; www.charlesdavid.com): High-heeled shoes for the well-heeled crowd. Second floor.

✔ **Club Monaco** (☎ 312-787-8757; www.clubmonaco.com): Minimalist fashions at affordable prices for the young crowd. Ground level.

✔ **Coach** (☎ 312-440-1777; www.coach.com): Everything leather, from handbags to luggage. Second floor.

✔ **Glove Me Tender** (☎ 312-664-4022; www.glovemetender.com): If you lost your mitts somewhere in your travels up and down

Michigan Avenue, this boutique has a huge selection to help you replace them. Fifth floor.

✔ **Gucci** (☎ 312-664-5504; www.gucci.com): From loafers and leather goods to leading-edge fashion, Gucci sets the styles. Ground level.

✔ **J. Crew** (☎ 312-751-2739; www.jcrew.com): Sweaters, slacks, hats, belts, and other clothing featuring the scrubbed-clean look. Second floor.

✔ **Mark Shale** (☎ 312-440-0720; www.markshale.com): Chicago's own upscale clothing store, with a fine selection of men's and women's casual and dress clothing. Especially good for men. Service is excellent, and the clothing is unique. Third and fourth floors.

✔ **Williams-Sonoma** (☎ 312-587-8080; www.williams-sonoma.com): Chefs love this store offering the latest in kitchen gadgets and high-quality cookware. Second floor.

Water Tower Place

Chicago's showcase mall at 835 North Michigan Ave., with cascading fountains and waterfalls and glass-cage elevators, contains more than 100 stores spread over seven floors. Marshall Field's and Lord & Taylor are the anchors. The innovative **foodlife** food court (see Chapter 10) contains more than a dozen stations, offering everything from burgers and pizza to Mexican and Moroccan, plus the **Mity Nice Grill,** a faux-1940s diner. One movie complex contains four screens. The mall contains standard mall offerings, such as the Gap and Banana Republic, plus the following:

✔ **Accent Chicago** (☎ 312-944-1354): T-shirts, pizza pans, logo sports gear, and other souvenirs that say "Chicago."

✔ **Avventura** (☎ 312-337-3700): Men's shoes from Italy, Spain, and elsewhere in Europe, made exclusively for the store.

✔ **Eileen Fisher** (☎ 312-943-9100; www.eileenfisher.com): Women's clothing in luxurious fabrics and rich colors from a suburban Chicago-born designer.

✔ **Gymboree** (☎ 312-649-9074; www.gymboree) and **Jacardi** (☎ 312-337-9600; www.jacardi.com): Stylish children's clothing, not available in department stores.

Chicago Place

This 8-floor, 50-store mall at 700 North Michigan Ave. has **Saks Fifth Avenue** as its anchor. A small supermarket called **Bockwinkel's** (☎ 312-482-9900) on the lower level is a good spot for made-to-order sandwiches and daily soup selections, and it has a small dining area. Skip the food court on the eighth level; it's depressing and smells greasy. But if you need a watch battery, you'll find a little shop on that floor that will replace yours while you wait. Stores include

✔ **Ann Taylor** (☎ 312-335-0117; www.anntaylor.com): Conservative career clothing and accessories for women. Ground level.

✔ **The Body Shop** (☎ 312-482-8301; www.thebodyshop.com): All-natural shampoos and lotions. Ground level.

✔ **Talbots** (☎ 312-944-6059; www.talbots.com). Conservative, classic women's clothing in a wide range of sizes. Ground level. A **Talbots Kids** is also located here (☎ 312-943-0255).

Westfield North Bridge mall

Chicago's newest high-rise mall, at 520 North Michigan Ave., features 35 stores with popular urban men's and women's clothing, jewelry, and specialty items. The third level is dedicated to children's fashions, accessories, and toys; kids love the oversized LEGO models on this floor! The fourth floor is Chicago's "Magnificent Meal," an upscale food court. Shops include

✔ **A/X Armani Exchange** (☎ 312-467-5702; www.armaniexchange.com): Urban wear for the hip among us at reasonable prices. First floor.

✔ **The LEGO Store** (☎ 312-494-0760; www.lego.com): Anything your child can imagine can be built with these little, colored blocks. Kids can easily spend an hour here. Third floor.

✔ **Sephora** (☎ 312-494-9598; www.sephora.com): *The* makeup mecca. You can find the latest and greatest from many small, chic makeup companies here. First floor.

✔ **Vosges Haut-Chocolat** (☎ 312-644-9450; www.vosgeschocolate.com): Truffles to die for in pretty packaging. Second floor.

Oak Street

If you want sophistication and high fashion and are prepared to pay for them, you'll be in heaven along the short stretch of Oak Street between Michigan Avenue and Rush Street. In 1 block you can find more than 40 stores in converted brownstone mansions. Included are

✔ **Barneys New York,** 25 East Oak St. (☎ 312-587-1700; www.barneys.com): A mini-version of New York's Barneys, the store has the latest, from makeup to shoes, bags, and clothes. If you want top-of-the-line men's suits, this is the place. Not for those who faint at high prices. Excellent for spotting trends and people-watching.

✔ **Elements,** 102 East Oak St. (☎ 312-642-6574): High-end, high-design gifts and home decorating items.

✔ **Hermès of Paris,** 110 East Oak St. (☎ 312-787-8175; www.hermes.com): Hermès makes the world's most sought-after scarves and ties. Don't be intimidated: Walk in and take a look at the displays of color and design that make these silk scarves and ties stunning, season after season.

✔ **Jil Sander,** 48 East Oak St.(☎ **312-335-0006;** www.jilsander.com): Ultramodern clothing and shoes.

✔ **Kate Spade,** 101 East Oak St. (☎ **312-654-8853;** www.katespade. com): From plaid to gingham to basic black, Kate Spade does lovely bags. Her shoes are adorable, too.

✔ **Prada,** 30 East Oak St. (☎ **312-951-1113;** www.prada.com): So chic it's almost painful. The ultimate spot for buying the designer's signature bags.

✔ **Sugar Magnolia,** 34 East Oak St. (☎ **312-944-0885**): Women's clothing boutique that also has small gifts, jewelry, and handbags. Casual clothes for relaxing, and sexy clothes for going out.

✔ **Ultimo,** 114 East Oak St. (☎ **312-787-1171**): Chicago's best-known upscale clothier offers women's clothing by big-time labels such as John Galliano, Dolce & Gabbana, and Agnona.

✔ **Wolford,** 54 East Oak St. (☎ **312-642-8787;** www.wolford.com): Women swear by the quality and durability of these European-made bodysuits and hosiery.

River North

Furniture, art, and objects are in abundance in the River North gallery area. Shops include

✔ **Mig & Tig,** 549 North Wells St. (☎ **312-644-8277;** www.migandtig. com): Monumental furniture that manages to be very charming at the same time.

✔ **Paper Source,** 232 West Chicago Ave. (☎ **312-337-0798**): Come here to find out how to make your own scrapbook, buy cards and small gifts, choose among reams of exotic papers, and add to your collection of rubber stamps.

✔ **Primitive Art Works,** 706 North Wells St. (☎ **312-943-3770;** www. primitiveartworks.com): The owner of this store packs a brownstone with furniture, rugs, jewelry, beads, and objects from his world travels. One day you may find a giant Buddha head rescued from a Korean temple that was being destroyed; another day may reveal an exquisite embroidered rug from Turkmenistan.

✔ **Room & Board,** 55 East Ohio St. (☎ **312-222-0970**): This Minnesota-based furniture company has contemporary furniture. Its sister store, **Retrospect** (☎ **312-440-1270**), in the same building, offers more-traditional furniture.

✔ **Sawbridge Studios,** 153 West Ohio St. (☎ **312-828-0055;** www. sawbridge.com): Stunningly crafted furniture with stunning prices to boot. Boasts some of the most beautiful woodworking I've ever seen.

State Street and the Loop

Before falling on hard times, State Street, in the heart of the Loop, wore the shopping mantle that now belongs to the Mag Mile. But "that great street" — according to an old Chicago song — is reversing its fortunes and luring back shoppers.

State Street

Although a number of State Street department stores closed or fled to the 'burbs in the '70s, Marshall Field's and Carson Pirie Scott stuck it out. They now lead the renaissance along State Street. Other shops include

✔ **Filene's Basement,** 1 North State St. (☎ 312-553-1055; www.filenes basement.com): The East Coast discount department store chain's first Chicago branch.

✔ **Old Navy,** 35 North State St. (☎ 312-551-0522; www.oldnavy.com): Casual wear at low, low prices.

✔ **T.J. Maxx,** 1 North State St. (☎ 312-553-0515; www.tjmaxx.com): As the ads say, get the max for the minimum price. Bargain-hunter heaven with stock that changes constantly.

Elsewhere in the Loop

As State Street becomes revitalized, its environs are taking on a new shine, too. New hotels, restaurants, and theaters attract crowds to the area even on weekends. Shops include

✔ **Gallery 37 Store,** 66 East Randolph St. (☎ 312-744-8925; www.gallery37.org): Paintings, jewelry, ceramics, decorated furniture, textiles, and sculptures are all made by Chicago residents ages 14 to 21 who are part of Gallery 37, a nonprofit arts training program. Experienced artists mentor these young artists, and proceeds from the sales benefit the program.

✔ **Mallers Building,** 5 South Wabash Ave.: Tiny jewelers' shops cram into 16 of the 21 floors in this building that dates from 1911. Stop for breakfast or lunch at the **Mallers Building Coffee Shop & Deli** (☎ 312-263-7696), a time-warp diner on the third floor.

✔ **Sydel & Sydel Ltd.,** 208 South LaSalle St. (☎ 312-332-4653): Beautiful high-quality jewelry.

Lincoln Park

Yuppie heaven must include shopping, right? Right. You find some of Chicago's best boutique shopping near Lincoln Park's tree-lined residential streets.

Starting at the intersection with Halsted Street and going west, Armitage Avenue in Lincoln Park hosts a string of charming boutiques that sell everything from shoes and designer clothing to tableware and decorations for the home. Going north on Halsted from Armitage Avenue, you find more shops, including chain stores such as the Gap, Banana Republic, and Ann Taylor, as well as more boutiques and restaurants. Shops include

- ✓ **Cynthia Rowley,** 808 West Armitage Ave. (☎ 773-528-6160; www.cynthiarowley.com): Feminine (but not too girlie) styles from the designer who's originally from Chicago.

- ✓ **Endo-Exo Apothecary,** 2034 North Halsted St. (☎ 773-525-0500; www.endoexo.com): Colorful, fun makeup store. Let the aspiring makeup artists who work there try some of the store's latest products on you.

- ✓ **Findables,** 907 West Armitage Ave. (☎ 773-348-0674; www.findables.com): Out-of-the-ordinary home and kitchen accessories.

- ✓ **Fresh,** 2040 North Halsted Ave. (☎ 773-404-9776; www.fresh.com): A fragrance boutique that puts aromatherapy to work in the form of candles, soaps, and perfumes in scents like redcurrant basil. Customize your own scent.

- ✓ **Lori's Designer Shoes,** 824 West Armitage Ave. (☎ 773-281-5655; www.lorisdesignershoes.com): Shoe mecca. Discounted shoes from major designers. On the weekend, the store is swarming. Happy hunting!

- ✓ **Shabby Chic,** 2146 North Halsted St. (☎ 773-327-9372; www.shabbychic.com): The famous decorating look is for sale in this furniture store.

- ✓ **Tabula Tua,** 1015 West Armitage Ave. (☎ 773-525-3500; www.tabulatua.com): Everything you need to set the perfect table.

Old Town

One of my favorite shopping strips is North Wells Street in Old Town. Take a jaunt down one of the side streets to admire the neighborhood's restored brownstones. Shops include

- ✓ **Fleet Feet Sports,** 210 West North Ave., in Piper's Alley (☎ 312-587-3338; www.fleetfeet.com): Runner's heaven. They'll videotape you running on the treadmill and give you the verdict on shoes that work best for you.

- ✓ **Handle With Care,** 1706 North Wells St. (☎ 312-751-2929; www.shophwc.com): Located in a little strip of shops on Wells Street north of North Avenue, this shop boasts gift items and colorful clothing.

- ✓ **A New Leaf,** 1818 North Wells St. (☎ 312-642-8553): One of Chicago's top florists has a breathtaking storefront with a carriage house in the back, all packed with flowers, plants, pots, candles, glassware, and more.

State Street/Loop Shopping

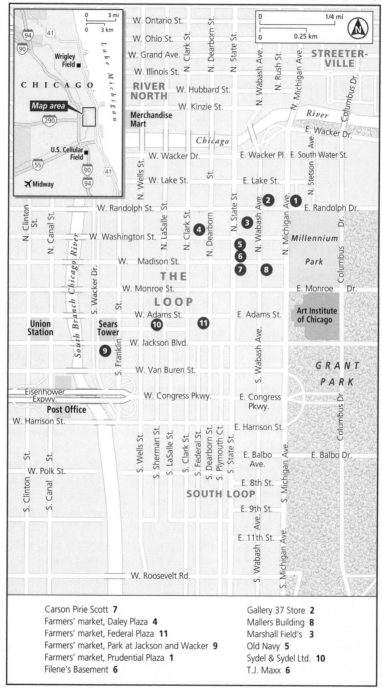

Carson Pirie Scott **7**
Farmers' market, Daley Plaza **4**
Farmers' market, Federal Plaza **11**
Farmers' market, Park at Jackson and Wacker **9**
Farmers' market, Prudential Plaza **1**
Filene's Basement **6**

Gallery 37 Store **2**
Mallers Building **8**
Marshall Field's **3**
Old Navy **5**
Sydel & Sydel Ltd. **10**
T.J. Maxx **6**

Southport Avenue

As recently as the early 1990s, this area was considered off the beaten path. Now fully gentrified, Southport Avenue retains some of its funkier past with eclectic boutiques for clothing and home accessories. Shops include

- ✔ **Fly Paper,** 3402 North Southport Ave. (☎ 773-296-4359): A card and gift store featuring exquisite gift wrap and stationery.

- ✔ **P.O.S.H.,** 3729 North Southport Ave. (☎ 773-529-7674; www.posh chicago.com): Tableware, including never-used vintage silver and commercial-grade china from European and American hotels, restaurants, and cruise ships.

- ✔ **The Red Head Boutique,** 3450 North Southport Ave. (☎ 773-325-9898; www.redheadboutique.com): Women's specialty boutique featuring clothes, purses, and jewelry.

- ✔ **She One,** 3402 North Southport Ave. (☎ 773-549-9698): Boutique for chic yet inexpensive women's clothing.

West Lakeview

The West Lakeview neighborhood, between 1100 and 2400 West, is known as "antique row." More than 20 shops offer a mind-boggling range of antiques and collectibles, from books and furniture to Depression-era glass and dolls. Destinations include

- ✔ **The Antiquarians Building,** 159 West Kinzie St. (☎ 312-527-0533): Fine antiques for big bucks.

- ✔ **Armitage Antique Gallery,** 1529 West Armitage Ave. (☎ 773-227-7727): The Midwest's largest restorer of vintage and antique timepieces and clocks. Come here for antique timepieces, from pocket watches to wristwatches, and a full selection of antique furniture, from Victorian to Deco — with an emphasis on Deco.

- ✔ **Broadway Antique Market,** 6131 North Broadway (☎ 773-743-5444): Two floors of funky, fun, somewhat pricey antiques and collectibles.

- ✔ **Father Time Antiques,** 2108 West Belmont Ave. (☎ 773-880-5599): Come here for unique antique timepieces.

- ✔ **The International Art & Antiques Center,** 2300 West Diversey (☎ 773-761-4901): Antiques from across the planet.

- ✔ **Olde Chicago Ltd. Antiques,** 3110 North Kedzie Ave. (☎ 773-935-1200): This importer of furniture from Europe specializes in the years prior to 1900. The shop is a well-kept secret that mostly serves the trade — in fact, much of the furniture is sold to out-of-town dealers — but now that you're in the know, make sure to stop by.

✔ **Antique Resources,** 1741 West Belmont Ave. (☎ 773-871-4242): This spot specializes in antique lighting fixtures.

Bucktown/Wicker Park

Fun, funky, and off-the-beaten-path purchases are best found in Bucktown and Wicker Park, Chicago's artist enclaves. Shops include

✔ **Apartment Number 9,** 1804 North Damen Ave. (☎ 773-395-2999): Modern menswear, on the mostly casual side. You'll find suits here (jackets and pants can also be purchased separately), plus dress shirts and ties, mixed in with more casual garments.

✔ **Pagoda Red,** 1714 North Damen Ave., 2nd floor (☎ 773-235-1188; www.pagodared.com): Imported antique furniture and art objects from China, Tibet, and Burma.

✔ **p45,** 1643 North Damen Ave. (☎ 773-862-4523; www.p45.com): A cool little boutique that has received acclaim from East Coast fashion editors. Women's and men's clothing by young designers.

✔ **Red Hen Bread,** 1623 North Milwaukee Ave. (☎ 773-342-6823): Homemade bread that's so good it's used by some of the city's best restaurants, including Café Absinthe (reviewed in Chapter 10).

Index of Stores by Merchandise

Art and Antiques

Antique Resources
The Antiquarians Building
Armitage Antique Gallery
Broadway Antique Market
Father Time Antiques
Gallery 37 Store
The International Art & Antique Center
Olde Chicago Ltd. Antiques
Primitive Art Works

Books

Barnes & Noble
Borders

Cards and Stationery

Fly Paper
Paper Source

Clothing and Accessories

Active Endeavors
American Girl Place
Ann Taylor
Anthropologie
A/X Armani Exchange
Banana Republic
Brooks Brothers
Burberry's Ltd.
Club Monaco
Coach Store
Cynthia Rowley
Diesel
Eddie Bauer
Eileen Fisher
Glove Me Tender
Gucci
Gymboree
H & M
Hermès of Paris
Jacardi
J. Crew
Jil Sander
Kate Spade
Mark Shale
Old Navy

Original Levi's Store
p45
Polo Ralph Lauren
Prada
The Red Head Boutique
She One
Sugar Magnolia
Talbots
Talbots Kids
Ultimo
Urban Outfitters
Wolford

Cosmetics and Perfume

Aveda
The Body Shop
Endo-Exo Apothecary
Fresh
Sephora

Department Stores

Barneys New York
Bloomingdale's
Carson Pirie Scott
Lord & Taylor
Marshall Field's
Neiman Marcus
Nordstrom
Saks Fifth Avenue

Discount Clothing

Filene's Basement
T.J. Maxx

Electronics

Apple Computer Store

Food and Candy

Chalet Wine & Cheese Shop
L'Appetito
Red Hen Bread
Vosges Haut-Chocolat

Footwear

Avventura
Charles David
Fleet Feet Sports

Lori's Designer Shoes
Niketown
Salvatore Ferragamo
Timberland

Gifts and Toys

Accent Chicago
American Girl Place
Anthropologie
Handle With Care
Hello Chicago
The LEGO Store

Home Accessories

Crate & Barrel
Eddie Bauer
Elements
Findables
Material Possessions
Mig & Tig
A New Leaf
Pagoda Red
Polo Ralph Lauren
P.O.S.H.
Pottery Barn
Retrospect
Room & Board
Sawbridge Studios
Shabby Chic
Tabula Tua
Williams-Sonoma

Jewelry

Cartier
Georg Jensen
Mallers Building
Sydel & Sydel Ltd.
Tiffany & Co.

Malls

Chicago Place
900 North Michigan
Westfield North Bridge Mall
Water Tower Place

Music

Borders

Chapter 13

Following an Itinerary: Four Great Options

● ●

In This Chapter

▶ Hitting the highlights for those with limited time
▶ Shopping along the Magnificent Mile
▶ Enjoying Chicago with your kids

● ●

*L*et's say you have limited time in our fair city, and you want to see as much as possible. Perhaps the holidays are near and shopping is tops on your list. Or maybe you want to arrange a day of touring with your kids. Either way, you came to the right chapter.

Chicago in Three Days

This itinerary covers the best that Chicago has to offer if you have a limited amount of time to visit the city.

Day 1

Spend the first day in the heart of downtown, known as the Loop. Thanks
to the Great Fire of 1871 and the city leaders' determination to rebuild
with style, Chicago has been a world leader in architecture for more than
a century. You find some of Chicago's best architecture in **the Loop.**
Assuming that you're visiting during nice weather, walk around the Loop
either on a self-guided tour or one organized by the **Chicago Architecture
Foundation** — the early skyscraper tour is a good primer (see Chapter
11). Finish your stroll at **Millennium Park,** Chicago's largest public-works
project in decades, which opened in 2004 (see Chapter 11). The park
begins at Randolph and Michigan Avenue and extends south to the Art
Institute. Catch your reflection in "The Bean" and walk over Frank Gehry's
curving pedestrian bridge, which has fantastic lake and city views.

When it's time for lunch, head to **Heaven on Seven** (see Chapter 10) for
some Cajun and Creole cooking. After lunch, visit one or two of the city's

Chicago in Three Days

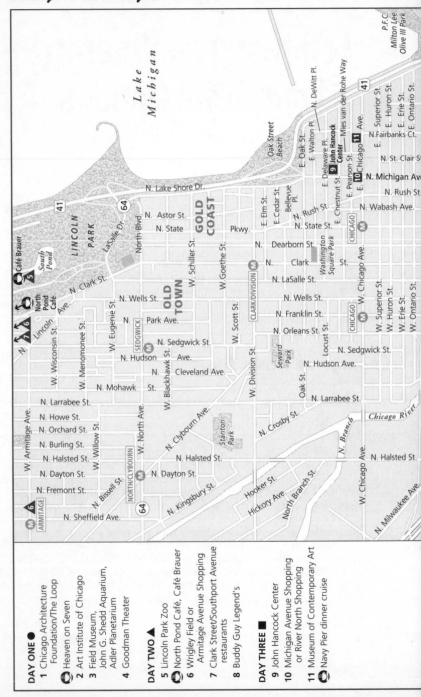

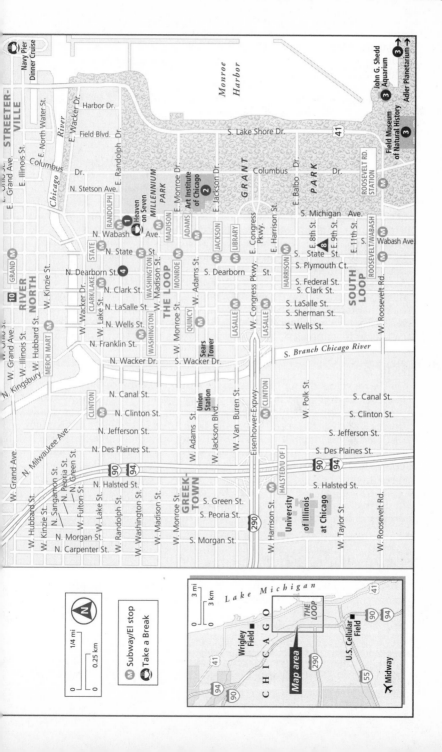

STREETER-VILLE

Navy Pier Dinner Cruise

Monroe Harbor

John G. Shedd Aquarium

Adler Planetarium

Harbor Dr.

E. Wacker Dr.

Field Blvd.

S. Lake Shore Dr.

41

Field Museum of Natural History

Chicago River

Columbus Dr.

E. Randolph Dr.

N. Stetson Ave.

MILLENNIUM PARK

GRANT PARK

Columbus Dr.

E. Balbo Dr.

ROOSEVELT RD. STATION

E. North Water St.

E. Illinois St.

E. Grand Ave.

E. Grand Ave.

E. Illinois St.

RANDOLPH

E. Monroe Dr.

Art Institute of Chicago

E. Jackson Dr.

MADISON

Heaven on Seven

N. Wabash Ave.

STATE

N. State St.

S. Michigan Ave.

E. 8th St.

E. 9th St.

E. 11th St.

Wabash Ave

N. Wabash Ave.

WASHINGTON

MONROE

N. Dearborn St.

N. Clark St.

N. LaSalle St.

N. Wells St.

N. Franklin St.

CLARK/LAKE

N. Lake St.

THE LOOP

W. Washington St.

W. Madison St.

W. Monroe St.

JACKSON

LIBRARY

S. Dearborn St.

E. Congress Pkwy.

E. Harrison St.

HARRISON

S. State St.

S. Plymouth Ct.

S. Federal St.

S. Clark St.

S. LaSalle St.

S. Sherman St.

S. Wells St.

SOUTH LOOP

ROOSEVELT/WABASH

W. Roosevelt Rd.

MERCH MART

RIVER NORTH

N. Kingsbury St.

W. Ohio St.

W. Grand Ave.

W. Illinois St.

W. Hubbard St.

N. Kinzie St.

W. Adams St.

W. Monroe St.

QUINCY

LASALLE

W. Congress Pkwy.

LASALLE

Sears Tower

N. Wacker Dr.

S. Wacker Dr.

S. Branch Chicago River

N. Canal St.

N. Clinton St.

N. Jefferson St.

N. Des Plaines St.

CLINTON

Union Station

W. Adams St.

W. Jackson Blvd.

W. Van Buren St.

Eisenhower Expwy.

CLINTON

W. Polk St.

S. Canal St.

S. Clinton St.

S. Jefferson St.

S. Des Plaines St.

W. Grand Ave.

W. Milwaukee Ave.

W. Hubbard St.

W. Kinzie St.

N. Sangamon St.

N. Peoria St.

N. Green St.

N. Fulton St.

90

94

N. Halsted St.

GREEK TOWN

290

S. Green St.

S. Peoria St.

S. Morgan St.

S. Halsted St.

University of Illinois at Chicago

HALSTED/U OF I

W. Harrison St.

W. Taylor St.

90

94

S. Des Plaines St.

S. Halsted St.

W. Roosevelt Rd.

W. Lake St.

W. Randolph St.

W. Washington St.

W. Madison St.

W. Monroe St.

N. Morgan St.

N. Carpenter St.

N

0   1/4 mi

0   0.25 km

M Subway/El stop

☕ Take a Break

Lake Michigan

3 mi

3 km

CHICAGO

Wrigley Field ■

THE LOOP

Map area

90

94

U.S. Cellular Field ■

41

290

55

✈ Midway

premier museums, such as the **Art Institute of Chicago** or one of the Museum Campus museums — the **Field Museum of Natural History,** the **John G. Shedd Aquarium,** or the **Adler Planetarium & Astronomy Museum,** depending on your particular interests (see Chapter 11). Next, return to your hotel for a little downtime before heading out to dinner (see Chapter 10 for options) followed by a show at one of the city's top theaters, like the **Goodman Theater** (see Chapter 15).

Day 2

On the morning of the second day, head for **Lincoln Park** (see Chapter 11), where you can stroll among the animals at **Lincoln Park Zoo,** stop and smell the roses at **Lincoln Park Conservatory,** and take a paddle-boat ride at one of the park's lagoons. When hunger strikes, have lunch at the **North Pond Café** (if money is no object) or **Cafe Brauer** (if sandwiches are more your style; see Chapter 10). If the Cubs are playing, and you secured tickets in advance, head to **Wrigley Field** for an afternoon game (see Chapter 11). You can also take a chance and try to buy tickets at the stadium. If you're not a sports fan, stroll among the boutiques of **Armitage Avenue** (see Chapter 12). For dinner, sample the fare at one of the city's many ethnic restaurants along Clark Street or Southport Avenue (see Chapter 10). Finish your day with some live, down-and-dirty Chicago blues. My personal favorite venue is **Buddy Guy's Legends**, which you can get to by hopping on the subway or taking a cab (see Chapter 16).

Day 3

On the morning of your last day, make a trip to the top of the **John Hancock Center** (see Chapter 11). Next, do some serious window shopping up and down **Michigan Avenue,** or go on a gallery-hopping expedition in **River North** (see Chapter 12). Both areas have plenty of excellent restaurants for lunch. If you're not in the mood for shopping, visit one of the major museums that you didn't see on the first day. Or perhaps check out the **Museum of Contemporary Art,** just off Michigan Avenue (see Chapter 11).

In the evening, head to **Navy Pier,** where you can board a boat for a **dinner cruise** with spectacular views of the skyline (see Chapter 11).

Chicago in Five Days

This itinerary hits more of the city's highlights. For the first three days, follow the itinerary in the preceding section.

Day 4

Begin the fourth day with a trip to **Hyde Park,** where you'll want to spend the majority of your day at the **Museum of Science and Industry** (see Chapter 11). If you also want to see the University of Chicago, make

Chicago in Five Days

DAY FOUR ●
1 Hyde Park
2 Museum of Science & Industry
3 Oriental Institute Museum
4 Robie House
● Meritage, Double Door

DAY FIVE ▲
5 Lakefront and
  Oak Street Beach
6 Bike Chicago
7 Chicago Mercantile Exchange
8 Glessner House
● Atwood Café,
  The Four Seasons Hotel
9 Green Dolphin Street

some time in the afternoon for visits to the **Oriental Institute Museum** (see Chapter 11) and Frank Lloyd Wright's **Robie House** (see Chapter 14), both on the university's campus.

After some relaxation time back at your hotel, make your way to the Bucktown/Wicker Park neighborhood for dinner. You can't go wrong at Pacific-Northwest–inspired **Meritage** (see Chapter 10). Afterwards, hit the music scene at Wicker Park fixture **Double Door,** a great place to see local and national indie-rock and jazz acts (see Chapter 10).

Day 5

If the sun is shining on your last day, head to the **lakefront** (see Chapter 11) and **Oak Street Beach**. Pitch your blanket on the sand and relax. Or, burn off calories from last night's dinner by renting a bike or in-line skates from **Bike Chicago** (see Chapter 11) at North Avenue Beach.

If the weather is inclement, take a taxi to the cozy **Glessner House** (see Chapter 11) for a tour of one of Chicago's architectural treasures. End the day with afternoon tea at the **Atwood Café** or **Four Seasons Hotel** (see Chapter 10).

Following dinner at the restaurant of your choosing, spend your last night at one of Chicago's outstanding jazz clubs, such as **Green Dolphin Street** (see Chapter 16), which also serves dinner.

Chicago for Families with Kids

The itineraries in this section are sure to please pint-size tourists — and their escorts. If you're visiting in winter, or if the weather is inclement, substitute the outdoor activities with some of the many indoor, kid-friendly attractions in Chapter 11.

Day 1

Begin your day with **a ride on the El** (subway). Most kids love trains, and riding high above the city streets gives them a bird's-eye view. One of the best is the brown line, which you can pick up at Lake and Clark streets and ride through the heart of downtown. After your tour, head south to the **Museum of Science and Industry** (see Chapter 11), the classic Chicago kids' attraction that never fails to enthrall. Spend the remainder of your day at this large museum, where you can also have lunch and catch an IMAX movie.

Return to downtown for dinner, perhaps at **Ed Debevic's** (see Chapter 6).

Day 2

On the morning of your second day, take a **Chicago Architecture Foundation** boat tour of the Chicago River and Lake Michigan (see

Chapter 11). Even small kids enjoy being on the water, while adults enjoy learning about the city's spectacular architecture. Back on land, stroll up the Magnificent Mile. Along the way, you pass such kid magnets as the **Disney Store** and **American Girl Place.** For lunch, head to the **Foodlife** food court in Water Tower Place (see Chapter 10), where the wide-ranging menu offers options for everyone in the family. Next, hop a ride on the elevator and head to the top of the **John Hancock Center** (see Chapter 11). In the evening, make your way to **Navy Pier** for dinner and more spectacular views of the city (see Chapter 11).

Day 3

If the Chicago Cubs are in town, spend day 3 at **Wrigley Field** (see Chapter 11). Dine on hot dogs or bratwurst while you sip a beer and the kids polish off cotton candy and licorice whips. If the Cubs aren't playing, take the brood to the **Art Institute of Chicago** (see Chapter 11). Make sure to check out the activity schedule at the Kraft Education Center. For lunch in the Loop, go to **Heaven on Seven** (see Chapter 10) or the food court on the eighth floor of **Marshall Field's** (see Chapter 12).

After two nights out, your kids probably need a quiet evening at the hotel (and you probably need an adults-only night out!). Try to arrange a **babysitter** through the hotel concierge so you can go out for dinner, maybe in the hotel where you're staying. Or have takeout food delivered to your hotel room — see the ethnic eats in Chapter 10 for options.

Day 4

On day 4, explore **Lincoln Park Zoo** and visit the Farm-in-the-Zoo. After lunch at **Cafe Brauer** (see Chapter 10), check out the **Peggy Notebaert Nature Museum,** with its spectacular butterfly house (see Chapter 11). In the evening, catch a show, such as a musical in one of the **North Loop theater district**'s many venues or the kid-pleasing **Blue Man Group** at Briar Street Theatre in Lincoln Park (see Chapter 15).

Day 5

If the sun is shining on your last day, head to the **lakefront** (see Chapter 11). Your kids can splash in the waves under the watchful eyes of lifeguards at Oak Street or North Avenue beaches. If your family is feeling more active, rent bikes from **Bike Chicago** (see Chapter 11) at North Avenue Beach. For lunch on the beach, you can pick up picnic supplies at **Bockwinkel's** (☎ 312-482-9900), a grocery store in the Chicago Place mall at Superior Street and Michigan Avenue.

Alternatively, if the day isn't beach-worthy, head to the Museum Campus and the **Adler Planetarium & Astronomy Museum, Field Museum of Natural History,** or **John G. Shedd Aquarium** (see Chapter 11). You can spend your whole day here, eating in one of the museum cafeterias for lunch.

Spend your last evening eating and playing games at **ESPN Zone** (see Chapter 11).

Chicago for Shopaholics

What could be more magnificent than strolling Michigan Avenue, admiring the shops and people-watching? For the true shopaholic, the experience can't be beat. The Magnificent Mile, Chicago's main shopping artery, makes a straight shot along Michigan Avenue from the Chicago River to Oak Street. Along the way are countless stores and four shopping malls.

 The Magnificent Mile is packed to the gills during summer weekends and holidays. Follow the cues of real Chicagoans and shop on weekdays to avoid the jostling crowds.

 Before hitting the stores, fortify yourself at the **Corner Bakery,** 676 N. St. Clair St. at Erie Street (☎ **312-266-2570**). Along with crowds of locals, you find dozens of breads, from olive ciabatta to walnut and raisin rolls, and an array of pastries. Among the many excellent choices are egg frittatas, scrambled eggs with smoked bacon and cheese, breakfast potatoes, and oatmeal studded with dried cranberries, almonds, and brown sugar.

Shopaholics can easily fill a day along Michigan Avenue. **Chain stores,** both on the high and low end, include Virgin Records, Crate & Barrel, Sony, Nike, Tiffany & Co., Pottery Barn, Banana Republic, and Borders. Among the **major department stores** are Nordstrom, Saks Fifth Avenue, Neiman Marcus, Marshall Field's, Lord & Taylor, and Bloomingdale's. Designer stores include everything from Burberry to Chanel. Rounding out the selections are **four big malls:** Westfield North Bridge, Chicago Place, Water Tower Place, and 900 North Michigan. For descriptions and locations of Chicago's best shops, see Chapter 12.

 For more details on the local shopping scene, check out the annual shopping guide on the *Chicago Magazine* Web site at www.chicago mag.com.

When hunger strikes and you don't want to waste valuable shopping time on a sit-down restaurant, head to **L'Appetito,** an Italian grocery store in the plaza of the John Hancock Center Observatory, 875 N. Michigan Ave. Order a sandwich to go and head across the street to the courtyard of the ivy-clad **Fourth Presbyterian Church,** between East Delaware Place and East Chestnut Street. Sit by the fountain to enjoy your mini-picnic.

If shopping wears you down, treat yourself to a little pampering at **Mario Tricoci Salon & Day Spa** (☎ 312-915-0960) on the lower level of the Bloomie's building, 900 N. Michigan Ave.

If you're still near Michigan Avenue at dinnertime, you may want a special dinner — so you can get decked out in all your new finery purchased that day. Try the nearby **Bice** or **Bistro 110** (see Chapter 10). After dinner, have a drink at **Cru,** 888 N. Wabash Ave. at Delaware Street (☎ 312-337-4078), a European wine bar that's decorated with a zebrawood bar, gold-tone paint accents, and chandeliers. Get a sofa next to a fireplace, watch the stylish crowd, and relax.

Chapter 14

Going Beyond Chicago: Five Day Trips

· ·

In This Chapter

▶ Exploring the roots of some great American literature and architecture: Oak Park

▶ Jonesing for chocolate: Long Grove

▶ Touring the tony North Shore

▶ Visiting university towns: Evanston and Hyde Park

· ·

*E*ven with all the city has to offer, if you're in town for more than a few days (or if you're staying with friends and relatives in the sub-urbs), you may want to explore beyond the city limits. In this chapter, I describe the best attractions in the Chicago suburbs and offer some day-trip suggestions.

Meeting Oak Park's Native Sons

Two fiercely independent men — both innovators with controversial personal lives — left their marks on this quiet, leafy suburb. Frank Lloyd Wright perfected his Prairie School style of architecture here, leaving behind numerous examples of his work. Ernest Hemingway was born in Oak Park and lived here into his late teens. For locations of the stops on this tour, see the "Oak Park" map in this chapter.

Getting there

Suburban Oak Park is 10 miles west of downtown Chicago. **By train,** take the green line El to Harlem Avenue, about a 25-minute ride from down-town. To reach the Oak Park Visitor Center (see the next section), get off the train at Harlem and walk 2 blocks north to Lake Street. Take a right onto Lake, and then walk to Forest Avenue, where you make a left.

By car, take the Eisenhower Expressway (I-290) west to Harlem Avenue (Ill. 43, about 10 miles from downtown) and exit north. Continue on Harlem north to Lake Street. Take a right on Lake Street and continue

Oak Park

0   0.1 mile
0   100 meters

╂─╂─╂ Commuter railroad
        and CTA Green Line
Ⓜ EL/Subway stop
ⓘ Information
🅿 Parking
✉ Post office

ATTRACTIONS ●
Ernest Hemingway Museum **3**
Frank Lloyd Wright Home and Studio **1**
Ginkgo Tree Bookshop **1**
Hemingway Birthplace **2**
Oak Park Visitors Center **4**
Unity Temple **5**

DINING ◆
Avenue Ale House **6**

to Forest Avenue. Turn left. Immediately on the right, you see the Oak Park Visitor Center.

Taking a tour

The **Oak Park Visitor Center,** 158 Forest Ave. (☎ **708-848-1500**), is open daily April through October from 10 a.m. to 5 p.m., and November through March from 10 a.m. to 4 p.m. You can pick up maps and guidebooks at the center, located only a few blocks from the heart of the historic district and the Frank Lloyd Wright Home and Studio.

Seeing the sights

The must-see attraction in Oak Park is the **Frank Lloyd Wright Home and Studio,** which is open by guided tour only (see Chapter 11 for details). You can also take a **guided walking tour** of the neighborhood on weekends from 10:30 a.m. to 4 p.m. (tour times are somewhat more limited Nov–Feb). You see houses designed by Wright, as well as the charming Victorian homes that he hated so intensely. Tours last one hour and cost $9 for adults and $7 for seniors and children 7 to 18 (free for children under 7). Tours depart from the **Ginkgo Tree Bookshop** in the Frank Lloyd Wright Home and Studio, 951 Chicago Ave. (☎ **708-848-1976**). At the shop, you can also rent an audiocassette for a self-guided tour of the historic district, available daily from 10 a.m. to 3:30 p.m. The rental cost is also $9 for adults and $7 for seniors and children.

Wright fans will also want to visit nearby **Unity Temple,** 875 Lake St. (☎ **708-383-8873**). Guided tours that last 45 minutes depart on Saturdays and Sundays on the hour from 1 to 3 p.m. Admission is $6 for adults and $3 for seniors, students, and children.

The other two highlights in Oak Park are the restored **Hemingway Birthplace,** 339 N. Oak Park Ave. (the home of his maternal grandparents), and the **Ernest Hemingway Museum,** just down the block at 200 N. Oak Park Ave., both operated by the Ernest Hemingway Foundation (☎ **708-848-2222**). The museum traces the author's life from his first job out of high school as a young reporter with the *Kansas City Star* to his work as a war correspondent in Europe during World War II. Videos of 15 films made from his work, from *A Farewell to Arms* (1921) to *Islands*

Wide lawns, narrow minds

At one time, the Oak Park city fathers shunned one of their most famous sons, Nobel laureate **Ernest Hemingway.** They apparently took umbrage at his supposed description of Oak Park as a town of "wide lawns and narrow minds." Today, all seems to be forgiven — the community welcomes visitors to Ernest Hemingway Museum, to tours of the Hemingway Birthplace, and to an annual festival that includes readings, a "Papa" look-alike contest, and other shenanigans.

in the Stream (1977), are shown. Both places are open Sunday through Friday from 1 to 5 p.m., and Saturday from 10 a.m. to 5 p.m. An admission charge of $7 for adults and $5 for seniors and students (children under 5 are free) covers both the birthplace and the museum.

Dining locally

 If you need to refuel between walking tours, many restaurants, cafes, and ice-cream shops are located on and around Oak Park Avenue, near Unity Temple. My favorite is the **Avenue Ale House,** 825 S. Oak Park Ave. (☎ **708-848-2801**), a tavern that specializes in steaks, chops, hearty sandwiches, homemade French onion soup, and giant salads. Eight beers are on tap, and 50 more are available bottled. An outdoor dining area is open in summertime.

Shopping in the Historic Village of Long Grove

Nestled among the northwest suburbs is Long Grove Village. Settled in the 1840s by German immigrants, Long Grove has preserved its old-fashioned character and makes a fine day trip for those looking for relief from the big-city noise and commotion. You feel like you stepped into a rural village at the turn of the 20th century. Set amongst 500 acres of oak and hickory tree groves, Long Grove is a browsers' and shoppers' mecca, and special events throughout the year keep the businesses hopping. The historic buildings contain more than 100 specialty shops, galleries, and restaurants.

Getting there

Long Grove is about 30 miles northwest of Chicago. From the Loop, take the I-94 tollway north until it separates at I-90, another tollway that travels northwesterly. Follow I-90 until you reach Route 53, and drive north on 53 until it dead-ends at Lake Cook Road. Take the west exit off 53 and follow Lake Cook Road to Hicks Road. Turn right on Hicks Road and then left on Old McHenry Road, which takes you into the center of town.

Taking a tour

The **Long Grove Tourist Information Center,** near the Fountain Square (☎ **847-634-0888;** www.longgroveonline.com), has information about events in town. You can pick up a map showing the locations of local businesses — many of the streets are small and winding, so addresses alone won't be of much help.

Seeing the sights

The village hosts several cultural and entertainment events, festivals, and art fairs during the year. The annual **Strawberry Festival** is the biggest, held during the last weekend in June. An **Apple Festival** is held in October, and a **Chocolate Festival** is held in May.

Don't miss the **Long Grove Confectionery,** 220 Robert Parker Coffin Rd. (☎ 800-373-3102), one of Chicago's last remaining candy companies, where you can eat hand-dipped chocolate-covered strawberries in the summer and gigantic caramel apples in the fall. Another standout is the **Pine Cone Christmas Shop,** 210 Robert Parker Coffin Rd. (☎ 847-634-0890), a year-round wonder of decorated trees and Charles Dickens villages.

Dining locally

For lunch, stop at **Village Tavern,** 135 Old McHenry Rd. (Route 22) at Country Lane (☎ 847-634-3117), a Long Grove institution offering soups, sandwiches, and other comfort food.

Discovering Evanston's College-Town Charm

Northwestern University contributes to the liberal, intellectual culture of Evanston, Chicago's oldest suburb — and one of the most scenic. Evanston manages to combine the peaceful feeling and green space of a suburb with the culture and lively atmosphere that you expect of an urban center. Evanston's downtown offers sophisticated dining and boutique shopping. From downtown Chicago, the drive to Evanston on Lake Shore Drive and Sheridan Road takes about 25 minutes. But time your trip, because at rush hour, it can take much longer — up to 45 minutes.

Getting there

By car from the Loop, drive north on Lake Shore Drive to Sheridan Road. Continue north on Sheridan. As you enter Evanston, Northwestern University is located along the lakeshore, on your right.

By public transport, take the Metra North train line from Northwestern Station in the Loop to the Davis Street stop, and walk east on Davis Street into the heart of downtown Evanston. The ride takes about 20 minutes. (See Chapter 8 for information on Metra.)

Taking a tour

Lighthouse Park, 2601 Sheridan Rd. at Central Street (☎ 847-328-6961), is the site of a lighthouse built in 1873 after the wreck of the *Lady Elgin.* Nature-center tours, a wildlife trail, a small museum, and an experimental greenhouse are all part of the park. Tours of the lighthouse start at 2, 3, and 4 p.m. on weekends from June to September. Admission to the lighthouse is $5 for adults and $3 for seniors and students, but kids under 8 are not allowed for safety reasons.

Seeing the sights

Relive college life at **Northwestern University** — the lakefront campus is worth wandering around for a couple of hours. From Sheridan Road, turn toward the lake on Campus Drive, and park in the lot that fronts Sheridan Road. From there, walk down Campus Drive toward the lake into the heart of the campus. Be sure to check out the stained-glass windows at **Alice Millar Chapel** and the art at **Mary and Leigh Block Gallery** during your walk.

The former mansion of Charles Gates Dawes, 225 Greenwood, now houses the **Evanston Historical Society** (☎ 847-475-3410), which gives free tours of this century-old national landmark. Dawes, a wealthy financier, served as vice president under Calvin Coolidge and won the Nobel Peace Prize in 1925 for his smooth handling of German reparations on behalf of the League of Nations following World War I.

Dining locally

While on the Northwestern campus, head to the **Norris Student Center** near the lake for quick snacks or ice cream. To experience Evanston's Bohemian side, grab a cup of coffee or enjoy breakfast or lunch at **Blind Faith Café,** 525 Dempster St. (☎ 847-328-6875), where organic and vegetarian specialties include scrambled tofu, huevos rancheros, granola, and pancakes. Stop in, soak in the atmosphere, and feel healthier by the minute.

Ambling Up the North Shore: Wilmette and Environs

A long string of suburbs run along Lake Michigan going north from Chicago; many of them are among the nation's wealthiest zip codes. As a friend of mine put it as we strolled Lake Forest, passing one expensive luxury car after another: Either everyone should live like this, or no one should live like this!

Getting there

By car, take Lake Shore Drive out of the city, which turns into Sheridan Road. Sheridan winds through the campus of Northwestern University in Evanston and into the upper-crust North Shore suburbs of Wilmette, Kenilworth, and Winnetka. (You'll recognize them by the multimillion-dollar homes that flank the road.)

Taking a tour

Admission is free at the **Baha'i House of Worship,** 100 Linden Ave. at Sheridan Road (☎ 847-853-2300), a gleaming stone temple, designed by the French-Canadian Louis Bourgeois and completed in 1953. Essentially a soaring nine-sided 135-foot dome, draped in a delicate lacelike facade, the temple strongly reveals the eastern influence of the Baha'i faith's native Iran. Surrounded by formal gardens, it is one of seven Baha'i temples in the world, and the only one in the Western Hemisphere.

The dome's latticework is even more beautiful as you gaze upward from the floor of the sanctuary, which, during the day, is flooded with light.

Temple members offer informal tours of the building to anyone who inquires; older children and adults with an interest in architecture will get the most out of a tour of the interior. Not only is the temple itself really a sight, but the drive on Sheridan Road is also one of the most beautiful in the Chicago area. The visitor center is open daily May through September 10 a.m. to 8 p.m. and October through April 10 a.m. to 5 p.m. The temple is open daily from 7 a.m., and devotional services are held Monday through Saturday at 12:15 p.m. and Sunday at 1:15 p.m. (with choral accompaniment).

A word of caution if you're driving: The temple seems to appear out of nowhere as you round a particularly tight curve on Sheridan Road, and it can distract even the most focused of drivers. Take it slowly, and wait until you're safely parked before gazing skyward.

Seeing the sights

If you're traveling with children, head to the **Kohl Children's Museum,** 165 Green Bay Rd, Wilmette (☎ **847-251-7781**). From Sheridan Road, turn left onto Central Street (at Evanston Hospital); go west to Green Bay Road; turn right and drive ¼ mile to the museum. This museum is a hands-on, dress-up-and-pretend, blow-bubbles sort of place where kids amuse themselves for hours. They shop at a "supermarket," take a simulated voyage on a Phoenician sailing ship, and join in puppet shows and sing-alongs. The museum is open Monday through Saturday from 9:30 a.m. to 5 p.m. and Sunday from noon to 5 p.m. Admission is $5 per person, $4 for seniors, and free for children under age 1. In the fall of 2005, the museum is slated to move to a dazzling new facility in Glenview, a suburb to the west of Wilmette, so call ahead for information if you're planning to visit after that time.

If you've made it up to the Baha'i Temple, take a stroll across Sheridan Road to **Gilson Park** for a taste of north-suburban life. Check out the sailors prepping their boats for a lake tour, families picnicking and playing Frisbee, and kids frolicking on the sandy beach. Access to the beach is restricted in the summer (the locals like to keep the Chicago riffraff out), but in the fall and spring you're welcome to wander (just don't expect to take a dip in the frigid water). You'll have a wonderful opportunity for a photo either in front of the lake or on one of the small grassy dunes.

Dining locally

 Next door to the Kohl Children's Museum is **Walker Bros. Original Pancake House,** 153 Green Bay Rd. (☎ **847-251-6000**), a favorite North Shore breakfast spot. Expect a long wait on weekends. Top choices are apple pancakes (a kid favorite), German pancakes served with fruit, and oven-baked omelets. The restaurant serves lunch and dinner, too.

Hanging Out in Hyde Park

Anchoring Chicago's Hyde Park neighborhood is the Museum of Science and Industry, a perennial favorite with kids and one of Chicago's most popular tourist attractions. What many visitors don't know is that the museum is located in a leafy neighborhood that is also the home of the sprawling 175-acre campus of the University of Chicago. Many fine attractions sit amid the Gothic architecture and tree-lined streets of the university campus. For the locations of the attractions in this section, see the "Hyde Park" map in this chapter.

Getting there

By car, take Lake Shore Drive south to 59th Street. Follow 59th Street west (you pass the Museum of Science and Industry) into the heart of the University of Chicago campus (59th Street and Ellis Avenue). The drive takes about 20 minutes from downtown.

By train, you can reach Hyde Park from downtown in 15 minutes with Metra. Trains run at least every hour Monday through Saturday from 5:15 a.m. to 12:50 a.m. and Sundays and holidays from 5 a.m. to 12:55 a.m. Pick up the train at Randolph and Michigan, Van Buren and Michigan, or Roosevelt and Michigan. The 55th-56th-57th Street Station is nearest the Museum of Science and Industry; the 59th Street Station is nearest the University of Chicago campus. Fare is about $1.95. (See Chapter 8 for information on Metra.)

By bus, the no. 6 Jeffrey Express from the Loop takes about 30 minutes. Pick up the bus on Wacker Drive on weekdays from 5:30 a.m. to 10:30 p.m., and on weekends and holidays from 7:30 a.m. to 7 p.m. Another way to go is local bus no. 1, which originates at Union Station on Jackson Boulevard and Canal Street.

By taxi, the fare to Hyde Park from downtown is about $15.

Taking a tour

Fans of Frank Lloyd Wright's Prairie School architecture will want to see the 1909 **Robie House,** 5727 S. Woodlawn Ave. (☎ **773-834-1847**), considered a masterpiece of 20th-century architecture. The house is undergoing a massive, ten-year renovation; although the house is open during

Hyde Park

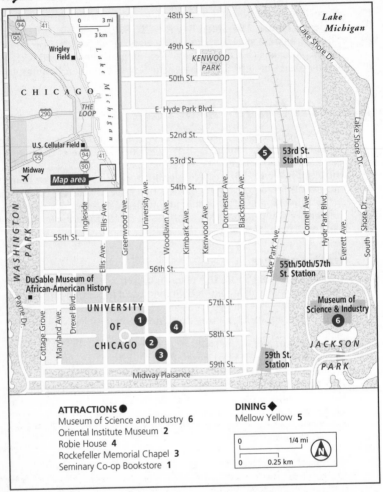

Inset map labels:
Wrigley Field ■
C H I C A G O
THE LOOP
U.S. Cellular Field ■
Midway ✈
Map area
Lake Michigan

48th St.
49th St.
KENWOOD PARK
50th St.
E. Hyde Park Blvd.
52nd St.
53rd St.
5 53rd St. Station
54th St.
55th St.
WASHINGTON PARK
DuSable Museum of African-American History ■
UNIVERSITY OF CHICAGO
1
2
3
4
56th St.
57th St.
58th St.
59th St.
Midway Plaisance
55th/50th/57th St. Station
59th St. Station
Museum of Science & Industry
6
JACKSON PARK
Lake Michigan
Lake Shore Dr.

Street names: Ingleside, Ellis Ave., Greenwood Ave., University Ave., Woodlawn Ave., Kimbark Ave., Kenwood Ave., Dorchester Ave., Blackstone Ave., Lake Park Ave., Cornell Ave., Hyde Park Blvd., Everett Ave., South Shore Dr., Cottage Grove, Maryland Ave., Drexel Blvd., Payne Dr.

ATTRACTIONS ●
Museum of Science and Industry **6**
Oriental Institute Museum **2**
Robie House **4**
Rockefeller Memorial Chapel **3**
Seminary Co-op Bookstore **1**

DINING ◆
Mellow Yellow **5**

0   1/4 mi
0   0.25 km

the process, your photos may include lots of scaffolding! Forty-five-minute tours start at 11 a.m., 1 p.m., and 3 p.m. on weekdays and every half-hour from 11 a.m. to 3:30 p.m. on weekends. Admission is $9 for adults, $7 for seniors and children 7 to 17. The former three-car garage (a rarity at the time) houses a gift shop stocked with Wright items.

Seeing the sights

For details on the main attraction, the **Museum of Science and Industry,** see Chapter 11.

About 10 blocks west of the Museum of Science and Industry on the campus of the University of Chicago is the stunning **Rockefeller Memorial Chapel,** 5850 S. Woodlawn Ave. (☎ 773-702-2100). The Gothic chapel, built in 1928, is home to the world's second-largest carillon, donated by John D. Rockefeller, Jr., in memory of his mother, Laura, in 1932. Choir concerts, carillon performances, and other musical programs are presented throughout the year, usually for a small donation. The building is open to the public daily from 8 a.m. to 4 p.m., except for religious services. Also on the campus of the University of Chicago is the **Oriental Institute Museum,** where you find mummies, gold jewelry, and other treasures of ancient Egypt, Syria, Iran, and other Middle Eastern countries. See Chapter 11 for details on this free museum.

Before his death in 2005, Nobel Prize–winning novelist Saul Bellow occasionally returned to the Chicago-area neighborhoods that he wrote about in novels such as *Herzog.* One of his favorite stops was the **Seminary Co-op Bookstore,** 5757 S. University (☎ 773-752-4381). This rambling bookstore has an amazing array of titles and is a treasure trove of academic and scholarly books.

Dining locally

For lunch, travel north to **Mellow Yellow,** 1508 E. 53rd St. (☎ 773-667-2000), where you can get a bowl of Cincinnati-style five-way chili. University of Chicago students and faculty members go to this Hyde Park institution for potent chili (including a vegetarian version) and to linger over coffee and dessert. Quiche and hamburgers are other reliable choices.

Part V
Living It Up after Dark: Chicago Nightlife

The 5th Wave   By Rich Tennant

"That's the third time tonight that's happened. They
start out playing the blues, but by the end, everyone's
playing a polka. I blame the new bass player from Milwaukee."

In this part . . .

Chicago after dark means world-class performances by the Chicago Symphony Orchestra and the Lyric Opera of Chicago. It means comedy at The Second City or a drama at the Steppenwolf or Goodman theaters. Chicago's theater district is booming in the North Loop, with shows on their way to Broadway — or touring after a successful Broadway run. Going out in Chicago can also be as simple as a game of pool at a neighborhood pub or a glass of Shiraz in front of the fireplace at a wine bar. Chicago has a thriving music scene, including first-rate jazz joints and some of the planet's best blues clubs. After reading this part, you'll be able to navigate Chicago's theater, performing arts, and bar and club scenes with ease.

Chapter 15

Applauding the Cultural Scene

● ●

In This Chapter

▶ Surveying the Chicago performing-arts scene

▶ Minding your manners: Theater protocol

▶ Finding out about performances and getting tickets

● ●

C ulture is alive and accessible in Chicago. The performing-arts scene — theater, symphony, opera, and dance — keeps things hopping just about every night, making Chicago a city that certainly doesn't sleep *much.*

With such fixtures as the Lyric Opera of Chicago, Joffrey Ballet of Chicago, Hubbard Street Dance Chicago, and Chicago Symphony Orchestra, the question is not so much "Should we see a performance?" as "How many of these fabulous performances can we see?"

Chicago's thriving theater scene offers something for everyone, from flashy musicals to low-budget dramas. Because Chicago audiences have a knack for mimicking the reactions of their Broadway audience counter-parts, the city has become a favorite pre-Broadway testing ground. Most recently, the success of *All Shook Up* and *Spamalot* in Chicago has led to those shows getting a chance on Broadway.

This chapter reveals the best of the local offerings and other helpful details, such as how to get tickets and find pre-theater dining.

Be sure to check out the "Loop After Dark" and "Lincoln Park and Wrigleyville after Dark" maps in Chapter 16 to locate this chapter's listings.

Getting the Inside Scoop

Chicago's performing arts scene is centered on the Loop, with another cluster of theatres on the city's North Side. The theater scene is chang-ing faster than you can shout "Bravo!" Not so long ago, the Loop was comatose after business hours. No more. Lively bars and bistros, splashy hotels, and a number of thriving theaters have pumped new life into the area.

Be sure to check out the "Dining before or after the show" sidebar for tips on where to eat.

Taking a look at Chicago's hot spots

Joan W. and Irving B. Harris Theater for Music and Dance, 205 E. Randolph Drive (☎ 312-334-7777; www.madtc.com), a sparkling new facility in Millennium Park, is up and running with a full slate of perform-ances from the 12 arts groups that are the theater's core tenants. From classic opera such as *Le nozze di Figaro* by Chicago Opera Theater, to modern dance by River North Chicago Dance and Hubbard Street Dance Chicago, and jazz dance by Giordano Jazz Dance Chicago, this brand-new theater and dance space boasts performances that are worth check-ing out.

The **Goodman Theatre** is located in an attractive building on Randolph and Dearborn streets (you'll recognize it by the exterior panels that change colors, creating a mosaic effect). The building was a total-gut

Dining before or after the show

I prefer dining before a show because sitting in a theater with a growling stomach for two hours is no fun. (I wind up thinking about food more than the entertainment in front of me!) Whether you choose to dine before or after the show, I have recommenda-tions for you.

Many establishments cater to the theater crowd and are accustomed to getting diners in and out quickly. A number of quality restaurants, such as **Atwood Cafe** and **Trattoria No. 10** (see Chapter 10), lie within walking distance of the large Loop theaters. Other good options are **Petterino's**, 150 N. Dearborn St. at Randolph Street (☎ 312-442-0150), a steakhouse in the Goodman Theatre building (call early for reservations), and **312 Chicago,** 136 N. LaSalle St. at Randolph Street (☎ 312-696-2420), an Italian restaurant in flashy Hotel Allegro.

If you're more comfortable eating after the show, Chicago has plenty of restaurants whose kitchens stay open late. Standouts open until at least 1 a.m. include **Bin 36, Café Iberico, Jake Melnick's, Kamehachi, Nine** (open until 3 a.m. on Sat!), and **Tango Sur.** See Chapter 10 for descriptions of all these spots.

If you crave more entertainment, nightclubs (see Chapter 16) usually are just getting up to speed around the time the curtain falls. Some clubs also provide good food late at night. Two notable examples are **Green Dolphin Street,** 2200 N. Ashland Ave. at Webster (☎ 773-395-0066), and **Harry's Velvet Room,** 56 W. Illinois St. at Dearborn Street (☎ 312-527-5600).

rehab of the historic Harris and Selwyn theaters. The focal point is the 830-seat main-stage theater, a limestone-and-glass structure in the center of the block. Completing the complex are a 400-seat studio theater, two restaurants, and retail space.

Another prominent and refurbished (as of 1999) Loop theater is the **Cadillac Palace Theater.** Connected to the hip Hotel Allegro, the Palace is a refurbished 1926 vaudeville house that offers 2,400 seats and stages first-run and touring Broadway musicals. The Palace recently played home to a nine-month run of *The Lion King.*

The **Lookingglass Theatre Company** also has a new space, in Water Tower Works. This convenient location on the Magnificent Mile next door to Water Tower Place has two stages to showcase the company's distinctive physical style.

Visitors to touristy Navy Pier will find the **Chicago Shakespeare Theater** — an intimate 550-seat space patterned after the Swan Theatre at Stratford-upon-Avon in England.

Despite all the change in Chicago's theater scene, you can rely on some constants. A robust contingent of long-running shows play here. Some of the most popular include *Late Night Catechism* (at Royal George Theatre Center), *Blue Man Group* (at Briar Street Theatre) and *Tony and Tina's Wedding* (at Piper's Alley, 210 W. North Ave., ☎ 312-664-8844).

Getting hip to theater etiquette

Ready for a big night at the theater? Before you face the bright lights, you may want to know a few things. First, some general tips:

- ✔ **Don't use cameras or camcorders in theaters.** Taping is prohibited by law.

- ✔ **Don't talk during a performance.** (Not that *you'd* ever do that!)

- ✔ **Do shut off all beepers and cellphones.** (When was the last time you were at a performance where one didn't go off?)

Chicago is a relaxed Midwestern city. Patrons of the theater and of theater-district restaurants dress relatively informally. In most cases, a sweater and slacks or jeans, perhaps with a light jacket, work for men. For women, similarly low-key attire is appropriate — pants and shirt or skirt and blouse.

For most theatergoers, the bottom line is how comfortable they feel about the appropriateness of what they're wearing. They're likely to dress up for a hot-ticket blockbuster musical and dress down for storefront repertory. Most prefer the safety of the middle ground to feeling self-conscious about being over- or underdressed.

Happy news: Ushers in Chicago theaters don't expect tips. Acknowledging their help with a thank-you or a pleasant nod or smile is all that's required. However, if you battle your way to the bar during intermission, the beleaguered bartender appreciates your tip.

The show must go on — and on time. Chicago-area theaters tend to be punctual, and tardy patrons usually must wait to be seated until the conclusion of the scene or musical number in progress. Arriving late for the opera can be especially troublesome. With acts lasting for over an hour, you'll be sitting outside watching the performance on a television.

Finding Out What's Playing and Getting Tickets

Getting connected to the Chicago fine-arts scene requires only a phone call. The **Chicago Dance and Music Alliance** information line (☎ 312-987-1123; www.chicagoperformances.org), can give you listings of upcoming events.

Fine arts in the Windy City pick up when the leaves start to fall. The **Chicago Symphony Orchestra** and the **Lyric Opera of Chicago** begin their seasons in September. The opera concludes its schedule in March; the symphony continues into June. (See "Raising the Curtain on the Performing Arts," later in this chapter, for information on all the organizations mentioned in this section.)

Area dance troupes are active all year. Highlights of their seasons include performances at the **Ravinia Festival** in late summer (see the "Bach in the 'burbs" sidebar in this chapter) and at the annual month-long festival **Dance Chicago,** which takes place at the **Athenaeum Theatre** (☎ 773-935-6860; www.dancechicago.com) in autumn. Other noteworthy happenings are **Joffrey Ballet of Chicago**'s *Nutcracker* over the holidays and the **Hubbard Street Dance Chicago**'s spring engagement.

In addition to the Ravinia Festival, summer traditions include concerts by the **Grant Park Symphony and Chorus,** which now take place in the Frank Gehry–designed Pritzker Pavilion. Featuring Gehry's signature sinuous lines, the pavilion is surrounded by dramatic ribbons of curved steel. The Grant Park Symphony will not only look better than ever, it should sound great, too — thanks to a state-of-the-art sound system. Concerts are held Wednesday through Sunday, with most performances beginning at 7:30 p.m. Seats (about 4,000 of them) are reserved for subscribers, but unclaimed places are offered to the public 15 minutes before the concert starts. There's also plenty of lawn seating; so bring a blanket and enjoy a picnic dinner.

Chicago's vibrant theater scene is in a constant state of flux, with openings, closings, revivals, and extensions. Useful tools to help you scope out a show are the *Chicago Tribune* (www.chicagotribune.com), *Chicago Sun-Times* (www.suntimes.com), and *Daily Herald* (www.dailyherald.com), which offer comprehensive weekly listings in their Friday entertainment sections. The papers also run reviews of larger shows around town; for older reviews, check their Web sites. Other reliable sources of reviews and commentary are *Chicago* (www.chicagomag.com) and *North Shore* (www.northshoremag.com) magazines. To find out about out-of-the-mainstream performances, pick up the *Chicago Reader* (www.chicagoreader.com) and *New City* (www.newcitychicago.com), the leading free alternative newspapers. These tabloids cover nearly every upcoming production, from traveling Broadway musicals to avant-garde performance art.

Some Chicago theaters have specially designed performances (usually on weekdays, or weekend matinees) that cater to families. These shows often offer discounted children's tickets or special discounts for large groups. You can find out about these performances in the papers (see "Finding Out What's Playing" earlier in this chapter). You can also get details on kid-friendly productions from the **League of Chicago Theatres** (☎ 312-554-9800; www.chicagoplays.com).

If you're surfing the Web, do as Chicagoans do and check out the following sites, which bring the Chicago theater world to your fingertips:

✔ www.metromix.com, supported by the *Chicago Tribune*

✔ www.centerstage.net/chicago, run by a group of Northwestern alumni in association with MediaOne

✔ www.chicago.citysearch.com, the local CitySearch Web site, offers valuable theater information and reviews

Getting tickets to symphony, opera, ballet, and theater performances is largely a function of what's hot and what's not. Try the **Ticketmaster** arts line (☎ 312-902-1500; www.ticketmaster.com) and the **Ticket Exchange** (☎ 800-666-0779 or, in Chicago, 312-902-1888) — if tickets are readily available, you can get them there. Another tactic is to wait until you get to town, show up at the venue around lunchtime on the day of the performance, and ask for turn-back tickets; you may luck out.

If you're unable to land the tickets you want, try contacting the concierge at your Chicago hotel. If that fails, try a licensed ticket agency. Brokers include **Gold Coast Tickets** (☎ 800-889-9100 or 312-644-6446) and **Union Tysen Entertainment Ticket Service** (☎ 800-372-7344 or 312-372-7344). Here, too, supply and demand rule. You could end up paying double or triple face value (or even more) for those coveted tickets.

Another good tactic is to stop at the box office around noon on the day you want to see the show. You can often pick up a cancellation. This is definitely the case at the Lyric Opera, where patrons have a long-standing tradition of turning in unused subscription tickets at the box office. You can purchase those tickets and often obtain great seats.

Traveling to the show by El or bus

For $1.75 (plus 25¢ for transfers), you can travel by bus or El (train/subway) to your venue. For details on Chicago's public transportation system, see Chapter 8. For a map of the El, see the Cheat Sheet at the front of this book. Following is a list of transportation directions to the major venues:

- **Chicago Theatre:** Green-, purple-, orange-, or brown-line El to State and Lake, or the State Street bus (no. 2, 6, 10, 11, 29, 36, 44, 62, or 146) to the corner of State and Lake.

- **Ford Center for the Performing Arts:** Green-, purple-, orange-, or brown-line El to Randolph, or the State Street bus (no. 2, 6, 10, 11, 29, 36, 44, 62, or 146) to the corner of Randolph and State.

- **Goodman Theatre:** Green-, purple-, orange-, or brown-line El to Adams, or the Michigan Avenue bus (no. 3, 4, 60, 145, 147, or 151) to the corner of Michigan and Monroe.

- **Lyric Opera of Chicago:** Metra train to Northwestern station, or take the green-, purple-, brown-, or orange-line El to Washington. Take the Madison Street bus (no. 14, 20, 56, 131, or 157) to the corner of Madison and Wacker.

- **Millennium Park's Pritzer Pavilion:** Green-, purple-, brown-, or orange-line El to Randolph, or the Michigan Avenue bus (no. 3, 4, 60, 145, 147, or 151) to the corner of Michigan and Randolph.

- **Shubert Theatre:** Red-line El to Monroe, or the State Street bus (no. 2, 6, 10, 11, 29, 36, 44, 62, or 146) to the corner of Monroe and State.

- **Steppenwolf Theatre Company:** Red-line El to North and Clybourne, or bus no. 33 or 41 to corner of North and Halsted.

- **Symphony Center:** Green, purple, brown, or orange line El to Adams, or the Michigan Avenue bus (no. 3, 4, 60, 145, 147, or 151) to the corner of Michigan and Jackson.

 Bargain hunters have several options for buying discounted tickets:

- The **League of Chicago Theatres** (☎ 312-554-9800; www.chicago plays.com) has a daily telephone listing of discounted shows, as well as information about upcoming shows and a current theater guide. The call costs $1 per minute, with calls lasting an average of three minutes.

- **Hot Tix** (☎ 312-554-9800; www.hottix.org), operated by the League of Chicago Theatres, sells same-day half-price tickets on the day of the show for about 125 city and suburban theaters. On Friday, you can buy tickets for shows throughout the weekend. Tickets are available starting at 10 a.m. Tuesday through Saturday and 11 a.m. Sunday at a number of center-city locations, including **Water Works Visitor Center,** 163 E. Pearson St.; in Lincoln Park at **Tower Records,** 2301 N. Clark St. and at all other Tower Records locations in the city; and in the Loop at 78 W. Randolph St., just east of Clark Street.

✔ The **Steppenwolf Theatre Company**'s box office (see the listing later in this chapter) usually has a limited number of half-price same-day seats.

✔ The "Tix at Six" program at the **Goodman Theatre** offers half-price, day-of-show tickets; many of them are excellent seats that have been returned by subscribers. Tickets go on sale at the box office at 6 p.m. for evening performances, or noon for matinees.

✔ Many theaters offer **discounts for full-time students and senior citizens** on off-peak days during the week. To find out if the show you want to see is discounted, call the theater. These specials aren't always well advertised, so many low-cost seats go unclaimed.

Raising the Curtain on the Performing Arts

Draw back the curtain on this town's theater scene and you find everything from splashy Broadway musicals to gritty small productions. This section guides you to the best of the offerings, organized by neighborhood.

Do you love the string section? Is your secret dream to become a professional dancer or to belt out "La Donna e Mobile" with the likes of Luciano Pavarotti? Symphony, dance, and opera lovers find plenty to love in Chicago.

Theater

You'll likely find yourself headed to one of several neighborhoods that form the base of Chicago's theater scene. What follows is the lowdown on each.

Civic duty

The Civic Opera House has played host to scores of famous operas, and when it comes to staging great plays, the adjoining Civic Theatre is no slouch. Perhaps best known for the 1944 premiere of Tennessee Williams's classic *The Glass Menagerie,* the Civic Theatre continues to put on plays, dance performances, and films. The theater (☎ 312-419-0033; www.civicoperahouse.com) is now part of the Civic Opera House. See the "Opera" section for information on the opera house.

The Loop: An awakening theatrical giant

Chicago's Loop imports the best and biggest of Broadway's musicals and dramas. The largest theaters often play host to extended runs of popular shows, filling out their schedules with special events and one-night-only performances by big-name artists. Major Loop theaters include the following:

- ✔ **Auditorium Theatre,** 50 E. Congress Parkway at Michigan Avenue (☎ 312-922-2110; www.auditoriumtheatre.org)

- ✔ **Cadillac Palace Theater,** 151 W. Randolph St. between North LaSalle and North Wells streets (☎ 312-384-1510)

- ✔ **Chicago Theatre,** 175 N. State St. at Lake Street (☎ 312-443-1130)

- ✔ **Ford Center for the Performing Arts/Oriental Theatre,** 24 W. Randolph St. at State Street (☎ 312-782-2004)

- ✔ **Goodman Theatre,** 170 N. Dearborn St. at Randolph Street (☎ 312-443-3800; www.goodman-theatre.org)

- ✔ **Shubert Theatre,** 22 W. Monroe St. at State Street (☎ 312-977-1700)

Lincoln Park: The cutting edge

Theaters in Lincoln Park leave the glitzy Broadway shows to larger venues and focus on original, edgy drama. **Steppenwolf Theatre**

Oriental Theatre's reversal of fortune

Among the success stories in the Loop theater revival is the **Ford Center for the Performing Arts,** a renovation of the former **Oriental Theatre.** But the road to success was long and winding:

1903 On December 30, fire sweeps through the Iroquois Theater killing 603 people during a Christmas show.

1926 On the site of the Iroquois, the Oriental Theatre opens — one of the first movie palaces to feature Far East–inspired décor, including turbaned ushers. The theater quickly becomes Chicago's top spot to see first-run films and elaborate stage shows. Bob Hope, Judy Garland, the Three Stooges, and Danny Kaye are among those who tread its boards.

1970s The theater falls into disrepair and is shuttered, thus becoming the terrain of theatrical ghosts and rodents.

1998 After a makeover, the theater reopens as the Ford Center for the Performing Arts with a lavish production of the smash Broadway hit *Ragtime.*

2005 The theater is home to the kickoff tour for the Tony Award–winning Broadway hit *Wicked.*

Finding a better seat

Most of Chicago's grand old theaters have balconies that go way, way up toward the ceiling — and if you're stuck in the cheap seats, you'll be straining to see what's happening on stage. Although theaters are very strict about checking tickets when you arrive, the ushers relax during intermission. So scope out empty seats during the first act, and then move down to better (and much pricier) spots for the rest of the show. (I've had great success with this tactic at the Auditorium Theatre, which is so huge that it rarely sells out.)

Company on Halsted Street launched the careers of Joan Allen, John Malkovich, and Gary Sinise, who often return to direct and act. In 2001, the **Victory Gardens Theater** became the third Chicago theater (after the Steppenwolf and the Goodman) to win a Tony for sustained excellence by a resident theater.

Other Lincoln Park theaters offer popular performances by traveling troupes, such as Blue Man Group at the **Briar Street Theatre.** Following are some key Lincoln Park venues:

- ✔ **Apollo Theater,** 2540 N. Lincoln Ave. (☎ **773-935-6100;** www. apollochicago.com)

- ✔ **Briar Street Theatre,** 3133 N. Halsted St. at Briar Street (☎ **773-348-4000**)

- ✔ **Royal George Theatre Center,** 1641 N. Halsted St. at North Avenue (☎ **312-988-9000;** www.theroyalgeorgetheatre.com)

- ✔ **Steppenwolf Theatre Company,** 1650 N. Halsted St. at North Avenue (☎ **312-335-1650;** www.steppenwolf.org)

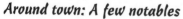

- ✔ **Victory Gardens Theater,** 2257 N. Lincoln Ave. at Belden Avenue (☎ **773-871-3000;** www.victorygardens.org)

Around town: A few notables

Other major theaters around town include

- ✔ **Chicago Shakespeare Theater,** 800 E. Grand Ave. at Navy Pier (☎ **312-595-5600;** www.chicagoshakes.com)

- ✔ **Lookingglass Theatre Company,** Water Tower Works, 821 N. Michigan Ave., Magnificent Mile (☎ **312-337-0665;** www. lookingglasstheatre.org)

- ✔ **Rosemont Theatre,** 5400 N. River Rd., in the northwestern suburb of Rosemont (☎ **847-671-5100**), a top stop for musicals and concerts

✔ **North Shore Center for the Performing Arts in Skokie,** 9501 Skokie Blvd., in the northern suburb of Skokie (☎ **847/673-6300**), home to the well-respected Northlight Theater, the Skokie Valley Symphony Orchestra, and a series of touring acts, including comics, dance troupes, and children's programs

Symphony

Tickets to the world-renowned **Chicago Symphony Orchestra** are always in high demand. (We're talking about the third-best orchestra in the world, so what do you expect?) Classical is far from the only kind of music on tap here, however. The "Symphony Center Presents" series has included some of the top jazz, world beat, Latin, and cabaret artists in the world in recent years.

Performances are held at the **Symphony Center,** 220 S. Michigan Ave. at Jackson (☎ **312-294-3000;** www.cso.org). Now entering its second century, the symphony reserves most seats for season subscribers — but don't fear. You can call in advance for a limited number of tickets or order tickets over the Web site. Good seats may also be available on the day of the performance at the box office. Call Symphony Center or stop by the box office to check availability.

The **Chicago Cultural Center,** 78 E. Washington St. (☎ **312-744-6630**), books a number of ensembles throughout the year, including the Chicago Chamber Musicians. Many performances are free. For schedules, call the **Chicago Dance and Music Alliance** (☎ **312-987-1123;** www.chicago performances.org).

Solti and Barenboim: Men with batons

If you try to conjure up the names of multiple Grammy winners, what performers spring to mind? Perhaps the Beatles, Whitney Houston, or Tony Bennett? How about the late, great Georg Solti? As the longtime director of the Chicago Symphony Orchestra (CSO), Sir Georg Solti won many honors during his illustrious career. His 32 Grammy Awards make Solti the most decorated musician in both classical and popular music.

After Solti's death in 1997, Daniel Barenboim from the Orchestre de Paris became the CSO's musical director. Barenboim has introduced more modern works by 20th-century composers to the orchestra's repertoire. But, of course, the ensemble still performs many of classical music's greatest hits by Beethoven, Brahms, and Mozart. Barenboim is set to leave the orchestra in 2006, so stay tuned for more developments in the Chicago Symphony's storied history.

Symphony Center: Convenient preshow dining

Symphony Center resulted from a $105 million renovation that connected the original Orchestra Hall, home of the Chicago Symphony Orchestra, to the surrounding buildings, expanded the stage and seating area, and created an on-premises education center and restaurant, **Rhapsody,** 65 E. Adams St. at Wabash Avenue (☎ **312-786-9911**). The restaurant serves contemporary American cuisine in a warm setting overlooking a small park. Concertgoers can savor every bite of the signature dessert — a chocolate brownie with a gooey, molten center, topped with chocolate sorbet and a treble-clef chocolate leaf — knowing that they're just steps from the concert hall.

Opera

The **Lyric Opera of Chicago** (☎ 312-332-2244; www.lyricopera.org) is one of the world's premier opera companies and performs at the Civic Opera House, at the corner of West Madison Street and North Wacker Drive. The Art Deco building is the country's second-largest opera house, with 3,563 seats, offering patrons a setting that's pleasing to the eye *and* the ear. Opening night in September remains the quasi-official kickoff of the Chicago social season, but don't be scared off by the snooty factor; audiences here are relatively casual (to the dismay of all those opera snobs).

You can always count on a spectacular set and outstanding music at the Lyric. The season sells out far in advance, but you can usually get turn-back tickets just before the performance.

Less highbrow than the Lyric Opera, **Chicago Opera Theater** (☎ 312-704-8414; www.chicagooperatheater.org) appeals to a broader audience that appreciates its emphasis on English-language productions, lower prices, and an abundance of available seats. Performances take place at the Joan W. and Irving B. Harris Theater for Music and Dance in Millennium Park, at 205 E. Randolph Drive, just north of the Pritzker Pavilion.

Dance

Millennium Park — the high-profile cultural and recreational center in Grant Park — is home to the Joan W. and Irving B. Harris Theater for Music and Dance, 205 E. Randolph Drive (just north of the Pritzker Pavilion), a state-of-the-art 1,500-seat music and dance theater where

---

Bach in the 'burbs

In summertime, music lovers pack their picnic hampers and spread their blankets on the lawns at the **Ravinia Festival** (☎ 847-266-5100; www.ravinia.org). Located in suburban Highland Park, the festival runs from mid-June through Labor Day weekend. Ravinia is the unofficial summer home of the Chicago Symphony Orchestra; the orchestra plays most weekends beginning at the end of June. The festival also features performances by the Joffrey Ballet and Hubbard Street Dance Chicago. Other offerings include jazz and pop performers such as Tony Bennett, Oscar Peterson, Lyle Lovett, and many more. A program of Saturday-afternoon performances is geared toward kids. Tickets for the lawn run from $8 to $10; pavilion seating costs $25 to $50. For big names, call well in advance for tickets.

To get to the festival, take the **Metra** (☎ 312-322-6777; www.metrarail.com) commuter train from the Loop to Ravinia. The train stops conveniently at the gate and has schedules to coincide with showtimes.

---

all of Chicago's major dance troupes perform. For complete information on local dance performances, call the Chicago Dance and Music Alliance information line at ☎ 312-987-1123 or check out www.chicago performances.org.

Founded in 1956 in New York and transplanted to Chicago, the **Joffrey Ballet of Chicago** (☎ 312-739-0120; www.joffreyballet.org) focuses on classic works of the 20th century and experiments with contemporary music by pop stars have made this troupe popular with a wide range of audiences. The Joffrey continues to draw crowds to its popular rock ballet, *Billboards,* which is set to the music of Prince, and continues to tour internationally. The company is usually in town in the spring (March or April), October, and December, when it stages a popular rendition of the holiday favorite *The Nutcracker.*

Dance lovers have flocked to contemporary dance performances by **Hubbard Street Dance Chicago** (☎ 312-850-9744; www.hubbardstreet dance.com) since 1978. The 22-member ensemble blurs the lines separating traditional forms and comes up with a truly American and original style. You see elements of jazz, modern, ballet, and theater dance in their performances. Sometimes whimsical, sometimes romantic, the crowd-pleasing 22-member ensemble incorporates a range of dance traditions, from Kevin O'Day to Twyla Tharp, who has choreographed pieces exclusively for Hubbard Street. Although the troupe spends most of the year touring, it has regular two- to three-week Chicago engagements in the fall and spring. In the summer, the dancers often perform at Ravinia Festival, the Chicago Symphony Orchestra's lovely outdoor pavilion in north-suburban Highland Park.

The **Old Town School of Folk Music,** 4454 N. Lincoln Ave. between Wilson and Montrose avenues (☎ **773-728-6000;** www.oldtownschool. org), covers a variety of indigenous musical forms, from country, folk, and bluegrass to Latin and Celtic. The school is best known as a training center offering a slate of music classes, but it also hosts everyone from the legendary Pete Seeger to bluegrass phenom Alison Krauss. Shows are reasonably priced, with tickets ranging from $10 to $25. The school's home, in a former 1930s library, is the world's largest facility dedicated to the preservation and presentation of traditional and contemporary folk music. The Old Town School also houses an art gallery showcasing exhibitions of works by local, national, and international artists; a music store offering an exquisite selection of instruments, sheet music, and hard-to-find recordings; and a cafe. The school hosts an annual **Chicago Folk and Roots Festival** in July in Wells Park at Lincoln and Montrose, with stage performances and an activity and craft tent for kids. Headliners are name-brand performers such as Patti Smith. The school maintains another retail store and a schedule of children's classes at its first location, 909 W. Armitage Ave.

Airwaves in the Windy City

While you're here, don't forget to tune in. Chicago's National Public Radio station WBEZ-FM (91.5 FM) is home to Ira Glass's This American Life program every Friday night at 7 p.m. and Saturday afternoon at 1 p.m. On your Chicago TV screen, WGN-TV (Channel 9), part of the Tribune Company media empire, can fill you in on Chicago's sports teams' progress — or lack thereof.

Chapter 16

Hitting the Clubs and Bars

. . . .

In This Chapter

▶ Hanging at Chicago's best bars

▶ Scoping out the music and club scene

▶ Yukking it up on the comedy circuit

▶ Checking out gay and lesbian bars and clubs

. . . .

*I*s your perfect night out spent in a seedy but exceedingly hip bar in an up-and-coming part of town, or nestled into a sofa in a wine bar? Do you want to dance the night away, or laugh until you cry at a comedy club? Maybe you'd like to experience the quintessential Chicago hangout — the neighborhood Irish bar, with patrons quaffing pints of stout as folk singers perform soulful ballads? Chicago has whatever gets you going after dark.

The legal drinking age is 21, and bars and clubs in the Lincoln Park area are especially tough on checking IDs. Some require patrons to be 23 — a policy aimed at circumventing the use of fake IDs. So if you're blessed with a baby face, don't forget your driver's license!

When stepping out for the night, consider leaving your rental car in the garage. You won't have to deal with parking — which can often be difficult to find — or assign a designated driver. Instead, travel to your destination by public transportation or taxi, and return to your hotel by taxi. (I don't recommend that you ride the bus or take the El [subway] late at night.)

Hanging Out: Chicago's Best Bars

Prime areas for bars include River North; the Clybourn Corridor (along Clybourn Avenue north of West North Avenue); Lincoln Park, especially along Lincoln Avenue and Halsted Street; Bucktown and Wicker Park; and the Randolph Street Market District west of the Loop.

Most bars stay open until 1 or 2 a.m. Unless noted otherwise, the bars in this section don't charge a cover.

The Loop after Dark

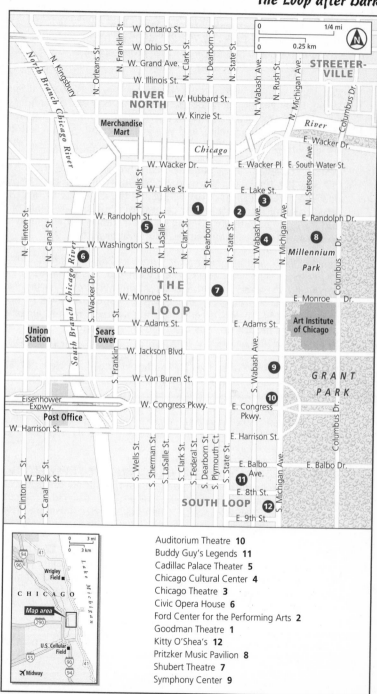

Auditorium Theatre **10**
Buddy Guy's Legends **11**
Cadillac Palace Theater **5**
Chicago Cultural Center **4**
Chicago Theatre **3**
Civic Opera House **6**
Ford Center for the Performing Arts **2**
Goodman Theatre **1**
Kitty O'Shea's **12**
Pritzker Music Pavilion **8**
Shubert Theatre **7**
Symphony Center **9**

A huge beer selection and a dance floor for cutting a rug later in the evening bring the crowds into the **Artful Dodger,** 1734 Wabansia Street, Bucktown/Wicker Park (☎ 773-227-6859). The 20- and 30-something crowd makes this a good singles and group scene, and the indie rock music really gets going after midnight.

The popular neighborhood pub **Brehon's,** 731 N. Wells St. at Superior Street, River North (☎ 312-642-1071), is a good place to shoot the breeze with the locals. Irish and Chicago memorabilia hang on the walls. Order a pint, get to talking, and you just may find that the fellow on the barstool next to you is a Chicago politician.

Celtic Crossings, 751 N. Clark St. near Chicago Avenue, River North (☎ 312-337-1005), is a warm, dark, friendly pub with two fireplaces and no TV. A diverse crowd of the young and the old, the corporate and the artistically minded, gathers for quiet conversation over pints of Guinness and Harp. Go on Sunday evening for the traditional Irish music jam, and you're sure to meet some natives of the Emerald Isle.

Baseball fans vent before or after games at **Cubby Bear,** 1059 W. Addison St. across from Wrigley Field, Wrigleyville (☎ 773-327-1662). Pool tables, darts, and TV screens are the focus. At night, the club is one of Chicago's premier rock venues, generally drawing a youngish crowd by booking popular bands. There's no cover during the day or after games; otherwise, tickets usually are less than $10 for most music, which really begins to rock after 10 p.m.

Cullen's Bar and Grill, 3741 N. Southport Ave., Lakeview (☎ 773-975-0600), is a classic Irish bar with great food, including grilled shrimp appetizers, huge Caesar salads, mashed potatoes, and the requisite Irish dishes such as shepherd's pie. Combine dinner here with a movie at the old-time **Music Box Theatre** next door (3733 N. Southport Ave., ☎ 773-871-6607), and you have a perfect evening. Sunday nights are among the liveliest here.

Delilah's, 2771 N. Lincoln Ave., Lincoln Park (☎ 773-472-2771), is a punk-rock bar ironically situated smack dab in the middle of yuppie Lincoln Park. Showcasing the best whiskey selection in town and arguably the most rocking jukebox as well, Delilah's is home to hardcore punk rockers, plus neighborhood regulars.

Fado, 100 W. Grand Ave. at Clark Street, River North (☎ 312-836-0066), is a reproduction of a Dublin pub. Traditional Irish music plays nonstop, and you can order up authentic Irish food and drink plus standard pub grub, including sandwiches, burgers, fries, and salads. The bar charges a cover on holidays.

Gamekeepers, 345 W. Armitage Ave. at Lincoln Avenue, Lincoln Park (☎ 773-549-0400), appeals to a young, sports-minded crowd intent on watching the game on big-screen TVs.

Located near the heart of Wicker Park, **Holiday Club,** 1471 N. Milwaukee Ave. (☎ 773-486-0686), is home to Chicago's most diverse jukebox, offering Englebert Humperdink, Social Distortion, Naked Raygun, and Ray Charles. Holiday not only shakes out gallons of martinis and manhattans a night but also has a decent beer selection. Groups of singles and couples in their 20s and 30s hang out here. There's a second location in Uptown at 4000 N. Sheridan Rd. (☎ 773-348-9600).

Hopleaf Bar, 5148 N. Clark St. (☎ 773-334-9851), is considered one of the best taverns in Chicago by those in the know. Serving excellent Belgian fare in a casual-cool Euro dining area, the bar offers an extensive Belgian beer list. Don't miss the mussels and frites.

Jake's Pub, 2932 N. Clark St., Lincoln Park (☎ 773-248-3318), is a classic Chicago neighborhood bar nestled on busy Clark Street. More than just a regular haunt for the local barflies, Jake's hops on Friday and Saturday nights with an eclectic mix of neighborhood regulars, college kids, and people looking for an alternative to the sports-bar scene. Imported beers, a nicely stocked jukebox, and a pool table in the back make Jake's a great hangout.

At **Kitty O'Shea's** in the Chicago Hilton and Towers, 720 S. Michigan Ave. between Balbo and Eighth streets, the Loop (☎ 312-922-4400), the brogues are as authentic as the Jameson and Guinness that are on offer. Most of the wait staff is hired through an Irish government work-permit program. You find live Irish entertainment, a jukebox stacked with favorite Gaelic tunes, a collection of shillelaghs, and Irish pub food such as lamb stew. Main courses range from about $8 to $12.

Lava Lounge, 859 N. Damen Ave., Bucktown/Wicker Park (☎ 773-772-3355), doesn't look like much from the entrance, where there's a pretty standard bar, but in the back you discover a bunch of rooms offering occupants some privacy. Bring a group and take over a back room. Lava is definitely a late-night place — great as your last stop on a tour of Bucktown and Wicker Park. The crowd is young and hip, but not trendy.

Lemmings, 1850 N. Damen Ave., Bucktown/Wicker Park (☎ 773-862-1688), is the Bucktown version of Jake's Pub. A perfect place to escape the craziness of other overpopulated Bucktown bars, Lemmings exemplifies the neighborhood's laid-back atmosphere.

Matilda, 3101 N. Sheffield Ave., Lincoln Park (☎ 773-883-4400), is a low-key hipster (but not hip) meet-market (but not meat-market) bar. The 20- and 30-something crowd downs drinks while listening to college radio selections from the jukebox. In two large rooms with ample seating, Matilda's serves food and a wide selection of beers. The menu boasts the famed 1-pound "Heartstopper" burger, plus sandwiches, salads, and appetizers. The bar offers 30 types of martinis, plus 26 beers on tap — with a heavy emphasis on Chicago microbrews.

Lincoln Park and Wrigleyville after Dark

Apollo Theater **21**
Athenaeum Theater **15**
Berlin **11**
B.L.U.E.S. **23**
Briar Street Theatre **18**
Closet **10**
Crobar **32**
Cubby Bear **5**
Cullen's Bar and Grill **1**
Elbo Room **16**
Delilah's **20**
Gamekeepers **27**
Green Dolphin Street **25**
Hogs and Honeys **30**
Hydrate **7**
Jake's Pub **19**
Improv Olympics **4**
Kingston Mines **22**
Matilda **13**
Metro **3**
Music Box Theatre **2**
North Beach **31**
Pops for Champagne **17**
Roscoe's **8**
Royal George Theatre Center **29**
Schuba's Tavern **14**
Second City **33**
Sidetrack **9**
Smart Bar **3**
Steppenwolf Theatre Company **28**
Vic Theater **12**

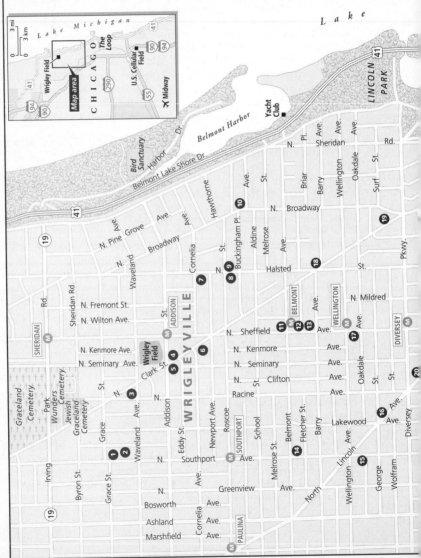

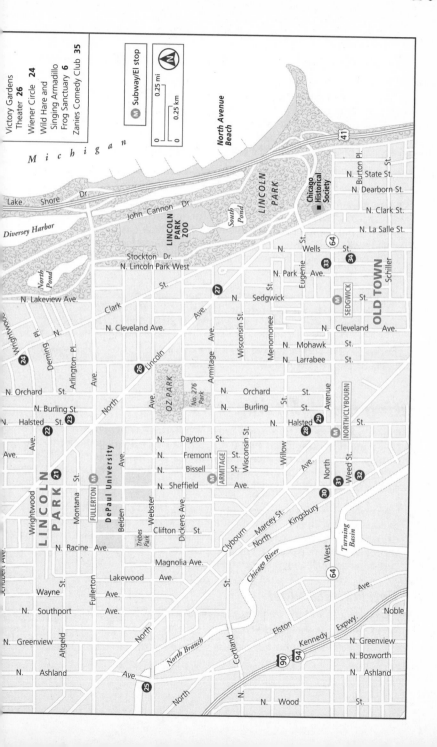

Victory Gardens
Theater **26**
Wiener Circle **24**
Wild Hare and
Singing Armadillo
Frog Sanctuary **6**
Zanies Comedy Club **35**

Ⓜ Subway/El stop

0   0.25 mi

0   0.25 km

Michigan

North Avenue Beach

Lake   Shore   Dr.

Diversey Harbor

John Cannon Dr.

LINCOLN PARK ZOO

South Pond

LINCOLN PARK

Chicago Historical Society

N. Burton Pl.   St.

N. State St.

N. Dearborn St.

N. Clark St.

N. La Salle St.

Stockton Dr.

N. Lincoln Park West

St.

N.   Wells   St.   64

33   34

N. Park Eugenie Ave.

27   N.   Sedgwick   St.

Schiller

OLD TOWN

North Pond

N. Lakeview Ave.

Clark   Ave.

N. Cleveland Ave.

Wisconsin St.

Menomonee

SEDGWICK

N. Cleveland   Ave.

N. Mohawk   St.

N. Larrabee   St.

24

Deming   Pl.

Arlington Pl.

Ave.

N.   Wrightwood

Lincoln

Armitage Ave.

26   Ave.

OZ PARK

No. 276 Park

N.   Orchard   St.

N.   Burling   St.

N.   Halsted   St.

Avenue

NORTH/CLYBOURN

29

N. Orchard   St.

N. Burling St.

North

Ave.

28

N.   Halsted   St.   23

22   Ave.

21

LINCOLN

PARK

Montana   St.

FULLERTON

DePaul University

Ave.

N. Dayton   St.

N.   Fremont   St.

N.   Bissell   St.

N. Sheffield   Ave.

Wisconsin St.

ARMITAGE

Willow

Ave.

North

Weed St.

32

30   31

Wrightwood

Webster

Belden

Triebs Park

Clifton   St.

Dickens Ave.

Clybourn

Marcey St.

North

Kingsbury

Turning Basin

West

64

N. Racine   Ave.

Magnolia Ave.

Lakewood   Ave.

Chicago River

Ave.

Noble

Wayne   St.

Fullerton

N.   Southport   Ave.

North

Elston

Kennedy Expwy.

N. Greenview

N. Bosworth

N. Greenview

Altgeld

North Branch

Cortland

90   94

N.   Ashland

Ave.

25

North

N.   Wood   St.

Late night bites in Lincoln Park

When the Lincoln Park bars shut down at 2 a.m., the action moves to the **Wiener Circle**, 2622 N. Clark St. (☎ **773-477-7444**). This hot dog stand is strictly no-frills: You shout your order across the drunken crowd, and the only spots to sit are a few picnic tables out front. Open until 4 a.m. during the week and 5 a.m. on weekends, the Weiner Circle is the center of pre-dawn life in Lincoln Park — and I know people who swear that the greasy cheese-topped fries are the perfect hangover prevention.

North Beach, 1551 N. Sheffield Ave. at North Avenue, Lincoln Park (☎ **312-266-7842**), is a cavernous bar and entertainment complex that provides outdoor sports indoors. Sand volleyball, basketball, bowling, table tennis, and miniature golf entertain a youngish, corporate crowd. North Beach charges a cover on some nights, but you get your money back via drink specials.

You find a cozy atmosphere of booths and tables, as well as an inviting bar that caters to the hipsters of Chicago, at the **Rainbo Club,** 1150 N. Damen Ave., Bucktown/Wicker Park (☎ **773-489-5999**). This place is packed to the gills with a mix of "scenesters" and young professionals on the weekends; you may have a better experience if you go on a weekday night. Be sure to take some photos in the antiquated photo booth.

Getting the Beat: Music Venues

Chicago is home to the world's most popular and widely heard style of blues and is an important venue for jazz. The city offers just about anything you're looking for, including music for listening, dancing, and damaging your hearing (not recommended!). You can find comfortable piano bars and wild clubs with wilder people.

Many music venues don't get hopping until after 11 p.m., but arrive between 9 and 10 p.m. to allow time to get seats in the club, have a drink, and relax before the show. Most clubs continue to pulse until the wee hours, depending on what's happening onstage. So you're not turned away, call ahead before heading somewhere at 2 a.m.

Catching the blues

Celebrate the women of blues at **Blue Chicago,** 736 and 536 N. Clark St., River North (☎ **312-642-6261**), which showcases top female talent. The cover charge ($5 to $8) is good for both locations.

B.L.U.E.S., 2519 N. Halsted St. between Wrightwood and Fullerton avenues, Lincoln Park (☎ **773-528-1012**), satisfies the most ardent fans with live music 365 days a year. The dark, narrow club places patrons up close to performers. As at Kingston Mines (described later in this section), expect to spend the evening standing. The cover is $5 to $8.

 If Chicago is the body and soul of blues music, then **Buddy Guy's Legends,** 754 S. Wabash Ave. between Balbo and Eighth streets, South Loop (☎ **312-427-0333**), is its heart. Everyone from Eric Clapton to Muddy Waters has stopped in to jam and listen to the best in blues at this club owned and operated by blues legend Buddy Guy. Every January, Guy plays a series of shows that sell out early. The cover charge is usually under $10.

Keep an eye out for Jake and Elwood at the **House of Blues,** 329 N. Dearborn St. at Kinzie Street, River North (☎ **312-923-2000**). Dan Aykroyd, also known as Elwood, is an owner. The hotel, restaurant, bar, and concert venue books a wide variety of acts and stages a popular Sunday gospel brunch for about $35 with seatings at 9:30 a.m. and noon. The cover varies from about $10 to $50 for a big name.

Kingston Mines, 2548 N. Halsted St. between Wrightwood and Fullerton avenues, Lincoln Park (☎ **773-477-4646**), has two stages' worth of blues greats. It may not be up to par with Buddy Guy's, but it's certain to satisfy your craving for down-home blues. Performances last until 4 a.m. on Saturdays. The cover charge is $12 Sunday to Wednesday, $12 on Saturday.

 Smoke Daddy Rhythm and Bar-B-Que, 1804 W. Division St., Wicker Park (☎ **773-772-6656**), serves dinner in plastic baskets like your favorite barbecue joint, and tops it off with live music seven nights a week. The result is great blues and jazz in a laid-back, intimate atmosphere.

A lesson in blues

Chicago grew to be a blues music center in the 1930s and 1940s, when thousands of Mississippians migrated north for factory work. Blues musicians from the Delta created a hybrid form that became known as Chicago-style blues, probably the most popular and widely heard style of blues. These early musicians captured the rawness of the Delta style and combined that with a fully amplified sound. In the 1950s and beyond, Muddy Waters, Willie Dixon, Big Bill Broonzy, Howlin' Wolf and other greats pioneered what became the early electric Chicago blues, featuring highly amplified harmonica, slide guitar, and piano. Today, Chicago bluesmen such as Buddy Guy, Lonnie Brooks, and the "Queen of Chicago Blues," vocalist Koko Taylor, continue to evolve the Chicago style. The blues is truly America's music — in fact, it's one of America's only indigenous art forms — so make sure to catch a show while you're in Chicago.

Jazzing up the night

Live jazz is performed virtually around the clock, mostly by nationally known musicians, at **Andy's Jazz Club,** 11 E. Hubbard St. between State Street and Wabash Avenue, River North (☎ **312-642-6805**). This loud, grungy hangout for serious jazz fans offers three-hour sets at lunch on weekdays and music throughout the evening all week. The kitchen stays open late; pizza and burgers are decent. The cover charge is $5 Sunday through Thursday and $10 and up Friday and Saturday; no cover is charged during lunch.

Green Dolphin Street, 2200 N. Ashland Ave. at Webster Avenue, Lincoln Park (☎ **773-395-0066**), is a retro supper club that's slick — and pricey. Stylish patrons in their 30s to 50s enjoy seafood and contemporary American cuisine from a celebrated kitchen and then head to an adjacent room that accommodates 200 people for live jazz. The music ranges from headliners, such as Wynton Marsalis, to experimental artists, plus Latin jazz and big-band music. The cover varies; on Sunday there is no cover charge. Main courses range from $20 to $30.

Known for great jazz in a historical setting, **Green Mill,** 4802 N. Broadway at Lawrence Avenue, near Andersonville (☎ **773-878-5552**), was established in 1907 and frequented by infamous mobster Al Capone. You hear Latin jazz, big-band jazz, jazz piano, and more. On Tuesday and Thursday nights, jitterbugging hipsters swarm to the club for Prohibition-era swing and big-band music. On Sunday, the club hosts Chicago's best-known poetry slam. The cover ranges from free to $8.

Joe Segal, founder of **Jazz Showcase,** 59 W. Grand Ave. at Clark Street, River North (☎ **312-670-2473**), has created this family-friendly venue that books some of the hottest names in the business. With two performances each night (open to audiences of all ages) and a 4 p.m. Sunday matinee, this club is ushering in the next generation of fans. The cover charge is usually $20.

If you're in the mood for bubbly, **Pops for Champagne,** 2934 N. Sheffield Ave. at Oakdale Avenue, Lincoln Park (☎ **773-472-1000**), offers more than 100 labels, plus live jazz combos. There's no cover Sunday through Tuesday; $5 Wednesday and Thursday; and $10 Friday and Saturday.

Rockin' 'n' rollin' to live music

Drawing a 20-something crowd for bands near Wrigley Field is **Cubby Bear** (see "Hanging Out: Chicago's Best Bars" earlier in this chapter), a popular bar during the day.

A Wicker Park fixture, **Double Door,** 1572 N. Milwaukee Ave. at North Avenue (☎ **773-489-3160**), attracts a broad audience by inviting edgy new groups to its stage nightly, from hip-hop to new country. The cover is $5 to $10, more for special performances.

Staying Up Late: The Club Scene

Prime areas for clubs are River North; the Clybourn Corridor (along Clybourn Avenue north of West North Avenue); Lincoln Park, especially along Lincoln Avenue and Halsted Street; Bucktown and Wicker Park; and the Randolph Street Market District west of the Loop.

Clubs generally open late and close in the early morning, so traveling to and from them by taxi is best.

Used to be that this club offered a taste of post-apocalyptic décor in an industrial neighborhood, but these days the atmosphere is open and airy, and a bit more welcoming. **Crobar**, 1543 N. Kingsbury St. south of North Avenue, Lincoln Park (☎ 312-337-5001), is where young, hip patrons wag their tails to trip-hop, techno, and old-school beats in one of Chicago's largest dance halls. Cover charge is $20.

Domaine, 1045 N. Rush St. (☎ 312-397-1045), caters to the slightly older and affluent Gold Coast crowd. Opened in late 2002, this club offers dinner as well as dancing — for a price. The drink prices are among the highest in the city. If you have connections, you may be allowed into the VIP section upstairs. The 18th-century French décor and theme are carried as far as two actors playing members of the French court — complete with powdered wigs. When charged, the cover varies — possibly depending on who you know.

Hogs and Honeys, 1555 N. Sheffield Ave. (☎ 312-377-1733), is styled after New York City's racy Hogs and Heifers bar in the Meatpacking District. Dance on the bar, ride the mechanical bull and enjoy the sounds of Kid Rock on the sound system. Cover is $5; if you're brave, you can pay $3 for a ride on the mechanical bull.

The music is throbbing, the dancing is rhythmic and the atmosphere is all '80s at **Rednofive,** 440 N. Halsted Ave., River West (☎ 312-733-6699), where the city's top DJs spin techno until 4 a.m. The cover charge is $5 to $20.

Smart Bar, 3730 N. Clark St., Wrigleyville (☎ 773-549-4140), in the basement of Metro (see "Rockin' 'n' rollin' to live music," earlier in this chapter), is one of the coolest clubs in Chicago. The bar often fills when shows end at Metro. The DJs here do some serious spinning. Every night features a different style of music, so ask before you enter. The bar stays open until 5 a.m. on weekends. There's no cover before 11 p.m. during the week; at other times, the cost is $2 to $5.

Dreadlocks and Red Stripe beer abound at the **Wild Hare** (the original name was The Wild Hare and Singing Armadillo Frog Sanctuary), 3530 N. Clark St. between Addison and Roscoe streets, Wrigleyville (☎ 773-327-4273). Chicago's premier reggae bar has hosted such notables as the Wailers and Yellowman. There's no cover until 9:30 p.m. on Monday and Tuesday; afterward, the charge ranges from $8 to $12.

Laughing the Night Away: Comedy Clubs

The Second City, 1616 N. Wells St. at North Avenue, Lincoln Park
(☎ 312-337-3992; www.secondcity.com), packs a comic punch line —
with a pedigree. Alan Alda, Alan Arkin, Ed Asner, Dan Aykroyd, John
Belushi, John Candy, Don Castellaneta (also known as "Homer Simpson"),
Chris Farley, Shelley Long, Elaine May, Tim Meadows, Bill Murray, Brian
Doyle-Murray, Mike Nichols, Gilda Radner, Joan Rivers, Martin Short,
George Wendt . . . whew! The list goes on and on, but you get the point:
The alumni of Second City — Chicago's comic breeding ground — read
like a laundry list of great American comedic talent. Some of the alums
hail from the Toronto branch, but they're all part of this improv factory,
one of the most prolific training grounds in American theater history. You
rarely see a bad show here. Tickets are easy to get, and shows change frequently — and no doubt you'll be seeing at least one rising star. You can

---

Mixing humor and history: The Second City Neighborhood Tour

Those who like their history sprinkled with improv comedy — and who doesn't? —
should not miss the Second City's Neighborhood Tour. A joint effort between the
Chicago Historical Society and the Second City, these humorous and historic guided
tours of Chicago's Old Town neighborhood (where the improv theater has been located
since 1959) take place on Sunday afternoons from April through September.

The tours are more than just fun: You can also gain real insight into the impact of popular entertainment on the history of Chicago and the role that humor has played —
sometimes unintentionally — throughout the decades.

The walking tours begin at the Historical Society, located at Clark Street and North
Avenue, and are led by actors from the Second City. The route starts with a rapid history of America since 1492, and includes stops at the Old Town Ale House (the favorite
bar of many Second City performers), Chris Farley's former apartment (above a
Mexican restaurant on Wells), St. Michael's Church, Twin Anchors (Frank Sinatra's
favorite rib joint), and the Crilly Court Apartments. The tours end with a visit to the
Second City on Wells Street.

Price is $15 for the two-hour tours, which begin at 4 p.m. each Sunday. I highly rec-
ommend buying the $30 discounted package deal for the tour plus a show at the
Second City (every tour ticket also allows free admission to the Historical Society galleries). After the tour, you'll have time to eat dinner in the Old Town neighborhood, then
catch the 8 p.m. performance. Tickets may be purchased directly from the **Second City
box office,** 1616 N. Wells Street, over the phone at ☎ 312-337-3992, via the Second City
Web site at www.secondcity.com, or through a link at the CHS Web site at www.
chicagohistory.org. Advance reservations are recommended, especially for
groups of eight or more.

choose between two sketch-comedy productions on the main stage and ETC (et cetera), a smaller venue. The cover charge runs $8 to $16.

A block away at **Zanies Comedy Club,** 1548 N. Wells St. between North Avenue and Schiller Street (☎ 312-337-4027), high-caliber comedians treat sold-out houses to the best in standup. The cover charge is $18 to $20, with a two-item food/drink minimum.

 ImprovOlympics, 3541 N. Clark St. at Addison Street, Wrigleyville (☎ 773-880-0199), engages the audience as the talented cast solicits suggestions and creates original performances. You pay a $5 to $14 cover charge.

Stepping Out: Gay and Lesbian Scene

The gay and lesbian scene plays out in clubs and bars in the Lakeview neighborhood (especially along Belmont Avenue) and along North Halsted Street, also known as Boys' Town.

At **Berlin,** 954 W. Belmont Ave. at Sheffield Avenue (☎ 773-348-4975), the party doesn't start until midnight. The dance club showcases male dancers (sometimes on tables in G-strings). The room is dark and the music loud. Weeknights, it's a mostly gay crowd, and weekends bring a more eclectic group. It's open nightly; with a $3 cover Tuesday to Thursday and a $5 cover on Friday and Saturday.

Big Chicks, 5024 N. Sheridan Rd. between Argyle Street and Foster Avenue (☎ 773-728-5511), appeals to the culture-hungry. The club generally attracts gay men and a few lesbians interested in checking out the artwork displayed on the bar and bathroom walls. There's no cover.

A bank of television monitors cycling through music videos and sporting events greets visitors to the **Closet,** 3325 N. Broadway at Buckingham Street (☎ 773-477-8533). The bar attracts mostly lesbian regulars. There's no cover.

A lounge and dance club, **Hydrate,** 3458 N. Halsted St. at Newport Avenue (☎ 773-975-9244), opens onto Halsted Street with garage-door-like windows.

One of Chicago's best-known gay bars, **Roscoe's Tavern,** 3356 N. Halsted St. at Roscoe Street (☎ 773-281-3355), has six bars, a huge dance floor and antique décor. Check out the patio garden. The $4 cover applies only after 10 p.m. on Saturday.

Across the street from Roscoe's, **Sidetrack,** 3349 N. Halsted St. (☎ 773-477-9189), draws a diverse gay crowd with its snappy video bar. The patio holds outdoor seating in the summer. There's no cover.

Part VI
The Part of Tens

The 5th Wave
By Rich Tennant

I enjoyed yelling out improvisational situations at Second City last night too. But this is the Chicago Ballet...

In this part . . .

*T*he Part of Tens will help you prioritize (with the top ten Chicago experiences) and brainstorm (with ten creative ideas for days when the weather isn't cooperating). Avoid tourist traps and Chicago clichés with my tips on ten Chicago experiences to avoid. Soon, you'll be experiencing Chicago as the locals do.

Chapter 17

Ten Oh-So-Chicago Experiences

*I*n this living, vibrant, diverse city, you'll be faced with a serious dilemma: One human being can't possibly see and do everything. (Particularly on summer weekends, when festivals, the beach, and Lincoln Park all beckon at once, I'd love to be able to clone myself!) To get you started, this chapter includes a list of what I consider the quintessential Chicago experiences.

Every activity in this chapter qualifies as a local pastime.

Strolling the Lakefront

Chicagoans use the lakefront in every possible way: for walking, rollerblading, biking, running, swimming, picnicking, and playing volleyball. Whatever you do, be sure not to miss Chicago's endless blue inland sea. The lake is a year-round destination. Summers on the lakefront can get a little crowded, but that's part of the fun. Even in winter, you can see hardy souls out for a run while waves crash onto the shoreline. Most activity takes place around Oak Street Beach (just north of the Magnificent Mile) and North Avenue Beach (several blocks north of Oak Street).

Sightseeing on the Chicago River and Lake Michigan

By far the best way to scope out the city is by taking a boat tour. My favorite is the Chicago Architecture Foundation's "Architecture River Cruise," which travels up and down the north and south branches of the

Chicago River. Getting onto the water gives you a fresh perspective on a city that grew up around a lake and a river. Nothing beats being on the water on a warm day with the sun glinting off Chicago's glorious sky-scrapers and a cool breeze at your back. Other options include dinner cruises, the "ducks" (amphibian land/water transports), speedboats, and tall ships. To find a boat trip, see Chapter 11 for more information, or head for the Michigan Avenue Bridge (Michigan Avenue and the Chicago River) or Navy Pier, where most tours start.

Shopping on Michigan Avenue

Tourists aren't the only ones crowding Michigan Avenue on the week-ends: Chicagoans love to shop. Whether you want to browse, buy, or people-watch, hit Michigan Avenue. And try, just try, to resist its tempta-tions, from Niketown to Nordstrom, Burberry's to Bloomingdale's. (See Chapter 12 for more on shopping.)

But don't get so caught up in retail frenzy that you miss the charming points of the avenue: Fourth Presbyterian Church, the plaza of the John Hancock Center, and Water Tower (the actual tower, not the mall of the same name). And do not — I repeat, *do not* — miss the best view of the city from the Michigan Avenue Bridge, looking up and down the Chicago River at the architectural gems lining the banks. Go at night when the colored lights shine on the river and the Wrigley Building, and I guaran-tee you'll fall in love with Chicago.

Visiting Marshall Field's around the Holidays

Marshall Field's State Street store puts on a real show during the holi-days. The unveiling of the windows is a much-anticipated event, and having breakfast or lunch around the gigantic Christmas tree in the stately Walnut Room is a time-honored tradition for generations of Chicagoans. (See Chapter 12 for more info.)

Cheering the Cubbies

Wrigley Field is not to be missed. In fact, Chicagoans regularly play hooky to hang out in the bleachers on a perfect summer afternoon. Eat a hot dog. Exercise your lungs during the singing of "Take Me Out to the Ballgame." Take a kid with you. I'm sure you'll leave agreeing with me that Wrigley Field is the most charming ballpark in America. (See Chapter 11 for more on Wrigley Field.)

Getting the Blues

This most American of music forms is venerated by Chicagoans, who keep the blues alive nightly in the city's clubs. Chicago-style blues is what most people think of when you mention live blues played in a nightclub setting. You can still find tiny bandstands in smoky bars where musicians jam away on electric guitar, amplified harp (or harmonica to the uninitiated), piano, bass, and drums. You can find a remarkable range of clubs, from down-to-earth Buddy Guy's Legends in the South Loop to Kingston Mines in Lincoln Park, where musicians perform continuously on two stages. (See Chapter 16 for more on the blues.)

Hearing Music under the Stars

Ah, summertime. In Chicago, summer is the season for spreading blankets and picnicking on the lawns at the Ravinia Festival, located in suburban Highland Park. Ravinia is one of the nation's best-known — and just plain *best* — summer music festivals. It runs nightly throughout the summer and offers Saturday matinee concerts especially for kids. Ravinia is the unofficial summer home of the Chicago Symphony Orchestra and also features pop performers, such as Tony Bennett, Lyle Lovett, and many more. On summer eves, you can see many people running with their picnic supplies to catch the Metra train to Ravinia from downtown. Grab your own refreshments and join them. (See Chapter 15 for more on the Ravinia Festival.)

Taking in a Show

Chicagoans love their homegrown theater companies, including the Goodman (which has a spectacular home in the Loop) and the innovative Steppenwolf Theater. You can also choose from shows in the revitalized North Loop Theater District with its Broadway-style theaters. The city's resident Shakespeare troupe is also well loved, and the theater is located in a stunning home on Navy Pier. (See Chapter 15 for the Chicago theater scene.)

Riding the El

New York City buried its elevated train decades ago, but the noisy, dirty El (Chicago's elevated train), which blocks sunlight from the streets beneath its tracks, is a quintessential part of Chicago. Even if you have nowhere in particular to go, hop on the El and ride around the Loop. The brown line heading south takes you on an up-close-and-personal view of Chicago's financial center. (See Chapter 8 for more on the El.)

Discovering Wonders at Chicago's Museums

Generations of Chicagoans recall permanent exhibits at Chicago museums with nostalgia. I remember Colleen Moore's Fairy Castle at the Museum of Science and Industry — the most fantastic dollhouse you'll ever see. My brother will never forget the Santa Fe Model Railway at the same museum. Whatever your fancy, you can find an exhibit about it somewhere among the Adler Planetarium & Astronomy Museum, Field Museum of Natural History, Art Institute of Chicago, Museum of Science and Industry, John G. Shedd Aquarium, or Museum of Contemporary Art. (See Chapter 11 for more on Chicago's museums.)

Chicago's Museum Campus is home to a trio of museums — the Field Museum, Adler Planetarium & Astronomy Museum, and John G. Shedd Aquarium — on a landscaped 57-acre area with terraced gardens and broad walkways. In my humble opinion, the Museum Campus is the most impressive collection of museums in the most beautiful setting anywhere in the United States, so don't miss out!

Chapter 18

Ten Things to Do in Bad Weather

In This Chapter

▶ Making the best of bad weather

▶ Hanging out indoors

▶ Keeping your spirits high when the wind blows

*L*et's face it: Chicago's weather can throw you a curveball at just about any moment. From sunny and warm to windy and cold, you can easily find yourself wanting to take shelter from the city's occasionally inclement weather. If the weather gets in the way of enjoying Chicago, try one of these indoor activities.

Taking Tea

For about $25, you can be served in one of Chicago's finest hotels and linger for hours over steaming pots of tea, finger sandwiches, scones, and pastries. Civilized, relaxing, and, best of all, sheltered from the storm, taking tea is a great way to while away the day. Try **The Drake, Ritz-Carlton, Peninsula,** or **Four Seasons** hotels. (See Chapter 10 for more on the best teas in town.)

Hitting a Michigan Avenue Mall

Chicago has a unique innovation: the downtown, high-rise mall. The **900 North Michigan, Water Tower Place, Chicago Place,** and **Westfield North Bridge** malls can keep you warm, dry, and entertained for hours. (See Chapter 12 for more on shopping.)

Immersing Yourself in the Art Institute

When storms lash the lakefront, head straight for the **Art Institute of Chicago.** The museum's renowned Impressionist collection includes one of the world's largest collections of paintings by Monet. A little Impressionistic romance is just the thing on a rainy or snowy day. (See Chapter 11 for details on the Art Institute.)

Luxuriating at a Spa

Indulge yourself in a massage, facial, or manicure at one of Chicago's many spas. Ask your concierge for a spa near you, or check out my favorite, **Mario Tricoci Salon and Day Spa,** 900 N. Michigan Ave. (☎ 312-915-0960). Also nearby is **Kiva,** 196 E. Pearson St. (☎ 312-840-8120), which is named after sacred healing places in the Southwest, and has a very peaceful, soothing atmosphere, featuring massage therapy, facials, and spa services.

Reading at a Cafe

Go to **Borders** on Michigan Avenue across from Water Tower Place, pick up a book, and head for a comfy cafe. A unique local favorite is **Julius Meinl Café,** 3601 N. Southport Ave. (☎ 773-868-1857). The first U.S. cafe by the venerable Viennese coffee and fine food purveyor, Mr. Meinl himself has a hand in translating the classic Viennese coffeehouse for the U.S. market. Pastries here are out of this world — I recently sampled a white chocolate mousse cake with layers of raspberry filling, covered in a soft and creamy white chocolate icing — and coffee is served to you on a silvery tray, accompanied by a small glass of water. Order a steaming *mélange* (coffee with milk), settle into a booth in front of the large picture windows that front Southport Avenue, and enjoy the live music that's frequently on offer here.

Working Out in a Health Club

Ask your concierge about your hotel's health-club facilities. If your hotel doesn't have its own club, it may have an agreement with a nearby club that you can visit for a minimal fee. Chicago's largest athletic club is the **East Bank Club,** located in River North at 500 N. Kingsbury (☎ 312-527-5800; www.eastbankclub.com). It features a mammoth 25,000-square-foot cardiovascular room, two large indoor pools, two restaurants, and a carryout food shop.

Seeing the Stars at the Planetarium

Even in cloudy weather, you can see the stars during the sky shows at the **Adler Planetarium & Astronomy Museum** (☎ 312-922-7827; www. adlerplanetarium.org). Choose from a tour of the solar system or of the Hubble Telescope's view of the visible universe. You can also take a voyage to the edge of a black hole. Shows change frequently, so call ahead for the latest. (See Chapter 11 for details on this museum.)

Catching Up on a Movie

Time it right, and you may even get the matinee rate at one of Chicago's many theaters (see Chapter 11 for some listings). To find out what's on, call MovieFone at ☎ 312-444-3456 or visit www.movies.channel.aol. com. Buy some candy and popcorn and you won't mind that rain and blowing wind so much.

One of my personal favorites is the **Music Box Theatre,** 3733 N. Southport Ave. (☎ 773-871-6604; www.musicboxtheatre.com). The ornate theater opened in 1929 and has a hodgepodge Spanish-Italianate décor built to suggest that you're watching a movie in an outdoor plaza somewhere in Italy. The theater, which shows mostly small, independent movies, still has its own organist who plays before shows.

During the holidays, the Music Box Theatre sponsors a holiday movie marathon and sing-along. In between showings of movies such as *White Christmas* and *Holiday Inn,* the organist and Santa lead the audience in singing carols. Bring your jingle bells and Santa hat and get into the spirit.

Watching the Weather from the Oceanarium

John G. Shedd Aquarium is home to a 3-million-gallon saltwater oceanarium. A wall of windows reveals the lake outside, creating the illusion of miles of sea. You'll find beluga whales, dolphins, otters, and seals, none of which could care less that it's raining or snowing outside. (See Chapter 11 for more on the aquarium.)

Going Out for Dinner

When the weather gets bad in wintertime, Chicagoans don't hole up at home. You'll find them overcoming cabin fever by dining at the city's many fabulous restaurants. Go out, lounge at the bar, eat a leisurely meal, and dream of the day that you can run off your meal on the lakefront. (See Chapter 10 for restaurants.)

Chapter 19

Ten Chicago Don'ts

In This Chapter
▶ Seeing the real Chicago
▶ Skipping tourist traps
▶ Spending money smartly

*1*t's easy to go astray when you're visiting an unfamiliar city. From coping with weather hazards to dressing the part, you can make a lot of missteps before you figure out how to do things the way the natives do.

In this chapter, I reinforce the importance of avoiding tourist traps. You'll be amazed at how much fun it is to bring your kids along, find out about architecture, delve into neighborhoods that aren't packed with chain stores and restaurants, and experience some of the new and exciting activities that Chicago offers, from Millennium Park to the newly remodeled John G. Shedd Aquarium, and the fast-gentrifying areas of Bucktown/Wicker Park, Lakeview, Southport Avenue, and more.

Don't Get Blown Away

True story: Chicago's famous winds once blew me off my feet and would have rolled me into traffic on Lake Shore Drive if it were not for a light pole, which I (fortunately) hit and then clung to for dear life. It seems there's one day each year, usually in February or March, when the Windy City becomes downright hazardous. I once saw a woman blown off her feet while crossing busy Michigan Avenue — she landed flat on her back in the middle of an intersection. Don't get yourself into that position. (On such days, construction sites, where building materials might come loose, should definitely be avoided). Severe winds don't usually last for more than a day. Take shelter, and see Chapter 18 for ideas on how to stay entertained inside, where it's safe and warm, until the winds subside.

Don't Fall Prey to the Chain-Store Mentality

Like most large cities, Chicago is bursting with chain stores and restaurants of every variety, from Niketown to the Hard Rock Cafe. Now, I am not against these places in every circumstance. (I once watched a great concert at the Hard Rock, and yes, I have purchased sporting goods at Niketown), but please make an effort to strike out into less-chartered territory during your stay. There are so many amazing stores, restaurants, and activities that can only be experienced in Chicago, from riding the El to eating a gigantic sundae in a conch shell at Margie's Candies, to checking out the toys and novelties at Uncle Fun and viewing the skyline from the 15-story Ferris wheel at Navy Pier. It's all about having an authentic Chicago experience, as opposed to having an experience that you could have in any one of a dozen big cities.

Don't Relive Tired Clichés about Chicago

Yes, gangsters did live here in the 1920s; and yes, our politics are stormy; and yes, a big fire caused by a cow did ravage the city once; and yes, we had stockyards that weren't particularly clean and nice; and yes, Michael Jordan did play here; and yes, Oprah does live here. But don't fall prey to a dozen gangster tours and spend all your money on Michael Jordan jerseys. You'll miss the cosmopolitan, forward-thinking place that Chicago is today. Head for Millennium Park, the newly renovated John G. Shedd Aquarium on Museum Campus, and the lovely tree-lined streets and refurbished brownstones of Lincoln Park, Lakeview, and Wrigleyville to see the people and places that are making Chicago great today.

Don't Fear that Appreciating Architecture Is beyond You

One of Chicago's main claims to fame is its skyline, and you'd be missing out by not learning a little about the buildings and architects who shaped our city. The docents for the Chicago Architecture Foundation's tours do a good job of making the tours enjoyable for visitors with all levels of architectural knowledge. In addition to pointing out famous buildings — Marina City, the Civic Opera House, the Sears Tower, and the Merchandise Mart, to name a few — they approach the sites thematically, explaining, for example, how Chicagoans' use of and attitudes toward the river have changed in the past two centuries. You'll hear not just about architectural styles, but stories that bring the city to life.

On a recent tour of South Michigan Avenue, a docent pointed skyward and asked us, "Did you notice that buffalo statue on top of that skyscraper?" It turns out that not only was there a buffalo statue perched on top of a skyscraper, but the skyscraper next door was topped by something just as interesting — a blimp port. Turns out that back in the day, blimps were thought to be the next great mode of transportation, and buildings installed landing ports in anticipation. Who knew? These and many more fascinating facts come to light during a tour.

Don't Leave Your Kids at Home

Of the three largest cities in the United States, I think Chicago is easiest to navigate with kids in tow. Our streets are busy but not impossibly congested, and you don't have to drive long distances on snarled freeways to get to attractions. Cultural attractions that please kids as well as adults are many, from the Museum of Science and Industry to Navy Pier to Millennium Park and Wrigley Field.

In the wintertime, stay in a hotel with a pool, and you'll find yourself in good company: Plenty of Chicago families check themselves in for the weekend to swim and escape cabin fever (and the city's great hotel deals in January and February make these getaways completely affordable).

Chicago has the added benefit of the lakefront and a long string of emerald parks — perfect for letting kids blow off steam after a day of touring. Midwesterners have a friendly attitude that's laid-back enough to put most parents and kids at ease, so bring the kids along. Soon you'll find you've established some family lore — from exploring the U-505 at the Museum of Science and Industry, to having brunch at Marshall Field's Walnut Room, to standing in the spray of Buckingham Fountain in Grant Park.

Don't Choose Vanity over Practicality

In the wintertime, even the most stylish Chicagoans dress for the weather. Parkas, scarves, boots with rubber soles, fuzzy hats, and mittens are all very much required here. If you're teetering along icy sidewalks in impossibly high heels and you've left your hat in your hotel room for fear of ruining your carefully coiffed hair, Chicagoans are going to look at you cross-eyed. Wear sensible boots so you don't slip and break your neck, and for goodness' sake, cover your head!

Don't Be Afraid to Venture into Neighborhoods

Some of the most authentic Chicago experiences can't be found along Michigan Avenue. Hyde Park's unique combination of academia and magnificent mansions, Andersonville's Swedish bakeries, Lincoln Square's German delicatessens, Pilsen's Mexican murals and taquerias, Greektown's candle shops and outdoor rooftop restaurants, Devon Avenue's Indian "chat" (or snack) shops in Rogers Park, Uptown's historic theaters and Asian grocery stores — there's a whole world of neighborhoods to explore. Try to visit at least one to gain an understanding of how Chicagoans really live.

Don't Be Naive about Dangerous Areas

 Now that I've encouraged you to explore, I have to add a caveat: Don't be naïve about the city. Hyde Park, for example, is one of Chicago's most interesting neighborhoods and definitely merits a visit, but venture beyond its borders, and you'll find yourself in some of the most blighted, crime-ridden areas of the city. It's no joke. Keep your head on straight, don't wander into new areas at night, and keep within established neighborhood borders. When in doubt, turn back to an area that you know is safe.

Don't Get Stuck in Tourist Traps

Chicago can drain your resources, from pricey museum admissions to pricey wares on the Magnificent Mile, to pricey meals in tourist areas (especially those tourist areas where you're a captive audience, such as Navy Pier). Even if you're not on a tight budget, who wants to feel like you're being taken advantage of? (And who wants to waste money on an overpriced cup of coffee when you could spend it on a souvenir in the Chicago Archicenter gift shop?) Use this book and its Bargain Alert icons to save yourself some cash. Take advantage of museum free days. Stock up on drinks and snacks at Bockwinkel's in the lower level of Chicago Place before you head to Navy Pier. That way, you can eat, drink, and be merry that night with dinner at Café Atwood and a show in the North Loop Theatre District — a much better use of your money.

Don't Go Fest-Crazy

In the summertime, Chicago becomes one big festival. By the middle of summer, one festival seems to blend right into the next — from Puerto Rican Fest to garden walks (really, just neighborhood street festivals in disguise) to music fests from country to gospel. Some of these festivals are worthwhile (Jazz Fest, Blues Fest, and the Air & Water Show come to mind) and some are not (Taste of Chicago is an example). There's a point when many festivals become one sticky, humid, mess of humanity, blended with the smells of grilled meat, funnel cakes, and Port-A-Potties. Yuck! Plan your fest-going carefully. Go early in the morning, exit before the crowds arrive, and head for another attraction. Think of it this way: If everyone else in Chicago is at Grant Park for Taste of Chicago, you'll have the Field Museum all to yourself.

Appendix

Quick Concierge

Fast Facts

AAA

For general information and emergency road service, call ☎ 800-222-4357.

Ambulance

Call ☎ 911.

American Express

You find two locations in Chicago: 55 W. Monroe (☎ 312-541-5440) and 605 N. Michigan (☎ 312-943-7840).

Area Codes

The **312** area code covers the Loop and all neighborhoods south of North Avenue. The rest of the city has a **773** area code. Suburban area codes are **847** (northern), **708** (west and southwest), and **630** (far west).

ATMs

ATMs are widely available. The Cirrus (☎ 800-424-7787; www.mastercard.com) and Plus (☎ 800-843-7587; www.visa.com) networks are the most popular. Check the back of your ATM card to see which networks your bank belongs to; then use the toll-free number to locate ATMs in Chicago.

Babysitters

Check with the concierge at your hotel, who is likely to have worked with sitters in the past. One referral service is American Registry for Nurses & Sitters Inc. (☎ 800-240-1820 or 773-248-8100), a state-licensed service that can match you with a sitter. Making a reservation 24 hours in advance is recommended.

Business Hours

Most businesses operate on a 9 a.m. to 5 p.m. schedule. Banks are open during the week from 9 a.m. to 5 p.m. and on Saturday from 9 a.m. to noon. Monday through Saturday, store hours are usually 10 a.m. to 6 p.m., with many stores open until 8 p.m. on Thursday. On Sunday, department stores are usually open from noon to 6 p.m., while smaller stores may close by 5 p.m. or not open at all.

Cameras and Photo Developing

Wolf Camera has a convenient downtown location at the corner of Chicago and Rush streets (☎ 312-943-5531). You can get instant reprints and enlargements as well as one-hour film processing.

Convention Centers

McCormick Place, located at 23rd Street and Lake Shore Drive (☎ 312-791-7000; www.mpea.com), is Chicago's major convention hall.

Credit Cards

Toll-free emergency numbers include: American Express, ☎ 800-528-4800, Visa, ☎ 800-847-2911, and MasterCard, ☎ 800-307-7309.

Doctors

Hotel concierges often keep lists of doctors (and dentists). If it's an emergency, call for the hotel physician or go to the nearest hospital emergency room. Northwestern Memorial Hospital has an excellent emergency room located at 250 E. Erie St. near Fairbanks Court (☎ 312-926-5188).

Emergencies

For police, fire, and ambulance, call ☎ **911.**

Hotlines

Travelers Aid Society is ☎ 312-660-1300. The Chicago police department runs a number of hotlines in addition to 311, the city's nonemergency number. One such number is the Superintendent's hotline, at ☎ 312-939-5555.

Hospitals

Northwestern Memorial Hospital is located right off North Michigan Avenue at 251 E. Huron St. (☎ 312-926-2000).

Information

See the "Getting More Information" section toward the end of this appendix.

Internet Access and Cybercafes

Open an account at a free e-mail provider, such as Hotmail (www.hotmail.com) or Yahoo! Mail (www.mail.yahoo.com), and all you need to check your mail is a Web connection. You can easily get on the Web at Net cafes and copy shops. In Chicago, Kinko's has many stores located downtown. For locations, call ☎ 800-254-6567 or visit www.kinkos.com. Visit www.netcafeguide.com for locations of hundreds of Internet cafes around the globe.

Liquor Laws

The minimum legal age to buy and consume alcoholic beverages in Illinois is 21. Most bars have a 2 a.m. license that also allows them to stay open until 3 a.m.

Sunday (Sat night). Others have a 4 a.m. license that also allows them to stay open until 5 a.m. Sunday.

Mail

Chicago's main post office is at 433 W. Harrison (☎ 800-275-8777) and has free parking. Other convenient branches are located in the Sears Tower, the John Hancock Center Observatory, the Federal Center Plaza at 211 S. Clark St., the John R. Thompson Center at 100 W. Randolph, and at 227 E. Ontario, 2 blocks east of Michigan Avenue.

Maps

Rand McNally has a retail store at 444 N. Michigan Ave. (☎ 312-321-1751), just north of the Wrigley Building. A Chicago map costs about $4; a smaller, laminated version is about $6.

Newspapers/Magazines

The two major daily newspapers are the *Chicago Tribune* (☎ 312-222-3232; www.chicagotribune.com) and *Chicago Sun-Times* (☎ 312-321-3000; www.suntimes.com). *Chicago Reader* (☎ 312-828-0350; www.chicagoreader.com) is a free weekly that has extensive entertainment listings. *Chicago Magazine* is the city's glossy monthly (☎ 800-999-0879; www.chicagomag.com).

Pharmacies

Walgreens, 757 N. Michigan Ave. (at Chicago Avenue) is open 24 hours.

Police

Dial **911** for emergencies and 311 for non-emergencies.

Radio Stations

WBEZ (91.5 FM) is the local National Public Radio station. WXRT (93.1 FM) is a progressive-rock station that deserves a listen. WGN (720 AM) and WLS (890 AM) are longtime talk-radio stations with solid sports coverage. WBBM (780 AM) has nonstop news, traffic, and weather.

Religious Services

Your hotel can provide you with the locations of nearby houses of worship and the times of their services. Episcopalians seeking to attend Sunday services may contact Chicago's Episcopalian Diocese at 65 E. Huron (☎ 312-751-4200; www. epischicago.org). Catholics can call ☎ 800-627-7846 (www.masstimes.org). Shabbat services throughout Chicago are listed online at www.jewishchicago. com; click on "Synagogue Guide."

Restrooms

Public restrooms do not exist on Chicago's streets. You need to visit a large hotel or fast-food restaurant. Department stores, railway stations, and museums are other safe bets.

Safety

At night, stick to well-lit streets in busy areas such as the Magnificent Mile, Gold Coast, River North, and Lincoln Park. Stay out of parks and off dark residential streets. Use caution when walking in the Loop's interior after dark (when the business district is empty) and in outlying neighborhoods. As for transportation, take a taxi late at night, instead of waiting for a bus or the El on a deserted platform.

Smoking

Chicago restaurants are more smoker-friendly than those in New York and Los Angeles. Most restaurants still have smoking sections. Most hotels have smoking and nonsmoking rooms.

Taxes

Chicago has an 8.75 percent sales tax. Restaurants in the central part of the city are taxed an additional 1 percent, for a whopping total of 9.75 percent. Hotel-room tax totals 14.9 percent in the city.

Taxis

You can easily catch a taxi in the Loop, Magnificent Mile, Gold Coast, River North, and Lincoln Park. If you're in outlying areas, you may need to call. Cab companies include Flash Cab (☎ 773-561-1444), Yellow Cab (☎ 312-829-4222), and Checker Cab (☎ 312-243-2537).

Time Zone

Chicago is on central standard time.

Transit Info

The Chicago Transit Authority (CTA) operates the train and bus systems in the city (☎ 312-836-7000 for information, 5 a.m.–1 a.m.; www.transitchicago.com). Pace buses (☎ 312-836-7000) cover the suburbs. The Metra commuter railroad (☎ 312-322-6777, Mon–Fri 8 a.m.–5 p.m.; at other times call the Regional Transit Authority at ☎ 312-836-7000; www. metrarail.com) has 12 train lines serving the six-county area around Chicago.

Weather Updates

For the National Weather Service's current conditions and forecast, call ☎ 312-976-1212 (for a fee) or check the weather on the Web at www.weather.com. Most television stations (CBS 2, NBC 5, and ABC 7) show the current temperatures in the bottom-right corner of the screen during morning news shows.

Toll-Free Numbers and Web Sites

Airlines

Air Canada
☎ 888-247-2262
www.aircanada.ca

Airtran Airlines
☎ 800-247-8726
www.airtran.com

American Airlines
☎ 800-433-7300
www.aa.com

American Trans Air
☎ 800-225-2995
www.ata.com

America West Airlines
☎ 800-235-9292
www.americawest.com

Continental Airlines
☎ 800-525-0280
www.continental.com

Delta Air Lines
☎ 800-221-1212
www.delta.com

Frontier Airlines
☎ 800-432-1359
www.frontierairlines.com

Jet Blue Airlines
☎ 800-538-2583
www.jetblue.com

Northwest Airlines
☎ 800-225-2525
www.nwa.com

Southwest Airlines
☎ 800-435-9792
www.southwest.com

United Air Lines
☎ 800-241-6522
www.united.com

US Airways
☎ 800-428-4322
www.usairways.com

Major car-rental agencies

Alamo
☎ 800-327-9633
www.goalamo.com

Avis
☎ 800-831-1212
www.avis.com

Budget
☎ 800-527-0700
www.budget.com

Dollar
☎ 800-800-4000
www.dollar.com

Enterprise
☎ 800-325-8007
www.enterprise.com

Hertz
☎ 800-654-3131
www.hertz.com

National
☎ 800-227-7368
www.nationalcar.com

Rent-A-Wreck
☎ 800-535-1391
www.rent-a-wreck.com

Thrifty
☎ 800-367-2277
www.thrifty.com

Major hotel and motel chains

Best Western International
☎ 800-528-1234
www.bestwestern.com

Clarion Hotel
☎ 800-262-7466
www.hotelchoice.com

Comfort Inn
☎ 800-228-5150
www.hotelchoice.com

Courtyard by Marriott
☎ 800-321-2211
www.courtyard.com

Days Inn
☎ 800-325-2525
www.daysinn.com

DoubleTree Hotel
☎ 800-222-8733
www.doubletreehotels.com

Econo Lodge
☎ 800-553-2666
www.hotelchoice.com

Fairfield Inn by Marriott
☎ 800-228-2800
www.marriott.com

Hampton Inn
☎ 800-426-7866
www.hampton-inn.com

Hilton Hotel
☎ 800-445-8667
www.hilton.com

Holiday Inn
☎ 800-465-4329
www.basshotels.com

Howard Johnson
☎ 800-654-2000
www.hojo.com

Hyatt Hotels & Resorts
☎ 800-228-9000
www.hyatt.com

Inter-Continental Hotels & Resorts
☎ 888-567-8725
www.interconti.com

Marriott Hotel
☎ 800-228-9290
www.marriott.com

Motel 6
☎ 800-466-8357
www.motel6.com

Quality Inn
☎ 800-228-5151
www.hotelchoice.com

Radisson Hotels International
☎ 800-333-3333
www.radisson.com

Ramada Inn
☎ 800-272-6232
www.ramada.com

Red Roof Inns
☎ 800-843-7663
www.redroof.com

Residence Inn by Marriott
☎ 800-331-3131
www.marriott.com

Ritz-Carlton
☎ 800-241-3333
www.ritzcarlton.com

Sheraton Hotels & Resorts
☎ 800-325-3535
www.sheraton.com

Super 8 Motel
☎ 800-800-8000
www.super8motels.com

Travelodge
☎ 800-255-3050
www.travelodge.com

Westin Hotels & Resorts
☎ 800-937-8461
www.westin.com

Wyndham Hotels & Resorts
☎ 800-822-4200
www.wyndham.com

Where to Get More Information

Everything you need to know, you can find right in this book. But if you really want to be thorough before you book your ticket or plan a driving route, you can arm yourself with stacks of free information, such as maps; brochures; calendars of events; and schedules for sports, theater, concerts, and other happenings in the Windy City.

Contacting and visiting tourist offices

Chicago has two major sources of tourism information. Both can be of service to the individual traveler, but information from the Chicago Convention and Tourism Bureau isn't as comprehensive because much of the content comes from the dining and lodging establishments that are its members.

 ✔ **Chicago Office of Tourism,** 78 E. Washington St., Chicago, IL 60602 (☎ 877-244-2246 or 312-744-2400; www.877chicago.com): The staff will mail you a free package of information that includes maps and details of upcoming events and attractions. Request the information and find out more on its Web site. The agency also operates visitor centers at 77 E. Randolph St. (in the north lobby of the Chicago Cultural Center) and at 163 E. Pearson St. (in the pumping station of Chicago's landmark Water Tower).

 ✔ **Chicago Convention and Tourism Bureau,** 2301 S. Lake Shore Dr., McCormick Place on the Lake, Chicago, IL 60616-1490 (☎ 800-226-6328 or 312-567-8500; www.choosechicago.com): The bureau distributes lodging, dining, and sightseeing information, as well as the free "Chicago Official Visitors Guide."

Surfing the Web

Type the keyword **Chicago** into any search engine and you may find yourself buried under an avalanche of information. This section points you toward the most useful sites, all packed with information including detailed maps and occasional sound effects!

 ✔ www.877chicago.com: Chicago from A to Z — art and architecture to zoos. The Chicago Office of Tourism site offers a calendar, a roundup of festivals, and listings of the current month's activities. An interactive clickable map of downtown features photos, addresses, historical information, and trivia about attractions and landmarks.

 ✔ www.choosechicago.com: Links connect with hotels, restaurants, attractions, and other members of the Chicago Convention and Tourism Bureau.

 ✔ www.enjoyillinois.com: The Illinois Bureau of Tourism will send you a packet of information about the city, the 'burbs, and beyond.

Hitting the books

You can probably find these two books at your local bookstore. Web shoppers can buy them online from www.amazon.com or www.barnes andnoble.com:

- ✔ *Frommer's Chicago* by Elizabeth Canning Blackwell (published by Wiley): This thorough guide features gorgeous color photos of the sights and experiences that await you. The book covers all the traditional tourist favorites but also lets you in on local finds, neighborhood hangouts, and little-known gems.

- ✔ *Frommer's Irreverent Chicago* by Elizabeth Canning Blackwell (published by Wiley): This guide is for young, sophisticated travelers who want a cutting-edge perspective on Chicago. It offers a wickedly irreverent, unabashedly honest, and downright hilarious take on the city.

Index

• *N* •

• *W* •

Walgreens, 288
walking in Chicago, 86–87, 194
walking tours, 203
wallets, lost or stolen, 44–45
Water Tower, 190
Water Tower Place mall, 214, 279
Water Tower Pumping Station visitor
    center, 82
weather
    activities for bad weather, 279–281
    and deciding when to travel, 22–25
    packing tips, 67,
    weather information, 289
    winds, 282
Web sites about Chicago, 292
Wendella Sightseeing Boats, 203
West Lakeview shopping, 220–221
Westfield North Bridge mall, 215, 279
WGN-720AM (radio station), 64
Where Chicago (magazine), 127
Wicker Park, 190
Wiener Circle, 264
Wild Hare, 269
Williams-Sonoma, 214
Wilmette and the North Shore
    Baha'i House of Worship tour,
        237–238
    restaurants, 239
    sightseeing, 238
    traveling to, 237
wind, 282
Windy City Times (newspaper), 60
Winfrey, Oprah (TV personality), 12,
    80, 185
winter, traveling during, 22, 25
wireless hotspots, 70
Wolf Camera, 287
Wolford, 216
Women and Children First book-
    store, 60
World Music Festival Chicago, 29
Wright, Frank Lloyd (architect),
    16–19, 20, 27
Wright Plus Tour, 27
Wrigley Field, 186, 195, 276

Wrigleyville
    attractions, 81
    map, nightlife, 262–263
    restaurants, 164

• *Y* •

Yellow Cab, 85, 289

• *Z* •

Zanies Comedy Club, 271
Zebra Lounge, 268
Zoo Lights Festival, 30
zoos
    Brookfield Zoo, 187
    Lincoln Park Zoo, 182

Accommodations Index

Amalfi Hotel, 102
Belden-Stratford Hotel, 100
Best Western River North Hotel, 117
Chicago Hilton and Towers, 100–101
Chicago Marriott Downtown, 101
City Suites Hotel, 89, 117
Comfort Inn and Suites Downtown,
    102, 118
Courtyard by Marriott, 90, 101, 102
The Crowne Plaza Chicago/The
    Silversmith, 10, 104
DoubleTree Guest Suites, 102, 104
The Drake, 10, 89, 102, 104–105
Embassy Suites, 9–10, 102, 105
Fairmont Hotel, 102, 105–106
Four Seasons Hotel, 10, 89, 106
Hampton Inn & Suites Hotel, 10,
    106–107
Hard Rock Hotel, 89, 102, 107
Hilton Garden Inn, 118
Homewood Suites, 118
Hotel Allegro, 89, 107–108
Hotel Burnham, 10, 89, 108
Hotel InterContinental Chicago, 10,
    89, 90, 102, 108, 109, 112–113

Restaurant Index

SPORTS, FITNESS, PARENTING, RELIGION & SPIRITUALITY

0-7645-5146-9

0-7645-5418-2

Also available:
- Adoption For Dummies
  0-7645-5488-3
- Basketball For Dummies
  0-7645-5248-1
- The Bible For Dummies
  0-7645-5296-1
- Buddhism For Dummies
  0-7645-5359-3
- Catholicism For Dummies
  0-7645-5391-7
- Hockey For Dummies
  0-7645-5228-7

- Judaism For Dummies
  0-7645-5299-6
- Martial Arts For Dummies
  0-7645-5358-5
- Pilates For Dummies
  0-7645-5397-6
- Religion For Dummies
  0-7645-5264-3
- Teaching Kids to Read
  For Dummies
  0-7645-4043-2
- Weight Training For Dummies
  0-7645-5168-X
- Yoga For Dummies
  0-7645-5117-5

TRAVEL

0-7645-5438-7

0-7645-5453-0

Also available:
- Alaska For Dummies
  0-7645-1761-9
- Arizona For Dummies
  0-7645-6938-4
- Cancún and the Yucatán
  For Dummies
  0-7645-2437-2
- Cruise Vacations For Dummies
  0-7645-6941-4
- Europe For Dummies
  0-7645-5456-5
- Ireland For Dummies
  0-7645-5455-7

- Las Vegas For Dummies
  0-7645-5448-4
- London For Dummies
  0-7645-4277-X
- New York City For Dummies
  0-7645-6945-7
- Paris For Dummies
  0-7645-5494-8
- RV Vacations For Dummies
  0-7645-5443-3
- Walt Disney World & Orlando
  For Dummies
  0-7645-6943-0

GRAPHICS, DESIGN & WEB DEVELOPMENT

0-7645-4345-8

0-7645-5589-8

Also available:
- Adobe Acrobat 6 PDF
  For Dummies
  0-7645-3760-1
- Building a Web Site For Dummies
  0-7645-7144-3
- Dreamweaver MX 2004
  For Dummies
  0-7645-4342-3
- FrontPage 2003 For Dummies
  0-7645-3882-9
- HTML 4 For Dummies
  0-7645-1995-6
- Illustrator cs For Dummies
  0-7645-4084-X

- Macromedia Flash MX 2004
  For Dummies
  0-7645-4358-X
- Photoshop 7 All-in-One Desk
  Reference For Dummies
  0-7645-1667-1
- Photoshop cs Timesaving
  Techniques For Dummies
  0-7645-6782-9
- PHP 5 For Dummies
  0-7645-4166-8
- PowerPoint 2003 For Dummies
  0-7645-3908-6
- QuarkXPress 6 For Dummies
  0-7645-2593-X

NETWORKING, SECURITY, PROGRAMMING & DATABASES

0-7645-6852-3

0-7645-5784-X

Also available:
- A+ Certification For Dummies
  0-7645-4187-0
- Access 2003 All-in-One Desk
  Reference For Dummies
  0-7645-3988-4
- Beginning Programming
  For Dummies
  0-7645-4997-9
- C For Dummies
  0-7645-7068-4
- Firewalls For Dummies
  0-7645-4048-3
- Home Networking For Dummies
  0-7645-42796

- Network Security For Dummies
  0-7645-1679-5
- Networking For Dummies
  0-7645-1677-9
- TCP/IP For Dummies
  0-7645-1760-0
- VBA For Dummies
  0-7645-3989-2
- Wireless All In-One Desk Referer
  For Dummies
  0-7645-7496-5
- Wireless Home Networking
  For Dummies
  0-7645-3910-8